Extending the Diaspora

THE NEW BLACK STUDIES SERIES

Edited by Darlene Clark Hine
and Dwight A. McBride

A list of books in the series appears at the end of this book.

Extending the Diaspora

New Histories of Black People

Edited by

DAWNE Y. CURRY, ERIC D. DUKE,

AND MARSHANDA A. SMITH

Foreword by

DARLENE CLARK HINE

UNIVERSITY OF ILLINOIS PRESS

Urbana and Chicago

Manufactured in the United States of America
1 2 3 4 5 C P 5 4 3 2 1
∞ This book is printed on acid-free paper.

Library of Congress Cataloging-in-Publication Data
Extending the diaspora : new histories of Black people /
edited by Dawne Y. Curry, Eric D. Duke, and
Marshanda A. Smith ; foreword by Darlene Clark Hine.
p. cm. — (The new Black studies series)
Based on conference papers.
Includes bibliographical references and index.
ISBN 978-0-252-03459-6 (cloth : alk. paper) —
ISBN 978-0-252-07652-7 (pbk. : alk. paper)
1. African diaspora—Congresses.
2. Blacks—History—Congresses.
I. Curry, Dawne Y., 1967–
II. Duke, Eric D.
III. Smith, Marshanda A.
DT16.5.E95 2009
305.896009—dc22 2008050479

Contents

Section Two: Diaspora Interactions

Section Three: The Black Presence in the Pacific

Section Four: Race and Nation

Foreword

DARLENE CLARK HINE

The palpable commitment and excitement of a cadre of Michigan State University graduate student organizers, specifically Dawne Y. Curry, Eric D. Duke, and Marshanda A. Smith, and the hundreds of students and professors who came from institutions around the world made the 2001 Comparative Black History (CBH)-sponsored "Diaspora Paradigms: New Scholarship in Comparative Black History" conference an unforgettable experience. Senior scholars joined with junior professors and dissertation-writing-graduate students in spirited exchanges about the origins and different meanings of diaspora: the significance of forced and voluntary migrations of African peoples from the days of the slave trade to the modern post-colonial era; the hierarchal structures of race, class, and gender; and the social, political, and legal resistance strategies of subject peoples. This memorable symposium featured keynote speakers renown for their seminal contributions to the emergence and evolution of the field of African Diaspora Studies. They included political scientist Michael Hanchard of Johns Hopkins University, anthropologist Michel-Rolph Trouillot of the University of Chicago, sociologist Ruth Simms Hamilton of Michigan State University (now deceased), historian Kim D. Butler of Rutgers University, historian Cassandra Pybus of the University of Sydney in Australia, historian Chana Kai Lee of the University of Georgia, and literary scholar Michelle M. Wright of the University of Minnesota to name only a few.

The conversations and debates the keynote speakers and panelists ignited continued long after each session ended, filling MSU's Kellogg Center with animated and impassioned voices. New friendships took root. Many graduate students stayed awake for days. As director of the Comparative Black History PhD degree program at MSU, I was enormously proud of how well the CBH students orchestrated the conference. My colleagues in CBH, Laurent DuBois, Daina Ramey Berry, David Bailey, Richard Thomas, David Robinson, and Peter Beattie shared in the conference deliberations and were as moved as I was by the frequent expressions of gratitude. We collectively savored the unique opportunity afforded by the gathering to learn of the new work in progress that promised to extend the diaspora far beyond the borders of the United States. Thus, we listened and learned much of value from members of the next generation of students and colleagues who are passionately and intellectually invested in extending the diaspora.

The joy from the success of the conference soon yielded to the much more challenging and difficult, indeed agonizing, selection process that produced *Extending the Diaspora: New Histories of Black People.* This splendid anthology of original, wide-ranging, and provocative essays deserves the attention of everyone interested in African Diaspora Studies and in developing comparative understandings of African American History. As editors, Curry, Duke, and Smith took great care to select the best papers from among the large number of illuminating conference presentations. Over the course of several months of group deliberations, the editors developed the requisite intellectual rigor to move the project toward publication. With CBH faculty assistance, they starred those papers that opened up new ways of understanding the myriad forces that shaped and were shaped by Black peoples in global contexts as they resisted oppression and sought new opportunities and freedom for themselves and those who would follow. Two superb external reviewers read and commented on multiple drafts of the manuscript, encouraging more cuts and suggesting important revisions for each essay.

The authors of the essays in *Extending the Diaspora* explore an array of new topics, spaces, personalities, and events, and thus broaden our understanding of complex theoretical and conceptual issues in diaspora studies and introduce new knowledge about diverse African diasporic peoples across time. The multidisciplinary approaches and the depth of the research displayed in these papers facilitate explorations into the convergences and disjunctions in the historical experiences and present conditions of diasporic peoples. This anthology will provoke discussions about future prospects of African descended peoples living and working in an array of societies and nation states, as well as the racial and economic policy changes needed to promote black striving. In sum, *Extending the Diaspora* builds upon earlier diaspora studies in ways that open space for a new and emerging generation of students and scholars to explore, debate, question, and thus contribute to a more inclusive discourse about hierarchal race, class, and gender structures, and ideologies of social, political, and economic transformation in the new millennium.

Finally, African American historians from the days of Carter G. Woodson to the more contemporary Black Studies scholars have consistently, across the decades of the twentieth century, investigated the multifaceted relations between Black people in the United States and the peoples of African descent in global societies. Today, this scholarship and the conversations it has provoked are integral in academic discourse around issues of race, identity, and citizenship. Contributors to *Extending the Diaspora* offer thoughtful and original information that broaden intellectual practice and public policy advocated by leaders and activists in global societies who wrestle with new opportunities and old conflicts surrounding adjustments to Black migrants and immigrants. Similarly, African peoples need deeper historical understandings of how earlier migrants, either forced or voluntary, made places for themselves in diverse sociopolitical economies and state formations. This historical knowledge provides armor for the new Diasporans as they encounter resistance in their quest for space, citizenship, and belonging in places outside their nations of origin. To be sure, recent Black migrants and immigrants, as in the past, must negotiate the conundrums animated by intersections of social status, gender, race, sexuality, ethnicity, and religion within their own communities as well as in larger host societies.

Extending the Diaspora is uniquely constituted to illuminate all of our journeys. In closing I would only add that I am enormously grateful to the magnificent University of Chicago historian Thomas C. Holt for his generous assistance, time, intellectual engagement, and critical readings that helped to transform this manuscript into a stellar contribution to African Diaspora and African American studies.

Acknowledgments

The publication of *Extending the Diaspora: New Histories of Black People* has involved much work. The results of this process surface on the pages that follow. However, none of this would have been possible without the many people who worked behind the scenes and in the forefront to make this volume and the conference it emerged from a success.

When acknowledging the various people who have made this volume's publication possible, we begin with a note of appreciation to the original sponsors of the 2001 Diaspora Paradigms conference at Michigan State University. We received overwhelming support from the university, and thus we note with tremendous gratitude the support of the many departments, schools, centers, programs, and offices that helped with the conference. Included in our collective "thank you" are the Comparative Black History Program, the History Department, the Center for Latin American and Caribbean Studies, MSU Black Alumni Association, the Affirmative Action Compliance and Monitoring Office (including Dr. Ralph W. Bonner), the Office of Minority Student Affairs (including Rodney Patterson and Murray Edwards), the College of Arts & Letters and Dean Wendy K. Wilkins, the Vice President for Student Affairs and Service (Lee N. June), the Graduate School and deans Patrick McConeghy and Karen L. Klomparens, and the Provost Office, which at that time was lead by Lou Anna K. Simon, the current president of Michigan State University. We also thank the support staff of all of these offices, including Linda M. Werbish, Barbara Harrison-King, Jo-Ann VandenBergh, and Rhonda Hibbitt. These women dedicated their time and energy to the conference's production and without their technical support, the event would not have been so successful.

We must also recognize and thank the various conference attendees and participants. Five keynote speakers established the theoretical framework that undergirded the Diaspora Paradigms conference through their presentations and their encouragement to expand the intellectual horizons of this burgeoning field of African Diaspora studies. This distinguished list of scholars included Kim D. Butler, the late Ruth Simms Hamilton, Chana Kai Lee, Larry E. Rivers, and Michel-Rolph Trouillot. We also want to acknowledge the support and efforts of our colleagues and fellow alumni of MSU's Comparative Black History Program as attendees (Felix Armfield, Jacqueline McLeod, Yasuhiro Okada, Kennetta Hammond Perry, Eric Washington), participants (Anthony Cheeseboro, Fikru Gerbrikidan, John Wess Grant, Mona Jackson, Regina Jones, Kenneth Marshall, Tamba M'Bayo, Dolores Sisco), and members of the organizing committee with the editors (Solomon Getahun, Leslie Rollins, Meredith L. Roman, Chantalle Verna, Matthew Whitaker). We acknowledge the support of MSU professors (at that time) including Bill E. Lawson, Susan Sleeper-Smith, and Christine Daniels, and especially the MSU faculty associated with the Comparative Black History Program: Laurent Dubois, Peter Beattie, Pero Dagbovie, Daina Ramey Berry, and Richard W. Thomas. We also note our gratitude for the musical nourishment that we received from the well-known talents of Chicago's Lynne Jordan and the Shivers and the Grammy-nominated vocalist Betty Joplin and Friends.

We thank the staff of the University of Illinois Press for their help in the publication of this volume. Of particular importance was the work of Joan Catapano (associate director and editor-in-chief), Rebecca Schreiber (assistant editor), and Marla Osterbur (acquisitions assistant). Additionally we note our appreciation for the thoughtful and insightful comments of the two anonymous reviewers who commented on this volume.

Finally we reserve our most appreciative and deepest thanks for the leadership and support of Darlene Clark Hine, the founder and director of Michigan State University's Comparative Black History PhD program. As a distinguished historian of African American women's history, Darlene Clark Hine has crossed boundaries and intersections to emerge as one of the most prolific scholars of her generation. Her tutelage knows no boundaries. She led by example, shared her eminent knowledge, and supported us as emerging scholars of our own professional endeavors and especially with this volume's publication. Without her belief in our abilities, our lives would not have been as enriched, productive or as expansive. Thus, we commend and respect the arduous hours that she expended to teach us about the historical profession. For that, we are eternally indebted.

Introduction

In September 2001, Darlene Clark Hine and the graduate students of the Comparative Black History PhD program at Michigan State University hosted an international conference titled "Diaspora Paradigms: New Scholarship in Comparative Black History." This conference provided a forum in which advanced graduate students, junior faculty, and seasoned scholars presented a wide range of research related to the histories of Black peoples within the African Diaspora. *Extending the Diaspora: New Histories of Black People* is a collection of select essays from that conference that contribute to the growing field of Diaspora Studies.

Over the past several decades, the study of "diaspora" has become increasingly popular, and developed different meanings and interpretations according to one's field of study. Many scholars have noted that diaspora began as a concept that explained Jewish dispersal throughout the world. From this beginning, the term evolved to include the historical dispersion of many other peoples, including African peoples. In the latter's case, some of the earliest discussions of an African Diaspora contained biblical roots. Robin D.G. Kelley and Tiffany Patterson explain, "Early activists, historians, and clergy frequently cited Psalms 68:31, which says 'Ethiopia shall stretch out her hands onto God' as a way of describing the black world." In the 1950s and 1960s, studies of the transatlantic slave trade, a major source of dispersal for African peoples, expanded the notion of an African Diaspora even further.[1] On the heels of such developments, scholars continued to expand concepts and studies of diaspora, moving beyond the American mainland and monolithic conceptions of diaspora to claim wider regions as part of the African

Diaspora.[2] For instance, scholars such as Herman Bennett, Robin D. G. Kelley, and Tiffany Patterson discerned that "Africa was not the only diaspora . . . [to which] Africans belonged." Similarly, Earl Lewis and Darlene Clark Hine articulate this assertion by emphasizing the "overlapping diasporas" of black peoples, and the need to "cross boundaries" to better understand these histories.[3] These scholars show how African dispersion included the development of culture and communities within spaces not traditionally recognized as African but that were African in content and scope.

In analyzing diaspora study, Kim D. Butler argues that five dimensions characterize the African Diaspora: (1) reasons for, and conditions of, the dispersal; (2) relationship with the homeland; (3) relationship with the host land(s); (4) interrelationships within diasporan group; (5) comparative studies of different diasporas.[4] The essays in *Extending the Diaspora* examine all of these intellectual considerations, including permanence or generational linkages that trace the trajectory of diaspora community formation. Diaspora is also shown within the context of African descendants returning to the motherland and finding themselves within the prism of discovery, that is, they play a role in race consciousness and oftentimes re-create the paradigms of politics within their respective societies. Analyzing the unique development and evolution of the African Diaspora highlights the fact that Black peoples represent a heterogeneous population not bound by monolithic constraints of identity. That heterogeneity accentuates the need to understand the African Diaspora holistically rather than as individual sums to parts to an intellectual whole that lacks depth.

Employing diaspora as an analytical category, the essays in *Extending the Diaspora* unite disparate regions into a metanarrative on race, politics, gender, and nationality among other related topics. This volume addresses both new and familiar topics with fresh perspectives to produce original and compelling scholarship on the diasporic histories of Black peoples. Through a variety of methodologies and theoretical constructs, the various contributors plumb a wide range of localities to engage many important subjects: slavery and emancipation, transnational and diasporic experiences, social and political activism, and political and cultural identity. In doing so, they offer insightful and thought-provoking studies, highlight new areas of inquiry in the African Diaspora, and in many cases, transcend geographical and national boundaries.

The probing and meticulously woven narratives of this collection combine to show the intertwined and vibrant histories of peoples of African descent that go beyond both geographical and national boundaries. With multiple essays centered on common themes but differing in geographical localities, these case studies also speak to each other across the thematic sections in which they are grouped. Indeed, each narrative represents a patch that stitches together the intellectual quilt that binds together these diasporic global conversations. Taken as a whole, *Extending the Diaspora* collectively and holistically plots the interconnections of people of African descent through their use of geographic region, subject analysis, and methodology.

The volume is separated into four thematic sections. In Section One, "Pursuing Freedom," John F. Campbell, Beatrice Mamigonian, and Afua Cooper provide case studies of the struggle for freedom by enslaved peoples in Jamaica, Brazil, and Canada. Each author offers a glimpse into the particular means by which their subject sought to escape their bondage, as well as the numerous obstacles they faced in achieving their goal. In doing so, these essays interrogate the very nature and attainability of "full freedom."

John Campbell's essay explores the limitations of manumission as a pathway to freedom for enslaved Africans in late eighteenth-century Jamaica. Relying heavily on the records of the Vanneck (Arcedekne) Estate, Campbell argues that while scholars frequently cite manumission as a popular means through which enslaved peoples attained freedom, its overall effectiveness as a tool of liberation was actually limited. Moreover, Campbell contends that manumission was not a challenge to the slave system as some scholars have assumed—instead, it actually acted as a tool of social control when dangled as an eventual reward for faithful service. Campbell's examination convincingly supports such arguments using various cases of manumission in which the actual emancipation was delayed, or outright denied, until it deemed most beneficial to the larger white society. By portraying manumission in these ways, Campbell's essay embodies the difficulties enslaved peoples faced in their pursuit of an often "incomplete freedom."

Beatriz Mamigonian's study investigates the lives and struggles of "Liberated Africans" in the service of the Brazilian state in the nineteenth century. Utilizing numerous petitions for emancipation from these Liberated Africans, Mamigonian shows how these "coerced laborers" (as Liberated Africans were not technically enslaved) still faced numerous difficulties in their push for full freedom after completing a mandatory apprenticeship period. Despite proclamations that limited their service to fourteen years, Mamigonian shows that the majority of the Liberated Africans worked well beyond this prescribed length of time. Moreover, compared to other Liberated Africans who worked for private hirers, Liberated Africans employed by the state worked even longer and lived in a more regimented and bureaucratic world that sometimes further complicated the process of emancipation. Much like the issue of manumission in Campbell's essay, Mamigonian shows how the push for freedom amongst Liberated Africans, especially those attached to the Brazilian state, proved to be a long and uncertain struggle.

Afua Cooper's essay provides a biographical account of Marie-Joseph Angélique, an enslaved "Black Portuguese" woman executed for allegedly setting the Montreal Fire of 1734. Cooper draws primarily upon judicial records to trace the journey of Angélique from her "homeland" in Portugal (where she was likely born into slavery) to her eventual new "home" in Canada. Broadening the scope of the African Diaspora to include less-commonly studied areas such as Portugal and Canada is an important issue in Cooper's essay; she primarily focuses on Angélique's life as an enslaved woman in Montreal, and her growing desire for freedom. Facing an increasingly contentious relationship with her "owners," Angélique initially tried to run away in hopes of returning to Portugal. When that plan failed and she was returned to bondage, Angélique allegedly resorted to arson, an act of resistance that led to her brutal torture and eventual execution. Whereas Campbell and Mamigonian probe the uncertainties of an "expected freedom," Cooper offers a more traditional study of slave resistance as a means to achieve freedom. However, her focus on Angélique, a European-born enslaved Black woman in Canada, makes her essay anything but traditional.

In Section Two, "Diaspora Interactions," Stephen Hall, Micol Seigel, and Iris Berger address diasporic relationships between African Americans, Haitians, Afro-Brazilians, and South Africans. In each essay, the authors offer case studies on the connections and relationships between African Americans and these other Black communities. Taken as a whole, these essays provide insight into the diverse types of diasporic connections, as well as both the cooperative *and* contested nature of such relationships.

Stephen Hall's essay explores how African Americans in the nineteenth century used the memory of the Haitian Revolution as a tool in their own antislavery activities. Utilizing the writings of African American activists James McCune Smith, George Boyer Vashon, James Theodore Holly, and William Wells Brown, Hall details how these authors sought to both legitimize and draw inspiration from the Haitian Revolution. In contrast to the racist "murder and mayhem" images of the revolution found in most white accounts of the era, these authors presented the Haitian Revolution as both a legitimate and far-reaching political revolution that embodied both the possibilities and capabilities of Black peoples for self-rule. Such positive accounts of the Haitian Revolution directly challenged widespread stereotypes of Black inferiority and savagery that African Americans faced in the United States in this era. Thus, Hall's essay provides an important example of early intellectual connections between Black freedom movements in the Diaspora.

Micol Seigel's study examines the diasporic connections between African Americans and Afro-Brazilians in the early twentieth century. Moving beyond a traditional discussion of comparative race relations between the two nations, Seigel explores the connections between these black communities through an examination of the relationship between the *Chicago Defender* (under the editorship of Robert Abbott) and some Afro-Brazilian presses (primarily in Sao Paulo). Seigel shows the cooperative nature of African Americans and Afro-Brazilians with both papers reporting on the activities of the other, as well as reporting wider news of the Black Diaspora. However, unlike Hall's essay, Seigel addresses some disagreements between the two Black communities. For instance, Abbott's 1923 visit to Brazil, in which he praised Brazil's supposed racial democracy, drew the ire of several Afro-Brazilians fighting for true racial equality. The opposition of many Afro-Brazilians to possible African American emigration to Brazil also showed some contestation between the two groups. In recognizing their similarities and differences, as well as the cooperation and contestation between African Americans and Afro-Brazilians, Seigel shows the complicated nature of purported diasporic connections.

Iris Berger's essay investigates the historical legacy of Madie Hall Xuma, an African American from North Carolina who became an important social activist in South Africa during the mid-twentieth century. Berger uses personal correspondence to trace Madie Hall Xuma's life from her emigration to South Africa in 1940 (upon her marriage to Dr. Alfred B. Xuma, then-President-General of the African National Congress) until her departure in 1963. During this period, Xuma successfully juggled roles as a wife, mother, political activist, and community leader. Despite the fact that Xuma's foreign status and her brown skin afforded her opportunities beyond what she attained in the American South, she remained determined to help the Black women of her newfound homeland. Following the example of many African American clubwomen before her, Xuma used her societal position to agitate, indoctrinate, and galvanize Black women in a broad project of "racial uplift," including the struggle against the rising tide of state-sanctioned segregation and discrimination. Berger pays particular attention to Xuma's establishment and leadership of the Zenzele clubs, self-help political organizations, where she worked alongside South African women in a fight for female empowerment through domestic science, moral standards, and political awareness. Through such examples, Berger captures both the intellectual and physical interaction personified in this diasporic connection.

Section Three, "The Black Presence in the Pacific," stretches the geography of the Black Diaspora beyond the usual focus on the Atlantic World. The studies of Cassandra Pybus and Yuichiro Onishi highlight two different eras and areas of the "Pacific World" (late eighteenth–early nineteenth-century Australia and twentieth-century Okinawa) in which Black peoples made significant impacts.

In a transnational tapestry, Cassandra Pybus's study weaves together the micro narratives of eleven African convicts who established a new community in New South Wales (Australia) in 1788. Tracing the journey of these convicts through the Atlantic World (including stops in Nova Scotia, Jamaica, the Bahamas, and England), these former slaves eventually landed at Sydney Cove, where they served out sentences for various crimes ranging from theft to impersonation. While these convicts provided no account of their multiple migrations, Pybus meticulously plumbed colonial records, transportation indentions, and "Negro Books" to excavate the narratives of her subjects from historical silence. She argues that because of imperial connections and the transnational process of empire building these convicts created a "Diaspora at the end of the world." Her acquisition of these micro narratives, as one reviewer suggested, enabled her to find "needles in a global haystack" that she used to "stitch together a careful and convincing account of her subjects."

Yuichiro Onishi's essay examines the role of African American GIs in the Okinawan freedom movement during the American occupation. Focusing on the years 1968–72, Onishi analyzes a transnational struggle against global whiteness, including a wide range of actors from various intellectual and social backgrounds such as peace activists, Okinawans, and African American GIs. Onishi pays particular attention to how activists in the Okinawan freedom struggle incorporated African American ideas of the "Black Liberation" struggle. For instance, he argues that the lessons learned from observing the African American civil rights campaigns, as well as the participation of African American GIs in the late 1960s and early 1970s were particularly key. Thus, Onishi offers a unique insight into the contribution of African Americans in a rarely studied anti-imperialist struggle.

In Section Four, "Race and Nation," Joel T. Helfrich, Fatima El-Tayeb, Matthew Smith, and Dawne Y. Curry offer essays on the relationships between race and national identities. Taken as a whole, their essays address this subject in England, South-West Africa, Haiti, and South Africa. Each author provides a different intellectual kaleidoscope on the subject.

Joel T. Helfrich's essay analyzes a series of early nineteenth-century boxing matches between Thomas Cribb (a white Briton) and Thomas Molineaux (an African American) to discuss a range of national and transnational issues. Helfrich moves beyond previous interpretations of these epic matches in which scholars largely characterized the events simply as a battle between the races. Instead, Helfrich uses these boxing matches as expressions of popular culture to examine broader issues of race, national identity, nationalism, and masculinity. He accomplishes this goal using the athletes' public persona, the audiences' reaction to the boxers, and the nations' honor. In such a presentation, international politics played out within the confined space of the boxing ring.

Fatima El-Tayeb's essay explores the creation of a German identity in the colony of South-West Africa (present-day Namibia) in the early twentieth century. Whereas Helfrich used popular culture to examine issues of race and nation, El-Tayeb uses German imperialism as the lens through which to review and analyze her subject. Her essay focuses upon the 1905 Anti-Miscegenation Law that provided the legal rationale for defining German citizenship in the colony and in the metropole. This policy, El-Tayeb argues, ultimately excluded the progeny of interracial unions in a concerted effort to solidify a German national identity based upon whiteness. Like Helfrich's study of race and British national identity, El-Tayeb's penetrating study exemplifies how a supposedly homogenous national identity is constructed though the exclusion of minority populations.

Matthew Smith's study explores the ways in which Haitian Marxist movements addressed issues of race and color within their political party platforms from the end of American occupation in 1934 to the dawn of the Duvalier era in 1957. Employing an array of communist and socialist sources in Haiti, Smith argues that these relationships were often evolutionary. For instance, the Communist Party of the 1930s presented color as less important than class issues, while in the 1940s, a reorganized Communist Party saw color as a key political issue and adapted itself to popular notions of black nationalism in Haiti. However, the rise of the Socialist Party in 1946 marked the return of a raceless, "class over color" focus. Unlike Helfrich and El-Tayeb, who examine the ways in which Black peoples were excluded from national identities because of racist ideologies, Smith examines how political movements in a self-proclaimed Black nation dealt with issues of race, color, and nation.

Addressing both historical and contemporary issues, Dawne Y. Curry's illuminating work discusses notions of identity, race, nationality, and gender as it pertains to both racial and national identities in post-apartheid South Africa. While the other essays in this section employ solely historical sources in their discussions of "race and nation," Curry draws from her own experiences as an African American researcher in South Africa to analyze the contested character and fluidity of racial categorization. She takes readers on an intellectual and introspective excursion into South Africa's rural areas and the urban center of Johannesburg. Through these journeys, readers see the ways in which "blackness" and "whiteness" are composed through various combinations of pigmentation, culture, and linguistic ability. Curry compliments and builds upon previous essays in this section as she inverts the power structure and turns the gaze onto herself and those people whom she encountered.

Extending the Diaspora presents multiple studies and interpretations on the social, intellectual, political, and spatial domain of areas inhabited by Black peoples. It synthesizes worldly issues, illustrating the various and far-reaching histories of Black peoples globally. In achieving this goal, the volume analyzes lesser- and well-known sites where Black people, either forcibly or voluntarily, created their own communities and cultures. The similarities and differences of these experiences speak to the richness of Black peoples' histories, as well as resurrect some of their marginalized voices.

In conclusion, this volume, like the conference from which it is modeled, serves as our contribution to the ongoing conversations on the history of Black peoples. The featured essays represent the interconnectedness of the Black experience demonstrating the significance of studying issues in tandem, rather than as isolated occurrences. Scholarship in the twenty-first century requires our engagement in "global conversations" if we are fully to understand the past and anticipate the future.

Notes

1. Tiffany Ruby Patterson and Robin D. G. Kelley, "Unfinished Migrations: Reflections on the African Diaspora and the Making of the Modern World," *African Studies Review* 43, no. 1 (April 2000): 14.

2. See for example, George Shepperson. "African Diaspora: Concept and Context," in *Global Dimensions of the African Diaspora*, ed. Joseph E. Harris. (Washington, D.C.: Howard University Press, 1982); Franklin Knight, *The African Dimension in Latin American Societies* (New York: Macmillan, 1974).

3. Judith Byfield, "Introduction: Rethinking the African Diaspora," *African Studies Review* 43, no. 1 (April 2000): 5; Earl Lewis, "To Turn as on a Pivot: Writing African Americans into a History of Overlapping Diasporas," *American Historical Review* 100, no. 3 (June 1995): 765–787; Darlene Clark Hine and Jacqueline McCleod, *Crossing Boundaries: Comparative History of Black People in the Diaspora* (Bloomington: Indiana University Press, 1999).

4. Kim D. Butler, "From Black History to Diaspora History; Brazilian Abolition in Afro-Atlantic Context," *African Studies Review* 43, no. 1 (April 2000): 127.

SECTION ONE

Pursuing Freedom

1

How Free is "Free"?

The Limits of Manumission for Enslaved Africans in Eighteenth-Century British Caribbean Sugar Society

JOHN CAMPBELL

The treatment of the topic of manumission within the literature of Caribbean enslavement often gives to the reader the impression that it was one of the early easily attainable avenues for freedom available to the enslaved. This idea, however, is not totally true. In questioning its truthfulness one has to realize that manumission was not usually in the planters' best economic interest and that it was practiced long before the appearance in the historiography of any "humanistic" argument. The subsequent illusion of attainability often given to manumission today, I argue, has largely been created by the writings of the apologists who wish to offer redeeming aspects for the ignoble act of Caribbean chattel slavery.

In this context then a dominant historiography has emerged in defense of the sugar plantocracy and which, by its emphasis on aspects of planter benevolence, has created a dominant and false idea of manumission in the British Caribbean prior to 1834. This essay locates itself outside of the traditional "manumission" scholarship of the British Caribbean and points out that the attainment of this desired goal of manumission was oftentimes far from easy for the enslaved. In challenging the traditionally accepted manumission scholarship, perhaps the best place to begin is with comments made on the topic of manumission by a leading enslaver of the period, Edward Long. He stated that "the slaves that most commonly gain a manumission here from their owners, are 1. Domesticks, in reward for a long and faithful course of service. 2. Those, who have been permitted to work for themselves, only paying a certain weekly or monthly sum; many of them find means to save sufficient from their earnings, to purchase their freedom. 3. Those who have effected some essential service to the public, such as revealing a conspiracy, or fighting valiantly against rebels and invaders. They have likewise generally been requited with an annuity, from the public treasury, for life."[1]

Edward Long's 1754 summation of the avenues available to enslaved people for manumission in the British Caribbean identified three main groups of enslaved beneficiaries. The first group comprised those who had rendered "domestic" services; the second, those who had sought self-manumission through the hiring out of their skills or through astute marketing of their meager commodity assets;[2] and the third, those enslaved people who had (in the minds of the "white" planter class),[3] turned their backs on their enslaved brethren and chosen instead to undermine resistance strategies by becoming informants for the white managerial class.

While categories two and three were open equally to both male and female enslaved persons, category one, that of "Domesticks" was usually dominated by females. This preponderance of females arose from the "reward" context manumission assumed when offered by the white male sugar management for the enslaved women's more intimate "domestic" services. Category two, that of enslaved "skilled" workers, was a proportionately smaller male-dominated group who provided additional revenues to the plantation management when hired out for their particular trades skills. Category three, comprising both males and females, and consisting simply of "those who have effected some essential service to the pubic," was also invaluable to white society.

This third category's importance was based on the security it gave to British Caribbean enslaved society—an important point to note especially in societies like Jamaica's where the seething enslaved community at times outnumbered the whites by as much as sixty to one on some estates![4] In this context white society was, within the primary literature, only too happy to reward "deserving" informants with the "gift" of manumission. Indeed, while manumission offered "freedom" to the enslaved person, in many cases it ultimately provided the planter management with a more than commensurate benefit.

Long's summation of the three main manumission categories thus reflected the white sugar management's broad aims of seeking gender exploitation and divisions amongst the enslaved classes, profit maximization from the labor of the enslaved, and colonial security through covert surveillance information. The planter management collectively used these categories more to buttress the hegemony of their society than to ease the conditions of the enslaved Africans and their descendents through the bestowing of manumission. By his noting that the third category of manumitted people had earned an annuity for life, Long also highlighted the partial solution to a dual concern that confronted white society over manumission. This concern arose over the way white society was expected to interact with the new "freedmen" and how these "freedmen" were to subsist as nonworkers within a society that traditionally saw their worth only in terms of their productive capacity within the sugar monoculture.

The presence of the first significant sets of manumittees coming off of the sugar estates in the eighteenth century brought these concerns to the fore. The manumittees were old or infirm people who had been mere liabilities rather than assets to the plantations' work regime. Their manumission was a simple way for the planters to avoid the cost of their subsistence. This early practice of manumission was frowned upon, not because it led to increased hardships for this vulnerable group of people, but because they became nuisances to white civil society as they wandered around waiting to die.

As a consequence colonial assemblies quickly drafted laws insisting that new manumittees be granted "pensions" from the estates that manumitted them.[5] Such laws were intended to take the pressure off of the community's general resources and to curb the number of people subsequently manumitted. Putting stringent manumission laws in place by the mid-eighteenth century helped resolve the problems incapacitated manumittees posed. However, the all-important issue of their "freedman" status was never adequately resolved and continued to form the basis of antagonistic black/white relationships throughout the entire period of British Caribbean chattel slavery and beyond. In light of this fundamental problem of social definition why then was the practice of manumission continued?

This chapter will argue that the freedom offered to enslaved Africans in the British Caribbean through manumission was, in practice, severely limited both in significance and scope to the enslaved community. As such its continued use within British Caribbean sugar society during the eighteenth century never really contradicted the inhumane profit-maximizing functioning of the "white" slave society. Indeed, the practice of manumission, taken as a whole, was perhaps more beneficial to white male sugar management than it was for the comparatively few enslaved people who are usually touted within the historiography as having "benefited" from it.

I

THE BASIS OF MANUMISSION

Manumission's ultimate goal—freedom—has many definitions and contexts. While having myriad perspectives ranging from the removal of physical constraints to those dealing with the problems of residual psychological restraints (which continue long after the physical shackles have been removed), these differing ideas all hold as their basis the belief that men are by nature born free. The move to manumit enslaved people in the eighteenth-century British Caribbean seemed to have an altruistic end—to return to fellow human beings that part of their liberty that was curtailed by the unfortunate circumstance of chattel slavery. Sadly, however, the British Caribbean sugar estate had no place for altruism especially as it related to the welfare of the enslaved people.

The act of manumission in the British Caribbean can be defined using, for example, Arthur Stinchcombe's definition, which states that it was " the establishment of a former slave as free by a governmental act initiated by the property owner."[6] Such a definition, while accurate in accounting for the bureaucratic process, only allows a de jure understanding of manumission within eighteenth-century British Caribbean sugar territories. To obtain a more complete understanding of how manumission worked de facto, it would be useful to analyze representative cases and critique the "freedoms" they actually bestowed upon the "freed" person.

Steering our analysis in this direction makes immediately apparent some startling revelations as to the limits of manumission for the enslaved. Perhaps the first limiting aspect of freedom offered by British Caribbean manumission stemmed from the fact that the property owner legally initiated whole process, not the enslaved person. As such, the granting of manumission always remained a discretionary act dependent on white sugar management's wills or whims. Thus, although an enslaved person could, in theory, have earned the right to manumission or secured her manumission price, the actual act itself still needed white management's consent—a consent sparingly given.

Indeed, one example of an institutional brake to management's discretion arose from the sugar plantations' constant need for more field labor. These labor demands on the estates stemmed from periodic inadequate supplies of local laborers due to the exigencies of Caribbean warfare and labor supply-related problems on the West African coast. The extremes of the tropical weather also ensured that there were more tasks at hand than the available labor supply on the Caribbean sugar estates could handle at any given time.

Simon Taylor, for example, summed up all that could go wrong for sugar management's labor supply on an average production day in Jamaica.[7] Having just visited his sugar plantation, he reported in October 1767 that "the Negroes had been very sickly, but were then on the mending hand but even then there were 36 in the Hott House & 21 in the Yaws which is a very great drawback on the Estate especially as there had been a very great flood in May which had laid almost every part of the Estate under Water and Caterpillars had very much hurt the young rattoons near the Riverside . . ."[8] To make up for the damage caused by the floods and for other maintenance work on the estate, he diverted already scarce labor from the production and preparation of sugar. At the end of the exercise he lamented to his absentee landlord, Chaloner Arcedeckne, about the lack of labor he had at his disposal for accomplishing the many tasks on the estate.

Taylor's preoccupation with the estate's labor supply was typical of most managerial correspondence of eighteenth-century British Caribbean sugar managers. Indeed, they were always complaining of the lack of labor at their disposal and how this forced them to adopt expensive labor strategies like "jobbing" to compensate.[9] Sugar management's labor woes were further compounded by the enslaved peoples' failure to reproduce and their high mortality rate along with the colony's demands on them to assist in hurricane repair and with many military and social building works.

From the outset during the eighteenth century, the practice of manumission in British Caribbean sugar colonies operated in the shadow of the particular sugar colony's constant need for estate labor. Over time, those colonies whose land fertility had been exhausted, and the immediate demand for labor lessened, exhibited higher manumission rates.[10] However, in a still highly productive colony like Jamaica, in its "Golden Age" in the mid-eighteenth century, labor demands always set stringent institutional limits on the manumission level.

Jamaica therefore offers a typical case study of how planter-inspired manumission operated within an active sugar colony. In this context we will see, firsthand, how the rare cases of manumission in practice were never really contradictory ends for the white profit-maximizing sugar management (even though they often complained of the lack of labor). Taylor's estate correspondence, for example, does not include many cases of enslaved manumissions. In fact his only reference in forty-one years of plantation correspondence on the Golden Grove estate concerned one long overdue case. This case, based on a sexual relationship between the plantation's doctor and an enslaved woman, is revealing as it highlights another institutional limit to manumission that was not immediately apparent from Edward Long's account or from definitions like Stinchcombe's.

CATHERINE'S LIMITS

Dr. Collins was the plantation doctor on the Golden Grove sugar plantation in Jamaica during the mid-eighteenth century. During his tenure, and according to the plantation's accounts, he secured the affections of a comely enslaved woman named Catherine. Their union was productive and, over the years Catherine bore him three sons: Johnny, Edward, and Isaac. As a plantation doctor serving a large parish, Collins's place with Catherine was not permanent; he eventually left the estate and was replaced by another doctor. But Collins never forgot Catherine and their children and, upon his death, directed the executor of his will, one Mr. John Archer, to use £350 from his estate to manumit Catherine and his children.

In 1771 Simon Taylor, the Golden Grove sugar manager, wrote to his absentee employer on this manumission matter. He pointed out that "One Dr. Collins, who I believe formerly lived at Golden Grove, kept a woman belonging to you named Catherine, and had by her three sons, whose names are Johnny Chaplin, Edward Kidvallide Collins & Isaac Collins. He left Archer his executor, and money in his hands to buy the freedom of these people. He gave himself no trouble about it in his life, but by his will he mentioned it, and desires they may be bought."[11]

Taylor's letter to Arcedeckne drew attention to the fact that following Collins's death, Archer, his executor "gave himself no trouble" about the manumission of Catherine and her children. Only on the death of John Archer in 1771, do his (Archer's) executors bring the matter of Catherine and her children's manumission to the attention of the Golden Grove management. Even so, Taylor, being already harassed by the labor shortages on the estate, was willing to ignore the subject as he had other more "productive" matters to be concerned with. However, his interest in Catherine's case was stimulated by the absentee owner's mother, Mrs. Arcedeckne, who, being resident on the island and on the estate, had taken a personal interest in the matter. As Taylor apologetically confessed to his absentee, "she (Mrs. Arcedeckne) seems anxious about the matter for the children to be free."[12]

Even with the interest of the white matriarch on the side of the enslaved woman, nothing more happened. Two additional written directives from the various subsequent estate executors appear in 1773 and 1776 stipulating the terms of the will and reminding the Golden Grove management that the terms of the manumission were for "the Freedom of a Sambo Woman Slave named Catherine . . . & her three Children . . . provided the said Freedom or Manumission can be purchased for the Sum of three Hundred & fifty pounds of Current Money of Jamaica . . . out of my (Dr Collins) Estate for that purpose & . . . during the term of her (Catherine's) natural Life an Annuity or yearly sum of Twelve pounds Current Money of Jamaica."[13]

In spite of the detailed manumission reminders in the intervening years following Taylor's first mention of the matter to Chaloner, absolutely nothing was done in terms of Catherine's and her children's manumission. In fact, by 1776 Mrs. Arcedeckne had passed on and it seemed that the matter of

Catherine's manumission was now also dead. Catherine, however, desperate for the manumission that was given and promised to her and her children so long ago, forced a new manumission appeal to the absentee owner.

She located one of her former white owners and persuaded him to pen, on her behalf, a stirring appeal to Chaloner Arcedeckne stating that she was now "growing in years," and out of respect for his own late mother's wishes Arcedeckne should see to have her manumitted. To this latter end Catherine's former owner reminded Arcedeckne that "your late dear Mother, . . . often promise[d] that she would use her endeavor, that Catherine & her children should have their Freedom."[14]

It was now five years since the death of Dr. Collins's executor and, an additional indeterminable amount of years since the death of Collins himself. The matter was allowed to rest for a further seven years, and only when Simon Taylor was temporarily away from the estate due to ill health did his proxy, Timothy Penny, make another mention made of the matter in 1783. Why did the Golden Grove management ignore the manumission of this enslaved woman and her children even though Dr. Collins had made adequate provisions for it in his will?

In 1771 when the matter was first mentioned, the Golden Grove estate was experiencing its customary labor shortage. In this context it was understandable (from the white sugar management's perspective) why the usually meticulous sugar attorney Simon Taylor could have ignored the legal matter of Catherine's manumission. Catherine was still a viable working asset on the estate at this time and her manumission would not have served any beneficial purpose to the estate—it would have benefited only her and her children. However, by 1783 (twelve years after the initial manumission request!) things had changed. The estate correspondence now refers to Catherine as "aging," and the estate would now benefit from manumitting her for the sum set aside for that purpose.[15]

As profit-maximizing entrepreneurs Taylor and his compatriots sought to derive as much utility as possible from each unit of often scarce labor. Manumission aided this project only insofar as it allowed them to purchase younger, more productive labor. Manumission, though promised to Catherine was perhaps never granted her or, granted at a time when the utility to be derived from her continued enslavement was in decline—a telling comment on how white planter management viewed the "humane" rationale underlying manumission.

Additionally, the time lag involved in actually manumitting an enslaved person was a convenient legal device that afforded the current estate management much leeway in their consideration of manumission bequests. As

Catherine's bequest demonstrated, the legal wording of many of these manumission documents stated that it was up to the executor of the will and the owner of the enslaved person to decide whether the terms and remuneration of the bequest was adequate. As the period of consideration had no limitation, an open-ended situation in favor of white sugar management was often created.

This lack of prompt action—or any action—on manumission bequests brings into question how free these de jure manumitted people were. Clearly, the promise of manumitted freedom, even though stated in a will or in correspondence, often never affected the lives of the candidates in the manner that it was supposed to.

We can only speculate as to whether or not Catherine and her children were ever manumitted but, as her case illustrates, the promise of manumission so routinely touted as one of the few benevolent actions of the planter management often became no more than just that—a promise. How freeing then, for Catherine, was her manumission? Perhaps if this was an isolated case we would overlook this consideration. But, sad to say, Catherine's case was not isolated. Thomas Thistlewood, another infamous Jamaican sugar planter adventurer, in his diaries also inadvertently writes of the oftentimes hollow affect of the manumission process.

JOHN AND PHIBBAH

Thomas Thistlewood, who resided in Jamaica from 1750 till his death in 1786, tried his hand at pen keeping and sugar management and, during his involvement in these activities was able to record his numerous sexual "adventures" and rapes of enslaved women.[16] Within the large number of escapades allegedly initiated, he noted his favorite sexual partner, an enslaved woman named "Phibbah" who subsequently became his "wife." With her he had a son in April 1760, a mulatto boy named John Thistlewood.[17]

Thomas readily admitted paternity of John and, in an entry dated May 3, 1762, he had the boy manumitted.[18] However, about a year later on April 12, 1763, Thomas noted in his diaries that to date he had only been given a "receipt for John's manumission" as it had "not been recorded yet."[19] Five months later (and a full seventeen months after he had sought to have the boy manumitted), Thomas still had not succeeded in procuring John's manumission papers.[20] Official manumission for John remained a hollow promise to him.

This example illustrates that even when plantation management had a vested interest in speeding up the manumission process, the length of time between the actual receipt of official manumission (through the procurement of the papers) and the promise of manumission was often long and drawn out. In the interim, no doubt, the manumitted "candidate" (especially if an adult) would have acknowledged it in his best interest to remain a model enslaved person. Thus, by ensuring continued "good" behavior, the promise of manumission also served, in a practical way, the security concerns of the estate.

The case of Phibbah, John Thistlewood's mother, was also illuminating. She became Thomas Thistlewood's "wife" in 1753 with his move as overseer to the Egypt sugar estate.[21] By mid-June 1757 Thistlewood was again on the move, this time to the Kendal estate. At that time (and according to his account) their relationship had advanced to the point where he wished to take her with him. To this end Thistlewood made offers to purchase or hire Phibbah from her owners, Mr. and Mrs. Cope. However, Mrs. Cope refused to entertain any such deal.[22] Finally, ten years later, in November 1767, Thistlewood "hired" Phibbah from Mr. Cope and she came to live with him at Breadnut Island Pen.[23]

This new "living in" arrangement worked quite satisfactorily for Thistlewood; and while he openly continued having sexual relations with other women, Phibbah remained monogamous to him while being kept "in house." Indeed, prior to Thistlewood's having her personally established in his home, she had clearly shown her preference for other men; it was perhaps only because he could guarantee her "home stability" that she was now prepared, in return, to be monogamous.[24] As such, her manumission was possibly not necessary while Thistlewood was alive as he was guaranteed her fidelity. Additionally, her owners felt that she was more profitable to them while rented out to Thistlewood.[25] Of importance to us is her eventual manumission through Thistlewood's will.

Thistlewood died on November 30, 1786, and in his will left provisions for Phibbah to be manumitted. However, as in the case of Catherine on the Golden Grove estate, Phibbah was not immediately manumitted. In fact, she was manumitted six years later in November 1792 when she was an old woman with poor eyesight and gastric and dental ailments.[26]

As these examples demonstrate, although promised at times when the enslaved person could have benefited from it, manumission was often not actually given to them at that point. Additionally, by promising to manumit these enslaved women (usually at the death of their white "husbands"), their good behavior was ensured during their husbands' lifetime. Therefore, insofar as the male plantation management was concerned, the promise of manumission often served far more effectively as a control device for their "relationships" than actual manumission would. These considerations thus bring us to question the underlying motives for manumission and, by so doing, help explain the often hollow context of its actual attainment.

In the first instance, manumission can be interpreted as a gendered tool of control which, when properly dangled by the sugar management, ensured greater submission of the often "own-minded" enslaved women. This control was furthered when, as Long stated, a fixed sum of money was bequeathed to the manumitted person for life to be drawn on an annual basis—an interesting twist because, in addition to providing some form of sustenance to the manumitted person, it also limited her ability to move far from the confines of the estate.[27]

While in theory manumitted people were often free to go where they liked, in practice this was not so. Just as the system of apartheid in South Africa set rigid limitations on the movement and enjoyment of people with "black" skins, so too did plantation society set limits on the movement of manumitted people. An immediate disincentive to their physical freedom to move around arose from the precarious nature of their "paper" freedom. A lost manumission paper or one callously destroyed by a vindictive or labor-starved white manager meant the end of manumitted freedom unless it could be otherwise proven. In this case, as Edward Cox argued, the fear of being mistaken for enslaved people in rural areas forced skilled free people of color to gravitate to towns while rural manumitted people's continued dependency on estate labor forced them to remain close to the plantation of their original servitude.[28]

Freed people of color were not as *free* to move about as their status should have allowed them. Former enslaved persons were well advised to stay within the proximity of bona fide witnesses willing to vouch for their free status. Thus, the manumitted person, in practice, was confined to a limited geographical area. Additionally, most manumissions had a yearly stipend attached to them that warranted physical presence for collection.

In most cases and, certainly by the mid-eighteenth century, it became a prerequisite that the manumitted persons be provided with a pension to ensure that they did not depend on the funds of the state.[29] While a practical consideration, this also facilitated another, more sinister managerial aim of the plantation society for it ensured that to collect their pension, the manumitted persons would remain near the estate, thereby serving as a living example and tangible proof to the remaining enslaved people of what could be achieved if they were "good" slaves. True geographical mobility or freedom for manumitted persons would have defeated this goal of plantation management.

Clearly then the terms of a manumission document sought not to grant total freedom to the enslaved person, but rather only a limited, hollow freedom from the regimented work on the estate. But what then of those enslaved people who had actually received their manumission papers? How free were they? To answer this question we turn to the examples of the manumitted offspring of planter management.

THE PROBLEM OF FREEDOM

From the outset we note that manumission served very important managerial functions over and above that of a "gift" to the enslaved. By manumitting their mixed-race offspring for example, plantation management actively sought to encourage a social practice of miscegenation that concretized the point of lighter skin color as beneficial to freedom. Manumission in this regard was more than just a paternal instinct, it was a necessary social tool that buttressed the all-important and necessary tenet of white supremacy within the color-based social order.

Indeed the limited paternalistic thrust inherent in this avenue of manumission came from the fact that the manumitted person remained always at a disadvantage within a society that, though it had changed her legal status, had not changed the all-important color of her skin.[30] Manumission in this case was more a matter of "up and out" of the social order, rather than "up and in" as was the case in some slave societies in West Africa.[31] This is the critical point. "How free is free?" considers the worth of manumission in a society that understood social relations and status primarily in terms of skin color. To be manumitted in such a society meant, ironically, only to become part of another alienated (and oftentimes despised) group.

Manumitted people in the context of the British Caribbean system of chattel slavery were less free as individuals in terms of their identity. They were forced to interpret their freedom as a means of becoming more accepted into white society—the unspoken assumption in a society in which "black = slave" and "white = free." Their freedom served to create a social group of "mimic men" who functioned as an artificial buffer between the polarities of enslaved and free people. For example, Mary Prince (the first enslaved Caribbean woman to write her autobiography) noted that in her opinion the free colored people she met often took on airs and isolated themselves from the rest of the enslaved community.[32] She wrote, for example, of Martha Wilcox, a hired mulatto woman working in the Wood household, who "was such a fine lady she wanted to be mistress over me. I thought it very hard for a colored woman to have rule over me because I was a slave and she was free

. . . she was a saucy woman, very saucy; and she . . . rejoiced to have power to keep me down. She was constantly making mischief; there was no living in for the slaves—no peace after she came."[33]

In this sense the freedom bestowed on these manumitted people, due to social conditioning, contributed to their alienation from the rest of the enslaved class. Freedom left one not free to be oneself. Mary Prince wondered how free really was the mulatto woman? In this context, one notes further the use white society made of the testimonies of the "properly" acculturated free black population for their own ends. An example of this can be discerned in the records of the proceedings held into the aftermath of the 1817 Rebellion in Barbados. From the recorded testimonies it was clear that the free people had parroted testimony buttressing white society's belief that the enslaved people were wrongfully stirred up by their misunderstanding of the Registration Ordinance and, thus, caused the rebellion. Further, these free colored "witnesses" all claimed that the enslaved people had been well treated and humanely kept.[34] As a consequence of their helpful testimonies the free colored population received additional "incentives" after the inquest.

Clearly manumitted people of color had a role within white society—that of acting as models for the rest of the enslaved community and buttressing white society whenever necessary. Manumission was therefore a viable and important social tool for proper black acculturation that white society depended upon. Indeed the societal benefits that derived from it more than made up for any marginal cost associated with granting freedoms to token enslaved people.

Considerations of sociopsychological and legal freedoms apart, it was clear that even the literal physical freedom of a manumitted person was also questionable. To this end we can take the example of John Thistlewood, the manumitted mixed-race son of Thomas, who demonstrated that even growing up as a free manumitted person did not mean the automatic acquisition of the rights of white society or its corollary: the removal of the disabilities inherent in black enslaved society.

As a lad of seventeen John was serving an apprenticeship with a Mr. Hornby and had been absent from the place of his apprenticeship without permission of the master tradesman. Hearing this news, the white plantation owner Thomas Thistlewood immediately instructed that his son be "put in the bilboes when he came from muster & kept . . . in all night . . ."[35] Additionally, Thomas Thistlewood had John returned to his place of apprenticeship securely bound with ropes. Revealingly, the same treatment was meted out to the recaptured enslaved man Jimmy, who was also returned to Mr. Hornby under the same guard and conditions together with John. Clearly then, for all his manumitted status, John was still fundamentally considered, and punished, in a similar manner to other enslaved people.

But this was not just an isolated case of an irate father responding to the misadventures of his mixed race offspring. In general, white society exhibited a low toleration for manumitted persons even though, as Long stated, white society appreciated them for their economic worth and their strength in terms of deficiency ratios.[36] However that was as far as it went. White society did not allow them the real freedoms to life and liberty that a free (white) man should enjoy. Manumitted people were thus less free, ultimately, to exhibit the freedom that their legal manumission had allegedly procured for them.

FURTHER LIMITS TO THE MANUMISSION PROMISE

In 1810 Mary Prince returned to Bermuda and, through the cultivation and sale of produce, she began to save for manumission.[37] Eighteen years later she still had not saved enough to manumit herself and so, as an enslaved woman, she accompanied her owners to London.[38] This observation on Mary Prince illustrates two other aspects of the manumission process. While the system allowed a minority of enslaved people to conduct business to save toward their manumission, this in itself did not mean success in their businesses or the attainment, ever, of the required funds for self purchase. As in the case of Prince and in most other examples, when manumission eventually came, the manumitted people were usually not fit enough to enjoy it to the fullest. For example, when she finally secured her quasi freedom in London, Prince was already severely crippled and almost blind.

White society itself also generated negative blocks in attaining manumitted freedom. As Moira Ferguson pointed out in the case of Prince's owners, "The Woods evaluated Mary Prince's desire to leave them and find another master who would manumit her as a reflection on the quality of their ownership. So they compelled her to remain their slave in order to protect themselves from a moral judgment about the quality of servitude in their house-hold."[39]

White owners thus placed hurdles in the path of the enslaved's access to the legal option of manumission. This was taken to an extreme in plantation managers like Thistlewood who also made demands on the meager capital earnings of the enslaved population through loans or through charging them for goods and services they used or for tasks he believed they had unsatisfactorily performed.[40] Lurking in the background of all these human activities was the weather that, particularly on sugar islands like Jamaica, devastated both land and limb and no doubt terminated many other manumission hopes through loss of life and the added expenses of survival.

Negative white attitudes and the vagaries of nature apart, to succeed manumission had to account for the human dimension of "the enslaved people as people."[41] To manumit an enslaved woman while keeping the rest of her family enslaved was often a hollow accomplishment. It meant freedom for the individual—but in a real sense the manumittees were still enslaved by association with the ongoing pain and suffering of their spouses and offspring. How free then was this type of manumitted freedom? Indeed as in the case of Phibbah, Thomas Thistlewood only manumitted her son while her daughter remained enslaved.

In light of the many considerations and hurdles that confronted manumitted people, manumission was perhaps not intended as an end in itself aimed at improvements for the enslaved persons. Other reasons may offer better justifications for enslaved manumissions by white sugar society.

II

THE MANAGERIAL SIDE OF MANUMISSION: CONTROLLING SEXUALITY

Manumission buttressed the sexual impropriety of the sugar estates. Planter Edward Long's mention of the rightness of manumitting enslaved Domesticks reflected a deviously veiled planter agenda. Historian Hillary Beckles convincingly argued that these Domesticks often became domestics in name only and were usually mistresses or hired sex slaves.[42] Sexual practices like these advocated the master's right to control the enslaved woman's body in the field as well as within the bedroom. However, while providing white male management a preferential access to the sexuality of the enslaved women, these arrangements did not guarantee management's exclusivity—a sore point that harbored ill on the male planters' ego and necessitated action.

Simon Taylor, in his daily account of the colony's sugar business, reported an illustrative incident that occurred in Kingston during the first half of 1768. According to him two local assemblymen "Bayly" and "Kennion" were involved in a fracas over a quadroon girl.[43] Apparently she chose to allocate her sexual favors between the two white men and their subsequent fighting over her caused quite a stir in Kingston. Their animosity toward each other centered on who had the proper "right of possession" of the enslaved girl. It is clear from Taylor's account that Bayly legally "owned" the girl. However, as far as she was concerned, he did not control her sexuality.

Hillary Beckles elaborated on the (ab)use made of enslaved women's sexuality during the period of enforced labor. He identified the association between sexuality and manumission in the prostitution taverns of British Caribbean sugar society where enslaved women were offered the boon of freedom as an incentive for maintaining their "enthusiasm" while in prostitution. He concluded that, in these cases, manumission was an appropriate incentive for them as "freedom was a legal status not easily rejected."[44] Though countless enslaved women were violated under these conditions, many enslaved women, far from being only victims, were also alleged to have used their sexuality to better their positions.

Long, for example, wrote: "In regard to the African mistress, . . . her dexterity consists in persuading the (white) man she detests to believe she is most violently smitten with the beauty of his person . . . and, by this stratagem, she is better able to hide her private intrigues with her real favorites."[45] While Long could be faulted for his racial bias, examples of white male "cuckolding" by enslaved women abound throughout the plantation literature. Historian Douglas Hall, for example, cites Thomas Thistlewood and the problems he had keeping his favorite mistresses faithful to him. Additionally, Hall points to other cases where the enslaved women had the better of many of the white estate managers. White plantation managers then, while in a position to abuse enslaved women's sexuality, were generally not in a position to control it. Enslaved plantation women were free to engage in other sexual liaisons with other men both black and white.

Thus, the move to "wifedom" and the associated manumission or promise of manumission that often came with it sought, in a real way, to restrict the enslaved woman's sexuality. For she now had a legal sponsor or "husband" who, in wanting to reserve her intimate favors for his exclusive use, took her off the sex "market." With the hope of manumission dangled before her, she would make every effort to ensure this desired hope was achieved even if it meant fidelity—a fidelity Long was clear to point out that the enslaved women were expert in feigning.

While white managers wished for fidelity from their enslaved women, it was oftentimes not their only wish. This point is exemplified in the case Thomas Sampson's wife. When Sampson, the overseer on the Amity Hall estate, decided to "marry" his enslaved mistress in Jamaica in 1818, the terms of the manumission document prepared for her were very clear. In addition to stating that she and her children were under "bond of Thomas Sampson," it also stated that she and her children were also the "property of Amity Hall." In a strange twist then, her annuity was to be matched by the estate itself.[46] As such she was now indebted both to the estate and to Sampson for her freedom. In ways like this we see collusion between male absentee plantation owners and local white male managers in buttressing a practice that benefited primarily their personal ends rather than those of the manumitted person. In this case the estate benefited as the enslaved woman would still be around the estate and Sampson benefited as he now had an "obedient" wife.

The practice of allowing white employees to purchase and manumit enslaved women and their mulatto children was also a mark of favor to maintain harmony between owners (usually absentees) and local managers. As Lord Barham told one of his managers: "I have to confess very strong objections to sell my slave in whatever case—but I should be sorry to let the opportunity escape of expressing my regard for you and opinion of your services."[47] In this context manumitted freedom provided an incentive to the white worker rather than a reward for the enslaved person who was manumitted. Attitudes like these shaped the degree and type of freedom offered.

As incidents like these illustrate, manumitted women became legally bound to their benefactors as their papers clearly identified who manumitted them and paid their pensions. Additionally, by manumitting an enslaved woman or by promising to manumit her, white managers not only made her freedom dependent on them, but also made the women more "monogamous."[48] Again, the question could be asked of these women after manumission—how free was free?

Indeed the Barbadian Legislature clearly summed up the ego-based phallocentric reasoning that underlay manumission when they debated the continued status of female enslaved manumission in the colony. Beckles noted:

> In 1774, a bill was introduced into the Assembly aimed at curtailing the number of females being manumitted. It was designed to raise the manumission fee to £100, but was rejected on the grounds that slave owners should not be deprived of the right to assist the "most deserving part" of their slaves—"the females who have generally recommended themselves to our 'kindest notice.'" It was defeated by a vote of eleven to five; opposition was led by Sir John Gay Alleyne who argued that female slaves who gave their loyalty, love and service to masters should not be denied the opportunity to gain freedom.[49]

III

CONCLUSION

Manumission during the period of British Caribbean slavery was the practice of granting legal freedom to a very small group of enslaved Africans and their enslaved descendents. This numerically small group, in the Anglophone

Caribbean, hardly affected the ranks of enslaved people, in contrast to the large numbers of manumitted people within Greek slavery. Indeed in many cases, the promise of manumission, rather than the benefits of the act itself, was the closest that many of these enslaved people ever came to actually receiving their freedom. While many writers have argued that manumission was a widespread practice in the Anglophone Caribbean during the period of enslavement, this chapter argued that its impact was negated because of its use as a managerial and social conditioning tool. Even further, historical methodology calls for the discerning historian to more critically interrogate the plantation records and statistics to understand the reality of manumission or, as was shown, the hollow nature of the promise of manumission. This redirected focus clearly showed the secondary context of the planters' benevolence and why the manumitted freedom was in itself a limited one.

Even at the best of times, manumission was a lengthy, drawn-out process that the manumission request carried in wills or noted in plantation papers seldom reflected. Too often researchers viewed the provisions for or promises of manumission within wills and legacies as proof of manumission. Often, the high demand for plantation labor and the gross indifference of white plantation managers made manumission a dead letter in the lives of the vast majority of enslaved people. This is not to say that the enslaved people never wanted their freedom. Indeed the reality of almost daily revolts and widespread marroonage by the enslaved, coupled with the their own attempts for self-purchase, demonstrated the indelible will of the human spirit, wherever it be, to be free. Sadly, however, even in the act of manumission these people were still denied their right to be truly free.

Ultimately the practice of manumission in white plantation society respected white rights of ownership and pleasure and the exigencies of plantation labor and security above that of the welfare of the enslaved person. Primarily these factors and not any sense of misguided passion or loyalty largely determined who was manumitted and when they would be so. These considerations prompted our query, How free was free? Within a society that believed in a false inequality of the races, the manumitted person would never automatically belong to the free society by virtue of a legal device.

A necessary corollary to manumission concerns the related avenue of the subsequent level of social absorption. This determined not only the extent to which manumitted persons would be considered equal but also the means they would have to enjoy freedom within the society. In the British Caribbean, as the struggle of the "colored's" right through to the nineteenth century demonstrated, proper enjoyment of manumitted freedom was never the case nor, as this chapter contends, was it ever a desirable goal underlying planter-sponsored manumission in these societies.

This chapter also comments on the state of the dominant historiography surrounding Caribbean enslaved manumissions before 1834 that often offers a simplistic understanding of this historical process. Caribbean historians need to become more vigilant in analyzing planters' statements and need to routinely interrogate evidence that may or may not justify their many assertions. Only by properly reconciling statements within the primary sources with the evidence can we ever really have a true, and free, Caribbean historiography.

Notes

1. Edward Long, "Freed Blacks and Mulattos," in *Slaves, Free Men, Citizens,* ed. Landros Comitas, David Lowenthal (New York: Anchor Books, 1973), 75–93.

2. The usual means to saving enough for manumission via the "commodity" route came through the marketing of crops obtained from the gardens of the enslaved people or through sales of animals they owned.

3. In this chapter the markers "white" and "black" are viewed as relatively inaccurate nouns or adjectives for groups of people as these signifiers tend to be too general and do not force identification with specific cultural traits and worldviews that may affect historical interpretations and understandings of various groups of people. For a more detailed understanding of nomenclature and historical interpretation in Caribbean history see John Campbell, "Textualising Slavery: From 'Slave' to 'Enslaved People' in Caribbean Historiography" in *Beyond the Beach, the Blood and the Banana,* ed. Sandra Courtman (Kingston: Ian Randle, 2004), 34–35.

4. Craton points out that by 1780 the population ratio had stabilized "to around 10:1 overall but being up to six times as high on the estates and those farthest inland." Michael Craton, *Empire Enslavement and Freedom in the Caribbean* (Kingston: Ian Randle, 1997), 165–66.

5. In 1739 for example, the manumission fee in Barbados was legally set at £50 plus an annuity of £4 local currency; poor law officials insisted upon the annuity as one way to prevent holders of enslaved people from freeing old and infirmed persons who could not, reasonably, be expected to earn their subsistence on their own.

6. Arthur Stinchcombe, *Sugar Island Slavery in the Age of Enlightenment* (Princeton, N.J: Princeton University Press, 1995), 139–40.

7. Simon Taylor was a creole planter born in Jamaica in 1740; he owned four plantations in addition to those he managed for absentee owners like the English landowner Chaloner Arcedeckne. For a detailed insight into his career and plantation interests see Betty Wood and T. R. Clayton, "Slave Birth, Death and Disease on Golden Grove Plantation, Jamaica, 1765–1810," *Slavery and Abolition* 6, no. 2 (September 1985): 99–121.

8. Simon Taylor to Benjamin Cowell, October 3, 1767, Vanneck Papers, Jamaican Estate Records 1765–1810. (J.E.R.), 2 Boxes. Cambridge, Cambridge University Library, Manuscripts Room. Contains letters, maps, estate records, and slave lists for the period. Offers a rare, continuous focus on the managerial business of an estate and the management of the estate's labour force.

9. "Jobbing slaves" were gangs of enslaved people usually owned by another planter or overseer and rented out to neighboring estates to extend their labor supply as and when required.

10. Additionally, an overall increase in manumission rates occurred on all islands on the eve of emancipation, once again emphasizing the profit-maximizing aspect of the act as it occurred at a time that was financially beneficial to bankrupt (and soon to be compensated) white sugar management.

11. Taylor to Arcedeckne, Kingston, December 3, 1771, Vanneck Papers.

12. Ibid.

13. Extract of will dated May 24, 1773, and contained in Timothy Penny to Chaloner Arcedeckne, February 6, 1783, Vanneck Papers.

14. Extract of letter dated October 31, 1776, and contained in Timothy Penny to Chaloner Arcedeckne, February 6, 1783, Vanneck Papers.

15. The usual practice was to manumit aged enslaved people when their utility was low and their purchase price could be used to finance the purchase of younger workers. See, for example, Hibbert & Taylor to Sir Hugh Smyth, August 19, 1797, County Council Record Office, Bristol (BCCRO), A C/WO 16 (27), 117(a); see also Fearon to Penhryn, October 25, 1805, University of North Wales: Penhryn MS, 1366 University of North Wales at Bangor, Penhryn MS, 1207–1442 letters to Richard Pennant (Lord Penhryn) from Jamaica on all aspects of estate management.

16. Shepherd points out that "his physical and sexual abuse of enslaved women leaves us in no doubt about his attitude toward them" and that he, "like other white men, seemed to have believed that one advantage of coming to the island was the chance of sexually exploiting many black and coloured women." V. Shepherd, "Gender and Representation in European Accounts of Pre-emancipation Jamaica," *Caribbean Slavery in the Atlantic World* (Kingston: Ian Randle Publishers, 2000), 706.

17. Douglas Hall, *In Miserable Slavery: Thomas Thistlewood in Jamaica 1750–86* (Kingston: University of the West Indies Press, 1999), 94.

18. Ibid., 314.

19. Ibid., 129.

20. Ibid.

21. This followed his separation from his first "wife," Jenny. Ibid., 32, 51.

22. Ibid., 79.

23. Ibid., 146.

24. Thistlewood did note that he suspected her having a tryst with Egypt Lewie in May 1777 and later, in January 1785, with "Strap." The illicit context of these epi-

sodes clearly implied that she was not entitled, as he was, to outside affairs. Ibid., 250, 302.

25. No doubt the Copes used Phibbah's involvement with Thistlewood to keep him involved with the management of their affairs as well.

26. Ibid., 314.

27. Edward Long, *The History of Jamaica,* 3 vols. (London: Frank Cass & Co Ltd., [1774] 1970), 2:322–33

28. Edward Cox, *Free Coloreds in the Slave Societies of St Kitts and Grenada, 1763–1833* (Knoxville: University of Tennessee Press, 1984), 29–32.

29. Even in later-acquired British territories like Grenada, new legislation was quickly introduced to bring them up to par with the other islands' practices in this regard. For example, a 1764 law stipulated that persons manumitting enslaved people by last will were to pay an additional £100 for each manumission (ibid., 33–37). In Antigua during the eighteenth century, "the law there compels landless manumitted people 'to enter themselves into the service of some family'" (Long, "Freed Blacks," 321). In Barbados a 1739 law fixed the manumission fee at £50 plus an annuity of £4 local currency (Hillary Beckles, "Property Rights in Pleasure: The Marketing of Enslaved Women's Sexuality," in *Slavery in the Atlantic World,* ed. Verene Shepherd, Hillary Beckles [Kingston: Ian Randle, 2000], 699). Jamaica had perhaps the most elaborate laws; from 1711 it passed legislation for the entire group of free coloured people that set severe restriction on them (Douglas Hall, "Jamaica," in *Neither Slave nor Free: The Freedmen of African Descent in the Slave Societies of the New World,* ed. David W. Cohen, Jack P. Greene [Baltimore, Md.: The John Hopkins University Press, 1972], 197–98).

30. Newly liberated, the manumitted person entered at the bottom of an already existing social hierarchy which was itself, highly stratified according to skin color and wealth. Karl Watson, *The Civilised Island Barbados: A Social History 1750–1816* (Bridgetown, Barbados: Caribbean Graphic Productions Ltd., 1979), 105.

31. James L. Watson, *Asian and African Systems of Slavery* (Berkeley: University of California Press, 1980), 10.

32. Mary Prince, *The History of Mary Prince: A West Indian Slave Related by Herself* (Ann Arbor: University of Michigan Press, 2000), 1–4.

33. Ibid., 79–80.

34. See, for example, the testimonies of Jacob Belgrave, a "free" mulatto (38); Thomas Harris, a "free" man of color (39); William Yard, a "free" black man (39); and Thomas Brewster, a "free" colored man (40) cited in Barbados House of Assembly, *The Report from a select committee of the House of Assembly appointed to inquire into the Origin, Causes and progress of the late insurrection* (Bridgetown, 1818). Unpublished manuscript.

35. Hall, *In Miserable Slavery,* 251; also 261 where in addition to being put in the bilboes and tied, John was also "pretty well flogged" and denied the use of his shoes.

36. Long pointed out that they also provided a source of skilled apprentices who would undercut the exorbitant prices charged by white tradesmen.

37. Prince, *The History of Mary Prince,* 9.

38. Ibid., 21.

39. Ibid., 18.

40. See, for example, May 19, 1781, where he forced his enslaved people to pay for limes he thought they had stolen. See also February 10, 1784 where he also made the estate's fisherman, Dick, pay him for "bringing such bad fish." For references see Hall, *In Miserable Slavery,* 284, 298.

41. Douglas Hall rightly stressed this point in "People in Slavery," in *Inside Slavery, Process and Legacy in the Caribbean Experience,* ed. Hillary Beckles (Kingston: Canoe Press, 1985), 12–30.

42. Beckles, "Property Rights in Pleasure," 694.

43. Simon Taylor to Chaloner Arcedeckne dated July 25, 1768, Vanneck Papers.

44. Beckles, "Property Rights in Pleasure," 697.

45. Long, "Freed Blacks," 87–88.

46. Correspondences of Amity Hall, Vere and the Bogue Pen, Jamaica May 20, 1818, 304/ Box 42, Surrey Record Office, Surrey, UK.

47. Barham to White & Webb, July 1, 1804, Bodl. MS, Clarendon dep. c. 357 Oxford, Bodleian Library, Clarendon MSS, Barham Family papers. Letters and papers pertaining to their Jamaican estates, 1747–1835. (MS. Clar. Dep.): Mesopotamia and island plantations. Letterbook—contains letters between Barham and estate managers.

48. As Beckles demonstrated in his analysis of late eighteenth-century Barbadian slave prostitution, women were less likely to become slave prostitutes when their status changed to "mistresses" or "married." Beckles, "Property Rights in Pleasure," 697.

49. Ibid., 699–700.

2

A Harsh and Gloomy Fate

Liberated Africans in the Service of the Brazilian State, 1830s–1860s

BEATRIZ G. MAMIGONIAN

In June 1855, among dozens of petitions for emancipation, Brazilian Ministry of Justice officials received one from Desidério, a man from the West Coast of Africa with a long story to tell. He was brought to Brazil as a slave in 1835 and was seized by authorities in Bahia charged with repressing the slave trade, then illegal. He was emancipated and, as a "liberated African," he served for fourteen years at the Bahia Navy Arsenal. Then, with fellow liberated Africans, he was transferred to Rio de Janeiro and sent into the interior of the province of São Paulo, to work in the Imperial Iron Foundry of Ipanema. From there, he returned to Rio. He was serving in the First Cavalry Regiment at the time he filed the petition. He, as had his mate João, had served the imperial government for almost twenty years, and yet a previous petition for their emancipation had been rejected on the grounds that they "belonged" to a public institution, and were, therefore, not entitled to emancipation.[1]

Similar petitions filled the offices of the 3rd section of the Brazilian Ministry of Justice. They represented a special legal category: liberated Africans ("*africanos livres*") who had been seized either from the ships condemned for illegal slave trading or soon after disembarking. They were emancipated and put under the custody of the Brazilian government for a term of mandatory service that was to last fourteen years.[2] The Africans distributed among private hirers and public institutions in the 1830s and early 1840s had already completed the prescribed terms. Yet, the decree that prompted that flow of petitions (decree n. 1303 of December 28, 1853) granted emancipation to all liberated Africans who served private hirers for fourteen years and purposely excluded the liberated Africans who worked at public institutions.[3]

Desidério and João, like many other liberated Africans who served their terms in public institutions, had their petitions refused despite the fact that they had completed, and often surpassed, the prescribed terms. For this reason, in his new petition written in June 1855, Desidério included not only the references to all treaties and legislation that conferred on him special rights based on his place of origin in Africa, but also a special plea in the name of all liberated Africans who served in public institutions. He declared that he had suffered through "years of unreasonable service and unfair punishment" and asked for the personal intervention of Emperor Pedro II. Desidério predicted that without royal assistance, he and the other liberated Africans in service to the imperial government would "be forever true slaves of the same government, at its mere discretion; and with all resources exhausted they would perish under the harshness of such a gloomy fate."[4]

Desidério's eloquent plea calls attention to the fate of the liberated Africans in Brazil, and particularly to those in service to the Brazilian government. This essay examines the confined and hard-laboring lives of the liberated Africans who served in public institutions and contrasts their experiences to those of the liberated Africans who worked for private hirers and those elsewhere in the Atlantic. Besides inspiring reflection on state-sanctioned compulsory labor, this essay aims to show that liberated Africans were a group of coerced laborers peculiar to the age of abolition and that in Brazil this status carried a particular significance that contributed to their fate. The sources, petitions for emancipation filed by the liberated Africans in the 1850s and 1860s and rich documentation from the Brazilian Ministry of Justice on the group, allow a "microscopic" examination of the Brazilian version of the system that, under the name of apprenticeship, kept free persons as coerced laborers, and offer unprecedented insight into how liberated Africans experienced the contradictions related to their peculiar category in the harshest of working environments, that of the public institutions.

The Principle of Liberated African Apprenticeship and Its Application in Brazil

The creation of the category of liberated Africans was a direct, although unforeseen, consequence of the British abolitionist campaign in the nineteenth century. Legally derived from legislation and international treaties designed to prohibit the continuation of the Atlantic slave trade, the category of liberated Africans was handled differently in the various Atlantic and Indian Ocean territories where it existed, such as Sierra Leone, the Cape Colony, Mauritius, and the Seychelles in Africa; and Cuba, the Bahamas, Jamaica,

British Guiana, Surinam, and Brazil in the Americas. Nevertheless, even though they were often taken for slaves, liberated Africans throughout the Atlantic shared the special legal status of free persons who had to remain under the guardianship of the state for a period of time before attaining "full freedom."[5]

The bilateral agreements signed by Great Britain with Spain, the Netherlands, and Portugal in 1817–18 and with Brazil in 1826 to abolish the slave trade made each government responsible to "guarantee the liberty" of the Africans emancipated in its territory and determined that they were to be "employed as servants or free laborers."[6] Deemed by imperial administrators as "barbarous" and unfit to enjoy their right to freedom, liberated Africans were forced to endure a transition period before they could enjoy the status of freedpersons with full privileges. Recruitment and apprenticeship seemed ideal for achieving this goal, since responsibility for, and protection and control of, the Africans' insertion into the labor market were distributed among military units, private parties, and public institutions encouraged to employ and educate the Africans in crafts or trades. The compulsory term of service varied by place and was formulated to facilitate the adaptation of the recaptives, socially and geographically displaced by enslavement, to their new places of residence. Combining labor training, social control, and cultural adaptation in a compulsory labor system, imperial authorities expected the liberated Africans to "prove themselves worthy of enjoying their complete right to freedom."[7]

To serve their terms of apprenticeship in Brazil, liberated Africans were distributed among private individuals and public institutions, mainly in the city of Rio de Janeiro. A close look at their labor experience reveals that they lived and worked alongside private slaves at their hirers' houses or alongside crown slaves at public institutions and were treated as slaves in many ways: liberated Africans could not be bought or sold, but the transfer of their "concessions" was often a monetary transaction; they often hired out or put to hire themselves out in the streets of Rio and never kept their earnings, and they were not trained to take on skilled occupations.[8] Significantly, until the 1860s, the children of liberated Africans inherited the ambiguous status of their parents instead of being considered free.[9] Moreover, in the late 1840s, Brazilian authorities changed their policy and refused to recognize liberated Africans' right to "full freedom" after fourteen years of service. In other Atlantic territories where this category existed, with the exception of Cuba, the treatment of the liberated Africans was adjusted to new ideas on free labor during the nineteenth century, and the terms of apprenticeship were shortened.[10] In Brazil, much like in Cuba, the presence of liberated Africans among the slaves, particularly the newly arrived Africans, was resented by masters, and avoided by the authorities whenever possible. Thus, they were kept under increased control.

The reason for tensions in dealing with liberated Africans was the continuation of the slave trade that renewed legislation and international agreements failed to curb. In fact, the slave trade to Brazil thrived despite the bilateral treaty signed between Great Britain and Brazil that became effective in March 1830 and the subsequent national law for the abolition of the trade passed by the Brazilian Parliament in November 1831. Approximately 11,000 Africans were "rescued" from the slave trade between 1821 and 1856, while during the two decades of illegal activity, the 1830s and 1840s, the trade brought 760,000 Africans to Brazil who were illegally held in slavery. The Brazilian government's policy toward liberated Africans was a direct reflection of this considerable legal problem; following the 1831 law, their free status should have been extended to all Africans who entered Brazil after abolition. But, for political reasons, it was not.[11]

Life under the Watchful Eyes of Public Institutions' Overseers and the Brazilian Government's Labor Policy

Ministry of justice officials collected information on the individual fates of the liberated Africans to compile a register in 1865. The careful analysis of the information on the Africans first emancipated in the 1830s from the *Duquesa de Bragança, Continente, Novo Destino, Rio da Prata, Cezar, Angélica,* and *Amizade Feliz* shipments, and from small seizures made by local authorities reveals details about the liberated African experience never examined until now. The separation of the liberated Africans by place of service and by sex, and moreover, the calculation of the length of their terms of service until their deaths or emancipation, provide a striking picture of the harshness of life in public service.

The labor experience of the liberated Africans serving in public institutions was considerably different from that of liberated Africans granted to private hirers. Liberated Africans in public institutions did not have the "master" figure of a hirer; instead, they worked under the orders of administrators and overseers who also dealt with slaves and free laborers. Their socialization was also very different from that experienced by liberated Africans granted alone or in small groups to private hirers; liberated Africans in public institutions often lived and worked in large groups, which in some cases facilitated the formation of stable families. In the 1830s, only one-fifth of all the liberated Africans distributed for service by the imperial government were sent to public institutions. In the 1850s all the liberated Africans emancipated in the last years of the slave trade were engaged by public institutions and colonization projects.

The judge of orphans and the Ministry of Justice distributed the Africans emancipated by the Mixed Commission Court (the British and Brazilian tribunal charged with enforcing the slave trade treaty) or by Brazilian judicial authorities in Rio de Janeiro to work in institutions subordinated to the central government or located in Rio de Janeiro. They served at the House of Correction (in the construction of the prison building), at the Navy and War Arsenals, in public works, in the Gunpowder Factory, in many nongovernmental institutions such as brotherhoods and other civil societies, and also in the Ironworks of Ipanema, located in the interior of the province of São Paulo.[12] The compiled data on 955 liberated Africans distributed for service in the 1830s shows that 28.4 percent of liberated Africans serving public institutions died in the first five years after emancipation, while considerably fewer of those serving private hirers (15 percent) died during the same period.

The disproportion in mortality rates, particularly during the first year after arrival, can be attributed partly to the fact that hirers received liberated Africans who enjoyed better health and partly to the precarious care for the infirm in public institutions. While one hirer would probably oversee the

Table 2.1. Distribution of Liberated Africans for Service According to Sex

	Male	%	Female	%	Unknown	%	Total	%
Hirers	437	74.2	317	93.8	19	67.8	773	81.0
Institutions	145	24.6	17	5.0	7	25.0	169	17.7
Not Distributed[1]	5	0.8	3	0.9	2	7.2	10	1.0
Not Registered[2]	2	0.4	1	0.3	0	0	3	0.3
Total	589	100.0	338	100.0	28	100.0	955	100.0

[1] Deceased before distribution for service.

[2] Place of work not registered.

Source: Tables with information on the liberated Africans of the *Duquesa de Bragança* (1834), *Continente* (1835), *Novo Destino* (1835), *Rio da Prata* (1835), *Angélica* (1835), *Amizade Feliz* (1835), *Cezar* (1838), and of apprehensions made by local judges between 1835 and 1837 prepared by the Ministry of Justice probably in 1865. They compiled information on where each liberated African was put to work (name of the hirer or institution), what became of him or her (death, emancipation, escape, unknown), and when (date of death or emancipation). Those tables were completed with information gathered from petitions of emancipation and registries of death of liberated Africans. The total number of Africans listed is 955; AN, IJ6 471—Ofícios, relações e processos sobre Africanos livres, 1834–1864.

Table 2.2. Terms of Service of Deceased Liberated Africans According to Place of Work

Years	Hirers	% of Total Distributed	Institutions	% of Total Distributed
0–4	116	15.0	48	28.4
5–9	76	9.8	15	8.9
10–14	56	7.2	6	3.6
15–19	38	4.9	9	5.3
20–24	37	4.8	12	7.1
25–29	10	1.3	2	1.2
Total	333	43.0	92	54.5

Source: See Table 2.1. Sample of 425 deceased liberated Africans with known terms of service and places of work. Total distributed to hirers, 773; to institutions, 169.

care dispensed to the few liberated Africans he or she received, directors of institutions or overseers would not give the same attention to individuals in the groups assigned to them. The heavy work performed by liberated Africans, particularly in public works, road projects, and in the arsenals, was also one possible reason for their high mortality in the first years. Overall, the variation in mortality rates reflects the differences between the lives of liberated Africans in institutions and those serving private hirers; documents from the institutions and the Africans' own petitions provide further details of their labor experience.

The majority of the liberated Africans in service to the state worked alongside other liberated Africans within the larger group of laborers employed by the institutions. Thus, not only did they often spend their terms of service with some of their shipmates, but also they had to relate to slaves and free persons who worked with them. In establishments such as the Gunpowder Factory, the Navy and War Arsenals in Rio, or the Ironworks of Ipanema in the province of São Paulo, liberated Africans were part of a complex industrial labor force producing vital military equipment and supplies for the country and that employed not only state slaves and liberated Africans but also Brazilian-born and foreign skilled laborers. The labor arrangements and occupations of the liberated Africans show, however, that they were treated as slaves rather than as free laborers.

In the major public institutions of the empire, liberated Africans joined existing groups of state slaves. Known as *"escravos da nação"* ("nation slaves"), state slaves had been acquired through purchase, donation, and natural reproduction; they lived and worked in public establishments of the crown or the imperial state, such as the Santa Cruz Farm, the Navy and War Arsenals of Rio de Janeiro, the Gunpowder Factory, and the Ironworks of Ipanema.[13] Through marriage and the bonds created by their common status, state slaves appeared to have formed stable communities in the institutions they served. They had little access to manumission until the first half of the nineteenth century, particularly because their opportunities to earn cash were limited. Administrators reported "behavior problems" and complained of their inefficiency. The solution adopted was to break their bonds by moving them from one institution to the other. Their numbers not augmented by the purchase of new Africans, but only by births and the occasional acquisitions of Creole slaves, the groups of state slaves tended to age and to decrease in number by natural death from 1830 onwards. The arrival of the liberated Africans at the institutions filled the void left by the deceased and aging state slaves; they supplied labor for the indispensable tasks that required a reliable labor force and that were rejected by free laborers.

Although they sometimes had a special overseer, and their records were kept in separate registries, liberated Africans usually shared lodging, food, and occupations with state slaves. In 1844, in the Navy Arsenal of Rio de Janeiro, a sizeable military complex located on *Ilha das Cobras* (Snakes' Island) and in adjoining buildings on the shore of the city's harbor, the 61 existing liberated Africans shared their daily lives with 170 state slaves, of whom 110 were adult Africans, 37 were adult Creoles, and 18 were children.[14] The Navy minister's report for that year showed that the largest group of liberated Africans was employed on board the frigate *Cábrea;* others served in the Navy hospital, on the launches, and at the arsenal; and a few were employed in the workshops. In all locations, liberated Africans worked alongside slaves; a strong evidence of their labor engagement lies in the fact that there were proportionally more male slaves than liberated Africans employed in the workshops, that is, engaged in skilled trades. A more detailed account of the occupations of the liberated Africans and the state slaves at the Navy Arsenal was given by the arsenal's inspector in 1849:

> Those staying at the *Cábrea* are employed daily in the various and diverse jobs of that frigate, in the launches and tug boats, in transportation, in lifting and mooring ships and boats; those quartered on board the brig *Imperial Pedro* are employed, some in the workshops, other on the launches, and some with the slave women in the ordinary cleaning of the Arsenal; while it is from those serving on land that we select those who go to the pen with carts to transport the meat to all the war boats, other transports and unarmed ships, to carry the sick and the dead; and finally, [they are also employed] in running aground ships, launches, antennas, masts, large rods, and [for that] I order them removed from all the workshops . . . ever since the galleys who performed these and other heavy labors were removed to the construction of

> the dike on *Ilha das Cobras;* adding to that the fact that many times these jobs are reinforced by the colonists who are employed as servants in the works of *Ribeira Nova,* where they usually don't stay.[15]

According to the arsenal's inspector, therefore, liberated Africans and nation slaves were employed in the heavy work of assisting the ships' operations and for menial tasks such as cleaning and carrying the sick and the dead. Liberated Africans, state slaves, and galley prisoners performed all the services that were refused by free persons.[16] The inspector explained that liberated Africans and slaves were removed from the workshops whenever they were needed for simpler tasks, demonstrating how fundamental their manpower was and yet how unimportant and dispensable their training was regarded by administrators.

Slaves and liberated Africans received the same compensation for their labor: food and clothing. In the budget for slaves and liberated Africans, the Navy Arsenal had provisions for the men's clothing (they received two shirts, two pairs of trousers, and one coat twice a year, plus one cover and one hat every year) and for daily payments of 140 réis for every adult and 110 réis for every laboring child. It was from the money of their daily payments (which apparently did not reach the laborers) that the slaves and liberated Africans' food was purchased by the arsenal. According to the inspector, they were served three meals daily: dried meat and manioc flour porridge at lunch, beans with meat and pork fat at dinner, and rice with pork fat at night. Women's and children's clothing, medicine, or special chicken meals for pregnant women were not in the budget but were bought with leftover money.[17]

There can be no doubt that the liberated Africans received the same treatment as the state slaves in the Navy Arsenal: not only did they perform the same functions and receive the same food and clothing, but they also received (or failed to receive) the same amount for their services. The chronic need for laborers felt throughout the first half of the nineteenth century at the arsenal led to different solutions for the performance of many of its functions, for example, the recruiting of native Indians, free unemployed laborers, and prisoners or the hiring of private slaves. Instead of receiving training to perform skilled functions, which would allow them greater autonomy, liberated Africans were employed among those involuntary laborers. Skilled laborers were in high demand both in the public and private sectors. Several sections of the Navy Arsenal employed free laborers, and their payment varied according to their level of specialization. While an experienced ironworker was employed in 1843 for the daily sum of 4000 réis, in the late 1840s, colonists from the Azores were engaged as oarsmen and servants for the monthly sum of 8$000 to 10$000 réis plus food in their first year of contract. For practically the same type of service performed by the liberated Africans, the Azorean colonists received in the first year of their contract twice the amount paid to the Africans, and probably more in the following years, demonstrating that liberated Africans were treated not as free but as involuntary laborers.[18]

That the labor regime in the public institutions was more rigid than the one practiced by private hirers is clear from various sources. Liberated Africans who became insubordinate and refused to obey their hirers' orders were often transferred to institutions where, it was expected, they would be subjected to stricter discipline. That was the case of Maria Benguela, who, according to hirer João de Almeida Brito, "was unworthy of being in a respectable home" and was moved to the House of Correction "for the sake of improving her conduct."[19] In many institutions, liberated Africans and other workers were subject to military discipline, which limited their spatial mobility; they needed special authorization to leave the institutions and were punished for disobeying their overseers. Those seen as "unfit" were never authorized to circulate freely in the city; for example, Firmina Benguela did not leave the House of Correction for four years because, according to the director, "she had given herself in to the vice of drunkenness."[20] Moreover, liberated Africans in the service of public institutions had less chance than others to accumulate cash, for not only did they receive little or no pay for their labor, but they could work outside the institutions only on Sundays and holidays.[21] In fact, the rigorous regime of the public institutions must have given liberated Africans the impression that there was no way out, for not only was emancipation a dim perspective, but running away also rarely guaranteed freedom for long: of the twenty-nine liberated Africans reported as runaways in 1865, only one belonged to a public institution, and that was Ambrósio Benguela, who ran away from the works at the House of Correction in 1837, three years after being emancipated from the *Duquesa de Bragança*.[22]

What explains the fact that liberated Africans were kept as involuntary workers in public institutions by the same administration that should have fostered their treatment as free laborers? That which was justified in the beginning by the need to protect and guide the newly arrived Africans during a period of adaptation soon took the shape of permanent indenture. Liberated Africans not only did not collect compensation for their labor, but they were also not allowed to leave the institutions or choose other occupations or employers. The fact that the Brazilian imperial government kept liberated Africans under strict control and employed them in various government projects could have been a response to the lack of free laborers in the market. However, the influx of a significant mass of free immigrants, particularly Portuguese, starting in the second quarter of the nineteenth century, challenges the hypothesis that the continued coercion exerted over liberated Africans was due to the lack of voluntary laborers. Indenture contracts with Portuguese as well as with other foreign colonists on plantations and in cities became more common than ever in the 1840s. It has been argued that the income of Portuguese laborers into Rio de Janeiro drove wages down and induced the sale of slaves away from the city, where they could be more profitably worked and more efficiently controlled.[23] The coercion of liberated Africans was not to be attributed to the lack of free laborers in the market; instead, it responded to the imperial government's growing need for laborers for public works and frontier projects and to the perceived need to keep the liberated Africans under strict control, independent of their labor value. The Brazilian government's labor policy toward the liberated Africans in the 1850s and 1860s reinforces this interpretation.

In the 1850s, the government changed its distribution policy and no longer favored private hirers with the concession of liberated Africans.[24] All those emancipated during the captures made in the last years of the slave trade were assigned to the state and were distributed among public institutions in Rio de Janeiro and various government-sponsored ventures in the provinces. In Rio, the distribution of liberated Africans benefited numerous sectors of the imperial and provincial administrations located in and around the city, such as Rio's Municipal Chamber, the Military School, Hospital Pedro II, the departments of public works in the city and in the province of Rio, and the newly founded Institute for the Blind and Institute for the Deaf. Yet, many more liberated Africans were sent in groups to new ventures away from the turbulent capital of the empire. They were granted in large numbers to the sectors engaged in the economic exploration of the country's inland potential. Liberated Africans were sent to the northern region to work as servants in the newly founded Steam Navigation Company of the Amazon River, and to the west as colonists in military outposts and native Indian reserves, meant to pave the way for white settlement in the provinces of São Paulo, Paraná, and Mato Grosso.[25] In sending the liberated Africans away from Rio de Janeiro ("the theater of their vices" as one official put it)[26] and having them engaged in the economic development of the country, the imperial government combined social control and an effective labor policy. The concern about their individual apprenticeships contained in the earlier legislation had gradually disappeared from the government's handling of the group.

From the military colony of Itapura come the life histories of André Lualle and Honorata Benguella, which illustrate the experience of liberated Africans on the frontier.[27] In 1864 the two were listed as a married couple, André and Honorata Pirataca, in the documentation of the military colony of Itapura, located between the provinces of São Paulo and Mato Grosso. André was engaged in the opening and maintenance of the road to Avanhandava, and Honorata worked as a washerwoman. He was forty-six years old and she was over sixty years of age. Honorata had two daughters: Marciana, age twenty and single, who made tallow candles; and Maria do Rosário, age twenty-five, married to Cantidiano Lualle, and who worked in the field. Her two daughters were born when Honorata served at the Ironworks of Ipanema. Honorata had been emancipated from the *Orion* in January 1836 and arrived in Ipanema in early April of that year, with at least twenty of her shipmates. In Ipanema, she worked in the field, probably cultivating the factory's grounds, maybe raising animals. All the other women in Ipanema, except for Joaquina who was the factory's cook, worked in the field too. André had also come to Itapura after having served in Ipanema. André was probably emancipated from the *Subtil* in July 1845 and arrived in Ipanema in the following month, with a group of at least forty of his shipmates. In 1854, the "Imperial Iron Foundry" of Ipanema had 155 state slaves and 133 liberated Africans at its service, and engaged free laborers for many of its functions, specialized or not.[28] Proportionally more slaves than liberated Africans were engaged in skilled occupations, and director Raposo attributed that distribution to the fact that the slaves in Ipanema "are the most intelligent and practical in those occupations [the internal, specialized functions at the factory], for they had been trained to perform them ever since their childhood, as children of the institution that they are."[29]

André and Honorata served their terms in Ipanema amidst a large group of other liberated Africans and an established community of state slaves. They were among the first to be recruited for the new imperial venture, projected to "establish direct communications through the interior of the country with the province of Mato Grosso."[30] Honorata, her daughters, and André left Ipanema in mid-1858, along with twenty-eight other liberated Africans and a number of slaves. They had all been carefully chosen for their age and strength for the pioneering work in the opening up of a road farther west and the founding of the projected "colony and military establishment" of Itapura. In the following years, more liberated African families were transferred from Ipanema to Itapura, lured by the promise of an independent peasant life. Yet they continued to be employed as compulsory laborers in the essential functions of the colony: the maintenance of the road that linked Avanhandava to Itapura and the cultivation of foodstuffs. In 1864, when Honorata and André were finally emancipated by an order of the Ministry of Justice along with seventy other liberated Africans from Itapura, they had served the imperial government for twenty-eight and nineteen years respectively. Despite having been formed into the "Labor Corps of Itapura" in the previous year and having been promised the same treatment as 3rd class colonists, including a plot of land, the liberated Africans of Itapura did not see those promises fulfilled.[31] Their work had fostered the settlement of small proprietors along the Avanhandava road and had initiated contact with the native Indian tribes that would soon be expelled by the expansion of white settlement. Yet the liberated Africans left Itapura after emancipation without reaping the benefits of their own labor.

Liberated Africans in the service of the imperial government in frontier projects had a distinctive labor experience, possibly the harshest of all. They had virtually no mobility. The work in which they were engaged showed no intention on the part of the government to train them for skilled occupations or for autonomous labor. In fact, the transfer of liberated Africans away from Rio de Janeiro and their continuous engagement as servants or as involuntary laborers in military colonies, Indian settlements, public works, and arsenals demonstrates the imperial government's disposition to optimize the use of that pool of involuntary laborers in its service by employing them in some of the major imperial ventures of the time. Given the economic boom of the 1850s and early 1860s and the imperial government's commitment to economic development in the form of subsidies, political support, or direct involvement, it can be said that the involuntary labor of liberated Africans greatly contributed to the country's economic development during those decades.[32] Moreover, the transfer of liberated Africans to the frontier reinforced the unwritten policy that they should be kept subordinated and under close government control, preferably away from the imperial capital.[33] Taken as a whole, the labor experience of the liberated Africans in Brazil from the 1820s to the 1860s represented one particular form of involuntary labor within the range of labor relations existing in the country during that period.

For the liberated Africans, what did it mean to serve the Brazilian state instead of a private hirer? It surely meant having a "faceless" master and being subjected to the orders of different administrators and overseers through successive years and in such subordinate administrative positions that negotiating any arrangements other than ordinary daily ones was very complicated. Anastácio Abondo, for example, had to petition for permission to marry Eufrásia

Ganguela, while they both worked at the Lepers' Hospital in Rio de Janeiro. His petition was examined and judged by not only the administrator of the hospital, but also by an official in the police department, by the judge of orphans, and by an official at the Ministry of Justice. Opposition was raised against the marriage, for it could stir up problems with the other Africans serving at the hospital and because the hospital had no accommodations for them to live as a couple there. The judge of orphans and the ministry's clerk, however, preferred to support the official marital engagement of the two liberated Africans for moral reasons; the two were finally emancipated a few months after the petition because they had completed their terms of service.[34]

The only notable advantage of serving at a public institution was, for some, the chance to be part of a larger community of liberated Africans and state slaves, and therefore to have the opportunity to constitute stable families. Liberated African families of three generations could be found in the 1850s and 1860s in such places as the Gunpowder Factory, the Ironworks of Ipanema, the Military Colony of Itapura and the War Arsenal. Interestingly, the firm grip exercised over the liberated Africans working for institutions also applied to their children who, though born free, were recruited to work at age seven and also had great difficulty leaving the institutions. That happened with Lauriana, the daughter of liberated African Felisberta. Born in Ipanema in 1842, she was already working the field at age seven; in 1864 she was in the Military Colony of Itapura, married to Deolindo Lualle, and had her own children. After her mother was granted final emancipation, she petitioned, too. Only in 1864 did the Ministry of Justice issue orders regarding the children of liberated Africans born in Brazil: they should not be prevented from leaving the institutions, for they were born free.[35] Up until then, their status was uncertain and they were held at the closed confines of the institutions where they were born.

In collective groups, liberated Africans in institutions were also able to articulate everyday resistance to the harsh labor regime. From the recurrent complaints of administrators about the bad behavior and inefficiency of liberated Africans and state slaves alike, particularly in the late 1840s and early 1860s, it appears as if they were successful in challenging the government's attempts to impose military discipline on their lives. Yet, once their term of service expired, attaining emancipation, that is, receiving permission to leave the confines of the institutions and lead independent lives was much more complicated for them than it was for those who had served private hirers.

The information compiled in 1865 shows that those working for the state fared worse. Only 19 percent of those who worked for public institutions

Table 2.3. Terms of Service of Emancipated Africans According to Place of Work

Years	Hirers	% of Total Distributed	Institutions	% of Total Distributed
15–19	57	7.4	0	0
20–24	66	8.5	3	1.78
25–29	99	12.8	28	16.6
30+	16	2.1	2	1.2
Total	238	30.8	33	19.5

Source: See Table 2.1. Sample of 271 emancipated Africans with known terms of service and places of work. Total distributed to hirers, 773; to institutions, 169.

obtained their final emancipation, compared to 30 percent of those who worked for private hirers. Moreover, those who had served in public institutions worked longer terms (at least twenty-four years instead of fourteen) before receiving what they called "full freedom" than did the liberated Africans who worked for private hirers. There were gender differences too. Men worked longer terms than women did. Although this sample of liberated Africans emancipated from institutions is small (twenty-eight men and three women), it is clear that women received their emancipation first. Among the women, 67 percent of them worked between twenty and twenty-four years and 33 percent worked between twenty-five and twenty-nine years, while 93 percent of the men worked between twenty-five and twenty-nine years and 7 percent worked more than thirty years.

In general, liberated Africans who served public institutions worked longer terms than those who served private hirers because the government withheld emancipation from those in institutions until the last years of the 1850s. Desidério's emotional plea was not just a rhetorical act; he was "an insider," and he knew that the prospects for liberated Africans were, as he said, to become "true slaves of the government," when they were actually freed persons who had completed their compulsory terms of service and should have complete autonomy. Tertuliano and Catarina, liberated Africans working and living as a couple in the War Arsenal in Rio de Janeiro, for example, had their petition for emancipation turned down in 1857. He had been emancipated from the *Ganges* in 1839, and she had been emancipated from the *Orion* in 1836; they had served for eighteen and twenty-one years respectively and, despite having completed and surpassed the prescribed term, their request for freedom was denied because "their services belonged to a public institution." There seemed to be no way out. Tertuliano attempted suicide in 1862 and shortly thereafter, a new petition had positive results.[36] Likewise, Onofre and Suzana Cabinda, a married couple with two small children, had served at the War Arsenal and at the Gunpowder Factory but had their first petition turned down in 1857. They had been shipmates across the Atlantic on board the *Leal*, were emancipated together in 1839, and only obtained their "full freedom" in 1862.[37]

Complaints from the liberated Africans about their living and working conditions fell on deaf ears every time they were voiced and were usually dismissed by the authorities. In a collective petition to their curator, the person responsible for their well-being, the liberated Africans who served at the House of Correction voiced their complaints, in 1853, about their sufferings and ill-treatment, declaring they had been living in "quasi-slavery . . . with no guarantee of their freedom" for twenty years. The director of that public establishment, however, justified the treatment conferred to the liberated Africans by the need to keep laborers under military discipline and denied the accusation of keeping them for twenty years, declaring that the first liberated Africans arrived at the House of Correction in 1835. Nobody in the Ministry of Justice, not even their curator, considered the idea of examining individual cases and granting full emancipation to those who had completed their fourteen-year terms.[38]

Upon close examination, the documentation reveals a very bleak picture of the service for the state and of the state as a master. Why should that have been the case? The only reasonable explanation beyond the state's need for compulsory laborers is the imperial administrators' overwhelming obsession with social control. Freed persons could not go unrestrained for fear that they would stir up the slaves. Considering that liberated Africans were special freed persons, who held the status that should be extended to a great proportion of the country's slave population, the potential disruption that their release represented becomes clearer.[39] During the liberated Africans' petitioning for emancipation between 1853 and 1864, Ministry of Justice officials and the chief of police carefully selected the liberated Africans who would be entitled to emancipation from those who had served private hirers and who showed records of self-employment and obedience. Many of them were kept in public service after having completed their fourteen-year terms, for the ministry officials did not recommend their emancipation. Liberated Africans who had served in public institutions had to wait until 1860 for their petitions to be accepted, and even then, had to go through all the steps in the bureaucracy, as the cases discussed above suggest. The state, as a master, was much more rigid than a private one, for it took into consideration the social, and not just the private, implications of manumission. In this sense, both liberated Africans and state slaves were at a great disadvantage in relation to the slaves of private masters. Moreover, liberated Africans paid for the symbolic meaning of their status.

Conclusion

Overall, the labor experience of the liberated Africans in Brazil was not very different from that of the liberated Africans who served their apprenticeship during slavery in Cuba or in British colonies before slave emancipation.[40] Everywhere liberated Africans worked and lived alongside slaves and performed the same occupations at the bottom of the labor hierarchy. Their places of engagement varied: unlike in other places, in Brazil liberated Africans never worked extensively on plantations, but instead served their hirers and the state mostly in cities. The engagement of liberated Africans in public works and state service has yet to be explored for Cuba and the British Caribbean in order to allow for a balanced comparison. So far, what seems to distinguish the Brazilian experience (from the British West Indian one) is the length of their term of service: liberated Africans in Brazil served between fifteen and thirty-one years before their final emancipation, instead of the prescribed fourteen years. Data from the British colonies points to the enforcement of the fourteen-year limit and to the practice of shorter indentures after the 1820s, while data from Cuba has yet to be properly assessed but seems to point to long indentures. The comparative assessment of the liberated African labor experience provides a window into the decline of slavery and the emergence of different forms of coerced labor across the Atlantic during the nineteenth century.

There is little doubt that the terms of engagement under which liberated Africans worked could not be classified as "free labor." However, it was not slavery either, at least in legal terms. Liberated Africans were a peculiar group of coerced laborers. They formed a separate legal category, created during the campaign for the abolition of the Atlantic slave trade. As laborers, they never had to be recruited; instead, their obligation to serve for a limited time was a by-product of their emancipation. The imperial government was at the same time the guardian of their freedom and their employer. During their terms of service, they were employed in the same occupations as slaves, in tasks that free persons would refuse to perform, for the tasks were either menial or dangerous, and the pay would not attract laborers free to choose their occupations. Severely limited in their spatial mobility, liberated Africans were kept as coerced laborers by the threat of physical punishment and by collusion among government officials, who turned a blind eye to their complaints. Most of all, they stayed because they believed they would be freed after completion of the term of compulsory service. It was after having endured what they believed to be their term of temporary captivity and not seeing the fulfillment of the promised emancipation that their "unfreedom" became most clear. Because they worked alongside slaves, liberated Africans may have seen their own legal freedom as an advantage; if they had contact with other groups of coerced laborers such as sentenced prisoners, native Indians, Army and Navy involuntary recruits, for example, they would have realized it was not.[41]

This examination into the experience of the liberated Africans in Brazil shows a significant difference between the experience of the recaptives who served private hirers and that of those who served in public institutions and suggests that the peculiar labor conditions in public institutions and imperial ventures should be further explored. State-sanctioned coerced labor represents an understudied portion of the experience of Africans in the diaspora, one in which slaves and liberated Africans were engaged along with convicts, native Indians, indentured European laborers, and recruited "nationals." Further study of labor for the state will explore the changes in policy during the nineteenth century, and illuminate the important interplay of race, class, and gender in the post-abolition policies for social control.

Notes

This essay stems from research conducted for my doctoral dissertation, "To Be a Liberated African in Brazil: Labour and Citizenship in the Nineteenth Century," completed in 2002 at the University of Waterloo, in Canada. I thank Mary Karasch, Charles Beatty Medina, and an anonymous reviewer for their comments on an earlier version of this essay. I wish to acknowledge the financial support I received from CAPES (Brazilian Ministry of Education Agency) to conduct doctoral studies in Canada.

1. Desidério, Mina, Petição de emancipação, 4 June 1855, Arquivo Nacional, Rio de Janeiro, Brazil (hereafter AN), Diversos SDH—cx. 782 pc. 3. Desidério and his mates' collective quest for emancipation has been discussed at length in Beatriz G. Mamigonian, "Do que 'o preto mina' é capaz: etnia e resistência entre africanos livres," *Afro-Ásia* 24 (2000): 71–95.

2. On liberated Africans in Brazil, see Robert Conrad, "Neither Slave nor Free: The *Emancipados* of Brazil, 1818–1868," *Hispanic American Historical Review* 53 (1973): 50–70, reprinted in Robert E. Conrad, *World of Sorrow: The African Slave Trade to Brazil* (Baton Rouge: Louisiana State University Press, 1986), 154–70; Luciano Raposo Figueiredo, "Uma Jóia Perversa," in *Marcas de escravos: listas de escravos emancipados vindos a bordo de navios negreiros, 1839–1841* (Rio de Janeiro: Arquivo Nacional, 1989), 1–28; Afonso Bandeira Florence, "Nem Escravos, Nem Libertos: os 'Africanos Livres' na Bahia," *Cadernos do CEAS* 121 (1989): 58–69; Jaime Rodrigues, "Ferro, trabalho e conflito: os africanos livres na Fábrica de Ipanema," *História Social,* no.

4–5 (1998): 29–42; Jorge Luiz Prata de Sousa, "Africano livre ficando livre: trabalho, cotidiano e luta" (PhD diss.; Universidade de São Paulo, 1999); Enidelce Bertin, "Os Meia-Cara: Africanos Livres em São Paulo no século XIX" (PhD diss., Universidade de São Paulo, 2006). On the diplomatic struggle for the abolition of the Brazilian slave trade and the background for the creation of this legal category, see particularly Leslie Bethell, *The Abolition of the Brazilian Slave Trade: Britain, Brazil and the Slave Trade Question, 1807–1869* (Cambridge: Cambridge University Press, 1970); Pierre Verger, *Flux et reflux de la traite des nègres entre le golfe de Bénin et Bahia de Todos os Santos du XVIIe au XIXe siècle* (Paris, The Hauge: Mouton, 1968); Jaime Rodrigues, *O Infame Comércio: Propostas e experiências no final do tráfico de africanos para o Brasil (1800–1850)* (Campinas: Editoria da UNICAMP/CECULT, 2000).

3. "Decreto n. 1303 de 28 de Dezembro de 1853—Emancipação dos africanos livres que tiverem servido por quatorze anos a particulares," *Coleção de Leis do Império do Brasil de 1853,* tomo XVII, Parte II (Rio de Janeiro: Typographia Nacional, 1853), 420–21.

4. Desidério, Mina, Petição de emancipação, 4 June 1855, AN, Diversos SDH—cx. 782 pc. 3.

5. See John Peterson, *Province of Freedom: A History of Sierra Leone, 1787–1870* (London: Faber and Faber, 1960); Rosanne Marion Adderley, *"New Negroes from Africa": Slave Trade Abolition and Free African Settlement in the Nineteenth-Century Caribbean* (Bloomington: Indiana University Press, 2006); Marina Carter, V. Govinden, and Satyendra Peerthum, *The Last Slaves: Liberated Africans in Nineteenth-Century Mauritius* (Port Louis, Mauritius: Center for Research on Indian Ocean Societies, 2003); Howard Johnson, "The Liberated Africans in the Bahamas, 1811–1860," *Immigrants & Minorities* 7, no. 1 (1988): 16–40; Alvin O. Thompson, "African 'Recaptives' Under Apprenticeship in the British West Indies, 1807–1828," *Immigrants & Minorities* 9, no. 2 (1990): 123–44; Christopher Saunders, "Liberated Africans in Cape Colony in the First Half of the Nineteenth Century," *International Journal of African Historical Studies* 18, no. 2 (1985): 223–39; Christopher Saunders, "'Free, Yet Slaves': Prize Negroes at the Cape Revisited," in *Breaking the Chains: Slavery and its Legacy in the 19th Century Cape Colony,* ed. Nigel Worden and Clifton Crais (Johannesburg: Witwatersrand University Press, 1994), 99–115.

6. "Regulations for the Mixed Commissions annexed to the Additional Convention to the Treaty of the 22nd January, 1815, between Great Britain and Portugal, for the purpose of preventing the Slave Trade," 28 July 1817, reprinted in "Instructions for the Guidance of Her Majesty's Naval Officers employed in the Suppression of the Slave Trade" (1844), *British Parliamentary Papers—Slave Trade* (Shannon: Irish University Press, 1968), vol. 8.

7. United Kingdom of Portugal, Brazil, and Algarves, "Alvará com força de lei de 26 de janeiro de 1818," *Coleção das leis do Brasil de 1818* (Rio de Janeiro: Imprensa Nacional, 1889), 7–10.

8. Beatriz Gallotti Mamigonian, "Revisitando a 'transição para o trabalho livre':

a experiência dos africanos livres," in *Tráfico, Cativeiro e Liberdade: Rio de Janeiro, séculos XVII-XIX*, ed. Manolo Florentino (Rio de Janeiro: Civilização Brasileira, 2005), 389–417.

9. Alinnie S. Moreira, "Liberdade tutelada: os africanos livres e as relações de trabalho na Fábrica de Pólvora da Estrela, Serra da Estrela/RJ (c. 1831–c.1870)," (Master's Thesis, Universidade Estadual de Campinas, 2005).

10. Liberated Africans elsewhere in the Atlantic served under similar regulations, but their experience varied according to local conditions. See references on note 5.

11. The fact that there were repeated attempts to repeal the 1831 law, and failing that, a long public campaign to deny its validity, attests that it was not "para inglês ver" ("for the English to see") as the current interpretation holds. See particularly Lenine Nequete, *Escravos & Magistrados no Segundo Reinado* (Brasília: Fundação Petrôneo Portella, 1988); Elciene Azevedo, *Orfeu de Carapinha: A Trajetória de Luiz Gama na Imperial Cidade de São Paulo* (Campinas, Editora da UNICAMP, 1999); Elciene Azevedo, "O Direito dos Escravos: Lutas Jurídicas e Abolicionismo na Província de São Paulo na Segunda Metade do Século XIX," (PhD diss., UNICAMP, 2003); and Beatriz Gallotti Mamigonian, "O direito de ser africano livre: os escravos e as interpretações da lei de 1831" in *Direitos e Justiças no Brasil: Ensaios de História Social*, ed. Silvia H. Lara and Joseli Mendonça (Campinas, Editora da Unicamp, 2006), 129–60.

12. On the labor regime of the liberated Africans in the public institutions, see particularly Rodrigues, "Ferro, trabalho e conflito"; Afonso Bandeira Florence, "Resistência Escrava em São Paulo: A luta dos escravos da Fábrica de Ferro São João de Ipanema, 1828–1842," *Afro-Ásia* 18 (1996): 7–32; and part 2 of Prata de Sousa, "Africano livre ficando livre," which contains case studies on the House of Correction, the Ironworks of Ipanema in São Paulo, the Gunpowder Factory, the Navy and War Arsenals in Rio, and the military colony of Itapura in Mato Grosso.

13. There is no comprehensive study of the experience of state slaves in the colonial or the imperial periods. References to their existence are scattered in works dealing with public institutions or the crown. See, for example, Juvenal Greenhalgh, *O Arsenal de Marinha do Rio de Janeiro na História*, 2 vols., vol. 2 (1822–1889) (Rio de Janeiro: Arsenal de Marinha, 1965), 179–85; Carlos Engemann, "Os Servos de Santo Ignácio a Serviço do Imperador: Demografia e relações sociais entre a escravaria da Real Fazenda de Santa Cruz, RJ (1790–1820)," (Master's Thesis, UFRJ, 2002); Lilia Moritz Schwarcz, *As Barbas do Imperador: Pedro II, um monarca nos trópicos* (São Paulo: Cia. Das Letras, 1998), 234.

14. "Quadro dos Escravos da Nação e Africanos livres de ambos os sexos existentes no Arsenal de Marinha da Corte, bem como de sua distribuição pelos diferentes serviços em que se acham empregados." Prepared by Antônio Pedro de Carvalho, Inspector of the Navy Arsenal, 15 Apr. 1845, printed in Brazil, Relatório [do ano de 1844] da Repartição dos Negócios da Marinha Apresentado à Assembléia Geral Legislativa na 2a sessão da 6a legislatura pelo respectivo Ministro e Secretário de Estado

Antônio Francisco de Paula e Hollanda Cavalcanti d'Albuquerque. (Rio de Janeiro: Typographia Universal Laemmert, 1845). The report is reproduced and discussed in Sousa, "Africano livre ficando livre," 119.

15. Greenhalgh, *O Arsenal de Marinha,* 2: 177–78.

16. Galley prisoners (*galés*) had been condemned to serve in public works with their legs permanently chained. It was the second worst punishment listed in the Criminal Code, after the death sentence. Thomas H. Holloway, *Policing Rio de Janeiro: Repression and Resistance in a 19th-century City* (Stanford, Calif.: Stanford University Press, 1993).

17. Silvestre José Nogueira to Inspector Antônio Pedro de Carvalho, 19 Nov. 1844, in Brazil, Relatório [do ano de 1844] da Repartição dos Negócios da Marinha Apresentado à Assembléia Geral Legislativa na 1a sessão da 6a legislatura pelo respectivo Ministro e Secretário de Estado Antônio Francisco de Paula e Hollanda Cavalcanti d'Albuquerque. (Rio de Janeiro: Typographia Nacional, 1845).

18. Greenhalgh, *O Arsenal de Marinha,* 2: 174. It is possible that these Azorean colonists were the ones mentioned previously as being employed in the works of the *Ribeira Nova* and recruited by the inspector to perform the hard work alongside liberated Africans and slaves.

19. João de Almeida Brito, Pedido de exoneração de responsabilidade sobre Maria, 25 Oct. 1856, AN, Diversos SDH—cx. 782 pc. 2. Even if she had been serving for the previous sixteen years since her emancipation from the *Paquete de Benguela,* the director of the House of Correction did not recommend her final emancipation, feeling that her presence in the institution benefited "public morality." Maria Benguela, Petição de emancipação, 24 Dec. 1856, AN, Diversos SDH—cx. 782 pc. 2

20. Firmina Benguela, Petição de emancipação, 07 Mar. 1862, AN, GIFI 5E-130.

21. The director of the House of Correction reported that the liberated Africans in the service of that institution had the authorization to work for private persons on Sundays and holidays, and that they kept the money they earned from this extra labor; Carlos Honório Figueiredo to Luís Antônio Barbosa, 4 July 1853, AN, IJ6 523.

22. Record of Ambrósio Benguella, n. 267 of the Duquesa de Bragança, AN, IJ6 471.

23. Luiz Felipe de Alencastro, "Proletários e Escravos: imigrantes portugueses e cativos africanos no Rio de Janeiro, 1850–1872," *Novos Estudos—CEBRAP* 21 (1988): 30–56; Rosana Barbosa Nunes, "Portuguese Migration to Rio de Janeiro, 1822–1850," *The Americas* 57, no. 1 (2000): 37–61. In the Navy Arsenal there were Chinese and Portuguese indentured laborers. Greenhalgh, *O Arsenal de Marinha,* 2: 155.

24. The change was inscribed in the new law for the abolition of the slave trade. Brazil. "Lei n. 581 de 4 de setembro de 1850—Abolição do Tráfico de Escravos," *Coleção de Leis do Império do Brasil,* 1850, Tomo XI, parte 1a. (Rio de Janeiro: Typographia Nacional, 1851), 267–71.

25. A sample of the institutions that received liberated Africans can be found in Conrad, "The *Emancipados,*" in a transcription of a list obtained by the British offi-

cials in Rio de Janeiro, enclosed to Hunt to Russell, 22 Mar. 1865, FO (British Foreign Office) 84/1244.

26. Sidney Chalhoub, *Visões da Liberdade: Uma história das últimas décadas da escravidão na Corte* (São Paulo: Companhia das Letras, 1990), 198.

27. The following description comes from a combination of different sources, from emancipation records to listings produced in Ipanema and Itapura. See Zacharias Góes e Vasconcellos to Juiz de Órfãos, 25 June 1864, AN, IJ6 16; "Relação nominal dos Africanos livres, maiores e menores, extrahida do livro de matrícula dos mesmos, organizado em julho de 1849, declarando os que actualmente existem nesta Fábrica, os que tiverão destinos e os que falleceram, 27/10/1851," Arquivo do Estado de São Paulo, São Paulo, Brazil (hereafter AESP), lata 5216; Maria Apparecida Silva, "Itapura—Estabelecimento Naval e Colônia Militar (1858–1870)" (PhD diss., Universidade de São Paulo, 1972), 105; List of Africans emancipated from the *Orion,* AN, Cód. 184 vol. 3.

28. See "Mappa dos escravos e Africanos livres existentes no Fábrica d'Ypanema" and "Quadro da actual distribuição do serviço," 30 Oct. 1854, AESP, lata 5216.

29. Francisco Antonio Raposo to José Antôntio Saraiva, 30 Oct. 1854, AESP, lata 5216.

30. "Viagem de exploração aos Rios Iguatemy, Escopil e Ivinheima," attached to Brazil. Relatório que tinha de ser apresentado à Assembléia Geral Legislativa na Terceira Sessão da Décima Primeira Legislatura pelo Ministro e Secretário de Estado dos Negócios da Marinha [1862], o Chefe de Divisão Joaquim Raimundo de Lamare (Rio de Janeiro: Typographia Perseverança, 1863).

31. Silva, "Itapura—Estabelecimento Naval e Colônia Militar," 102–7. British consul William Christie criticized the continuous engagement of liberated Africans emancipated by the mixed commission court and the imposition by the regulation of the corps of six more years of compulsory service. For the diplomatic exchange regarding the Africans at Itapura, see United Kingdom, "Correspondence respecting liberated slaves in Brazil," Parliamentary Papers LXXIII (1863).

32. Caio Prado Jr., História Econômica do Brasil, 37 ed., (São Paulo: Brasiliense, 1970), 192–204.

33. Since there were no economic factors pushing liberated Africans from the city or pulling them toward the interior, it can be assumed that the government was driven by its concern with social control. This conclusion reinforces Sidney Chalhoub's argument that the expansion of slave autonomy and frequent acts of slave resistance influenced masters in selling their slaves away from Rio de Janeiro; Chalhoub, *Visões da Liberdade,* 175–248.

34. Anastácio Abondo, Pedido de permissão para casar-se com Eufrásia Ganguela, Aug. 1862, AN, IJ6 468.

35. Zacharias Góes e Vasconcellos to Ministro da Marinha, 28 July 1864, AN, IJ6 16.

36. Tertuliano e Catarina, Petição de emancipação, 27 Jan. 1857, AN, GIFI 6D-136; Ministro da Justiça to Ministro da Guerra, 8 Feb. 1862, AN, IJ6 15.

37. Onofre e Suzana, do Arsenal de Guerra, Petição de Emancipação, 28 Oct. 1856, AN, Diversos SDH—cx. 782 pc. 3; Onofre Cabinda, pedido de emancipação para Suzana Cabinda, Sept. 1862, AN, Diversos SDH—cx. 782 pc. 3.

38. Carlos Honório Figueiredo to Luís Antônio Barbosa, 4 July 1853, AN, IJ6 523.

39. Numerous works on slave resistance in Brazil point to the potential disruption of freedpersons and the particularly turbulent years from 1830 to 1860. See João José Reis, *Slave Rebellion in Brazil: The Muslim Uprising of 1835 in Bahia,* trans. Arthur Brakel (Baltimore, Md.: Johns Hopkins University Press, 1993); Chalhoub, *Visões da Liberdade;* Flávio dos Santos Gomes, *Histórias de Quilombolas: Mocambos e Comunindades de Senzalas no Rio Janeiro—século XIX* (Rio de Janeiro: Arquivo Nacional, 1995); Dale T. Graden, "An Act 'Even of Public Security': Slave Resistance, Social Tensions, and the End of the International Slave Trade to Brazil, 1835–1856," *Hispanic American Historical Review* 76, no. 2 (1996): 249–82. It is the first time, however, that the significance of the presence of liberated Africans among slaves is discussed. This point is further explored in my dissertation, Beatriz G. Mamigonian, "To Be a Liberated African in Brazil in the Nineteenth Century" (PhD diss., University of Waterloo, 2002), 182–275.

40. Besides the works cited on note 5, see Roseanne Marion Adderley, "'A Most Useful and Valuable People?': Cultural, Moral and Practical Dilemmas in the Use of Liberated African Labor in the Nineteenth-Century Caribbean," *Slavery and Abolition* 20, no. 1 (1999): 59–80; Monica Schuler, "Liberated Central Africans in Nineteenth-Century Guyana," in *Central Africans and Cultural Transformations in the American Diaspora,* ed. Linda Heywood (Cambridge: Cambridge University Press, 2002), 319–52; David R. Murray, "A New Class of Slaves," in *Odious Commerce: Britain, Spain and the Abolition of the Cuban Slave Trade* (Cambridge: Cambridge University Press, 1980), 271–97; Ines Roldan de Montaud, "Origen, Evolucion y Supresion del Grupo de Negros 'Emancipados' en Cuba (1817–1870)," *Revista de Indias* 42, no. 167–68 (1982): 559–641; Teresita Martínez Vergne, "The Allocation of Liberated African Labour through the Casa de Beneficencia—San Juan, Puerto Rico, 1859–1864," *Slavery and Abolition* 12, no. 3 (1991): 200–16.

41. Peter M. Beattie, *The Tribute of Blood: Army, Honor, Race, and Nation in Brazil, 1864–1945* (Durham, N.C.: Duke University Press, 2001); Hendrik Kraay, *Race, State, and Armed Forces in Independence-era Brazil, Bahia, 1790s-1840s* (Stanford, Calif.: Stanford University Press, 2001); Hendrik Kraay, "Reconsidering Recruitment in Imperial Brazil," *The Americas* 55, no. 1 (July 1988): 1–33; Álvaro Pereira do Nascimento, *A Ressaca da Marujada: Recrutamento e Disciplina na Armada Imperial* (Rio de Janeiro: Arquivo Nacional, 2001); Manuela Carneiro da Cunha, "Política indigenista no século XIX," in Manuela Carneiro da Cunha (Org.), *História dos Índios no Brasil* (São Paulo: Fapesp/Cia. das Letras/Secretaria Municipal de Cultura, 1998), 133–54.

3

A New Biography of the African Diaspora

The Life and Death of Marie-Joseph Angélique, Black Portuguese Slave Woman in New France, 1725–1734

AFUA COOPER

Studies of the African Diaspora have traditionally focused on groups and communities of people as opposed to individuals. But this essay looks at the life of one Black enslaved woman whose life had diasporic resonance and implications. Marie-Joseph Angélique was a slave woman who was hanged for allegedly setting fire to Montréal in 1734. Angélique did not come from Africa as part of a general group of captives destined for enslavement. She was born in Portugal, crossed the Atlantic to New England where she was owned by a Flemish or Dutch master, and later was bought by François Poulin de Francheville, a Montréal merchant. Angélique lived the last nine years of her life in Francheville's household in Montréal.

New World African diaspora studies have for the longest time focused on the Atlantic slave trade and its impact. Diasporan communities and experiences are created due to migrations, forced or otherwise. The construction of these experiences "is an organic process involving movement from an ancestral land, settlement in new lands, and . . . [sometimes] renewed settlement and movement elsewhere."[1] Angélique embodied "double or triple diasporic" identities, which resulted from her origins and migratory experiences of enslavement. Her forebears migrated from Africa to Portugal where they formed diasporic communities. Later, she left Portugal and Europe to migrate and resettle elsewhere, in this case, the Americas.

Because Canada has been rarely theorized as a part of the African Diaspora, Black people in that country, slave and free, have been missing from discussions about this diaspora. For example, Paul Gilroy in his celebrated book *The Black Atlantic* failed to engage Canada as part of an extended Black world, even though he gave a detailed discussion of the Black intellectual and medical doctor, Martin Delany. Yet Delany lived in Canada for eight years and from there formulated much of his plans for a colony in Africa. Further, it was in Canada that Delany wrote *Blake,* his first novel.

That slavery existed in Canada for over two hundred years is not a well-known, though documented, fact. That over seventy-five slave ships used in the British slave trade were built in Nova Scotia, Québec, and Newfoundland is known by only a few. Canada might not have been a slave society like the West Indies or the United States, but it was a society with slaves. Like virtually all other New World societies, slavery in Canada was an institutionalized part of life. The story of slavery in Canada is locked in the national closet—a well-guarded secret—so well guarded that even scholars who have made slavery their business do not know about the Canadian variant.

Scholars of the African Diaspora can remedy this by examining Angélique's story as a chronicle of slavery, of Blacks in the African Diaspora, and also as a Canadian story. But a word of caution. Though Angélique's story can be studied as an aspect of Canadian history, to place it solely within that context would be to miss specifics of her history. Given her many and varied transnational identities and experiences, using the diaspora as concept and method in writing her story is useful because such a framework brings together many critical strands of her narrative that otherwise could not be contained by a national history paradigm.[2] In addition, Angélique's story brings together the disparate branches of Atlantic slavery: Portuguese, Dutch, French, and English. Using the experiences of one slave woman to African diasporize Canada brings a gender reading and perspective to the African Diaspora and eighteenth-century Black transnationality.

The story provides a unique opportunity to place at the center of a historical investigation an analysis of the "interlocking system" of oppression—gender, race, and class—as embodied in one slave woman in eighteenth-century Canada (called New France before the 1760 British conquest). Angélique was an obscure slave woman who rose to prominence and gained notoriety because of the spectacular Montréal fire that she was accused of setting. Her trial, sentencing, and hanging speak volumes about the nature of early Canadian slavery and of crime and punishment in the colony.

* * *

On April 10, 1734, a fire blazed through the house of Thérèse de Couagne de Francheville, a Montréal bourgeois. Madame Francheville, a widow, lived in her house on Rue St. Paul with her servants and one slave woman, Marie-Joseph Angélique. The fire spread and destroyed much of the town. Accused of setting the fire, Angélique was arrested, charged, and thrown in jail. For the next six weeks she endured a grueling trial. Found guilty, she was hanged on June 21. Though the fire and the hanging were both spectacular events, very little has been written about them either in traditional Canadian or women's history.[3] The same is true for the history of the Black or African Diaspora. Angélique's story allows us to take a critical look at the African Diaspora in Canada.

Kim Butler and others have identified five dimensions of diasporic research: (1) reasons for, and conditions of, the dispersal; (2) relationship with homeland; (3) relationship with host society; (4) interrelationships within diaspora groups; and (5) comparative studies of different diasporas. These five dimensions, especially the first three, are well suited for the study of Angélique's experience and I will analyze each within this essay.[4]

The Atlantic Slave Trade, the African Diaspora, and Slavery in New France

The Atlantic trade in African captives is ultimately responsible for the arrival of Marie-Joseph Angélique in the New World. The trade in African captives to the Americas and Europe began in earnest along the western coast of Africa from the middle of the fifteenth century to 1865. Holland, France, Britain, and Portugal dominated the slave trade, with Britain, by the middle of the eighteenth century, taking the lion's share. Estimates of the number of Africans forcibly transported across the Atlantic ranged from a low of 10 million to a high of 50 million. A median range is 15 million.[5] The greatest number of captives were taken to Brazil, Haiti, and the Caribbean, though the United States also received a significant number. As the decades and then centuries rolled by, the number of forced migrants increased dramatically, and peaked in the last half of the eighteenth century. The forced migration of Africans to the Americas occurred in direct response to the unceasing labor demands of white-owned mines, farms, plantations, and households in the Americas.[6]

But there was a European preamble to the trans-Atlantic trade. In the early years of the trade in Black bodies, most of the captives were taken to Europe.

At least 200,000 people were taken to Iberia in the fifteenth, sixteenth, and seventeenth centuries.[7] Portugal was the first European country to initiate the African slave trade. Around 1440 some of her seamen kidnapped unsuspecting Senegalese people who were working on a beach.[8] The sailors took these captives to Lisbon and sold them in the slave market there. The trade grew, with the bulk of the victims taken and sold within Europe (Portugal and Spain in particular) and in Mediterranean countries. The import of African human merchandise to Portugal led to the spectacular growth of the Black population in that country. By 1650, roughly one-third of the population of Lisbon (10,000) was black.[9]

For most of the fifteenth century and the first decades of the sixteenth, the majority of African captives were taken to Lisbon, the capital of the country and center of its maritime trading activities. Many remained in the capital and were sold to residents there, but others were transported to different parts of the country, fulfilling the demand for African captive labor. Along with Lisbon, the Algarve and Évora were the main centers of Black enslavement in Portugal.

Enslaved Africans worked in a variety of occupations and for a variety of owners. A. Saunders, an expert on Black slavery in Portugal, informs us that "except for beggars, people of all classes, from laborers to kings, owned black slaves."[10] Even Muslim and Jewish Portuguese (in theory New Christians), people who normally faced various proscriptions, owned Black slaves along with their Christian neighbors. In the rural areas, the bulk of the enslaved population worked in agriculture or in households.

Though primarily the province of women, both sexes labored as house servants, cooks, and cleaners. Men and women also worked in hospitals as nurses, servants, and maids—in fact, during periods of infections and plagues, they were placed at the front line. Men especially worked as retainers in the entourages of the nobility, and both sexes served various capacities at court. Queens and princesses had slave women as ladies-in-waiting; these women apparently had a good life. Enslaved men also worked as shepherds, and guarded vineyards and olive fields. Bonded laborers monopolized these occupations as free men found them distasteful and monotonous. Black male slaves too worked as sailors and stevedores, but as salaried laborers. Their owners took their pay, usually giving them just a percentage of their salaries. Throughout the sixteenth century, the government sought to restrict slave men from working in the nautical professions because many enslaved mariners used their access to the rivers and seas to effect their escape. Male slaves also worked as carpenters, masons, goldsmiths, blacksmiths, silversmiths, and in a variety of other craft occupations.

Black women, both enslaved and free, had a monopoly on certain occupations, especially in the urban areas. The distasteful work of removing garbage and excrement from the homes of whites was one such job that was reserved for slave women for obvious reasons. The women carried the excrement in tall wicker baskets from the homes down to rivers to dispose of it. Women also monopolized the *regateiras* or street vending occupation. Black women, free and enslaved, sold stewed plums, cooked beans and pasta, cooked seafood, olive oil, fruits, and vegetables. Enslaved women needed their owners' permission to engage in vending, and had to turn over their earnings to them.[11] But the good citizens often complained about these women. In Lisbon, the charge was that these street vendors were "unreasonable" and "insulted" ladies of rank—not the first time that white citizens in the Atlantic world would hurl this kind of accusation against Black women. Apparently, it was not so much that Black women insulted white women of rank, but that they were not, or did not appear, docile and subservient enough to their betters.[12]

Slavery was not the only defining feature of Black Portuguese life. Free people composed a significant portion of the Black population. But there was a strong bond between the free and the enslaved as they often were related by blood or marriage. Free African Portuguese founded various fraternal organizations to press for improvements in their lives and those of their enslaved brethren. In 1515, when King Manuel restricted the movement of the Black street vendors, a fraternal organization petitioned him to reconsider. He did. These fraternities also buried their members, assisted with marriages and baptisms, and functioned as a general race upliftment society. They held dances, rallies, religious marches, and participated in the carnivals. Moreover, members gave shelter to runaway slaves and assisted in their escape. It was not long before the fraternities came under government suspicion and legislation was enacted to restrict their activities.[13]

Marie-Joseph Angélique was born in Portugal around 1705, very likely into slavery. It is not known where in Portugal she was born or lived, though probably in one of the main centers of Black life and habitation—Lisbon, Évora, and the Algarve. Black descendants of the Moors, called Moriscos, and recently imported Africans and their descendants were the chief Black populations of these regions. They would have spoken diverse African languages, Portuguese, and a Portuguese-creole based on African linguistic structures. If Angélique originated from one of these places, she would have been part of a vibrant Afro-Portuguese culture and a steadily growing cosmopolitan environment.[14] In the year of her birth and for many decades after, Black slavery was still a fact of life in Portugal; no one thought that it would end, or that it was not the "natural condition" of Africans.[15]

Sometime during her youth Angélique was removed from her native country. It could be that she was in the employ of a foreign trader and so left with him. More likely, she was sold to a foreigner who took her out of Portugal. In any event, she crossed the Atlantic and ended up in North America. In her trial transcript, Angélique names New England as a place where she lived after her Atlantic crossing—but in 1725 the Portuguese-born enslaved woman arrived in Montréal, New France. Her journey to Montréal was an odyssey. According to her trial transcript, "she was born in Portugal then sold to 'a Flemish man' who then sold her to Sieur Francheville."[16] We do not know whether the Fleming owned her while she was in Portugal or if he became her owner in New England. We can assume she was sold to him in Portugal, since, in the transcripts, immediately after naming her place of birth, she went on to say she was sold to a Flemish man. What we do know is that while she was living in New England her Flemish owner sold her to Francheville. According to Angélique, the Fleming *sent* her from New England to Montréal in 1725.

We have to be wary of the term "New England" in mid-eighteenth-century Canadian colonial parlance. French officials often refer in a generic way to any of the northern English colonies as "New England." Therefore we find the same name given to the area defined geographically today as New England, New York, or even Pennsylvania. For example, the Marquis de Beauharnois, governor-general of New France, in a letter to his superior in France, the Comte de Maurepas, minister of the marine, described a Dutch-speaking Albany merchant, John Henry (Johann Hendricks) Lidius as "a native of Orange in New England." In 1725, Lidius arrived in Montréal, settled there, took on French citizenship, married a French woman, and in 1730 converted to Roman Catholicism. However, his conversion was false and he turned out to be a notorious fur smuggler. Lidius was subsequently expelled from New France to the Netherlands. Three critical events link Angélique and Lidius. Both arrived in Montréal in the same year, both were baptized in 1730, and by the same priest. It could be that it was Lidius himself, a Dutch New Yorker, who brought Angélique to Montréal. The Dutch connection is intriguing. Nonetheless, the point is that Governor Beauharnois named Orange (Albany) as in "New England" and not New York.[17] Therefore when the French authorities stated that the bondswoman lived in New England before she came to Montréal, they could very well have meant that the she came from the colony of New York—the Hudson Valley in particular. That her previous owner was a Fleming (a Dutch-speaking man) makes it all the more likely.

I believe we can understand Angélique's North American wanderings by looking at the colonial fur trade between the French, Dutch, and English. The key to Angélique's life could lie within this matrix.

* * *

In colonial North America, especially in the Great Lakes region, the French, English, and Dutch competed with each other for land and other resources, but also traded with each other. Fur gave meaning to their trading nexus. The Montréal merchants had the best furs because they controlled a vast fur-bearing hinterland west of Montréal known as *Les Pays en haut* (the Upper Country). This region extended west to present-day Wisconsin, and north to Lake Superior. Though in theory, all furs were to be shipped to France via the port of Québec, Montréal merchants developed a lucrative trade with Dutch-speaking merchants of Albany and the Hudson Valley. Dutch merchants did obtain furs in the area west of the Alleghenies, but these furs were inferior to those obtained from the Canadians. The main trading route between Montréal and New York was the Richelieu/Lake Champlain road. And on this road, Canadian merchants or their agents brought furs to the Albany merchants in exchange for English manufactures and luxury goods, which were better made and cheaper than the French variant. The French kept most of the luxury goods for themselves but used rum and manufactures in exchange for furs obtained from the First Nations of the Upper Country.[18]

The Montréal-Albany trade was so lucrative that even when the respective governments in New York and Canada ruled against it for whatever reason (usually because of war or other hostilities), French and Dutch merchants simply used the Native people, the Iroquois or Five Nations in particular, as their agents and go-betweens. The Five Nations were not bounded by the white man's laws and their ancestral homeland bordered on and included the vast territories the whites claimed as theirs. As "natives of the land," the Five Nations knew of and often traversed secret routes to Albany, in addition to the more public ones like the Richelieu/Lake Champlain corridor, without fear or restrictions. Further, many members of the Five Nations had removed themselves to one of the several Christian missions close to Montréal, making them well-situated, as Christians and Iroquois, to play an important role in the fur trade—legally or illegally—to Albany.[19]

Manufactured goods and luxury items were not the only goods that returned to Montréal. Slaves also trekked through the Hudson Valley to Montréal and other parts of the St. Lawrence Valley. Because the New York merchants had better access to enslaved labor, they sometimes furnished slaves to the French in the St. Lawrence.

If slaves were exchanged through the legal means of trade, they also changed hands through the violent process of war. Take the Schenectady massacre for example. In 1690, the French from Canada attacked the village of Schenectady, pillaged, killed, and then took slaves—Black and Indian—with them to Canada. Many of these enslaved people were "Dutch" given that Schenectady and most of the settlements in the Hudson valley at the time were populated mainly by people of Dutch descent. Even in the early decades of the eighteenth century, the Canadians obtained slaves, through legal or aggressive means, from the Dutch and English. *Couriers de Bois* (French Canadian trappers), notorious for their illegal trade with Albany, soldiers, diplomats, and merchants, were the principal people who obtained slaves from the English colonies.[20]

* * *

Slavery existed in Canada from the beginning of its colonial history. The first record of Black enslavement in Canada pertains to Olivièr Le Jeune, a nine-year-old Madagascan boy, bought to Québec by the Kirke brothers. The Kirkes, French Huguenots, working for the English Crown, sailed to Canada in 1628. Arriving in the settlement of Québec, they quickly rounded up the few inhabitants, and "conquered" the colony for England. On board their ships, the Kirkes had a young African boy whom they sold to a French clerk. By 1632, Canada was returned to France, and as the decades passed, more and more Black slaves began arriving in the colony. The white settlers felt slavery was an answer to their labor needs and petitioned the Crown to have Black slavery regularized. They themselves wanted to send ships directly to Africa to purchase captive Africans. However, nothing came of that plan and colonists had to procure slaves by other means—through war and trade with the English colonies, the First Nations, and by buying enslaved Africans directly from the West Indies and Louisiana. Of course, slaves were also born in the colony.[21] "Slavery was given its legal foundation in New France between 1689 and 1709" as the colonial and imperial governments sought to regulate the institution.[22] Sections of the *Code noir* of 1685, the legal code that regulated slavery in the French plantation empire, was used in New France to manage Black slavery.[23]

However, given the nature of the colony's economy, slavery did not evolve into a large-scale enterprise. The colony existed solely to produce furs (not a labor-intensive venture) and no one, certainly not in Versailles, thought otherwise. In New France, since most of those who owned slaves were town dwellers, slavery tended to be urban in nature. Two-thirds of all slaves lived in the three urban centers of Montréal, Québec, and Trois-Rivières. In the Upper Country, most enslaved Africans lived in Detroit and Michillimackinac; and in Acadia, Louisbourg had the largest number of enslaved workers. Because slavery was urban, it was domestic, familial, and sometimes paternalistic. Merchants, the government, and the Church held the largest number of enslaved people, but colonists from every echelon of society owned slaves. Among these were military officers, innkeepers, shopkeepers, voyageurs, notaries, sea captains, seigneurs, and artisans.[24]

Enslaved persons tended to live in the same household as their owners, at least during the winter. This arrangement allowed for intimate interactions between both groups. Slaves in the colony were used for a variety of purposes. As Kenneth Donovan has shown, "they became servants, gardeners, bakers, tavern keepers, stone masons, musicians, laundry workers, soldiers, sailors, fishermen, hospital workers, ferry men, executioners, and nursemaids." Many, especially male *Panis* (Aboriginal slaves) were used as boatmen in the fur trade.[25] According to one authority on slavery in French Canada, the life of slaves, especially the *Panis,* was short—most did not live beyond twenty years.[26]

It is hard to determine the number of enslaved Africans living in Montreal in 1734, but the census of 1731 showed 142 slaves (both *Panis* and Africans) living in the settlement.[27] What is known is that during the decades of the 1720s and 1730s when Angélique lived in Montréal, most, of the leading families living in town and in the suburbs were slaveholders.[28] Under the ancient regime, enslaved *Panis* in New France were more numerous than enslaved Blacks. This trend reversed itself after the Conquest of 1760 when enslaved Blacks became the majority in the servile labor force.[29]

Montréal, given its strategic location on the St. Lawrence River between the city of Québec and the Upper Country, became the center of the Canadian fur trade long before Angélique's arrival in 1725. From Montréal, traders outfitted fur expeditions to the interior of the continent. Once there, they bartered trade goods with Native people in return for pelts, mainly beaver. However, by the time of the fire of 1734, though the fur trade was still significant, agriculture was emerging as an important economic activity.[30]

About three thousand people lived in Montréal at the time of the fire. It was a hierarchical community. Members of the nobility, Church, and the military dominated society, and were conscious of their superior rank and status. The bourgeois class, composed of important merchant families, formed a second significant echelon. The mercantile elites often intermarried with the upper class, and both classes—having members in each group—"ruled" the community. Artisans and small merchants occupied the third level, with indentured laborers or engagés forming the fourth level. And below them were the slaves—Black and Aboriginal—who composed the lowest echelon of the society.[31]

Colonial Montréal was a rectangular-shaped block, the southern portion of which fronted the St. Lawrence River. The city was spatially divided into "Lower Town," and "Upper Town." A narrow ridge separated the two entities. In the Upper Town were the Sulpician seminary, the Recollet fathers, the Jesuits, and the Sisters of the Congregation (a teaching order). The cemeteries lodged in the northern outskirts of Upper Town. In Lower Town lived the principal merchants. Rue St. Paul, "the merchants' street," was the main thoroughfare of the Lower Town. The Hôtel-Dieu, the town's hospital, also lodged in Lower Town. Poorer merchants, domestics, and artisans made sectors of both Lower and Upper Town their home. The nobility, military officers, and the intendant, in their grand mansions lived in the eastern quarter of the settlement. After the governor-general, the intendant was the most important official in the colony. He had his official residence in the capital, Québec, but he also maintained a Montréal home.

Angélique's owners, François Poulin de Francheville and his wife Thérèse de Couagne were part of Montréal's mercantile elite. Sieur Francheville was one of the town's principal fur traders who outfitted trading brigades to the interior, sent men to discover new fur resources, and loaned money to other merchants engaged in the trade. Francheville was also a seigneur. He inherited his grandfather's seigneury or estate, at St. Maurice, near Trois-Rivières. Francheville subdivided his estate into numerous plots that he rented or sold to settler-tenants. However, it was not for that reason that seigneury became important, but rather because at St. Maurice Francheville discovered iron ore and went on to build and operate an iron forge that eventually produced utensils and other iron goods for the domestic market and the fur trade. Francheville, with the assistance of the Crown, invested heavily in the forge, which eventually emerged as the leader in Canada's industrial development. Francheville also owned a farm in St. Michel, a village in the Montréal suburbs.[32]

The Franchevilles also came from wealthy Montréal merchant families and were well connected to other important families from both the business elite and nobility. Their wedding, held at the chateau of Claude de Ramezay, governor of Montréal, indicates their social standing. The couple had one child who did not survive infancy.[33]

Francheville acquired Angélique in 1725. The slave woman worked as a domestic in the Franchevilles' household, and also as a laborer on the St. Michel farm. Angélique performed an unrelenting round of duties. She cooked, fetched firewood, cleaned, laundered, sewed, wove, ran errands, and performed other household chores. As a domestic she was on call twenty-four hours a day. Though her work schedule was restrictive she still had a measure of freedom. She found time to take walks along the banks of the St. Lawrence, visited the sick in the hospital, and participated in carnival. Her "frenchification" appeared complete when on June 28, 1730, her owners baptized her in the Roman Catholic faith.

The second article of the *Code noir* declared that all slaves in the colonies "were to be baptized and instructed in the Catholic religion." Owners were to prepare their slaves for baptism within a week of purchase.[34] Yet it was five years after Angélique's arrival in Montréal that Francheville attended to that duty. She was named at her baptism "Marie-Joseph-Angélique"— Marie-Joseph, in honor of her godmother, Marie-Joseph de Couagne, sister of Madame Francheville. Angélique was also part of her name but it functioned somewhat as a surname. Her godfather was Sieur Francheville, her master. The priest was the Sulpician Father Dulescoat.[35]

Undoubtedly, her name was not Marie-Joseph Angélique when she came to Montréal. She could have had an English name (coming from New England) or a Portuguese name (being born in Portugal) or even a French or Dutch name (being previously owned by a Flemish man). She could also at some point have had an African name. Angélique lost a name in her renaming in Montréal. Her Montréal owners, in their naming of her, manifested the power they held over her. The renaming of slaves by owners was a "major feature of the ritual of enslavement," states sociologist Orlando Patterson. "The changing of name is almost universally a symbolic act of stripping a person of his former identity. . . . The slave's former name died with the former self."[36] In renaming his slave, Francheville, once and for all, claimed her for himself.

The bondswoman's Montréal baptism raises several questions about the nature of her early religious upbringing or lack thereof. Being born in Portugal, she should already have been baptized a Catholic. In early sixteenth-century Portugal, the monarch Manuel I instituted a series of reforms pertaining to slave life and master-slave relationships. Manuel mandated that all enslaved persons in Portugal be baptized and instructed in the Catholic faith. If owners reneged on their duty, they faced the courts.[37] Therefore, if Angélique was not baptized in Portugal, it could be that she was (secretly?) raised in a Protestant, or more likely, a Jewish household. It could also be that once in the English colonies, she was indoctrinated into Protestantism, the Dutch Reform faith. Finally, her previous owners may not have cared a whit about her spiritual life and raised her a "pagan." Whatever the case, when she arrived in New France, she was not a Catholic (or even a Christian) and her new owners therefore had the responsibility to bring her into the Church of Rome.

It is noteworthy that Angelique's baptism took place five years after she came to Montréal. The long interval between Angélique's arrival in Canada and the date of her baptism suggests that some owners did not always baptize their slaves out of Christian conviction, but rather for pragmatic reasons. Slaves in New France were often baptized on their death beds.[38] It could also be that Angélique herself resisted baptism. Her trial transcripts reveal that she was proud, feisty, and determined—qualities she could invoke if she did not want to be coerced into Catholic baptism.

The baptism, an act of paternalism, looks like a cozy arrangement. The owners or relatives were godparents with the slave appearing as an adopted child. But the owners were merely carrying out a religious and judicial obligation since they purportedly were responsible for the spiritual life of those they enslaved. Baptism did not translate into more humane treatment for slaves, nor did it mean that they would partake in communion. For example, Jacques-César, father of Angélique's children, was also baptized in 1730, but took his first communion in 1756, fully twenty-four years after his baptism. It appeared that in order for slaves to receive communion they had to prove their Christian worthiness.[39]

Angélique was pregnant when she was baptized at the end of June 1730, and that could be the reason for her baptism. In January 1731, she gave birth to a son named Eustache. This child lived for only one month. Angélique also named Jacques-César, a fellow Black slave, as father. Jacques-César belonged to Ignace Gamelin, Jr., a prosperous merchant and close friend and business associate of Francheville. When a slave woman had children, the children belonged to her owner, irrespective of the father's status. Slave women as mothers had no legal rights over the children to whom they gave birth. By 1710, law and custom in New World slavery determined that children born to slave women inherited their mothers' status. This was also the case in New France.[40]

Angélique proved a fertile slave. In May 1732, she gave birth again, this time to twins, Louis and Marie-Françoise. If Angélique had intended to create a family for herself with the birth of her children, she was to be disappointed. Francheville owned the children, and they also died soon after birth—Louis lived for only two days, while Marie-Françoise lived until October of the same year.[41] Further, Angélique lived in a separate household from Jacques-César.

The slaveholders of Montréal baptized their slaves; but they rarely encouraged them to marry and create lasting families. One feature of slavery, the breaking apart of families through sale, militated against the enslaved creating families; for slaveholders, the creation and maintaining of families was not their primary motivation.

We can never know how Angélique felt in giving birth, and watching the demise of her children soon afterwards. Perhaps she felt a sense of loss at their death. She might also have been pleased that death released her children from a life of perpetual servitude. And, if Francheville had bought Angélique with the intention of increasing his stock of slaves, he was to be disappointed because her three children died in infancy.

Two other major changes occurred in the bondswoman's life a year after —Françoise's death. Sieur Francheville, her master, died in November 1733, and she began an affair with Claude Thibault, a French contract worker in Francheville's employ. These changes set in motion a series of events that would forever alter the slave woman's life and future.

Immediately after Sieur Francheville's demise, Angélique asked her mistress, Madame Francheville, for leave or congé (vacation or permission to go elsewhere to work). Angélique's request was audacious because congé was permitted to free laborers, not enslaved persons. Her mistress refused. Why did Angélique make the request? She discovered that Madame Francheville had sold her, and insisted that her mistress release her from slavery. It could be that Sieur Francheville had promised Angélique her freedom, but died before granting it. Or it could be that the sale was underway even before Francheville's death. Angélique begged her mistress not to sell her. But Madame Francheville would not relent, telling Angélique that she had sold her because she was rude, disobedient, and incorrigible. Angélique fired back, "If you sell me, I will 'burn' you." The slave woman had moral and "tactical" support in the form of her lover and fellow worker, Claude Thibault. He too challenged his employer's authority, and spoke "insolently" to her.[42]

Fear-filled, Madame Francheville took Angélique's threat seriously. In the second week of February, unable to control either Angélique or Thibault, Madame Francheville turned to her friends and relatives for help. She arranged for Angélique and Thibault to live with her relative Sieur Monière. The slave woman would work for Monière, while Thibault was contracted out to work for one Sieur de Berey. Angélique would remain in Monière's household until spring when the ice broke on the river and the fishing fleet was ready to head to the Gulf of St. Lawrence. Angélique would travel on one of the boats to Sieur Cugnet in Québec. Her mistress had sold her to Cugnet for six hundred pounds of gunpowder.

François-Étienne Cugnet was a French-born lawyer. He migrated to the colony in 1719, and in no time became a senior judge in the Superior Court. He was also a director of the king's domain (royal resources of fish, fur, timber, and other resources) in the region east of Québec City. Cugnet was an elite merchant with connections in the West Indies and France, and was one of the men that Sieur Francheville chose to sit on his board of directors for the St. Maurice forge initiative. When Francheville died, Cugnet rearranged the firm and named it "Cugnet and Company." In short, this man, firmly ensconced in the judiciary, administration, and maritime trade, was one of the richest and most important men in the colony.[43]

Angélique knew the reason for her removal to Moniere's and while she was there, a servant informed her that she was to be shipped to Québec and from there transported to the West Indies. Unwilling to remain a defenseless target, Angelique, upon arriving at Monière's, fled in the company of Thibault, intent on making it to New England or another English colony. From there, she had planned to board a ship for Portugal. Thibault himself planned on returning to France.

Thibault played a significant role in Angélique's life. A contract laborer from France, he was serving out his contract in Sieur Francheville's employ. It is not known whether Francheville recruited him directly in France or later, upon his arriving in the colony. Thibault did not like New France, and like Angélique, wanted to return to Europe. As a white male, it was easier for him to escape his servile condition than could a Black female slave.[44] Thus both Thibault and Angélique had something in common. Both chaffed under their servitude, both were European and desired to return to the "old country." They conspired.

Thibault's and Angélique's flight represented a collaboration between two sets of servile workers. Flight from bondage between these two groups was a common feature of early colonial history. Bulletins and memos from the Carolinas, Maryland, and Barbados regularly announced the escape of slaves in the company of indentured servants. Likewise, in Canada, during the English regime, the Québec and Montréal gazettes regularly broadcasted the joint flight of these two sets of servile laborers. Thibault and Angélique ran away during the French regime (there were no newspapers in the colony at that time), and their collaboration suggests that others like themselves could also have escaped or attempted to escape. We know also that enslaved persons and contract laborers often worked in partnership to undermine their employers and the system. For example, in Montréal in 1735, enslaved African Jean-Baptiste-Thomas was arrested along with three indentured laborers. Thomas and his white friends were in the habit of stealing goods from whites and fencing them. Thomas was hauled in front of the courts, pronounced guilty, and hanged.[45]

Servant and slave who joined forces saw themselves as oppressed workers against a common enemy—their owners or employers. To some degree, slaves and servants had more in common as bonded persons than a white indentured servant had with his white owners or employers. Whites in power feared this bond between Black slaves and white indentured workers and tried to break it by diverse means, including legislation. Powerful whites felt that if those persons most marginalized teamed up to resist, rebel, and revolt, then the whites would lose their grip on society and their control over the lower classes.[46]

For Angélique and Thibault, rank and status prevailed over considerations of race. However, the two were connected in ways that muted race. They were lovers and thus joined by bonds of passion. They supported each other's goal—to flee from Canada. Angélique wanted to return to Portugal and Thibault to France, more specifically, to his native province of Franche-Comté. And yet, the court record reveals that they planned to live together in Europe. One wonders how they were going to live together if their ultimate destinations were different. Angélique seemed to have thought about that, for during her trial, a witness, Jacques Jalleteau, told the court that Angélique had told him while she was at Sieur Monière's that she would stop in Franche-Comté on her way to Portugal.

It made sense for Angélique, in her escape from Montréal, to travel in the company of a white person, especially a white male. A lone Black woman traveling would definitely arouse suspicion. She would immediately be taken for an escaping slave. No sea captain would assist her, for example, unless he had abolitionist leanings. As a white male, Thibault could pose as her owner.[47]

Angélique remained a fugitive for two weeks in the snowy woods of Chambly, about eighty kilometers from Montréal. Chambly sits on the Richelieu River, which flows into Lake Champlain. From Lake Champlain, the couple could reach a port in Maine, New Hampshire, or Massachusetts—or more likely, New York City. From a New England or New York port, Angélique hoped to board a ship for Portugal. As mentioned earlier, the Richelieu River/ Lake Champlain route was very popular among traders and travelers, and was one of the principal fur trade and military routes from Montréal to Albany and New England.

Meanwhile, in Montréal, the authorities broadcasted the flight of Angélique and Thibault and organized a hunt for their capture. Officers of the constabulary searched the countryside, and after two weeks caught the fugitives in

Chambly, arrested and returned them to Montréal. Thibault was lodged in prison and surprisingly, Angélique was sent back to her mistress.

Angélique's flight and death threat to her owner illustrate the tensions building in the Franchville household between slave and owner.[48] Thérèse Francheville may have been Angélique's owner, but clearly she was not her master.[49] Matters only worsened in the Francheville's household upon Angélique's return. The bondswoman begged her mistress not to sell her. Angélique promised to be "good" and to please her mistress. Madame Francheville refused to budge from her position, telling Angélique that she did not want her in the house any longer, that she was rude and impolite, and that she behaved like a "mongrel." Furious at her mistress's response, Angélique "lost" it and began a reign of terror in the house. Again, she told her mistress that she would "grill and barbecue" her, and furthermore that the French were "dogs and not worth anything." Thérèse Francheville could only bide her time and wait for the river to thaw. She had the upper hand and she would use it.

* * *

With the sale to Cugnet complete, Madame Francheville made arrangements for her bondswoman to be removed to Québec on April 11. But this was not to be. The two women had a furious quarrel on the morning of April 10, with Angélique's impending departure as the likely source of the quarrel. Anxious and agitated, Madame Francheville left the house for a walk.

During Angélique's trial, Marie-Manon, a *Panise* of the neighboring de Berey's household, told the court that in the early afternoon of April 10, Madame Francheville stopped to greet Madame Desrivieres, a neighbor. Angélique had come over to the de Berey's house on an errand and stopped to speak with the *Panise*. The two slave women noticed Mesdames Desrivieres and Francheville chatting and laughing. Marie-Manon related that Angélique then said to her that Madame Francheville would not sleep in her home that night. When the *Panise* asked Angelique why she said that, the latter replied that she was going to "burn Madame Francheville in her own house." The *Panise* also said that Angelique called Madame Francheville "a bitch."[50]

In any event, around seven o'clock that evening, someone saw smoke curling from the roof of the Francheville's house and raised the alarm. Madame Francheville had gone to the evening mass, leaving Angélique in the house babysitting ten-year-old Marguerite de Couagne, Madame de Francheville's niece, and her two playmates. By the time the residents of the lower town organized themselves to fight the fire, the Francheville house was in flames. The fire spread with appalling speed, driving the frightened residents of the neighboring houses into the streets. It blazed through the lower portion of the town, where most of the merchant families lived, destroying forty-six houses in its wake, and a portion of the convent hospital, L'Hôtel-Dieu.[51]

People saved what they could and took what they saved to the hospital's courtyard where most of those who lost their homes spent the night. Even before the embers cooled, suspicion fell on Marie-Joseph Angélique. Louis Bellefueille, the gardener of L'Hôtel-Dieu, told Angélique (who had joined the others in the courtyard) that "everyone was saying she set the fire." Angélique replied that she did not. Others present said that Angelique had publicly threatened her mistress with burning. Claude Thibault, who was among the homeless, said nothing.

The night grew late, and the nuns of the hospital walked among the refugees distributing blankets. The priests of the Sulpician seminary and the Recollet fathers arrived with warm food for the fire victims. After eating, those who could found shelter among the hospital's ruins and slept for the night. Angélique made her way to the chapel of the Virgin Mary, which miraculously had escaped the blaze. She wrapped herself with the blanket that the nuns gave her and tried to sleep. But morning came early and brought with it the knowledge that the townspeople were pointing their collective finger at her. This made Angélique uneasy.

Early on morning of April 11, the authorities began their investigations and determined that Angélique and Thibault were the prime suspects. Officers of the constabulary quickly organized a search. At dawn, they found Angélique huddled in the small chapel, whom they promptly arrested. But they could not find Claude Thibault —he had disappeared.[52] They brought the bondswoman to the prison and lodged her there.[53] Her trial began the morning of the next day, April 12.

In the English criminal justice system, the suspect was presumed innocent until proven guilty. In the French system the reverse was true: the suspect was presumed guilty and was treated in the most hostile fashion by the prosecution. Further, the accused did not have the assistance of a lawyer (Louis XIV banned lawyers in the colony).[54] In French criminal cases, the accused had to undergo a series of "interrogations" or questions that she was bound to answer, a process known as the "question ordinaire."[55] These interrogations were usually very aggressive—sometimes torture was used "to help the accused remember." Next, the prosecution called on witnesses, who made their depositions without the accused being present. Later, the accused was confronted with the witnesses, and would deny or confirm their allegations.[56]

François Foucher, the king's attorney, was responsible for gathering evidence and making a case against the accused. Before he launched his investigations, as a formality, he sought permission to do so from Pierre Raimbault, the king's judge and lieutenant-general in charge of civil and criminal matters for the jurisdiction of Montréal. Raimbault granted Foucher's request and the attorney began summoning witnesses and taking depositions. Jacques-Cyprien Porlier, a scribe or court recorder, wrote down all the information.

Angélique's trial began with the interrogations—a series of questions posed by Raimbault. Porlier recorded the exchange. Here is the first entry:

> The Year one thousand seven hundred and thirty-four, the afternoon of the twelfth of April, we, Pierre Raimbault, official of the king, Lieutenant General, civil and criminal for the royal jurisdiction of Montreal, we were transported to the court chamber of the jail of this city, where we had brought before us, the negresse of demoiselle de Francheville, named Angelique, the latter, prisoner in virtue of our order of yesterday, at the request of the king's prosecutor. The aforementioned, after pronouncing an oath to tell the truth, was interrogated by us as follows: asked about her name, her age, her qualities and her residence. She stated that her name was Marie-Joseph, her age twenty-nine, that she had been born in Portugal, and that she had been sold to a Flemish man who sold her to the late Seigneur de Francheville about nine years ago, where she remained ever since.[57]

It is this stunning piece of narrative recorded by the royal court that highlights in no uncertain terms Angélique's multiple diasporic and transnational consciousnesses and identities: Black, Portuguese, European, multilingual, multicultural, New World, and thoroughly Atlantic. But she was an enslaved woman, sharing the status of the vast majority of her fellow Blacks in the Western Hemisphere.

In his interrogations Raimbault often repeated the same questions, hoping to hear a confession. But Angélique denied setting the fire. She also firmly answered "non" when asked whether Thibault was her accomplice.[58] But Raimbault pressed on. If the slave woman would not tell him what he wanted to hear, he would get the information from the witnesses. With Foucher's help, he called nearly two dozen witnesses who gave their testimonies without the accused present.

Madame Francheville was the first, testifying that Angélique had cursed her and threatened to "burn" her if she did not grant the enslaved woman freedom. She said her fear of Angelique led her to sell her slave. Other witnesses followed. The *Panise,* Marie-Manon, told Raimbault that Angélique said she would burn down the house of her mistress, and called Thérèse Francheville a "bitch" and a "whore." Marie-Louise Poirier, who once worked as a house servant for Madame Francheville, said that she quit her job eight days before the fire because Angélique had also threatened her. She had reprimanded Angélique for drinking brandy and leaving the house without permission. Angélique responded, saying that she if ever returned to Portugal and found any French people there, she would "burn them all like dogs." Five-year-old Amable Monière, one of the children whom Angélique babysat on the evening of the fire, also testified, saying that while in the house she saw Angélique carry live coals up to the attic. (The fire started in the attic.) A neighbor, Sieur Radisson, related that when the alarm was raised, he went over to the Francheville's house to help put out the fire. But Angélique told him there was no ladder in the house and refused to help him carry the buckets of water to throw on the blaze. Another witness claimed to have seen Angélique on the street just before the alarm was raised, fixing her gaze two or three times at the precise spot on the roof where the fire broke out. This same witness also said that Angélique tried to prevent Marguerite de Couagne and her playmates from running to warn Madame Francheville.

When "confronted" with the witnesses, Angélique's reactions ranged from denial to defiance and manipulation. To Madame Francheville, she said, "Madame, however nasty I might be, I'm not wretched enough to commit an act of that sort." She told another witness, Louis Langlois Traversy, "My dear Traversy, you could be mistaken," and to Amable Monière, "Little Amable, someone told you to tell a lie on me; come let me give you some candy so you may speak the truth."[59]

After hearing from the witnesses, the court continued haranguing Angélique, sometimes on a daily basis. Convinced that she was the culprit, the king's representatives wanted her to confess to the crime. But she did not. Having called all its witnesses and done its research, the court then weighed the evidence. On the morning of June 4, the Montréal tribunal presided over by Raimbault handed down a terrible judgment on Angélique. Based on the eyewitnesses' evidence and Angélique's behavior before and during the fire, she was found guilty of arson and given the death penalty. Historian André Vachon sums up the punishment: "She was sentenced to make honorable amends, to have her hand cut off, and be burnt alive."[60] Her ashes would then be thrown to the four winds.[61]

The sentence was part of the grisly French medieval punishment practices. Bodily mutilations, burning at the stake, and the casting of the ashes to the four winds were usually reserved for witches, heretics, arsonists, and those accused of other grave crimes. Joan of Arc, for example, was burned at the stake as a witch and heretic. This punishment meant that one's soul would be forever damned to roam the earth in agony, with no hope of entering

Purgatory, where it would have had a chance to repent and then possibly enter Paradise.

In New France, all those sentenced to die had the right to appeal. And so did Angélique. Foucher, the king's attorney, launched her appeal to the Superior Court (*Conseil Supérieur*) housed in Québec, the capital of the colony.[62] Angélique traveled to Québec by boat to make her appeal.[63] On June 12, the court handed down its decision upholding the death sentence, but modifying aspects of the gruesome punishment. There would be no bodily mutilation or live burning. Instead, the slave woman would still make honorable amends and then be hanged. Later, her dead body would be burnt and the ashes cast away.[64] François-Étienne Cugnet, Angélique's intended new owner, was one of the *Conseil*'s judges. He seemed not to have found his presence on the bench a conflict of interest. Angélique returned to Montréal after the *Conseil Supérieur* made its decision. All she had to do now was to wait for her death.

June 21, 1734, was set as the day of the execution. At six o'clock in the morning, Raimbault, four of his assistants, the doctor from L'Hôtel-Dieu, the royal executioner, and the scribe met Angélique in the *sale de chambre* (interrogation room or court room) of the prison. (We will learn later why a doctor was present.) Raimbault once more harangued her, and not getting the confession he desired, subjected her to *la question extraordinaire*—interrogation under torture. Authorities in New France used this method in cases where the accused being questioned "proved reluctant to talk." The court was still convinced that she had set the fire, and also that she had not acted alone. The tribunal hoped that *la question extraordinaire* would force her to confess to setting the fire and naming her accomplice.[65] She was tortured with the *brodequins*,[66] a popular instrument used by the authorities in France and New France and consisting of planks that were bound to the defendant's shins, forming a wooden "boot" to fit the leg and foot. Wedges were then inserted between the planks and struck with a heavy hammer to crush the bones of the reluctant confessor. The interrogator sat in front of the accused ready to fire his questions. A scribe was also on hand to record both questions and answers. And the torturer waited ready with his hammer. After each question, if the interrogator was not satisfied with the answer, the torturer would smash the hammer onto the defendant's limbs.[67]

The "master of the means of torture" (king's executioner) placed Angélique on the "seat of torture" and fit the *brodequins* around her legs. This torturer was Mathieu Leveille, an enslaved African from the island of Martinique.[68] Raimbault began questioning her once more. Did she set the fire, and who was her accomplice. Angélique's response: "No one helped me set the fire because I did not do it." Raimbault gave the signal and the torturer smashed the hammer on the wedges of the *brodequins.* She screamed, "It's me and no one else. I want to die!" Raimbault asked about her accomplice. She denied having any. Again the smashing, accompanied by screams. Angélique had confessed to setting the fire but Raimbault wanted her to also say Thibault was her partner in crime. Because of that he continued the torture.

One round of the *brodequins* consisted of four smashings. The first round passed and still Angélique did not name an accomplice. After this round, the slave woman was in a weakened state. Her knees and legs were battered and bruised and she was in extreme agony. Feverish, trembling, and crying out in pain, Angélique was unable to sit upright any longer. Leveile laid her out on a mat and the doctor gave her "reviving" medicines.

When Raimbault determined that the slave woman had sufficiently revived, he ordered another round of smashings. This was unnecessary. Angélique was in extreme pain and her body, if not her will, was broken. The last time the torturer smashed the heavy iron onto Angelique's knee, she screamed in agony and once more confessed to the crime: "I did it, it was me *monsieur,* me and no one else. A bad thought came to me. I did it with a small stove. I have no accomplice." Raimbult, frustrated that Angélique would bend no further, stopped the questioning and the smashings.

Angélique at first denied having set the fire, but later "confessed" under torture. Her first thought under *la questionne extraordinaire* was perhaps that if the authorities believed she did not set the fire, they would release her, or waive the death penalty. During the first application of the *brodequins,* Angélique replied that she had set the fire. One can speculate that she confessed only because she could not endure any more of the torture. If indeed she was guilty, she probably also confessed because now she felt she had nothing to lose. After all, she had been judged guilty and condemned to death. Nothing could save her.

Still, even under torture, Angélique would not budge on one point. She insisted that Claude Thibault was not her accomplice and that he was not involved in any way with the destruction of the town. Did she refuse to implicate Thibault because she loved him? And is she to be believed that Thibault was not involved? Angélique was protective of Thibault, though he did not deserve her consideration. The Frenchman disappeared from Montréal the night of the fire and was never seen again. The authorities named him as Angélique's accomplice and for two years had a warrant out for his arrest. But he was never caught. Angélique would face the gallows alone.

At three o'clock in the afternoon, the prison clerk came to her cell and ritualistically read the death sentence to her. Father Navetier, a Sulpician priest accompanied him. Navetier heard Angélique's confession and gave her final rites. Leveille, the royal hangman, was also on hand with the rubbish cart to take her to the gallows. Angélique was readied for her role. She wore a long white chemise with the word "arsonist" embroidered at the front. In her hand she held a flaming torch. The cart took her on a "tour" of the area devastated by the fire and then stopped in front of the parish church of Notre Dame. Here she carried out the ritual of making honorable amends. On the steps of the church, on bended wounded knees, she cried in a loud voice, "I beg pardon of God, the king, and Justice, for the crime I committed!" She repeated this three times. Angélique was then taken to the gallows and hanged. Her body was later burnt and the ashes cast to the four winds.

Revisioning the New World African Diaspora

Even though Marie-Joseph Angélique, under torture, admitted to setting the fire, we will never know for sure if she did it. Was she a vengeful slave or a scapegoat? She had at least two motives for setting the fire. The first was her desire for freedom. The other was vengeance. Angélique was upset and angry when she discovered that her owner had sold her and vowed to get even.

Arson was also a chief mode of resistance used by New World enslaved Africans in their struggle against enslavement. Enslaved Africans burnt their owners' plantations, homes, cities, and settlements in their struggle against slavery. Angélique repeatedly spoke about "burning" or "barbecuing" her mistress and the French—there is no reason to think that she was unwilling to carry out her threats. By February 1734, she had reached the point of no return and simply did not care anymore.

On the other hand, she could have been scapegoated. From all accounts, Angélique was not a docile slave. She was unwilling to be subservient to those who had power over her. She was indeed a slave, but did not have a servile mind.[69] She was defiant, feisty, foul-mouthed, and bad-tempered. She talked of burning her mistress and all French people. Her attitude and behavior endeared her to no one, least of all her mistress. So when the fire burned out of control, all fingers pointed conveniently to Angélique, Madame Francheville's incorrigible Negress.

The bondswoman's desperate desire to return to Portugal reveals the centrality of Portugal in her mind. Even if she was enslaved in Portugal, she likely had relatives there and would have been part of a larger Black community. In New France she was isolated and alienated from society. Her insistence on returning to Portugal raises the question about why she would want to return if she was going back to slavery. But perhaps she had not been a slave in Portugal. Could it be that Angélique was free or indentured in Portugal but was tricked, sold, or kidnapped into slavery?

Unfortunately, this question cannot be answered with any certainty. But what we are sure about is that the bondswoman was desperate to return to the land of her birth. Often upon arriving in the New World, Africans yearned to return to "Guinea" or Africa. But not Angélique—her "Guinea" was Portugal.

The discovery and recovery of Angélique's story provides us with knowledge, information, and insight into an understudied area of the Black Diaspora—Canada. It also provides further understanding of New World slavery. Most studies of slavery in the New World explore the field and plantation variant. Since slavery in Canada was primarily domestic, researching Canadian slavery offers a wonderful opportunity to examine another type of domestic slavery. Angélique's life connects different areas of the Black Diaspora and the Atlantic. Her story offers a global perspective into the lives of African-descended people in the Americas.

Notes

This paper benefited greatly from the insights and comments provided by Bernard Moitt. I also extend my appreciation to Sethe Witherspoon, Franca Iacovetta, and Rosalyn Terborg-Penn for reading previous drafts.

1. Colin Palmer, "Defining and Studying the Modern African Diaspora," *Perspectives* (AHA Newsletter) 36, no. 6 (September 1998), 22.

2. See Kim Butler, "Defining Diaspora, Refining a Discourse" (paper presented at the 113th Annual Meeting of the American Historical Association, 1999), p. 7, for a discussion on the usefulness of diaspora as concept.

3. Jan Noel, in her essay on women in New France, has white French women as her unit of analysis. She mentions Black and Aboriginal people as *slaves* but not as gendered persons. Slave women therefore did not figure in her discussion, and when mentioned, their gender was erased. Jan Noel, "Women in New France," Canadian Historical Association Booklet, No. 59.

4. Butler, "Defining Diaspora," 8.

5. Some standard texts on the Atlantic trade, and that also discuss the "numbers question" are Philip Curtin, *The Atlantic Slave Trade: A Census* (Madison: University of Wisconsin Press, 1969); Herbert S. Klein, *The Atlantic Slave Trade* (New York: Cambridge University Press, 1999); David Eltis, *The Rise of African Slavery in the Americas* (New York: Cambridge University Press, 2000); James Rawley *The Trans-*

atlantic Slave Trade (New York: Norton, 1981); Hugh Thomas, *The Slave Trade: The Story of the Atlantic Slave Trade: 1440–1870* (New York: Simon & Schuster, 1997); J. E. Inikori, *Forced Migration: The Impact of the Export Slave Trade on African Societies* (London: Hutchinson University Library, 1982); Walter Rodney, *West Africa and the Atlantic Slave Trade* (Cambridge: Africa Research Group, 1974), 3–27.

6. Robin Blackburn, *The Making of New World Slavery from the Baroque to the Modern, 1492–1800* (London: Verso, 1997).

7. A.C de C.M. Saunders, *A Social History of Black Slaves and Freedmen in Portugal, 1441–1555* (London: Cambridge University Press, 1982); Blackburn, *Making of New World Slavery,* 95–114; David Eltis, *The Atlantic Slave Trade, a CD-Rom Database* (New York: Oxford University Press, 2000).

8. Bailey W. Diffie and George D. Winus, *Foundations of the Portuguese Empire, 1415–1580* (Minneapolis: University of Minnesota Press, 1977), 76–88; Basil Davidson, *The African Slave Trade* (Boston: Little, Brown, 1980), 53–59.

9. Linda M. Heywood, "The Angolan-Afro-Brazilian Cultural Connections," in Sylvia Frey and Betty Wood, ed. *From Slavery to Emancipation in the Atlantic World* (London: Frank Cass, 1999), 9–23; Saunders, *Social History,* 54, 55, 59; Edward Scobie, "The Black in Western Europe," *African Presence in Early Europe,* ed. Ivan Van Sertima (Edison, N.J.: Transaction Publishers, 1993), 193.

10. Saunders, *Social History,* 62–63.

11. Saunders has an extensive discussion on slave occupations. Ibid., 63–88.

12. Ibid.

13. Ibid, 78.

14. On Black life and culture, see ibid., 89–107.

15. Slavery would not be abolished in Portugal until 1773 as part of Prime Minister's Pombal's sweeping reforms. Ibid., 178.

16. Angélique's Trial Transcript, 11 April to 21 June 1734, *Registre Criminel,* IV: 24–26; *Procédures Judiciaires, Matieres Criminelles,* IV: 237, housed at the Archives Nationales de Québec, at both the Montréal and Québec branches (ANQM and ANQQ).

17. Beauharnois to Maurepas, in Edmund B. O'Callaghan, ed. *Documents Relative to the Colonial History of the State of New York, Vol. 9* (Albany, 1856–1887), 1019–20. Also in 1727 Intendant Dupuy issued an ordinance prohibiting "foreign" merchants from trading in Montréal. Dupuy was particularly incensed about the trading activities of the merchants of Albany, "New England" (985–86).

18. For a thorough discussion on the trade between the Montréal and New York merchants during the French regime, see Thomas Elliot Norton, *The Fur Trade in Colonial New York: 1686–1776* (Madison: University of Wisconsin Press, 1974) 121–51.

19. Jean Lunn, "The Illegal Fur Trade Out of New France, 1713–1760," *Canadian Historical Association Report* (1939), 61–76.

20. Thomas E. Burke, Jr., *Mohawk Frontier: The Dutch Community of Schenectady, 1661–1710* (Ithaca, N.Y.: Cornell University Press, 1991), 68–108.

21. Marcel Trudel, *L'esclavage au Canada Francais: Histoire et Conditions de*

l'esclavage (Quebec: Presses Universitaires Laval, 1960) gives a comprehensive treatment of French Canadian slavery. William Riddell's "The Slave in Canada" (*Journal of Negro History* 5, no. 3 [1920]: 261–377) offers a thorough treatment in English on Canadian slavery. Riddell also includes a discussion of slavery in the Maritimes. Maureen Elgersman has gendered Canadian slavery with *Unyielding Spirits: Slave Women in Canada and Jamaica* (New York: Garland, 1999). Kenneth Donovan brings a new, fresh, and very necessary perspective to the examination of Canadian slavery, focusing on Acadia, with his "Slaves and their Owners in Ile Royale, 1713–1760," *Acadiensis* 25, no. 1 (Autumn 1995): 3–32.

22. Robin Winks, *The Blacks in Canada* (Montreal: McGill-Queens University Press, 1971), 3.

23. See William Riddell, "Le Code Noir," *Journal of Negro History* 10, no. 3 (1925): 321–29.

24. Trudel, *L'esclavage,* 126–159. See also Marcel Trudel, *Dictionnaire de Esclaves et Leur Proprietaires au Canada Francais* (La Salle, Quebec: Editions Hurtibise, 1990).

25. Kenneth Donovan, "Slaves and Their Owners," 4; Trudel, *L'Esclavage,* 168–70. Slavery in New France was very much akin to New England slavery regarding climate and economy. For New England slavery, see Lorenzo Greene, *The Negro in Colonial New England, 1620–1776* (New York: Columbia University Press, 1942).

26. Trudel, *L'esclavage,* 168–86.

27. Louis Dechene, "The Growth of Montreal in the 18th Century," in J. M. Bumsted, ed. *Canadian History Before Confederation* (Georgetown, Ontario: Irwin-Dorsey, 1979), 165.

28. Yet, in the colonial towns of North America, town and country were very close to each other. Many town residents owned farms on the outskirts of the city. With town and country being in such close proximity, slaves would be engaged in both town occupations and on the farm.

29. Trudel, *L'Esclavage,* 87–98; James Walker, *A History of Blacks in Canada* (Hull, Quebec: Ministry of Supplies and Services, 1980), 19.

30. W. T. Easterbrook and Hugh G. J. Aitken, *Canadian Economic History* (Toronto: University of Toronto Press, 1988, reprint), chaps. 4, 5, 6.

31. Andre Lachance, *La Vie Urbaine en Nouvelle-France* (Montreal: Boreal, 1987), 66; Dechene, "Growth of Montreal," 165.

32. Cameron Nish, "François Poulin De Francheville," *Dictionary of Canadian Biography* 2 (Toronto, 1969), 529–30; letter from Beauharnois et Hocquart, 25 October 1729 to Le Comte Maurepas, Minister of Marine; letter of Poulin de Francheville to Maurepas, National Archives of Canada, C11 A, vol. 51, pp. 99–100, 101–3. See also "Beauharnois et Hocquart au Ministre" 15 October 1732, NAC, C 11 A, pp. 200–4.

33. Trudel, *Dictionnaire,* 400–1.

34. Riddell, "Le Code Noir," 322.

35. Trudel, *Dictionnaire,* 113.

36. Orlando Patterson, *Slavery and Social Death, A Comparative Study* (Cambridge, Mass.: Harvard University Press, 1982), 54–55.

37. On the Manueline reforms see Saunders, *Social History,* 40–41.

38. Donovan, "Slaves and Their Owners," 7.

39. Trudel, *Dictionnaire,* 103.

40. Riddell, "Le Code Noir," 323; Thomas D. Morris, *Southern Slavery and the Law, 1619–1860* (Chapel Hill: University of North Carolina Press, 1996), 43.

41. According to Trudel, at the baptism of Marie-Françoise, Angelique declared that she did not know who the father of this child was. This is strange considering that Marie-Françoise was a twin to Louis, whom she said was fathered by Jacques-César. Perhaps, at the time she conceived the twins, Marie was already involved with Claude Thibault, a white indentured laborer from France, and thought he could possibly be the twins' father. Her owner, François Poulin de Francheville, was also a possible candidate. However, Trudel states that all of Marie's children were fathered by Jacques-César. Trudel, *Dictionnaire,* 113.

42. Angélique's trial transcripts.

43. Cameron Nish, *François-Étienne Cugnet: Entrepreneur et Entreprises en Nouvelle-France* (Montréal: Fides, 1975).

44. Thibault's white skin enabled him to take advantage of escape opportunities. Note that Thibault disappeared after the fire and was never seen again and therefore never caught.

45. Rulings of the Conseil Supérieur, May 1725: "Jean-Baptiste-Thomas, Negre," Archives des Colonies, Serie C11A, Vol. 64, ANQQ.

46. On collaboration between enslaved and indentured laborers in colonial America, see Hilary Beckles, *White Servitude and Black Slavery in Barbados, 1627–1715* (Knoxville: University of Tennessee Press, 1989); Robert Middlekauf, *Bacon's Rebellion* (Rand McNally, 1966).

47. William and Ellen Craft, American fugitive slaves, used subterfuge to effect their escape from slavery. The light-skinned Ellen posed as a white male and owner of her much darker-skinned husband, William. Their story is recorded in William Craft, *Running a Thousand Miles for Freedom* (New York: Arno Press, 1969, reprint).

48. See the trial transcripts, 12 April 1734: Dossier du Conseil Supérieur, *Matieres Criminelles,* IV, 237.

49. To "mistress" her fails to convey the meaning of control, authority, and domination that the word "master" implies. The sexist and gendered nature of the English language ensures that "to mistress" would have less of an impact than "to master."

50. The narrative pertaining to the fire is taken from the trial transcripts.

51. A series of fires destroyed Montréal, or sections of it, during its colonial history. L'Hôtel-Dieu was always victimized. *La Presse* (Montreal), February 7, 1988; Pierre-Georges Roy, "Les Catastrophes dans La Nouvelle-France," *Le Bulletin des Recherches Historiques* 53, no. 2 (1947): 35–48.

52. The Marechaussée "constituted the police force of the time and was attached

to the royal jurisdictions." Andre Vachon, *Taking Root: Canada from 1700–1760* (Ottawa: Minister of Supplies and Services, 1985), 111.

53. It is curious that she was put in prison instead of under the "care" of the nuns of the Hospital General, where female offenders were typically placed. Perhaps Raimbault felt Angelique was too "dangerous" to be confined at the Hospital General. Thus, her sex was obscured by considerations of the severity of the crime she allegedly committed, and possibly her race and servile status.

54. Marcel Trudel, *Introduction to New France* (Toronto: Holt, Rinehart and Winston,1968), 218,

55. New France adopted its legal code from the Coutume de Paris, or French legal code.

56. Trudel, *New France,* 218.

57. Trial transcripts, 12 April 1734, translated from French by Jonas Stefan and Afua Cooper.

58. Trial transcripts, 21 June 1734.

59. "Confrontations" between Angelique and witnesses translated by Adrienne Shadd and Afua Cooper.

60. Andre Vachon, "Marie Joseph Angelique," *Dictionary of Canadian Biography,* Vol. 2, 457–58. See also Trial Records, 4 June 1734. This document was also signed by the four notaries who assisted Raimbault Nicolas: Auguste Guillet de Chaumont, Francois-Michel LePailleur, Charles-Rene Gaudron de Chevremont, and Jean-Baptiste Adhemar. Honorable amends (*L'Amende honorable*) was considered a part of the death penalty and was carried out before the actual execution. Each condemned person had to endure *L'Amende honorable.* The criminal was usually driven around the town in a cart with a rope around her neck and a torch in her hand, and then left in front of the court house or the main church. Here, she publicly confessed her crime and asked pardon of God, the king, and Justice. *L'Amende honorable* was ordered for crimes against religion (blasphemy, for example), sorcery, public scandal, the abuse of children, and for other grave acts like arson. Raymond Boyer, *Les Crimes et Les Chatiments au Canada Francais du XVII au XX Siecle* (Montreal: Le Cercle du Livre de France, 1966), 183–86

61. Trudel, *L'Esclavage,* 227.

62. The Conseil Superieur was composed of the governor-general, the intendant, the bishop, twelve counselors, and the lieutenant-general of the jurisdiction in question. Vachon, *Taking Root,* 104.

63. The four notaries whom Raimbault employed to assist him with the trial prepared her appeal.

64. Trial Records, 12 June 1734; Vachon, "Marie Joseph Angelique."

65. Boyer, *Les Crimes et Les Chatiments,* 240–68.

66. Pierre Raimbault, "Procedure Criminelle de Marie Josephe Angelique—Incendiere," 21 June 1734, APQ; Trudel, *L'Esclavage,* 227. For a description of the *brodequins* see Andre LaChance, *La Justice Criminelle Du Roi au Canada au XVIII* Siecle

(Quebec: Les Presses de L'Universite Laval, 1978), 81–83, and "Tout Sur La Torture," *Le Magazine Maclean* (December 1966), 36–42.

67. R. Douglas Francis, *Origins: Canadian History to Confederation* (Toronto: Holt, Rinehart & Winston, 1992), 92.

68. In 1733 Leveille was transported from Martinique to work as New France's executioner. After her conviction, he became Angélique's executioner. Trudel, *Dictionnaire*, 175–76.

69. Thomas J. Davis made that same observation about Caesar, the slave implicated in the "plot" to burn down New York City in 1741. Davis, *A Rumor of Revolt: The "Great Negro Plot" in Colonial New York* (New York: The Free Press, 1985), 2.

SECTION TWO

Diaspora Interactions

4

Envisioning an Antislavery War

African American Historical Constructions of the Haitian Revolution in the 1850s

STEPHEN G. HALL

The Haitian Revolution was one of the most compelling events in the revolutionary annals of the modern Western hemisphere. Born of slavery, one of the West's most loathsome institutions, and stirred in the cauldron of unceasing oppression, the Haitian Revolution featured not only an uprising of slaves in the French colony of Saint Domingue against the tyranny of their masters, but the waging of a sustained slave revolt that led to the subsequent defeat by these slaves of highly trained armies from France, Britain, and Spain. The proclamation of the Haitian Republic in 1804 sent tremors and shockwaves through the hearts of early-nineteenth century republicans in the Western hemisphere.[1]

Determined to erase the revolutionary memory of the Haitian Revolution, the United States, because of its proximity to Haiti and the fact that slavery was firmly entrenched in its social, political, and economic institutions, not only failed to recognize Haiti diplomatically until 1862, but also attempted to deny the legitimacy of the revolution. Some argued that the revolution represented a spontaneous outburst of the unrestrained passions of the slaves. Others pointed to the tales of the white refugees who offered lurid accounts of masters murdered in their beds and slaves run amok killing, butchering, and burning. These sentiments forestalled any serious discussion in the public sphere among majoritarian populations about the meanings of the Haitian Revolution. It was, for all intents and purposes, relegated to the margins of Western revolutionary history.[2]

As a result of its marginal position, Haiti remained an uncertain sign and symbol. As a sign it wielded great power. For republicans it meant the possibility that the system of slavery might be toppled if a spark or an ember from the Haitian conflagration took hold and began to burn in other parts of the Western hemisphere. For African-descended populations, Haiti served as a symbol of the possibilities for erecting a black republic and maintaining it in the face of colonial intrigue, cataclysmic upheaval, and governmental nonrecognition. These signs and symbols served as the canvas upon which ideas about the meanings of the revolution and the destiny of free blacks were written.[3]

While the markings and etchings on the canvas seemed uncertain or indecipherable, many of these descriptors became more legible and understandable with the sea change in national discourse on slavery in the late 1840s and throughout the 1850s. A period characterized by the ascendancy of expansionist and Manifest Destiny ideologies that shaped the national debate on African Americans in the republic, and revolutionary upheaval in Europe in 1848, which toppled the monarchy in France for good, brought expanded rights for women in England and fostered nationalism with the Austria-Hungarian empire. Accustomed to defining their issues in an international manner, African American intellectuals seized this propitious opportunity.[4]

The Haitian Revolution surfaced again as a viable tool in an expansive Antislavery War for two distinct reasons: black intellectuals viewed it as a tangible example of what persons of African descent could accomplish in the face of great odds, and the revolution's pre- and post-history offered a refutation of the dominant discourse on black moral and mental capacity. This essay, then, explores accounts of the war not simply as objective historical accounts, but instead examines the ways they seek to use the memory of the Haitian Revolution as a tool to wage an Antislavery War in the United States. My goal here is not to talk about the historiography of the Haitian Revolution as written by African Americans and Haitians. Rather it is to focus on a highly charged political moment and excavate how African American writers used a single revolutionary moment in the Western hemisphere to intervene decisively in a contemporary Antislavery War. By doing so, I hope to show how these intellectuals contributed to rereading the Haitian Revolution as a legitimate revolutionary construct and the importance of their relationship to the growth of historical understanding about persons of African descent in the Western hemisphere.[5]

Rereading the Haitian Revolution

While the American Revolution served as a recognizable component of the Antislavery War, a legitimate site of revolutionary discourse (at least from the vantage point of black intellectuals), Haiti offered other possibilities—possibilities that threatened to ignite the already catalytic agents of revolutionary fervor. Haiti's reemergence in the nation's public discourse as a harbinger of revolutionary possibilities demonstrated the urgency as well as the uncertainty of black intellectuals whose civic prospects literally hung in the balance. Haiti, the site of the only black republic in the Western hemisphere, offered a place for potential emigration as well as a metaphorical symbol (in the present) and actual symbol (in the past) of ultimate triumph in the Antislavery War.[6]

As African American intellectual discourse in the Antislavery War suggests, the war meant more than a simplistic contest between anti- and proslavery forces; rather it operated as a war of ideas and rhetorical strategies that revolved around defining, appropriating, and applying terms usually reserved for majoritarian populations and extending them to African American populations and other diasporic communities of color. Ideas such as patriotism, republicanism, self-government, moral propriety, and civic and social responsibility figured prominently in the social reform lexicon of the day. Like their counterparts who held up the American Revolution as an example of black service to the nation, black writers also used the Haitian Revolution in the same way.[7]

The most visible writers on the intersections between the Haitian and American revolutions included George Boyer Vashon, William Wells Brown, and James Theodore Holly. All of these writers built on Martin Delany's *Condition, Elevation, Emigration and Destiny of the Colored People of the United States* (1852) and William Nell's *Colored Patriots of the American Revolution* (1855) in affirming the sense of exclusion and uncertainty experienced by African Americans. Highly visible in the abolitionist community, two of the three, Vashon and Holly, traveled to Haiti in the late 1840s and 1850s. Brown did not travel to Haiti, but actively participated in the transatlantic abolitionist community, traveling extensively in Europe and lecturing on the abolitionist circuit.[8]

Haiti in the Hemispheric Mind Before 1850

To understand the development of African American ideas about Haiti and the fluid meanings of the Haitian Revolution requires an examination of the relationship between Haiti and the United States prior to the 1850s. Initially a site of fear and uncertainty for the slavocracy of the Western hemisphere and a source of pride for African-descended populations, Haiti's independence in 1804 did not assure it unfettered entry into the community of republican nations. Rather, its incendiary meanings threatened to destabilize the institution of slavery in the Western hemisphere. Many white planters fled the island with their families and slaves carrying with them lurid tales of a violent slave uprising complete with stories of planters murdered in their beds by bloodthirsty slaves. These individual stories as well as emigrant tales of the destruction and plunder of the town of Cape François in 1792 quickly melded into an archetypal sensibility about the revolution's impact known as the "horrors of Saint Domingue" (the "horrors" as opposed to the possibility informed the relationship between Haiti and the United States).[9]

Although it is commonly believed that African Americans uncritically embraced Haiti and its incendiary meanings from the republic's inception up to the 1850s, this popular perception is much more complex than commonly presented. Haiti's fortunes ebbed and flowed during the tumultuous period following its establishment. Chronic instability, periodic changes in government, and colonial intrigue, as well as the refusal of the United States to recognize the fledging nation, complicated an already difficult situation. Clearly aware of this tenuous situation, black intellectuals embraced the Republic as an example of black governance, but tended to downplay its origins as the culmination of a successful slave revolt. The Haitian government's pledge of citizenship to persons of African descent, however, proved attractive and beginning in the 1820s numerous African Americans emigrated to the island. While some remained, many did not, and the island received a mixed reputation in this regard.[10]

Despite these problems, black intellectuals remained optimistic about Haiti's prospects. They also understood the nation's importance as an example of the capacity of black people to govern themselves and often went to great lengths to refute the erroneous characterization of the revolution, at least from the vantage point of black intellectuals, as simply the "horrors of Saint Domingue." James McCune Smith's "A lecture on the Haytien revolutions," dramatizes this point because it embodied many of the ideological themes and positions that subsequent writers in the Antislavery War used. Smith, a distinguished member of New York's free black community, received medical training at the University of Glasgow. After returning to the United States, he affiliated with several abolitionist organizations, including the American Anti-Slavery Society, the Society for the Promotion of Education among Colored Children, the Statistics Institute, and the Philomathean Literary Society.[11]

From the outset, drawing on articles from the *British Quarterly,* D. M. Brown's *History of St. Domingo,* and Vide's *History of St. Domingo,* Smith's "lecture" hoped to vindicate the struggles of the Haitian people to establish a republican government and situate Haiti as an indisputable example of the benefits of immediate emancipation. In the introduction to the lectures, Smith not only examined the plight of slaves, but other issues such as caste distinctions, the treatment of the free colored population, and the topographical features of the island, which facilitated the revolution.[12]

In the minds of many black Americans, Haiti remained an important symbol of black vindication in the Western hemisphere. Smith's lecture clearly operates at this level. It not only reconfigured the meanings of the Haitian Revolution in light of the "horrors of Saint Domingue," but offered an objective and dispassionate account of a deeply contentious historical event. I argue that Smith's mediations on the Haitian Revolution fall within the stream of the Antislavery War envisioned by black intellectuals during this period. By drawing on issues of self-elevation, moral propriety, and fitness for citizenship, it highlighted issues of importance to the African American community.[13]

Rather than a single explosive event, a central component of the "horrors of Saint Domingue" legend, Smith convincingly presented the revolution as one influenced by multiple actors including Saint Domingue's *grand blancs* (planters and slave owners), *petit blancs* (small farmers, artisans, and overseers), and *affranchis* or *gens de coleur* (the free black population), as much as it was by the servile population—a reality Smith linked to events on the island that preceded the revolution. Concerned more with the profitability of sugar cultivation than the condition and plight of the slaves, the *grand blancs* seemed unaware of the ramifications of importing large numbers of African slaves into the colony. This fact coupled with the growing animosity between the *petit blancs* and free people of color added further fuel to the fire.[14]

In Smith's genealogy, the outbreak of the French Revolution in 1789 inspired dissension and class warfare among *petit* and *grand blancs*. They, not the servile population, exacerbated an already tense situation. The refusal of the *grand blancs* to allow *petit blancs* representation in the new government sparked an armed conflict between the two groups. Smarting from their rebuttal by the *grand blancs,* the *petit blancs* organized themselves into an army with the intention of expelling the attorney general and the intendant at Port-au-Prince. Rather than face expulsion, both men voluntarily left the island.[15]

The situation was further complicated by the arrival of Vincent Oge, a member of the *affranchis* who had traveled abroad seeking support for the demands of the free people of color. Oge returned to the island to secure compliance with the 1790 decree of the French National Assembly allowing all persons twenty-five and older to vote in the formation of a national assembly. Instead of complying with the request, the Colonial Assembly sent a force of six hundred men to capture Oge. After his capture and execution, the National Assembly decreed equal rights for all French citizens regardless of race. Rather than implementing the new law, the governor and colonial assembly in Saint Domingue convened to circumvent the law's passage and tighten restrictions on the servile population.[16]

Smith's presentation of Saint Domingue's internal politics of class and race is designed to provide a more complex genealogy of the Haitian Revolution; however, the account masks as much as it presents. This is especially true in his discussion of Vincent Oge. Smith is notably silent about the initial revolt of the free blacks after it became clear that the Colonial Assembly would not recognize, nor even accept Oge's petition. Oge is not simply a humble petitioner who throws himself on the mercy of the colonial assembly; he is a hesitant insurgent whose vastly inferior force is defeated by a greatly superior one. Smith's attempt to present Oge as a humble servant in the cause of liberty comments as much on the patience of the educated free black population in Haiti as it does on the free black community in the United States. How long can one justifiably wait for freedom without acting to make it a reality? This question seems to lie at the heart of Smith's inquiry.[17]

The question's answer is embedded in Smith's genealogy of the Haitian Revolution. This account aids the reader in believing that this "insurrection was the legitimate fruit of slavery, against which it was a spontaneous rebellion. It was not therefore the fruit of emancipation, but the consequence of withholding from men their liberty." Following from this supposition, Smith turned to settling questions surrounding the destruction of Cape François in 1792, the central component of the "horrors of Saint Domingue." Smith's awareness that survivors' tales of this ordeal formed the basis for the belief "that the first use of their liberty made by the slaves, was ruthlessly to imbrue their hands in their former master's blood" further strengthened his resolve to dispense with the veracity of this claim once and for all. He pointed out that although the servile army consisted of more than one hundred thousand people, only three thousand actually attacked the town—an event no different, in Smith's thinking, than the uprising of Spartacus in the level of violence visited upon slaveholders. In fact, Smith believed the damaged inflicted on the planters by the slaves paled in comparison to the number of serviles killed by white insurgents.[18]

Having legitimized the right of human beings to rise up and throw off the yoke of oppression, situated Haiti as a legitimate revolutionary example in hemispheric history, and deflated the potency of the "horrors of Saint Domingue" legend, Smith turned to shoring up the vindicationist edifice he erected to glorify the Haitian Revolution by celebrating the ability and capacity of blacks for self-government. For Smith, Toussaint L' Ouverture embodied this capacity. L' Ouverture's fame proved the one constant in African American and Haitian relations. L' Ouverture, unlike his successors Jean-Jacques Dessalines, André Rigaud, and Henry Christophe, remained above reproach. He not only defeated French, British, and Spanish forces on the island, but proved a capable administrator. His imposition of strict labor laws allowed the colony to regain much of its former strength as a site for sugar, coffee, and indigo production. He also promulgated a new constitution guaranteeing equality before the law.

In Smith's account, L' Ouverture's changing fortunes boded ill for Haiti—a reality he attributed to Napoleon's behavior, his "dark spirit . . . glutted but not satiated with the gory banquet afforded at the expense of Europe and Africa . . ." Although Napoleon's plan to reinstate slavery never reached fruition, his capture of L'Ouverture set the stage for the bloodiest portion of the revolt led by generals Dessalines and Christophe (upon which Smith does not comment).[19]

Smith's "lecture on the Haytien revolutions" represented a framing of the revolution that commented as much on its successes as it did on the efforts of free blacks to achieve a similar result in the United States. Throughout the lecture, Smith is careful to legitimize the efforts of oppressed people to achieve freedom, a necessary approach because he is part and parcel of a similar struggle in the United States. He also spends a considerable portion of the lecture deflating the "horrors of Saint Domingue" legend. This, too, demonstrates his use of the Haitian Revolution as a mirror for the Antislavery War. He wants to show that armed revolution is the last resort, not the first. Even though the Haitian Revolution involved violence, the situation emanated not from the uncontrollable and ungoverned passions of the slaves, but the intrigue and class warfare engaged in by Haiti's white citizenry. Smith masks the fact that Oge finally resorted to taking up arms in the cause of liberty by presenting him as a supplicant who was rebuffed, captured, and executed, rather than a free black whose hands are dripping with blood—an image anathema to those who opposed the use of politics or violence to effect the abolition of slavery. Instead, Smith's account privileges free blacks like Toussaint L' Ouverture, even though he began his life as a slave, by portraying them as models of self-restraint, moral propriety, and capable of self-elevation and self-government.[20]

Other writers followed Smith's lead in presenting the Haitian Revolution as an integral part of the Antislavery War. Like Smith, each of the prominent intellectuals of this period came from communities actively engaged in antislavery struggle. These struggles informed their work and colored their use of the Haitian Revolution as a template for the Antislavery War. An 1840 graduate of Oberlin College, George Vashon briefly, in 1844, worked with Martin Delany's short lived newspaper, *The Mystery.* Although trained for a career in law, he, like so many of his contemporaries, overcame numerous obstacles. Denied admission to the bar in Alleghany County, due to an 1838 provision in the Pennsylvania constitution limiting the franchise to white men, he journeyed to New York. Once there, Vashon became the first African American admitted to the bar in that state.[21]

While not born free, William Wells Brown rapidly rose from slavery. He first attracted public attention with the publication of *The Narrative of William Wells Brown.* An abolitionist and compiler of antislavery songs, Brown worked as an agent for the Massachusetts Anti-Slavery Society and published a songbook, *The Antislavery Harp* (1847). Best known for his controversial novel, *Clotel or the President's Daughter* (1852), he spent considerable time on the European antislavery circuit during which he published *Three Years in Europe or, Places I Have Seen and People I Have Met* (1852) and *The American Fugitive in Europe.*[22]

Like Vashon, James Theodore Holly was born free in Washington, D.C., in 1820. He enjoyed the benefits of a classical education in his youth, and after completing his formal education in Burlington, Vermont, took increased interest in the work of the American Colonization Society. Less interested in emigrating to Liberia than Canada, Holly soon became a voluntary correspondent for Henry Bibb's *Voice of the Fugitive.*[23]

Haitian politics also exerted a great influence on the historical production of these writers. Elected in 1848, Faustin Soulouque proclaimed himself Emperor Faustin I in 1849. During his ten-year reign, he associated himself with the island's black tradition, which led him to curtail the influence of local and foreign merchants in the economy, impose a state monopoly on the importation of sugar and coffee, and organize state-controlled houses to regulate imported goods. Faustin employed Freemasons, and the practice of Voodun became more pronounced during his reign.[24]

Not surprisingly, each of the three writers interacted with Faustin. Vashon did not meet the emperor, but commented favorably on the early years of Faustin's regime in a series of epistolary exchanges that appeared in Frederick Douglass's *North Star.* One of the most poignant of these observations presented Vashon's personal feelings about the island's emancipatory and incendiary meanings: "It would be impossible for me to describe the rapture with which I beheld Haiti for the first time, this land, unpolluted by the foul stain of slavery, and upon which the insults and cruelties of the tyrants had been washed out in the blood of himself and his children." Holly arrived in Haiti six years after Vashon on a mission sponsored by the Episcopal Church. He presented a plan to the emperor for settling emigrants on the island, complete with stipulations to exempt settlers from the military and facilitate the importation of tools and other personal possessions. Although Faustin never officially endorsed Holly's plans, Holly remained optimistic about Haiti's prospects for African American settlement. Of these writers, Brown had the least personal experience with Faustin. He never met the leader, but his rhetoric reflected many of the leader's pro-black assertions.[25]

In addition to concerns regarding the pro-slavery enactments of the 1850s in the United States (especially the Compromise of 1850), the philosophy of self-elevation and emigration also informed African American discourse on the Haitian Revolution. After returning from Haiti, Vashon immersed himself in the work of elevation. Working closely with his father, he joined in the "Call for a North American Colored Convention" held in Rochester, New York, in July 1853, one month prior to the publication of "Vincent Oge." The forceful denunciation of black exclusion affected Vashon's historical production. The same is true of James Theodore Holly. He attended Bibb's North American Convention of Negroes in Toronto, Ontario, in September 1851. Composed of delegates from five states and Canada, the convention adopted Holly's proposal calling for the establishment of a League of Colored People from the Americas and the Caribbean. The league's goals included construction of an agricultural union to purchase and cultivate land.[26]

Each of these writers, then, came from activist communities, expressed explicit concerns about the perilous course that United States was embarking upon, and read the Haitian Revolution into the possibilities of the Antislavery War. One of the most interesting of these interventions was George Boyer Vashon's poem, "Vincent Oge." First published in Julia Griffiths's *Autographs for Freedom,* the poem offered a highly romanticized portrait of the Haitian mulatto leader Vincent Oge.[27]

Like his predecessors, Vashon understood the importance of positioning Haiti in the stream of legitimate revolutionary activity in the Western hemisphere. He begins his poem by drawing tangible connections between the French and Haitian Revolution. He portrays freedom as a teleological force often preceded by tyranny and undemocratic systems of government which then blossomed into a positive force—a reality that was embodied in the splendor and power of the French monarchy beginning with Louis XIV (also known as the Sun King) and ending with the beheading of Louis XVI. Vashon wrote:

> The visions of grandeur which dazzlingly shone,
> Had gleamed for a time, and all had suddenly gone.
> And the fabric of the ages—the glory of the kings,
> Accounted most sacred mid sanctified things,
> Reared up by the hero, preserved by the sage,
> And drawn out in rich hues on the chronicler's page,
> Had sunk in the blast, and in ruins lay spread,
> When the altar of freedom was reared in its stead.

The consummation of the this marriage between freedom and destiny lay in the fact that

> a spark from that shrine in the free-roving breeze,
> Had crossed from fair France to that isle of the seas.[28]

Once freedom's spark crossed from France to the Haiti, it integrated itself into the island's realities. Its liberatory light gave rise to feelings of "vengeance, hatred and despair," most strongly felt among free blacks and slaves due to their exclusion from the island's political life. Vashon felt that freedom's spark ignited the need for the redress of previous grievances. So much so that

> when they burst, they wildly pour
> Their lava flood of woe and fear,
> And in one short—one little hour,
> Avenge the wrongs of many a year.

In Vashon's mind, free blacks—a population ably represented by Vincent Oge—held the destiny of the race in their hands.[29]

Vashon's romantic portrait of Oge is designed to intervene in the contemporary politics of the Antislavery War. Oge represents the nobility of free black populations. Educated, sophisticated, and a member of the highly influential Friends of the Negro (a prominent group of French abolitionists that included Abbé Grégoire; Antoine Pierre Barnave, a lawyer and a liberal; and Jacques Pierre Brissot de Warville, founder of the Friends and a Girondon leader in the General Assembly), Oge embodies all of the qualities of a leader. The voice of the mulatto elite, Oge intended to return to Haiti and force the Colonial Assembly to accept the Proclamation of March 8, 1790. Rebuffed by the assembly, according to Vashon, free blacks were left with no other choice but to let "other torrents louder roar." These "other torrents" symbolized the recourse to armed revolution.[30]

Amid the clamor for this course of action, the voice of the Spartan mother is heard, another of Vashon's romantic devices designed to locate the Haitian struggle in the mainstream of revolutionary discourse. Here, the Spartan mother is transformed into the Afro-Caribbean woman whose support of the mulatto revolt through the production of strong male and female children is manifest. Oge's mother bids the troops—the freeman, her figurative sons—into battle. By doing so, she played a traditional role in the nation as citizen. It is her voice that authorizes and sanctions the struggle for freedom, and sacrifice for freedom is viewed as a noble cause:

And there's the mother of Ogé,
Who with firm voice, and steady heart,
And look unaltered, well can play
The Spartan's mother's hardy part;
And send her sons to battle-fields,
And bid them come in triumph home,
Or stretched across their bloody shields,
Rather than bear the bondman's doom.[31]

Vashon's romanticism constructs Oge's actions as heroic and, by extension, celebrates the leadership qualities of the free black population; however, this heroic characterization hides much that is problematic about Oge's project. As historian C. L. R. James has noted, Oge, despite having procured weapons and support from abolitionist Thomas Clarkson, seemed unsuited to the contingencies of revolution. Instead of initiating a revolt, which he was equipped to do, Oge voiced support for the slave system by issuing two high-sounding proclamations calling for mutual cooperation between blacks and whites to alleviate some of the odious restrictions on the free black population. Despite this compromise, the island's white citizenry remained determined to block free black participation in the political forum.[32]

Vashon again deploys romantic imagery in capturing the desperation of the freedmen after their rebuff by the white factions on the island. Despite the nobility of their cause,

Their virtuous strength availeth them nought
With the power and skill the tyrant brought.

The freeman, like "Sparta's brave sons in Thermopylae's strait" failed to overcome the power of a superior foe. The comparison is striking because Oge's force consisted of far fewer men than that assembled by the white citizenry.

The Spartans, consisting of Leonidas and a force of 350 men, were unable to secure the pass at Thermopylae because of the treachery of a fellow Greek who showed the Persians a route around the Spartan soldiers. Like the Spartans, the freeman represented the most privileged class. Although they did not possess the military genius of the Spartans, they occupied the best position from which to launch an insurrection against the white planters. As the Spartans sacrificed themselves for Greece, so the free blacks sacrificed themselves for Haiti.[33]

Oge's martyrdom is captured in compelling tones. These brave "Spartans," as Vashon conceived them, gave their all to the cause of freedom in Haiti. Following their capture, Oge and Jean-Baptist Chavannes experienced a grueling trial. Afterwards, under torture, both were made to confess their crimes with a candle in their mouths. Chavannes never submitted, but Oge broke down under pressure and begged for mercy. The next day, Oge's brother was condemned along with other conspirators. Whereas Leonidas's body, after a great struggle for possession of it by the warring parties, was preserved by the remaining Greeks, the full power of the state literally destroyed the bodies of Oge and his brother: both men were placed on the rack and their limbs broken. Yet, like the Spartans whose preservation of Leonidas's body ensured his fame, the brutal execution of Oge and his compatriot preserved their names for posterity and served as the catalyst for subsequent developments in the Haitian Revolution.[34]

Brown and Holly continued the heroic presentation of free blacks in their respective accounts, making even more tangible connections with the American Revolution. Brown's speech, "St. Domingo: Its Revolution and Its Patriots," offered a telling commentary on the inclusionary and exclusionary legacy of the American Revolution. He points out the participation of Haitian patriots in the Siege of Savannah in 1779. The linkage between the American and Haitian revolutions cannot be denied given that several participants in the Siege at Savannah later played important roles in the Haitian Revolution. Brown's use of the term "patriots" is a deliberate attempt to expand and extend its meaning. In the American context, the term's connection seemed strongest with the American Revolution. But Haitian patriots occupied the same ambivalent space as African American patriots of the Revolutionary War. By linking the two patriotic traditions, Brown hoped to clarify and exonerate the contributions of both to the revolutionary history of the Western hemisphere.[35]

Brown makes more concrete connections between the Haitian and American revolutions in his analysis of the debates preceding the issuance of the

March 8 decree, and the actions of various components of the Haitian populace. Brown quotes Barnave, who in seconding the claims of mulatto rights put forth by Vincent Oge, exclaimed "Perish the colonies rather than the principle!" Brown added: "Noble language this! Would that the fathers of the American Revolution had been as consistent." In another instance when describing the massacre of five hundred faithful servants who refused to bear arms in the conflict, Brown pointed out that the struggle was for "liberty or death." Here Brown echoed the sentiments of Patrick Henry, a member of Virginia's House of Burgesses, and signer of the Declaration of Independence. The urgency of the slogan "liberty or death" manifested itself in the massacre of innocent people as demonstrated by the Haitian example, and in the imminent death of many Americans in the cause of liberty from Britain.[36]

James Holly's "Vindication of the Capacity of the Colored Race for Self-Government," published two years after Brown's lecture, used historical devices common to the era when comparing the Haitian Revolution to the Antislavery War. Holly's lecture included several common features in historical presentations of the period: he viewed the revolution as progressive in size, scope, and import, and focused on the importance of presenting a contributionist and vindicationist portrait of black involvement in the revolutionary uprising. Religious imagery also figured prominently in Holly's account. In an invocation of the jeremiad, the servile population was characterized as being directed by the "Lord of Hosts," who "directed their arms to be the instruments of His judgment on their oppressors, as the recompense of his violated law of love between man and his fellow . . ." Apart from the historical devices he used, Holly also linked the Haitian Revolution to its American counterpart. In Holly's mind, the revolution's occurrence and aftermath not only vindicated the mental and moral capacity of blacks for self-government, but "was one of the noblest, grandest, and most justifiable outbursts against tyrannical oppression that is recorded in history."[37]

Like Vashon, Holly also viewed the free black population as the class of destiny. After describing the restrained behavior of the servile population toward the rapidly growing tide of revolution on the island, he turned to the free black population. This population exercised even more restraint, Holly thought, because their wealth and education did not translate into political power in the colony. Aware that patience might be misunderstood and labeled as ignorance or cowardice, Holly pointed to the fact that this class of men was "educated in the seminaries of France" and that they were "patrons of that prodigy of literature, the Encyclopedia of France." Nor were they cowards, because they served, as Brown pointed out in "St. Domingo: Its Revolutions and Its Patriots," as the "voluntary compeers of the Revolutionary heroes of the United States; and who, under the banners of France, mingled their sable blood with the Saxon and the French in the heroic battle of Savannah."[38]

Holly also seemed more trenchant than Brown in his claim that the Haitian Revolution "surpasses the American Revolution, in an incomparable degree." Here, he hoped to deflate the importance of the American Revolution while trumpeting the benefits of the Haitian one. Doing so further strengthened his case for the legitimacy of the Haitian revolutionary project. In this reading, the Haitian Revolution is what the American Revolution could never be. The fact that Americans were free, highly enlightened, and that their greatest grievance seemed "the imposition of the three pence pound tax on tea," paled in comparison to the rationale for the Haitian Revolution. He argued the leaders of the Haitian Revolution were slaves, largely menial and uneducated, and that the tax imposed on them not only affected their unrequited labor, but usurped their bodies. Their opponents consisted of the mother country and the colonial government, which played an active role in attempting to suppress the revolt. Given the sum total of these observations, Holly concluded that the America Revolution was but a "tempest in teapot" when compared with the Haitian one.[39]

Arguing for the inherent ability of African Americans to govern themselves, and deeply committed to civilizationist projects, Holly focused on presenting Vincent Oge as representative of the ability of free blacks to skillfully negotiate contested political terrain. Aware of the opposition in the colony to black rights, Oge appears here as a calculating politician, one who attempts to judge the mood of the people and take the most appropriate action. Rather than returning immediately to Haiti, Oge sought support from other European nations, namely Holland, where he received the rank of lieutenant colonel and the Order of the Lion. Holly's focus on Oge's class position, rank, and the honors bestowed on him by European nations is also indicative of his belief in the superiority of free blacks to their less fortunate enslaved brethren. Returning to Haiti with an armed escort, Oge immediately became aware of opposition to his position. His selfish attempt to privilege the position of free blacks by suggesting a Faustian bargain (the tacit acceptance of black slavery) with the landed whites proved unfruitful. Glossing over the inherent betrayal of the servile population by the free black population, Holly attributed this move to a political strategy no different than that employed in the Antislavery War of the 1850s: "This specific assurance on the part of Oge, although its does not speak much for his high sense of justice . . . yet it shows as much wisdom and tact in the science of government, as evinced by the sap headed legislators of this country, who make similar compromises to the oligarchic despots of this nation."[40]

Oge's demise was swift, but Holly constructs it in masculinist and heroic terms. He fell "against the overwhelming odds of the sanguinary tigers, with a manly heroism only equaled by the Spartans at the pass of Thermopylae." His trial, a mock trial, akin to fugitive slave trials in Boston, Philadelphia, and Cincinnati, left him condemned to death and "broken alive on the wheel." Holly, in an attempt to encourage selective historical remembrance, urged the reader to essentially forgive Oge for his actions toward the servile population, but to focus instead on "the ignoble and unworthy fate, received at the hands of those monsters of cruelty in St. Domingo."[41]

Brown's "St. Domingo" also portrayed the mulattoes as an oppressed and grieving class while also situating them in relationship to freedom's spark. He concurred with Holly, saying that despite their education, they received few benefits as a result of their class position. Largely teleological in his presentation, Brown located the spark of freedom in England as opposed to France. This locale change had much to do with Britain's role in the humanitarian and abolitionist movement and Brown's admiration of the reformers he had no doubt met during his travels in Europe in the early 1850s.[42]

As mentioned earlier, both men examine the role of slaves in the revolt; however, they viewed this population's role in the war in different ways. Brown, probably because of his background as a fugitive slave, identified more directly with their plight. His lecture presented the slaves as a tempestuous factor in the revolt. The slaves awoke, Brown wrote, "as from a dream, and demanded their rights with sword in hand." Fire consumed the island destroying villas, factories, and farms. The slaves' fury seemed justified to Brown because their "ancestors had been ruthlessly torn from their native land and sold in the shambles of St. Domingo." Holly, on the other hand, offered a more cautious view of slave involvement in the insurrection. Suspicious of the capacity of slaves to conduct themselves rationally, he presented them as awakening "from [their] slumber of degradation to the terrific power of brute force." Bouckman, the "Spartacus of his race," directed the work of devastation on the island. In a manner almost indicative of brute, unthinking force, like a hurricane that gradually loses it punch, he "continued to ride on the storm of the revolution in its hurricane march, with a fury that became intensified as it progressed." Unfortunately, he, too, like Oge, fell under the vindictive weight of the colonists. His death cleared the way not only for a "triumvirate of negro and mulatto chieftains," but for what Holly termed "The Auspicious Dawn of Negro Rule," the ascendancy of Toussaint L' Ouverture.[43]

"The Auspicious Dawn of Negro Rule" had a different starting point for Brown than for Holly. For Brown, the revolutionary legacy began not in 1804, but 1799, the year L' Ouverture emerged as a leader of the colony. L'Ouverture's comrades, André Rigaud, the mulatto general, and Christophe and Dessalines, former slaves, also figured prominently in the discussion. These patriots, as Brown termed them, fought not merely for independence but for an Antislavery War. The Haitian Revolution leaders, like their American counterparts, maneuvered shrewdly when faced with danger. When the main contingent of the French army landed at Cape City (Cape François), and a smaller force at Port-au-Prince, Toussaint and Christophe like "Nat Turner, the Spartacus of the Southampton Revolt," fled into the mountains.[44]

In another instance when describing the numerous atrocities committed by the black general Dessalines against white planters, Brown pointed out that this should serve as an omen for American slaveholders: "Let the slaveholders in our Southern states tremble when they call to mind these events." In his mind, fear had tangible manifestations. Given the belief in the tangible and ongoing nature of the American Revolutionary heritage, Brown applied this same concept to the Haitian revolutionaries. He believed Toussaint L' Ouverture, the father of the Haitian Revolution, and the patriots of the Haitian Revolution would reappear in the southern United States. Their spirits were already there, and when they combined with the impulses from the American Revolution, Brown believed the "day is not far distant when the revolution of St. Domingo will be reenacted in South Carolina and Louisiana."[45]

Brown also judged the revolution's effectiveness not only in terms of cyclical notions of history, but by the legacy it bequeathed to the Western hemisphere. For Brown, then, the overarching question became, What traditions did the French and American revolutions produce? Were they consistent with liberty or opposed to it? In this analysis, both George Washington, the father of the American Revolution, and Napoleon Bonaparte, the inheritor of French republicanism, paled in comparison to Toussaint L' Ouverture. While Napoleon and L' Ouverture shared a number of commonalities ranging from their humble origins to ending their careers in exile, the differences in how they achieved their fame seemed too striking to overlook: "Toussaint fought for liberty; Napoleon fought for himself. Toussaint gained fame by leading an oppressed and injured race to the successful vindication of their rights, Napoleon made himself a name and acquired a scepter by supplanting liberty and destroying nationalities, in order to substitute his own illegitimate despotism."[46]

Brown extended his critique to George Washington, inheritor of the American republican tradition, but he fared no better than Napoleon when compared with L' Ouverture. The America Revolution's outcome was the antithesis of the Haitian Revolution. Brown concluded that L' Ouverture was the true republican, for his government made "liberty his watchword, incorporated it in his constitution, abolished the slave trade and made freedom universal among his people." Brown argued that Washington's government took the opposite course and in doing so, perverted the true spirit of republicanism. His government "incorporated slavery and the slave-trade, and enacted laws by which chains were fastened on the limbs of millions of people." Washington's legacy not only perverted the revolution, but, in a direct reference to the contested ideological terrain of the 1850s gave "strength and vitality to an institution that would one day rent asunder the union that he had helped to form." Despite the fact that a slave revolt did not occur in the South in the 1850s, Brown opined that as a result of the failure to fulfill the revolutionary promise the "slave in his chains in the rice swamps of Carolina and the cotton fields of Mississippi burns for revenge."[47]

For Holly, L' Ouverture was, like Washington, "the regenerator and savior of his country," an individual eminently suited to the exigencies of revolution and the demands of statecraft. He argued that the power of L' Ouverture's government originated from his ability to impose strict regulation on land and quotas on sugar production to stabilize the island's commercial enterprises. Sensitive to the needs of the recently enslaved population, this course of action facilitated international commerce and paved the way for the enactment of the Rural Code. Under the Rural Code, the island returned to the prosperity it had known prior to the Haitian Revolution. This code compelled the unemployed to seek a private employer, and if one could not be found, to seek employment by the government on sugar plantations in rural areas. In Holly's opinion, L'Ouverture's success proved more enduring than that of the British. Haiti's labor regulations were fairer and did not resort to apprenticeship or encourage voluntary or forced immigration of Asians to meet the production goals of planters.[48]

That Haiti never resorted to an apprenticeship program or that L'Ouverture's plan of wealth distribution did not defraud the peasants in favor of the landed class boded well not only for claims of innate ability for self-government, but in ensuring democratic forms of government that treated all citizens fairly regardless of class. Holly's criticism also extended to the British during the Revolutionary War. Holly pointed out that William Pitt the Younger, England's prime minister during the Revolutionary War, satisfied the needs of the wealthy in the policies he pursued, but failed to meet the needs of the common people. L' Ouverture's foresight in this area assured his name would be emblazoned on the "historic page of the world's statesmanship."[49]

Holly believed that L' Ouverture's successors possessed the sophisticated qualities of statesmanship exhibited by their predecessor. But, similar to his presentation on Oge, Holly failed to mention the darker side of the diplomacy of Dessalines. He focused instead on Dessalines's ability to build an army of six thousand men, and his unsuccessful attempt to unite the French and Spanish portions of the island. Holly also glosses over the serious problems of class and caste in Alexander Petion's and Christophe's regimes. Despite their opposition to one another, they appeared united against a common external enemy. Although under Jean Pierre Boyer, the divisions between the Spanish and French portions of the island were healed, civil war and disorder erupted. Holly attributed these occurrences to "the animosities that the ancient regime of slavery had created among them." However, in Holly's mind, all dissension and discord were settled under the "vigorous specter of the present ruler, Faustin I."[50]

African Americans in writing about the Haitian Revolution in the 1850s focused on linking the realities of the past to the exigencies of the present. The Antislavery War proved to be one of the most challenging historical events for African Americans during the antebellum period. Black intellectuals, as they had done throughout the early republic and the first half of the antebellum period, turned to the history of persons of African descent in the Western hemisphere to make a case for preserving and extending their rights. The Haitian Revolution contained all of the elements necessary to do this.

Haiti, like the American mainland, had experienced discovery, exploration, and exploitation. The island's rapid rise as the crown jewel in the French sugar production project occasioned serious problems for its slave population. The brutal conditions on the island coupled with the French Revolution and colonial intrigue fanned the flames of revolt that eventually engulfed the island in its intensity. While African Americans could never mount a revolt similar in size, proportion, and scope to the Haitian one, its success buoyed hopes that they one day would be free.

Black intellectuals like James McCune Smith, George Vashon, James Theodore Holly, and William Wells Brown used the spoken and written word to reread the Haitian Revolution as a legitimate revolutionary construct. But it was more in their minds than a spontaneous outburst of slave fury, a charge that they constantly rebuffed in the United States. Rather it represented the legitimate desire of these individuals of color to achieve the much vaunted "Rights of Man." Moreover, they asserted, the revolution's lessons, if carefully assessed, provided a template or an incendiary warning for what could happen in the United States if the Antislavery War proved futile or if it was won.

Like other historical writers of the nineteenth century, these writers deployed historical knowledge in highly subjective and didactic ways. Closely wedded to cyclical and teleological understandings of history, they were less concerned with linear presentations of facts than with presenting a narrative that used the past to intervene in the realities of the present—in this instance, a past that had been denied as legitimate by majoritarian populations and a present that seemed contested and uncertain.

These accounts, then, provide insights into the importance of history as a tool in the Antislavery War. Rather than viewing this period simply as a moment of intense physical contestation between pro-slavery and antislavery forces, we would do better to look more closely at its intellectual signposts. For African Americans, these signposts involved proving their capacity for citizenship, self-government, and moral propriety. The pre- and post-history of the Haitian Revolution, despite the island's turbulent history, offered a tangible example for African Americans of the possibilities of a world of their own making. They envisioned the Haitian Revolution through the lenses of the Antislavery War in the United States to legitimize Haiti's revolutionary past in the annals of the Western revolutionary tradition as they sought to carve out a space for recognition of their own efforts to destroy the institution of slavery forever.

Notes

1. The literature on the Haitian Revolution is extensive. I am listing some of the works central to this study. C. L. R. James, *The Black Jacobins: Toussaint L'Ouverture and the San Domingo Revolution* (London: Allison & Busby, 1980); Eugene Genovese, *From Rebellion to Revolution: Afro-American Slaves Revolts in the Making of the Modern World* (Baton Rouge: Louisiana State University Press, 1979); Thomas Ott, *The Haitian Revolution, 1789–1804* (Knoxville: University of Tennessee Press, 1970); David Nicholls, *From Dessalines to Duvalier: Race, Colour and National Independence in Haiti* (New Brunswick, N.J.: Rutgers University Press, 1996); Brenda Gayle Plummer, *Haiti and the Great Powers, 1902–1915* (Baton Rouge: Louisiana State University Press, 1988), *Haiti and the United States: The Psychological Moment* (Athens: University of Georgia Press, 1996), and "The Haitian Revolution," in Franklin Knight and Colin Palmer, *The Modern Caribbean* (Chapel Hill: University of North Carolina Press, 1989), 21–50; Carolyn E. Fick, *The Making of Haiti: The Saint Domingue Revolution From Below* (Knoxville: University of Tennessee Press, 1990)

2. Rather than accept the idea that the Haitian Revolution has been written out of history, this essay shows that the treatment of the revolution is fairly complex. I build here on Michel-Rolph Trouillot's assessment of the ways in which the revolution was viewed primarily as shocking and surprising and then systematically ignored in the

literature of the West as a legitimate revolutionary construct, especially in the literature of the European metropoles and the republican literature in the United States. Trouillot's argument can be found in his *Silencing the Past: Power and the Production of History* (Boston: Beacon Press, 1995), 31–107.

3. Plummer, *Haiti and the United States,* 11–33.

4. African American interest in the wider world has a long genealogy. In the first chapter of her monumental study, *Rising Wind,* Brenda Gayle Plummer sketches out the contours of black interest in foreign affairs. See Plummer, *Rising Wind: Black Americans and U.S. Foreign Affairs, 1935–1960* (Chapel Hill: University of North Carolina Press, 1996), 9–36. Assessments of black thought as well as notions of rebellion, identity, and political theory in the 1850s are discussed in Maggie Montesinos Sale, *The Slumbering Volcano: American Slave Ship Revolts and the Production of Rebellious Masculinity* (Durham, N.C.: Duke University Press, 1997).

5. Haitian historical writing is explored in Gordon K. Lewis, *Main Currents in Caribbean Thought: The Historical Evolution of Caribbean Society in Its Ideological Aspects, 1492–1900* (Baltimore, Md.: Johns Hopkins University Press, 1983), 255–64. Writing on the revolution is also bound up in the rise of disciplinary constructs for scientific postulations on race; see Lee Baker, *From Savage to Negro: Anthropology and the Construction of Race, 1896–1954* (Berkeley: University of California Press, 1998). The best known Haitian account that not only responds to discourse on the Haitian Revolution but challenges Count Gobineau's *Inequality of the Human Races,* 4 vols. (1853–55) is Antenor Firmin's *The Equality of the Human Races* (1885; reprt. Urbana: University of Illinois Press, 2002). See also David Geggus, *The Impact of the Haitian Revolution on the Atlantic World* (Columbia: University of South Carolina Press, 2001).

6. Haiti's role as a site for emigration and the general relationship between the state and society in the nineteenth century is discussed in Plummer, *Haiti and the Great Powers,* 15–40. Also see Plummer, *Haiti and the United States,* 26–31.

7. Assessments of Haiti's influence on antebellum include Alfred Hunt, *Haiti's Influence on Antebellum America: Slumbering Volcano in the Caribbean* (Baton Rouge: Louisiana State University, 1988), 1–106. The noted African American historian Benjamin Quarles argued that African Americans were "keepers of the Revolutionary flame." I would extend Quarles's comments to the uses of the revolution a century after its occurrence. With democracy unfinished and the legacy of the revolution unfulfilled, black writers in the 1850s offered radically new rhetorical formations that awakened America and reminding Americans of the importance of living up to the revolutionary promise. For Quarles's initial characterization of the revolution to blacks, see Benjamin Quarles, "The Revolutionary War as a Declaration of Independence," in Ira Berlin and Ronald Hoffman, eds., *Slavery and Freedom in the Age of the American Revolution* (Charlottesville: University Press of Virginia, 1983), 283–301.

8. The transatlantic community is discussed in R. J. M. Blackett, *Building an Anti-*

slavery Wall: Black Americans in the Atlantic Abolitionist Movement, 1830–1860 (Ithaca, N.Y.: Cornell University Press, 1983). Assessments related to the antislavery war and black destiny are discussed in William Nell, *The Colored Patriots of the American Revolution* (Boston: Robert F. Wallcut, 1855) and Martin Delany, *The Condition, Elevation, Emigration and Destiny of the Colored People of the United States* (1852)

9. As Plummer has observed, the outcomes of both the Haitian Revolution and the French Revolution worried American republicans. Social leveling, radical and violent overthrow of the monarchy in France, and the ascendancy of former slaves to power in Haiti through an armed uprising raised a number of concerns. These issues were additionally compounded in the nineteenth century with the Denmark Vesey revolt in Charleston in 1822. Plummer, *Haiti and the United States,* 34–49.

10. In addition to the material that appeared in *Freedom's Journal* and *Rights of All,* Haiti was an active topic of discussion in the black press prior to 1850, especially in the *Colored American.* See "Hayti," *Liberator,* August 6, 1831; "The Republic of Haiti," *The Weekly Advocate,* March 11, 1837; "A Colored Community Taking Care of Themselves," *Colored American,* July 1, 1837; Robert Douglass, "Haiti," *Colored American,* March 3, 1838; and "The Hour and the Man: Toussaint L'Ouverture," *The National Antislavery Standard,* February 11, 1841. For an examination of Haiti's place in the Pan-African lenses of African Americans, see Elizabeth Raul Bethel, *The Roots of African-American Identity: Memory and History in Free Antebellum Communities* (New York: St. Martin's Press, 1999), 149–54.

11. James McCune Smith's activism is discussed in David Blight's "In Search of Learning, Liberty, and Self-Definition: James McCune Smith and the Ordeal of the Black Antebellum Intellectual," *Afro-Americans in New York Life and History* 9 (July 1985): 7–25. Also see assessments of Smith in Mia Bay's *The White Image in the Black Mind: African-American Ideas About White People, 1830–1925* (New York: Oxford University Press, 2000) and John Stauffer, *The Black Hearts of Men: Radical Abolitionists and the Transformation of Race* (Cambridge, Mass.: Harvard University Press, 2002).

12. Announcements of Smith's lecture appeared in "Notices: Lectures in Clinton Hall by James McCune Smith, M.D.," *National Antislavery Standard,* February 11, 1841. Smith delivered his talk as part of an institute lecture series for free blacks. See James McCune Smith, *A lecture on the Haytien revolutions with a sketch of the character of Toussaint L'Ouverture. Delivered at the Stuyvesant Institute, February 26, 1841* (New York: Daniel Farnshaw, 1841).

13. Smith's engagements with the larger issues of the period are more clearly discussed in *The Destiny of the People of Color A Lecture, Delivered Before the Philomathean Society and Hamilton Lyceum in January 1841*(New York: self-published, 1841).

14. Smith, "A lecture on the Haytien revolutions," 11–15.

15. Ott, *The Haitian Revolution,* 34–35.

16. Smith, "A lecture on the Haytien revolutions," 11–15.

17. Information on the Proclamation of March 8, 1790, can be found in David

Brion Davis, *The Problem of Slavery in the Age of Revolution, 1770–1823* (Ithaca, N.Y.: Cornell University Press, 1975), 139–40; and James, *The Black Jacobins,* 70–73.

18. Smith, "A lecture on the Haytien revolutions," 15–18.

19. Ibid., 19–27. For information on L' Ouverture's portrayal in intellectual circles, see Hunt, *Haiti's Influence on Antebellum America,* 84–106.

20. For a general assessment of black protest in the antebellum period, see Patrick Rael, *Black Identity and Black Protest in the Antebellum North* (Chapel Hill: University of North Carolina Press, 2002).

21. For biographical information on George Boyer Vashon, see William C. Nell, *Colored Patriots of the American Revolution* (Boston: Robert F. Wallcut, 1855), 328; and Catherine Hatchett, "George Boyer Vashon, 1824–1878: Black Educator, Poet and Fighter for Equal Justice, Part One," *The Western Pennsylvania Historical Magazine* 68 (July 1985): 205–19. Vashon later assumed a professorship at Central College in McGrawville, New York. For a prospectus of the college, see "New York Central College," *Impartial Citizen,* September 14, 1850.

22. Biographical information on William Wells Brown is found in William Edward Farrison, *William Wells Brown, Author & Reformer* (Chicago: University of Chicago Press, 1969); and L. H. Whelchel, *My Chains Fell Off: William Wells Brown, Fugitive Abolitionist* (Lanham, Md.: University Press of America, 1985).

23. Biographical information on Holly is found in David Dean, *Defender of the Race: James Theodore Holly, Black Nationalist and Bishop* (Boston: Lambeth Press, 1979). Some of Holly's thoughts on colonization are included in a series of articles in the *Voice of the Fugitive:* "Canadian Colonization," (April 12 and 21, 1848; July 16 and 30, 1851).

24. David Nicholls, *From Dessalines to Duvalier: Race Colour and National Independence in Haiti* (Cambridge: Cambridge University Press, 1979), 82–84; and Michel-Rolph Trouillot, *Haiti, State Against Nation: Origins and Legacy of Duvalierism* (New York: Monthly Review Press, 1990), 35–58.

25. Vashon's visit to Haiti is discussed in Hatchett, "George Boyer Vashon," 208–9. His letters in the *North Star* include April 21, June 9, August 8, and August 21, 1848; April 7 and September 28, 1849. Holly's journey to Haiti is discussed in Dean, *Defender of the Race,* 22–24. Brown's intellectual development is explored in Farrison, *William Wells Brown,* 255–58.

26. Dean, *Defender of the Race,* 11–12. The goals of Holly's African Civilization Society are discussed in "African Civilization Society: Objects and Prospects," in BAP, Reel 10. Vashon was intimately acquainted with the work of Reverend Jeremiah Loguen. See Vashon, "Reverend J. W. Loguen," Frederick Douglass Papers, February 1, 1856.

27. Julia Griffiths, *Autographs for Freedom* 2 vols. (Rochester, N.Y.: Wanzer, Beardsley & Company, 1854). Also see Joan Sherman, ed. *African American Poetry of the Nineteenth Century: An Anthology* (Urbana: University of Illinois Press, 1992), 153–54.

28. Vashon, "Vincent Oge," in Griffiths, *Autographs for Freedom,* 50.

29. Ibid., 51.

30. Ibid., 53–54.

31. Ibid.

32. James, *The Black Jacobins*, 70–73.

33. The Spartan defense of the pass of Thermopylae during the Persian War is discussed in Herodotus, *The Histories*, bk. 7 (New York: Wordsworth Classics, 1996), 586–601.

34. Oge's trial and torture are described in James, *The Black Jacobins*, 74–75.

35. For the best literary discussion of Brown's "St. Domingo: Its Revolutions and Its Patriots," see Eric Sundquist, *To Wake the Nations: Race in the Making of American Literature*, (Cambridge, Mass: Belknap Press of Harvard University Press, 1994), 31–36.

36. Brenda Gayle Plummer notes in her groundbreaking study of Haiti that the "American Revolution offered inspiration to the Haitian, but the revolutionary generation in the United States feared Caribbean upheaval. Eighteenth century conservatives perceived Haiti as a source of subversion and a threat to slaveholding societies." Plummer, *Haiti and the United States*, 4–5.

37. James Theodore Holly, *A Vindication of the Capacity of the Negro Race for Self-Government, and Civilized Progress as Demonstrated by Historical Events of the Haytian Revolution and Subsequent Acts of That People Since Their National Independence* (New Haven, Conn.: W.H. Stanley, printer, 1857; reprt. in Howard Holman Bell, ed. *Black Separatism and the Caribbean in 1860 by James Theodore Holly and J. Denis Harris* (Ann Arbor: University of Michigan Press, 1970), 30–35.

38. Holly, *A Vindication of the Capacity of the Negro Race*, 30–31.

39. Ibid., 25.

40. Ibid., 36–39.

41. Ibid., 39.

42. Brown, "St. Domingo: Its Revolutions and Its Patriots," 6–8.

43. Ibid.; Holly, *A Vindication of the Capacity of the Negro Race*, 41–42.

44. Brown, "St Domingo: Its Revolutions and Its Patriots," 22–23.

45. Ibid.

46. Ibid., 35–37.

47. According to William Farrison, Brown's principal biographer, Brown's characterization of L' Ouverture borrowed heavily from the work of John Beard, a minister who wrote *Toussaint L'Ouverture A Biography and Autobiography* (Boston: James Redpath, 1863).

48. Holly, *A Vindication of the Capacity of the Negro Race*, 45–46. The British colony of Jamaica imposed the most extensive apprenticeship program. For further information, see Thomas Holt, *The Problem of Freedom: Race, Labor and Politics in Jamaica and Britain, 1832–1938* (Baltimore, Md.: Johns Hopkins University Press, 1992), 55–114.

49. Holly, *A Vindication of the Capacity of the Negro Race*, 47–49.

50. Ibid., 55.

5

Comparable or Connected?

Afro-Diasporic Resistance in the United States and Brazil

MICOL SEIGEL

In 1923, a writer for *Getulino,* a São Paulo newspaper by and for readers "*de raça,*" called black North Americans "our brothers, to be sure, but of different habits, sentiments, and religion."[1] This statement of Afro-diasporic fraternity in difference was both descriptive and prescriptive. The author was working to convey a certain posture to his peers as well as to his government, to suggest how Afro-Brazilians might relate both to other fragments of the African Diaspora in the Americas and to the Brazilian nation. His doubled stance of identification and repudiation, a posture shared by an important contingent of his peers, gestures to a problem with the comparative approach popular in Diaspora Studies today. For heuristic and practical reasons, the field needs more imaginative transnational historical methods.

Comparative method has enjoyed great favor among students of Afro-diasporic resistance in Brazil and the United States. Countless observers have compared the two nations' Afro-descended citizens, concluding that they have chosen diametrically opposed strategies in the fight for racial justice. Scholars and nonacademics alike have practically reached consensus: people of African descent in the United States prefer collective, race-conscious confrontation, and in Brazil, individualist, nationalist assimilation.[2] This comparison, rather insulting to Afro-Brazilians, is misleading.[3] It shirks the full implications of the insights that subjectivity emerges in relation, and that the African Diaspora, like any collective identity, is an actively imagined community.

This essay proposes an alternative to comparative method, focusing on a small group of Afro-Brazilians in the city of São Paulo in the 1920s, readers and contributors to a modest set of racially organized newspapers. After exploring the contours of the "global vision" articulated by some among this diverse, never univocal group of diasporic thinkers, the essay explores one instance of transnational contact, a controversy precipitated by African American hopes for emigration to Brazil.[4] This exchange brought a small number of black people in both places squarely into each other's sights, with ramifications for state policy, national identity, and the lived experience of race.

The story of this interaction challenges both the form and substance of comparisons of Afro-Brazilians to African Americans: substance because it reveals Afro-Brazilians to have been more confrontational and race-conscious than they appear in comparative frames; form because careful reading of historical sources shows Afro-descended citizens of both Brazil and the United States elaborating self-presentations and antiracist strategies in tandem with each other, though not exactly in cooperation. Afro-Brazilians and African Americans, like many nationally defined subgroups of New World Afro-descendents, define themselves in part in relation to each other, and are therefore too inextricably related to compare.[5]

* * *

Afro-Brazilians and African Americans in the 1920s had ample opportunity to encounter each other.[6] Twentieth-century booms in communications technologies and mass culture amplified cross-talk between the United States and Brazil, while urbanization brought more people into these developments' reach. During the First World War, the exchange rate skyrocketed as it realigned trade routes and forced Americans to seek markets within their hemisphere for the goods they had previously shipped to Europe.[7] Increased trade boosted travel by businessmen and investors as well, including African Americans.[8]

The World War also magnified Afro-diasporic identification by showcasing the various conditions of black soldiers in segregated U.S. troops, the allies' African and Caribbean units, and European armies. The impact on black activism was marked, as was the wave of repression that followed.[9] The violence of the "Red Summer" of 1919 prompted another of the periodic waves of emigrationism that occasionally swept the United States. Like others before them, emigration proponents of the 1920s considered Brazil as a site for black settlement. The notion that Brazil was a place of "racial harmony" had long intrigued black North Americans; the idea itself provoked (and continues to provoke) further fascination among African Americans and Afro-Brazilians.[10] Asymmetries of ignorance kept most North American fans of Brazil unaware that they were projecting a desire for racial paradise onto a place far from that ideal.[11]

Afro-Brazilians and African Americans in the 1920s shared yet another means to mutual encounter: the black press. In this period, Afro-Brazilians as well as African Americans produced newspapers by and aimed at communities defined by race. These invaluable historical sources reveal the multiple imagined communities their readers engaged. They record the intersecting, competing loyalties these various affiliations demanded, and in the words of a student of the U.S. press, showcase "writers forming and reforming ideologies, creating and re-creating a public sphere, and staging and restaging race itself."[12] These papers both confirm and refine Benedict Anderson's insight that newspapers open a space for the reflection and direction that forge an imagined community.[13] The refinement comes from the painfully obvious inequality between these two media. The social boundaries of their worlds meant that the U.S. and Brazilian black presses could not constitute a sphere of interaction among equals, a true black public sphere. Global power imbalances in the news and entertainment industry, publishing, foreign language acquisition, and raw wealth structured even the press, their clearest channel of communication. Inequity was (as it remains today) not the barrier to but the condition of transnational exchange.

A word or two about each press is in order. The U.S. press was extensive and has been deftly analyzed. It thrived nationwide, representing all the major regions of the country. The larger papers enjoyed fair financial stability, publishing regularly. They were linked formally and informally to African American educational, financial, and legal institutions, constituting a network of race-based organizations, and their editors were often public figures, enjoying recognition and respect from people of all races, and sometimes even personal fortune.[14]

The Brazilian papers were less extensive and less affluent, many constantly on the brink of extinction. During the war, three papers opened and folded (*O Menelick, A Rua,* and *O Xauter*); in the years 1918–19, only *O Alfinete, O Bandeirante,* and *A Liberdade* were in circulation. *O Kosmos* began publishing in 1922, and probably folded in 1925; *Getulino* ran from 1923 to 1926; *Elite* started and stopped in 1924, the year *Clarim* began. *Clarim* ran longer than any of the others, putting out its final issue in 1935, but with several interruptions and new starts along the way.[15] *Auriverde, O Patrocinio,* and *Progresso* all began in 1928; while the first seems not to have survived into the new year, the second published until 1930, and the third, until 1933, also the year of the only microfilmed issue of *Evolução.*[16]

The Brazilian newspapers have received less scholarly attention overall, and less nuanced treatment. Key observers have asked them to serve as a window into "Afro-Brazilian psychology," and have found them signal proof of Afro-Brazilians' "essentially assimilationist" and "integrationist" tendencies.[17] The papers therefore lie at one crux of the comparison to the United States, and frequently provoke comparative gestures on the part of late-twentieth-century readers. Yet despite occasional overlap in personnel, the papers articulate great ranges of opinion and position, including frequent conflict. Even in the arcs of argument I trace through the rest of this essay, no consensus emerges. When situated in more of their local, national, and transnational contexts, the papers exceed the pictures scholars have drawn of them.

For example, the Brazilian papers were not fully "Afro-Brazilian," for they were not evenly distributed across Brazil. They were concentrated in the state of São Paulo, most of them in its capital city of the same name. They were *Paulistano* and *Paulista* (pertaining to the city and/or state of São Paulo), as many writers termed their papers and themselves. Their infrastructure and membership reflected a social phenomenon unique to São Paulo: the recreational societies, cultural centers, and mutual aid organizations Afro-Brazilians had organized there since at least the first decade of the twentieth century. These groups flowered thanks to cross-fertilizations of African associational traditions and the social organizations of the immigrant communities populating the teeming international metropolis that was São Paulo in this period.

In terms of readership, the press's audience was concentrated in São Paulo, but there were avenues of contact with people elsewhere. Connections to readers in other urban centers are the easiest to discern (scholars who focus on rural areas, rather than those who approach the topic through the press itself, may be better able to identify rural readerships). Individual journalists traveled, such as the poet Cyro Costa, or the peripatetic Vicente Ferreira. The Rio de Janeiro *Federação dos Homens de Côr* (Federation of Colored Men) had contacts with various clubs and papers.[18] *Clarim* had representatives in Rio de Janeiro, Santos (São Paulo state), and Salvador, Bahia.[19] The papers occasionally reached out intentionally to their mainstream counterparts in both Rio and São Paulo, provoking largely laudatory notice.[20]

Yet if this press was less than fully national in some respects, it was more than national in others. Afro-Paulista journalists reached beyond Brazil's borders, despite limited resources and meager educations, to pull the global into their local world. The São Paulo black press, though far from monolithic, tended to the cosmopolitan and the internationalist, in line with the postwar era and in conversation with the communities of recent immigrants and expatriates from around the world with whom its writers and readers shared the streets of São Paulo. Articles reported news from Europe, Africa, and throughout the Americas. Gestures in a specifically pan-Africanist direction included the work of Bahian polyglot Mário de Vasconcelos, who used the press to speed the travels of Marcus Garvey's diaspora-inducing appeal. He sent translations of articles on "the Negro movement in the U.S. and elsewhere" to *Clarim* for publication.[21] The press also communicated directly with organs of the U.S. black press, notably the *Chicago Defender,* the periodical of greatest circulation within the U.S. black press.[22] *Clarim,* along with at least one other organ of the Afro-Paulista press, *Progresso,* and one mainstream newspaper, Rio de Janeiro's *A Notícia,* all read the *Defender.*[23]

The Chicago paper's visibility in Brazil was due in good part to its editor, ardent Brazilophile Robert Abbott. Abbott himself was a powerful engine of transnational exchange between Brazil and the United States He visited Brazil in 1923, generating much publicity about the South American nation, especially in the pages of his own paper. Upon his return, he published the lectures he had given in Brazil and an extensive series of articles, and he would continue to translate and publish articles from both mainstream and Afro-Brazilian newspapers in the *Defender* in subsequent years.

Clarim and its fellow São Paulo black press organs and the *Chicago Defender* were therefore at once smaller and greater than a national label can convey. Neither journalistic community set neatly in the borders of its governing nation-state. When these papers spilled their ink over their urban and national borders and into each others' columns, they created something new. Their encounters were productive, but not in the ways one might imagine. While in the long run their conversations would reinforce the idea of the African diaspora, for immediate participants, they produced neither liquid clarity nor pan-African solidarity. Marked by asymmetries in power invisible to participants, these meetings yielded unpredictable consequences, misunderstandings, and political positions that can only be understood in the context of their generative transnational context.

Where Prejudice Is a Fact

The São Paulo black press's global vision was ample but unbalanced, for one nation hung so close on the horizon that it crowded out other stars. While articles in these papers referred to many European, African, and American countries, the United States earned more mention than any other. The North

American nation's position in the pages of the Afro-Paulista press reflected in part its power in the hemisphere—Brazilians looking past their own borders could not avoid the United States, even if they wanted to. Many of these journalists did not want to. To many Brazilians in the 1920s, the United States seemed an icon of modernity and progress, a beacon to follow down the righteous path to prosperity and happiness. Afro-Paulista journalists often agreed, calling the United States "the *leader* of progress," "the immense and formidable country of Washington . . . thinking brain of the Universe . . . formidable country of Lincoln, . . . solid and virile nation, of iron economic vitality"; "the entire world admires the rapid improvements of that extraordinary country."[24]

Afro-Brazilians also enjoyed pointing out the promising achievements of their "racial brothers," as they sometimes wrote. Reporting on African Americans was often fraught for them, however, for news of black people in the United States tended also to be news of violent racial hatred. Details of U.S. racial terror traveled the wires of international news information services widely in Brazil, thanks to their horrific, performative spectacularity, details of lynching in particular.[25] Such "news" found a receptive audience: Brazilians of various sorts appreciated it for the justification it seemed to provide for pride in their harmonious nation's moral superiority. Readers of most organs of the Brazilian press were therefore well acquainted with the terrible conflicts between blacks and whites in the most "modern" nation in the world.[26]

For Brazilians of African descent, the nexus of racism and modernity symbolized by the United States was both a problem and an opportunity. On the one hand, it fueled what Michael Mitchell has called the "discourse of conservative modernization," the idea that Brazil would progress only with "whitening," the gradual elimination of black people and culture from the body politic.[27] On the other hand, the United States was a foreign body whose ways could be rejected in the name of patriotism. Though many Afro-Paulista journalists praised growth in the United States, more denounced the horrors of U.S. racism and the damage it caused the entire society.[28] This comparison allowed these writers to take a nationalist posture that was at the same time unequivocally antiracist.

Thanks to the specter of racial violence raised by the U.S. contrast, positions that seem conciliatory and "integrationist" in strictly comparative frames could carry quite radical overtones. Consider this dramatic statement of national difference by *Clarim* writer Gervasio de Moraes: "While the North American Negro [*negro*] girds his chest and flings himself against the white [*branco*] in a barbaric and bloody war of extermination, dragged down by mortal hatred; while boiling gushes of brothers' blood run in the sewers, the Brazilian Negro extends a fraternal hand to his white brothers and they strengthen the characteristic friendship which unites them."[29]

Note whose helping hand is extended in this formulation. This is an offer proffered from a rhetorical position of some strength. De Moraes's violent images reminded *white* Brazilians of the dangers of white-supremacist racism. He borrowed news of Klan-type violence to compel not (only) Afro-Brazilians' obedient nationalism, but white Brazilians' cordiality and patronage. The performative qualities of lynching allowed North American racial terrorism to reach transnationally, with consequences the Klan could not have anticipated.

Understanding that the contrast to the United States was a constant frame of reference sheds new light on nationalist rhetoric in the Afro-Paulista press. De Moraes was unusually explicit, but the endless paeans to "the sacrosanct name of Brazil," "our beloved homeland," "the greatness of the beloved Brazilian homeland," so common that they became rhetorical flourish, extended de Moraes's "fraternal hand" of patriotism in exchange for racial justice.[30] Positive commemorations of slavery became grounds for demands to repudiate racial prejudice.[31] Another *Clarim* writer used a U.S.–Brazil contrast as a history lesson. Brazilian slave owners, he explained in 1925, were "not always benevolent, but, in any case, less barbaric than those of other countries, especially those from the United States. . . . They [slaves] contributed so much, so that Brazil would never have color prejudice [*preconceito de cor*]. . . . In the United States, even now, the inequality between blacks and whites [*pretos e brancos*] survives even after death; in some places there are different cemeteries for each!"[32]

This unnamed writer extended his contrast to turn the rhetoric of whitening into a markedly antiracist position. After listing a number of prominent Afro-Brazilians as proof of the race's mobility in Brazil, he rhapsodized, "What a beautiful gallery of illustrious Negroes and sons of Negroes [*negros e filhos de negros*] Brazil presents!"[33] This distinction between a Negro and his children, notoriously impossible in the United States where every black person's child is supposedly classified as black, patriotically turned a promise of black disappearance into a celebration of Afro-descended elements in the national community.[34]

Afro-Paulista journalists' minimization of Brazilian racism in contrast to the United States gave racism a more public airing than it earned in any other forum. José Correia Leite, coeditor of *Clarim,* wrote in 1926: "There in North America, where prejudice is a fact, what belongs to the black belongs to the black, what belongs to the white belongs to the white, here, no; everything

Brazilian is ours with the exception of some tiny little things that cannot qualify as prejudice."[35] Leite's exception, a sheathed accusation, exhorted white Brazilians to clean up their act, sweetened with a demonstration of Afro-Brazilian willingness to grant Brazil's good reputation in public.

Reading Afro-Paulista journalism in the overlapping local and transnational contexts of its production and reception undermines the comparison of Afro-Brazilians and African Americans as opposites. It shows the steel in Afro-Brazilians' seemingly conciliatory professions of nationalism and reveals the ways Afro-Brazilians as well as African Americans rested antiracist arguments on each other. Afro-Paulista writers folded the United States and their views of African American experience into their antiracist toolkit, just as African Americans made Brazil into a useful talking point. When members of the two groups actually met, these necessarily oversimplified visions of the other sparked a fascinating, potentially instructive tension. This happened in the 1920s, during the visit of *Chicago Defender* editor Robert Abbott, and in the wake of his exciting, confusing trip.

Teaching the Vicar

During his voyage to Brazil in 1923, Abbott met a host of Brazilian dignitaries of all shades of skin color and political affiliation. In Rio de Janeiro he was invited to speak before the "Press association of Rio" (probably the National Press Association) and was made an honorary member. He spoke to the *Federação dos Homens de Côr* and to groups he called "the Democratic conference of Brazil," and the "Progressive Union." Each lecture was followed by speeches by his hosts, receptions, interviews, and so on.[36]

The impressions Abbott took away from all these meetings with articulate, accomplished Brazilians were the conclusions he had drawn before his southbound steamer ever left port. Abbott loved Brazil because he had fully swallowed its claim to be free of racism. In fact, South American conditions were not what he expected. Abbott encountered a great deal of racial discrimination. He had a terrible time obtaining his visa, prevailing only after his congressman and senator sent repeated letters to the Brazilian Embassy in Washington. The Hotel Gloria in Rio de Janeiro refused him a room, the São Paulo Palace Hotel asked him to leave after just one night (blaming American tourists), and the Hotel Odeste would not let him eat in the dining room, nor would the porters there carry his bags.

Regardless, Abbott drew the conclusions from his experiences in Brazil that he wanted to draw. For the most part, he remained dedicatedly oblivious to anything contrary to his hopes. He wanted to see the lack of racism as a national trait, one shared uniformly across Brazil's scattered and diverse regions, so he judged the status of the "thousands of Negroes" he saw in São Paulo as "about the same as those of Rio de Janeiro," an evaluation few contemporaries or historians have shared.[37] When Abbott was forced to recognize prejudice, he blamed it on North American travelers or treated it as an aberration. He characterized the consular obstacles he encountered, for example, as "entirely contrary to the Brazilian National Constitution and shamefully at variance with the finely democratic temper of the Brazilian people."[38]

Abbott's wife, Helen, traveling with him, was far more attuned to the racism they met. She was light-skinned enough to pass (she bought their first-class steamer tickets, for example), and could eavesdrop on conversations people wouldn't hold within Abbott's earshot. She was painfully uncomfortable that Abbott "had been pushy and had often sought to go places he was frankly not wanted," a discomfort for which Abbott's biographer, Roi Ottley, had no patience, painting her as a wet blanket and a nag.[39] Helen Abbott's story remains to be told.

Robert Abbott's lectures in Rio de Janeiro managed to rub a large number of well-disposed listeners the wrong way. Unsurprisingly: Abbott was, forgive the anachronism, ethnocentric. He spoke in English, and encouraged Afro-Brazilians to learn English so that *they* could better understand black North Americans. During a public campaign to commemorate a certain Afro-Brazilian figure three years later, he urged Brazilian politicians to organize a ceremony and invite important black men, particularly North Americans.[40] Most important, he dared lecture Brazilians on Brazilian conditions, an affront his listeners resented for its arrogance as well as for its content.

Many Afro-Brazilians were unhappy with Abbott's myopia about Brazilian racism, and criticized him for it in the black press and elsewhere. In an article in the mainstream daily *A Patria*, for example, José do Patrocinio Filho, son of the well-known abolitionist of the same name, protested that Abbott should have offered Brazilian audiences less flattering, more realistic and productive words. Patrocinio Filho lamented the deception he feared Abbott's words would only deepen: "That this equality exists for blacks here—fantastic—purely fantastic. . . . The data gathered by Dr. Abbott will produce among North American blacks, a sign of evident happiness, but for those from Brazil, it will be a genuine let-down, keeping them under this illusion of equality in which they remain suspended . . . Resigned to the white's pious contempt, making him believe the racial struggle doesn't exist among us . . ."[41] This clear-sighted critique of the idea of racial democracy, fully aware of its differential significance abroad and in Brazil, predates by ten years the book that would supposedly introduce this myth.[42]

Even more vehement was a piece in the Afro-Paulista *Getulino*, angry that Abbott and others had allowed themselves to be swayed by appearances. This writer dryly compared Abbott's denying racial prejudice in Brazil to denying the defeat of Germany, and compared Abbott's lecturing Afro-Brazilians on their own racial situations to "teaching the Our Father to the vicar."[43] Blinded by an arrogance that made him feel he could speak authoritatively after only shallow investigation, Abbott, these authors charged, misunderstood the nature of racism in Brazil and harmed the very cause he thought he was helping.

When Abbott left Brazil, he stepped unknowingly even deeper into the mire. On the steamer home, he wrote a letter to the president of the Brazilian Press Association, the satirist Raul Pederneiras. Once back in the United States, Abbott promised, he would gather funds to send African Americans to Brazil: "It is my plan, upon my return, to gather capital resources in order to colonize other agricultural areas where cotton plantations may proceed. Southern blacks [*Os pretos do sul*] must be the principal factor in Brazil's cotton industry. I intend to initiate my campaign and the emigration of black American colonists with no less than 10,000,000 (ten thousand dollars) [sic]. . . . I plan to carry out my expectations in 1924 or 25. I will call it *The National Negro Business League of the Nort America* [sic]."[44]

With the best of intentions, Abbott blundered into a debate about Brazilian immigration policy that had been boiling for years. Brazilians had contemplated the possible arrival of African American colonists since at least the first years of the twentieth century, when African Americans and North American white supremacists both considered the possibility.[45] The threat of black North American migration prompted anthropologist Raimundo Nina Rodrigues to pen his influential *Os africanos no Brasil* (1905). His "immediate justification," historian Dante Moreira Leite explains, "was to prevent a plan then under discussion: to bring North American negroes to Brazil, which would be, he thought, an 'assault on our nationality.'"[46] Nina Rodrigues himself placed the offending proposal about "ten or fifteen years" prior to his book (around 1890–95), intriguingly near the formulation of Brazil's 1890 restrictions on African and Chinese immigration.[47]

Os africanos and Nina Rodrigues's oeuvre in general shaped elite views of the relationship between race and national progress, with great consequence for Brazilian domestic and foreign policy. He fanned fears of the debilitating African presence then weakening Brazil, and opinions such as his prevailed, preventing the feared settlement from taking place.[48] Here is further evidence of the inextricable relation between the social positions of African Americans and Afro-Brazilians. In the twentieth century's first moments, African

American actions, prompted by ideas about Afro-Brazilians or race in Brazil, shaped Brazilian state policies critical to questions of nation formation, and generated anthropological "knowledge" of local racial truths.

As the century progressed, Brazilian elites largely relinquished biological determinism in favor of environmentalist and culturalist paradigms that spelled a brighter future for their nation.[49] Neither innovation served to dent the widespread faith in whitening, however, nor the concomitant determination to restrict immigration of African descent. Especially resolute was the determination to rebuff African Americans, whom most perceived as a particularly noxious population of aggressively race-conscious activists. When the issue returned in 1920 with the formation in Chicago of a black emigration society, alarmed legislators introduced a bill to exclude immigrants of African descent, provoking raging debate in the Brazilian Congress.[50]

Though many legislators expressed approval for such a prohibition, more were reluctant to risk undermining Brazil's international reputation as a country without racism. They devised, instead, informal means to the same ends. By the time the bill was introduced, the Brazilian consul in St. Louis had already requested and received permission to deny visas, after alerting the Ministry in Rio de Janeiro of "the organization of a syndicate for the emigration of negroes" to Brazil.[51] The president of the state of Matto Grosso, where the colonists hoped to go, had simply refused to grant an extension on their contract for the land, as one of the bill's sponsors informed his colleagues by reading them the state president's reassuring telegram.[52] Debate in the Congress, then, was essentially only about the Brazilian state's right or need to codify a restriction already in place. Lawmakers nixed the redundant bill.

The Ministry of Foreign Affairs quietly advised its representatives to put the unlegislatable exclusion into practice, and Brazilian consuls throughout North America and the Caribbean began or continued to deny visas surreptitiously.[53] Brazilian politicians' overt acknowledgements of this subterfuge show how very actively the Brazilian state discriminated. It may never have legislated racism, as comparers so avidly note, but in many cases it worked no less hard to enforce it.[54]

Somehow, the telegrams the Brazilian government sent to consuls in St. Louis, Norfolk, New York, New Orleans, Baltimore, Chicago, San Francisco, and Barbados regarding the Brazilian American Colonization Syndicate (BACS), the Chicago emigration syndicate, were intercepted.[55] The response was furious and immediate. Attorneys for BACS brought a legal challenge, citing international treaties and the Brazilian constitution.[56] The National Association for the Advancement of Colored People (NAACP) sent a challenging letter to the Brazilian Consul in New York.[57] Brazil did not substantially alter its policies, and so over the course of the 1920s, civil rights groups, community organizations, and congressmen whose constituents had been offended staged letter-writing campaigns, filed legal actions, and registered plentiful complaints with representatives of both the Brazilian and the U.S. states.

When Abbott encountered this obstacle, he put his powerful shoulder to the wheel. He wrote to the Brazilian ambassador, and when the ambassador's response did not satisfy him, he approached the U.S. State Department. "There seems to be a secret understanding between the Brazilian Consuls in their country to not vise passports for Negroes," he complained, warning of significant public concern and urging that "appropriate diplomatic action [be] taken by the United States to protect the rights of . . . its citizens." Abbott menacingly insisted that he was "not willing to let this matter drop."[58]

Abbott's colonization plan terrified whiter Brazilians, and his challenges to their government made many Brazilians see red. The major urban newspapers reported on the "Effects of Mr. Abbott's visit to Brazil. American Negroes Intend to Provoke a Diplomatic Intervention to Force the Brazilian Government to permit their Entry and Permanence in national territories."[59] The foreign "*elemento negro*" would bring nothing but discord, "backwardness and retardation," they warned. In the view of most writers in Brazil's national press, African Americans brought the indignities they suffered upon themselves with their greed and belligerence, and would do so wherever they went. These "sons of Ham born in other lands [were] full of hatred for whites, battling them with iron and fire and desirous of the advantages offered by Brazilian lands."[60] A Brazilian government official likened this would-be migrant group to immigrants inadmissible based on "the corrosive principle of their tendency to crime." These were "undesirable negroes [*negros indesejaveis*] who in the United States feed prejudice and perturb the peace of the American family."[61]

The Afro-Paulista press reported both the visa challenges and the angry response at home. A *Getulino* editorialist reported the non-black press's notice of a diplomatic incident then being provoked by "the *leader* of the black race in the United States." Expressing no opposition to the racist immigration provision, this journalist sympathized only with his fellow Brazilians' concern for the damage Brazil would sustain in a conflict with "a nation as powerful as the 'American colossus.'"[62]

The beast Afro-Brazilians had to fear, however, was greater than a single state. As the press coverage shows, restrictionists in Brazil took the prospect of African American immigration as an opportunity to express and legislate the kinds of racist sentiments (e.g., black backwardness, Brazil's necessarily white future) that otherwise remained under cover or disavowed. The North American protestors challenged Brazilian sovereignty, allowing opponents to align the full force of nationalism against explicit antiracist activism. Helping to construct the idea of cordiality as a Brazilian national trait, African American activism offered the perfect illustrative contrast.[63]

Black press writers shifted their stance in an attempt to contain this outburst. During Abbott's visit, black press protests over his inappropriate intervention had focused on Brazilian racism. In response to his colonization plans a slate of writers toed the state line, leaving Brazilian racism entirely out of the picture. *Clarim* writer Gervasio Moraes charged Abbott with scheming to spread racial separation. Moraes didn't deny that Brazilians lived in the racial harmony Abbott observed, "the most sainted and significant fraternity," but sarcastically rejected his "offer" of inappropriate, even disastrous "social imports from our Sister America."[64] The *Getulino* writer who worried about the American colossus was furious at the "pretension" with which the "*millionario negro*" repaid the kind hospitality he had enjoyed in Brazil. He called African Americans "our brothers [*irmãos nossos*], to be sure, but of different habits, sentiments, and religion. If the *general in charge* is doing what the newspapers laconically say he is, what won't the *bulk of the army* do?"[65] This writer imagined a transnational diasporic community but one bracketed and essentially superseded by national borders.

Black press writers took Abbott's performance of racial identity as an opportunity to demonstrate elite and state interest in organizing Afro-Brazilian loyalties around shared "habits, sentiments, and religion." This claim to equal citizenship, contained within an offer of national loyalty, drew force from Abbott's threat of social disruption, which he generously demonstrated with his protests over visa denials. Afro-Brazilians' offer of national loyalty was an appealing bulkhead against a wave of militant, black-identified immigration. Rather than feeding transnational diasporic solidarity, then, North American activism, though transnational and antiracist, helped push some Afro-Paulista writers away from denunciations of Brazilian racism and toward professions of loyalty to the Brazilian nation.

Though there is no evidence that Abbott learned of the opposition his actions provoked, I imagine he would have been chagrined to hear criticism from Afro-Brazilians, especially those who identified as "black" in some way. Then again, Abbott did not see that some Brazilians of African descent refused to choose such an identity, whether they succeeded in avoiding its imposition by others or not. Abbott assumed that race would be the primary category of any Afro-diasporic identity. Ironically, proof to the contrary was close at hand: Abbott himself appeared to many Brazilians as something other than black, due to his own personal affluence and his nation's wealth. Abbott's biographer notes that the racial identity Abbott assumed he shared with Afro-Brazilians was often displaced by his national and class status. "Because of his wealth and his recognized position as a North American publisher, Abbott was given upper-class status; or, to use the Brazilian saying, 'A rich Negro is a white man, and a poor white man is a Negro!' His mulatto wife was . . . icing on the cake."[66]

Just as Abbott sometimes wrote as if all Brazilians were black, many in the Afro-Paulista press fantasized that all African Americans were rich. "Everyone talks enthusiastically about how North American blacks are millionaires, industrialists, doctors, pharmacists, engineers, etc.," wrote *Clarim*'s Horacio da Cunha. [67] If not "everyone," da Cunha's fellow journalists certainly did, marveling at the supposed "colossal fortunes" of Josephine Baker, Jack Johnson, "Stephin Fetchit," Abbott, and others.[68] These exaggerations reflect the great distance between even meager success in U.S. terms and the possibilities for financial mobility in the writers' communities, along with a dose of earnest desire for the United States to *be* the meritocracy of its claims. Projections of "racial paradise" could flow in both directions.

Still, as ignorance is the prerogative of privilege, Afro-Brazilians had a little more insight into their relationship with African Americans than vice versa. In 1929, *Progresso* reprinted a *Defender* piece praising Brazil's treatment of its black citizens. The *Progresso* writer understood the *Defender*'s intent exactly. "One can see," he pointed out, "that the journalist's intention—untruths aside—is to awaken in the spirit of the [North] American government the convention of equality, using as evidence the prestige enjoyed by black men [*homens pretos*] in our country, from which come practical advantages for the Nation [Brazil]."[69] Black press writers (and readers) knew precisely what Abbott was doing with his comparison, and understood that he was willing to distort conditions in Brazil to do it.

São Paulo black press writers expressed frustration at African Americans' overlooking of their relative power. Noting the NAACP's successful litigation against the "grandfather clause" in the U.S. Supreme Court in 1929, a *Progresso* contributor chided "North American Negroes and other NAACP allies" saying, "Unfortunately, they do not realize their prestige, which is much greater than they think."[70] While unconcerned with the class distinctions that made this statement true only for certain African Americans, this writer clearly conveyed the impact of national location. In relations with subjects of subordinate nations and when seen as acting in tandem with their state (as many Brazilian observers at the time wrongly assumed about visa protestors), even disenfranchised citizens of an imperial power would refract their nation's might.

Unaware of the ways Afro-Brazilians tailored their interventions to their specific ideological contexts, African Americans chose head-on confrontation to fight Brazilian racism. Most did not realize that their bluntness would play to a venerable tradition of national contrasts, helping to push Afro-Brazilians away from the Afro-diasporic sensibility they expressed at other times into a defensive posture that looked from afar like conciliatory Brazilian nationalism. African Americans could not have predicted that their challenges to Brazilian visa policies would align protests against racism with disloyalty to the Brazilian nation, lending the rhetorical crutches of nationalism to supporters of the vehicles of white supremacy in Brazil (immigration policy, health care priorities, urban reforms, and so on). So they could see neither the political context that made nationalist rhetoric a smart strategic choice for Afro-Brazilian activists nor the way some of those activists deployed that rhetoric as powerful antiracism.

What would it mean to recognize that Afro-Brazilians' "lack" of politicized racial identity (i.e., their nationalism) in this case was in part a result of transnational connections sown through the immigration debacle and the black press? It would certainly entail a recognition of their choices as political and antiracist, displacing notions of Afro-Brazilians and African Americans as opposites. It would problematize comparison as scholarly method, revealing comparison so deeply implicated in the construction of these contrasts as to be irredeemable as an analytical tool. This recognition reveals one of the pitfalls of comparative method: it too often conveys a collection of discrete national subgroups, obfuscating connections and portraying subjects as parallel when they are instead far more directly related.

Diaspora Studies and the history of race demand transnational methods that can articulate such associations. Scholars in these fields have carefully worked to elaborate the constitution of racial categories, mapping the borders separating racial categories from each other and charting their relations to other social categories such as nation, gender, or class.[71] Now they must incorporate conversations, cooperation, and conflict across imagined communities in far-flung places, for these too are formative, even in apparently peripheral, small-scale locales.

I realize as I write these last lines that I weave a mundane, contemporary prayer into this ostensibly academic and backwards glance. This essay, first delivered at a conference two weeks after September 11, 2001, and revised in the weeks following the 2004 U.S. presidential election, harbors a thinly camouflaged supplication to North American readers. It is the plea to recognize that the prejudices set deep in U.S. citizens by a privileged national location, despite other indices of subordination and deeply good intentions, can poison even the sorts of relationships that ought to produce solidarity and coalition. Failure to see this dynamic, added to the already arduous task of translating uncannily (un)familiar social categories, threatens alliances we cannot afford to squander.

Notes

I'm grateful to Jerry Dávila, Mark Wild, and the volume's anonymous reviewer for wonderfully smart, helpful comments. I would also like to thank the organizers of this volume and the terrific conference that sparked it. Errors are mine, of course; so are translations, unless otherwise noted.

1. *Getulino,* 19 August 1923.

2. This view is deeply inscribed in the academic historiography. See Oracy Nogueira, *Tanto Preto Quanto Branco: Estudos de Relações Raciais* (São Paulo: T.A. Queiroz, 1985), esp. "Preconceito racial de marca e preconceito racial de origem" [1956]; W. E. B. DuBois, "As the Crow Flies," New York *Amsterdam Star-News,* 20 December 1944; "Prospect of a World Without Race Conflict," *American Journal of Sociology* 49 (March 1944): 452, both cited in Hellwig, "Racial Paradise or Run-Around? Afro-North American Views of Race in Brazil," *American Studies* (1990): 52 and 60n35; Carl N. Degler, *Neither Black nor White: Slavery and Race Relations in Brazil and the United States* (New York: Macmillan, 1971); Roger Bastide and Florestan Fernandes, *Brancos e Negros em São Paulo; ensaio sociológico sôbre aspectos da formação, manifestações atuais e efeitos do preconceito de côr na Sociedade Paulistana,* 2d ed., rev. e ampliada (São Paulo: Companhia Editora Nacional, 1959), chap. 5; Roger Bastide, "A Imprensa Negra do Estado de São Paulo," in *Estudos Afro-Brasileiros* (São Paulo: Editora Perspectiva, 1973), 129–56; Miriam Nicolau Ferrara, "A Imprensa Negra Paulista (1915–1963): Estudo Monográfico" (master's thesis, University of São Paulo, 1981); Carlos Hasenbalg and Nelson do Valle Silva, "Notes on Racial and Political Inequality in Brazil," in *Racial Politics in Contemporary Brazil,* ed. Michael Hanchard (Durham, N.C.: Duke University Press, 1999), 163; Niani (Dee Brown), "Black Consciousness vs. Racism in Brazil," in *African-American Reflections on Brazil's Racial Paradise,* ed. David J. Hellwig (Philadelphia: Temple University Press, 1992), 225–48 (*The Black Scholar* [January–February 1980]: 59–70); Michael George Hanchard, *Orpheus and Power: The Movimento Negro of Rio de Janeiro and São Paulo, Brazil, 1945–1988* (Princeton, N.J.: Princeton University Press, 1994), 5–6, 41, 74; Howard Winant, "Rethinking Race in Brazil," and "Democracy Reenvisioned, Difference Transformed: Comparing Contemporary Racial Politics in the United

States and Brazil," both in Winant, *Racial Conditions: Politics, Theory, Comparisons* (Minneapolis: University of Minnesota Press, 1994), 130–31; 157–69; José Murilo de Carvalho, "Dreams Come Untrue," *Daedalus* 129, no. 2 (2000): 57–82.

3. Scholars able to see resistance outside the most narrow formulations of "the political" have refuted these demeaning suggestions by presenting Afro-Brazilians as agents of their own—and their broader society's—transformation. See, for example, Mary C. Karasch, *Slave Life in Rio de Janeiro, 1808–1850* (Princeton, N.J.: Princeton University Press, 1987); Dale T. Graden, "An Act 'Even of Public Security': Slave Resistance, Social Tensions, and the End of the International Slave Trade to Brazil, 1935–1856," *Hispanic American Historical Review* 76, no. 2 (1996): 249–82; Kim D. Butler, *Freedoms Given, Freedoms Won: Afro-Brazilians in Post-Abolition São Paulo and Salvador* (New Brunswick, N.J.: Rutgers University Press, 1998); and Rachel E. Harding, *A Refuge in Thunder: Candomblé and Alternative Spaces of Blackness* (Bloomington: Indiana University Press, 2000).

4. Robin D. G. Kelley, "'But a Local Phase of a World Problem': Black History's Global Vision, 1883–1950," *Journal of American History* 86, no. 3 (1999): 1045–77.

5. Readers may feel that I use awkwardly inequivalent terms for black people in the United States and Brazil. I find it less awkward to anglicize "*afro-brasileiro*," the term preferred by academics friendly to ongoing black liberation struggles, than to make up a Portuguese mirror image of "African American" (unhyphenated), the term standard in most U.S.-based Diaspora Studies work today. "African Brazilian" has no basis in usage. That I feel the need to explain this itself gestures to the untranslatability of racial categories across significant cultural distance. This untranslatability is also the reason I have occasionally included Portuguese racial terms in brackets within my translations of primary source material; it is also part of why I leave the Portuguese unmodernized.

6. Some of the routes of these encounters are detailed in my forthcoming *Uneven Encounters: Making Race and Nation in Brazil and the United States* (Durham, N.C.: Duke University Press, 2009).

7. Emily S. Rosenberg and Eric Foner, *Spreading the American Dream: American Economic and Cultural Expansion, 1890–1945* (New York: Hill and Wang, 1982); and Emily S. Rosenberg, "Anglo-American Rivalry in Brazil," in *World War I and the Growth of United States Predominance in Latin America*, ed. Emily S. Rosenberg (New York: Garland, 1987), 77–111.

8. There were enough African Americans in São Paulo in the 1920s to constitute a recognizable group of expatriates, according to José Correia Leite, "E, apoz a Liberdade . . .," *Clarim*, 30 August 1925; and Horacio da Cunha, "Os pretos da America do Norte e os Pretos da America do Sul," *Clarim*, 5 February 1928; see also Gervasio de Moraes, "Aos Negros Sensatos de S. Paulo," *Clarim*, 3 February 1929, 4.

9. For the United States, where this reaction is more documented, see William M. Tuttle, *Race Riot; Chicago in the Red Summer of 1919* (New York: Atheneum, 1970), esp. "The New Negro, the Police, and Militant Self-Defense"; Nell Irvin Painter,

Standing at Armageddon: The United States, 1877–1919 (New York: W.W. Norton, 1987), 364–65; Robin D. G. Kelley, *Hammer and Hoe: Alabama Communists During the Great Depression* (Chapel Hill: University of North Carolina Press, 1990), 228–31; period expressions include W. E. B. DuBois, "Returning Soldiers," *The Crisis* (May 1919), in Henry Lee Moon, ed., *The Emerging Thought of W. E. B. DuBois; Essays and Editorials from the Crisis* (New York: Simon and Schuster, 1972), 245; "Barred from French Fine Art School," Baltimore *Afro-American,* 27 April 1923, 1. For Brazil, see Bastide, "A Imprensa Negra," 131; and José Correia Leite and Cuti, *E Disse o Velho Militante José Correia Leite* (São Paulo: Secretaria Municipal de Cultura, 1992).

10. David Hellwig has shown that Brazil's image as a racial paradise "became a myth that served important functions for black Americans," most of whom had not visited and would never travel to South America. African Americans talked and wrote about Brazil, Hellwig documents, to attack "the fear of miscegenation," and to "affirm that the U.S. pattern of race relations was not universal," and could even earn the United States opprobrium abroad. Hellwig, *African-American Reflections,* xii, 17–18; see also Antônio Sérgio Alfredo Guimarães, "Brasil-Estados Unidos: um Diálogo Que Forja Nossa Identidade Racial," *Estudos Afro-Ásiáticos* 26 (1994): 141–47; Hellwig, "Racial Paradise or Run-Around?"; Hellwig, "A New Frontier in a Racial Paradise: Robert S. Abbott's Brazilian Dream," *Luso-Brazilian Review* 25, no. 1 (1988): 59–67.

11. "Asymmetries of ignorance" from Dipesh Chakrabarty, "Postcoloniality and the Artifice of History: Who Speaks for Indian Pasts," *Representations* 37 (Winter 1992): 1–26.

12. Todd Vogel, "Introduction" to *The Black Press: New Literary and Historical Essays,* ed. Todd Vogel (New Brunswick, N.J.: Rutgers University Press, 2001), 1–14, esp. 1, 3.

13. Benedict Anderson, *Imagined Communities: Reflections on the Origin and Spread of Nationalism,* 2nd ed. (London, New York: Verso, [1983] 1991).

14. Vogel, *The Black Press;* Frederick German Detweiler, *The Negro Press in the United States* (Chicago: University of Chicago Press, 1922); Irvine Garland Penn, *The Afro-American Press and Its Editors,* reprint ed. (New York: Arno Press, 1969 [Springfield, Mass.: Wiley, 1891]); Roland E. Wolseley, *The Black Press, U.S.A.,* 2nd ed. (Ames: Iowa State University, [1972] 1990); Armistead Scott Pride and Clint C. Wilson II, *A History of the Black Press* (Washington, D.C.: Howard University Press, 1997); William G. Jordan, *Black Newspapers and America's War for Democracy, 1914–1920* (Chapel Hill: University of North Carolina Press, 2001).

15. NB: *O Clarim da Alvorada* (1924–27) changed its name to *O Clarim d'Alvorada* (1928–30), ceased publication until 1935, and then returned as *O Clarim;* I have cited it as *Clarim* throughout.

16. Bastide, "A Imprensa Negra"; Ferrara, "Imprensa Negra Paulista," master's thesis; Ferrara, "Imprensa Negra Paulista," *Revista Brasileira de Historia (São Paulo)* 5, no. 10 (1985): 197–207; Ferrara, "A Imprensa Negra Paulista (1915–1963)," doctoral dissertation, University of São Paulo, 1986; George Reid Andrews, *Blacks and Whites*

in São Paulo, Brazil, 1888–1988 (Madison: University of Wisconsin Press, 1991); José Carlos Gomes Da Silva, "Negros Em São Paulo: Espaço Publico, Imagem e Cidadania (1900–1930)," in *Além Dos Territórios: Para um Diálogo Entre a Etnologia Indígena, os Estudos Rurais e os Estudos Urbanos,* ed. Ana Maria de Niemeyer and Emília Pietrafesa de Godoi (Campinas: Mercado de Letras, 1998), 65–96; Antonio Liberac, "As 'Associações dos Homens de Cor.' Política e 'Cultura Negra' no Brasil, na Primeira Metade do Século XX" (unpublished paper, UNICAMP, 1999); Leite, "Um Capítulo . . .," reproduced in Leite and Cuti, *E Disse,* 254–58. Two collections of these newspapers are preserved on microfilm, one compiled by Michael Mitchell and archived at Princeton University among other places; the other by the University of São Paulo (USP) under the direction, I believe, of Miriam Nicolau Ferrara, and available at USP, the Biblioteca Nacional in Rio de Janeiro, and other locations. There were a few other papers, before and after these dates and outside São Paulo, such as those discussed in Bastide, "A Imprensa Negra," 131–2, notably *A Voz da Raça,* the organ of the *Frente Negra,* whose years of publication fall outside the period considered here.

17. Quotes from Bastide, "A Imprensa Negra," 130; Hasenbalg and Silva, "Notes on Racial and Political Inequality," 163; and Ferrara, "A Imprensa Negra Paulista," master's thesis. See also Ferrara in the *Revista Brasileira de Historia;* Ferrara, doctoral dissertation; and Leite and Cuti, *E Disse.* Scholars who make excellent use of this source include Silva, "Negros Em São Paulo"; Andrews, *Blacks and Whites in São Paulo;* and Butler, *Freedoms Given, Freedoms Won.*

18. "Outr'ora," *Clarim,* 13 May 1926, 7, introducing Dr. Cyro Costa's poem, "Pae João," recited by its author in Rio at an event organized by the *Federação dos Homens de Côr.*

19. "Representantes," *Clarim,* 1 July 1928, 1.

20. "A Nossa Revista," *Clarim,* 3 June 1928, 1, notes congratulations on their May 13, 1928, issue from *O Globo* and *A Notícia* in Rio, and *O Combate, Diario Nacional, Jornal do Commercio* and *A Gazeta* in São Paulo.

21. In his memoirs, Leite claimed that Afro-Brazilians repudiated Garvey, finding his ideas inappropriate for their context. His position late in life seems to have caused him to flatten the heterogeneity of intent and reception suggested by the pieces themselves. Leite and Cuti, *E Disse . . .,* 78–80. See also "Os Negros Não Precisam de Protectores Brancos. Do 'Negro World' de Nova York," *Clarim,* 24 November 1929, 2; items from the *Negro World* and the *Chicago Defender* in *Clarim,* 25 January 1930, 4; on Garvey in *Clarim,* 13 May 1930; letter from Garvey and transcript from the *Washington Tribune* on imperialism and lynchings in *Clarim,* 28 September 1930, 4; and Frank St. Claire, "Sidelights on Brazil Racial Conditions," *The Negro World,* 13 January 1923, cited in Hellwig, *African-American Reflections,* 51–54.

22. Detweiler, *The Negro Press in the United States;* Theodore Kornweibel, Jr., "'The Most Dangerous of All Negro Journals': Federal Efforts to Suppress the Chicago Defender During World War I," *American Journalism* 11, no. 2 (1994): 154–68.

23. "The Chicago Defender. World's Greatest Weekly," *Clarim,* 24 November 1929,

1; see also the favorable review of James Weldon Johnson's novel in "A Questão das Raças nos Estados Unidos," *Clarim*, 3 February 1929, 4. The other paper is *Progresso;* see "A Formula Igualitaria Para Resolver a Questão Racial Americana," which mentions the *Defender;* Lino Guedes, "Illusão democratica *norte-americana*," *Progresso*, 28 July 1929 (on the invitation of a Chicago senator's wife to tea at the White House; bears the mark of the *Defender*'s interpretations). On the exchange with *A Notícia*, see Micol Seigel, "Black Mothers, Citizen Sons," in Flavio dos Santos Gomes and Olivia Gomes da Cunha, eds., *Quase-Cidadão: Histórias e Antropologias da Pós-Emancipação No Brasil* (Rio de Janeiro: forthcoming). Cf. Hanchard, *Orpheus and Power*, 95: "Prior to the 1970s, black Brazilians had little information about U.S. blacks due to the barrier of language."

24. Luiz Barbosa, "O Trabalho," *Clarim*, 20 June 1926, 3 ("*o* 'leader' *do Progresso*"; "*o immenso e formidavel paiz de Washington . . . cerebro pensador do Universo . . . formidavel paiz de Lincoln, . . . nação solida e viril, de ferrea vitalidade economica*"); *Clarim*, 14 November 1926 ("*o mundo inteiro admire a rapidez das edificações daquelle paiz extraordinario*"); also see celebrations of U.S. "civilization" and "ingenuity" in articles such as "O meio centenario da lampada electrica. Edison, o seu inventor, terá uma participação interessantissima," *O Patrocinio*, 28 September 1929, 3.

25. On the performative, terroristic qualities of lynching, see Trudier Harris, *Exorcising Blackness: Historical and Literary Lynching and Burning Rituals* (Bloomington: Indiana University Press, 1984); Phyllis Klotman, "'Tearing a Hole in History': Lynching as Theme and Motif," *Black American Literature Forum* 19 (1985): 55–63; Robyn Wiegman, *American Anatomies: Theorizing Race and Gender* (Durham, N.C.: Duke University Press, 1995). An earlier, eloquent articulation of this argument is Oliver C. Cox, *Caste, Class, & Race; a Study in Social Dynamics* (Garden City, N.Y.: Doubleday, 1948). On the disproportionate impact of terroristic violence policing another social category, see Eve Kosofsky Sedgwick, *Between Men: English Literature and Male Homosocial Desire* (New York: Columbia University Press, 1985).

26. One can regularly find articles such as Paulo Barreto, "O Problema das Raças nos Estados Unidos," *Patria*, Oct. 2, 1921; "Vida social," *O Paiz*, 13 March 1926, 6; "A resistencia dos negros," *Correio da Manhã*, 18 July 1925, 2; "Duas Biblias . . .," *Correio da Manhã*, 22 July 1925, 2; "Hoover," *Critica*, 21 December 1928, 3; "O chá presidencial," *Correio da Manhã*, 28 July 1929, 2.

27. Michael Mitchell, "Miguel Reale and the Impact of Conservative Modernization on Brazilian Race Relations," in Hanchard, ed., *Racial Politics in Contemporary Brazil*, 116–37; on "whitening," see also Thomas E. Skidmore, *Black into White: Race and Nationality in Brazilian Thought* (New York: Oxford University Press, 1974).

28. "Hatred" is ascribed to U.S. race relations in D'Alencastro, "Grave Erro!" *O Bandeirante*, n.d., September 1918, 2; "Cartas d'um Negro," *Getulino*, 21 October 1923; "O Ku Klux Klan," *Getulino*, 23 November 1924; Gervasio Moraes, "A inquisição moderna," *Clarim*, 14 November 1926, 2; "A questão de Raça," *Auriverde*, 29 April 1928, 3; "Os pretos são sympathicos á Candidatura Smith," *Progresso*, 15 November

1928, 3; "O odio de raça. Problema de funda raizes nos Estados Unidos. Será soluccionado por Hoover?" *Progresso,* 13 January 1929, 5; Pr[oprietário (probably Argentino Wanderley)], "A Formula Igualitaria Para Resolver a Questão Racial Americana," *Progresso,* 24 February 1929; "Lynchamento. É uma Aberração da Civilisação Americana," *Progresso,* 26 September 1929; "Separando o Joio do Trigo," *Progresso,* 24 November 1929, 5. Lynching and the KKK are mentioned in the first five of these articles (*O Bandeirante,* n.d., September 1918; *Getulino,* 21 October 1923; *Getulino,* 23 November 1924; *Clarim,* 14 November 1926; *Auriverde,* 29 April 1928) and in the *Progresso* article of 26 September 1929; they are mentioned as well in "Ku-Klux-Klan," *Clarim,* 2 December 1928, 2 (two articles with same title); Benedicto Florencio, "Os Pretos em São Paulo," *O Kosmos,* 19 October 1924; "A raça branca posta em cheque pela raça negra," *Progresso,* 7 September 1928, 3; untitled review of Rien que la terre, *Progresso,* 23 June 1929, 3; "Associação Nacional Para o Adiantamento da Raça Negra," *Progresso,* 31 August 1929, 4; Leite, "O Grande Problema Nacional," *Evolução,* 13 May 1933, 9. See also A. J. Veiga dos Santos, "A acção dos negros Brasileiros," *Clarim,* 15 January 1927, 5, which claims that the Brazilian situation is one of "social distinctions" [differentes sociaes], not racism; and Horacio da Cunha, "Os pretos da America do Norte e os Pretos da America do Sul," *Clarim,* 5 February 1928. This list is surely not exhaustive.

29. Gervasio Moraes, "A inquisição moderna," *Clarim,* 14 November 1926, 2.

30. Gervasio de Moraes, "A mocidade!" *Getulino,* 5 August 1923; "13 de maio," *Clarim,* 13 May 1930, 2; João Eugenio da Costa, "O Despertar do Gigante," *Clarim,* 25 April 1926.

31. T. Camargo, "Echos do Projecto F. Reis," *Elite,* 20 January 1924, 1; "A Redempção de nossa raça," *Clarim,* 13 May 1924, 1; Leite, "Capacidade dos incapazes," *Clarim,* 22 August 1926, 2, quoting Theodoro Sampaio; *A Noite* 13 April 1926 in "Monumento á Mãe Preta," *A Notícia,* 24 April 1926, 3; see also anon., untitled, *Clarim,* 13 May 1928, 1; "O Dia da Mãe Preta," *Clarim,* 28 September 1928, 1; Jayme de Aguiar, "O Negro no Brasil," *Clarim,* 3 June 1928, 1; Mario Beni, "A Contribução do Preto na Formação do Poderio Economio Paulista," *Evolução,* 13 May 1933, 4; "O Negro como factor do nosso Progresso," *Evolução,* 13 May 1933, 17; *A Patria* 8 April 1926 in "Pulicações de ultima hora. Glorificando a raça negra. A Idéa de um monumento á Mãe Preta suggerido pelos nossos collegas de 'A Notícia,'" *A Notícia,* 9 April 1926, 4; *A Folha* 6 April 1926 in "Tribuna Publica," *A Notícia,* 7 April 1926, 3. Wanting to convince white observers as much as to exhort Afro-Brazilian ones, Afro-Paulista journalists wrote to establish the survival of this tradition of black productivity into their present, praising their hardworking peers. Even musicians "in orchestras and jazz-bands" in Paris, *Clarim* illustrated, were performing "a veritable Herculean musical labor"; "Tumultuosa assembléa de negros," *Clarim,* 21 October 1928, 3.

32. "Os Negros," *Clarim,* 26 July 1925, 4.

33. Ibid.

34. On "whitening," see Skidmore, *Black into White.*

35. Leite, "Quem Somos," *Clarim*, 14 November 1926, 3.

36. Abbott met, among others, Rio's chief of police (unnamed); José do Patrocinio, Jr.; Juliana Moreira, a Bahian doctor; Eloy de Souza, a senator; Tito Carlos, a writer and journalist about to take a degree in medicine from the National University of Rio de Janeiro; the jurist Evaristo de Moraes; and Olympio de Castro, priest and scholar. "Sweet Liberty Wields Scepter Down in Brazil. Mr. Abbott Find Brazilians 'Sublime'; Sees the Spirit of Equality; Signally Honored," *Chicago Defender*, 14 April 1923, 2; "South America Gets Prejudice From the South. Mr. Abbott Tells Appomattox Club Members Interesting Stories of His Travels," *Chicago Defender*, 2 June 1923, 5; Abbott, "My Trip Through South America. Article 2—Personal Motives," *Chicago Defender*, 11 August 1923, 13–14; Abbott, "My Trip Through South America. Article 3—São Paulo," *Chicago Defender*, 18 August 1923, 13–14; Abbott, "My Trip Through South America. Article 4—Back in Rio de Janeiro," *Chicago Defender*, 25 August 1923, 13–14; Abbott, "My Trip Through South America. Article 4 (Continued)—Rio de Janeiro," *Chicago Defender*, 8 September 1923, 13–14.

37. Abbott, "My Trip Through South America. Article 3—São Paulo." On regional differences among Afro-Brazilians in São Paulo and Rio de Janeiro, see Florestan Fernandes, A. Brunel, Phyllis B. Eveleth, Arthur Rothwell, and Jacqueline D. Skiles, *The Negro in Brazilian Society* (New York: Columbia University Press, 1969); Clóvis Moura, *Sociologia Do Negro Brasileiro* (São Paulo: Editora Atica, 1988); Roger Bastide, "The Development of Race Relations in Brazil," in *Industrialisation and Race Relations; a Symposium*, ed. Guy Hunter (London: Oxford University Press, 1965), 9–29; Andrews, *Blacks & Whites in São Paulo;* Hanchard, *Orpheus and Power*, 29.

38. Abbott's *Defender* series, passim; quote from Roi Ottley, *The Lonely Warrior; The Life and Times of Robert S. Abbott* (Chicago: H. Regnery Co., 1955), 230–31. On African Americans' inability or unwillingness to see prejudice in Brazil, and Abbott's in particular, see Guimarães, "Brasil-Estados Unidos," esp. 143.

39. Ottley, *Lonely Warrior*, 240; see also 288.

40. "Brazilians are Told Meaning of Liberty Statue. Symbol of Liberty in Books Only; Millions Fight for Freedom and Get Oppression," *Chicago Defender*, 28 April 1923, 3; "Uma carta do director de 'The Chicago Defender,'" *A Notícia*, 23 April 1926, 1; "Monumento á MP. A grande repercussão, na America do Norte, da iniciativa de 'A Notícia.' 'O Brasil rende alta homenagem aos cidadões pretos,' diz o 'The Chicago Defender,'" *A Notícia*, 18 June 1926.

41. José do Patrocinio, Filho, "Preto e Branco," *A Patria*, 14 March 1923, 1; also reprinted in Abilio Rodrigues, "Preto e Branco," *O Kosmos*, 18 April 1923.

42. I am referring, of course, to Gilberto Freyre, *Casa-grande e senzala: formacão de familia brasileira sob o regimen de economía patriarchal* (Rio de Janeiro: Maia and Schmidt, 1933).

43. "Cartas d'um Negro," *Getulino*, 21 October 1923.

44. "Dr. Robert S. Abbott," *Jornal do Commercio*, 11 May 1923, n.p., in Maço (bundle) 9691/92 (629), AHI (Arquivo Histórico Itamaraty). Italicized words in English in the

original. The extra zeroes reflect the notation conventions of the currency in use in Brazil at that time, the milreis. A million thanks to Jeff Lesser for so generously sharing this AHI material with me.

45. Hellwig, *African-American Reflections;* anonymous to Booker T. Washington, 28 November 1906, enclosed in Booker T. Washington to S. L. Williams, 3 December 1906, Booker T. Washington Papers, vol. 9 (1906–08), 148–9. ALSr Con. 34 BTW Papers DLC. The "suggestion" this writer claims to offer is more of a threat than a collaboration.

46. Dante Moreira Leite, *O Caráter Nacional Brasileiro: História de uma Ideologia,* 5a. ed. (São Paulo: Editora Ática, [1954, 1968] 1992), 219, citing Raymundo Nina Rodrigues, *Os africanos no Brasil* (1905), 17–18.

47. Nina Rodrigues, *Os africanos no Brasil,* 6th ed. (Brasilia and São Paulo: Companhia Editora Nacional, 1982), 9.

48. Nina Rodrigues's other work bears these stresses, similarly. See Raymundo Nina Rodrigues, *L'animisme Fétichiste de Nègres de Bahia* (Bahia: Brésil Reis, 1900) or Gilberto Freyre, Rodrigues de Carvalho, and the Congresso Afro-Brasileiro, ed., *Novos Estudos Afro-Brasileiros Segundo Tomo: Trabalhos Apresentados ao 1. Congreso Afro-Brasileiro do Recife,* 2 vols., vol. 2 (Rio de Janeiro: Civilização Brasileira, 1937).

49. Skidmore, *Black into White;* Nancy Stepan, *"The Hour of Eugenics": Race, Gender, and Nation in Latin America* (Ithaca, N.Y.: Cornell University Press, 1991).

50. Andrade Bezerra et al., Congresso Nacional, *Annaes da Camera dos Deputados,* 1921, vol. 6 (20–30 July) (Rio de Janeiro: Imprensa Nacional, 1923), 623–35; Fidelis Reis, *Paiz a Organizar* (Rio de Janeiro: Typ. A Gloria, 1924).

51. Adriano de Souza Quartin, "Emigração de Negros Para o Brasil," instructions to consulates, n.d., c. 1929 (Maço 9691/92, AHI).

52. Bezerra (reading the *Correio da Manhã* article and Aquino's telegram) in *Annaes da Camera dos Deputados,* 1921, vol. 6 (29 July), 623.

53. Quartin, "Emigração . . ."; NAACP to Helio Lobo, in Lobo to José Manoel de Azevedo Marques, Ministro de Estado das Relações Exteriores, 19 April 1922 (Maço 9691/92, AHI); Jeffrey H. Lesser, "Are African-Americans African or American? Brazilian Immigration Policy in the 1920s," *Review of Latin American Studies* 4, no. 1–2 (1991): 115–37; Teresa Meade and Gregory Alonso Pirio, "In Search of the Afro-American 'Eldorado': Attempts by North American Blacks to Enter Brazil in the 1920s," *Luso-Brazilian Review* 25, no. 1 (1988): 85–110; Hellwig, "A New Frontier"; Hellwig, "Racial Paradise or Run-Around?"; and Skidmore, *Black into White.*

54. For other iterations of this point, see Michael Mitchell, "Racial Consciousness and the Political Attitudes and Behavior of Blacks in São Paulo, Brazil" (Ph. D. diss., Indiana University, 1977), 122–23; Richard Graham, "Economics or Culture? The Development of the U.S. South and Brazil in the Days of Slavery," in Shearer Davis Bowman and Kees Gispen, *What Made the South Different?: Essays and Comments,* (Jackson: University Press of Mississippi, 1990), 97–124; Richard Graham, "Free African Brazilians and the State in Slavery Times," in Hanchard, *Racial Politics in Con-*

temporary Brazil, 30–58; Jerry Dávila, "Expanding Perspectives on Race in Brazil," *Latin American Research Review* 35, no. 3 (2000): 188–98; Anthony W. Marx, "Race-Making and the Nation-State," *World Politics* 48, no. 2 (1996): 180–208; and Anthony W. Marx, *Making Race and Nation: A Comparison of South Africa, the United States, and Brazil* (Cambridge & New York: Cambridge University Press, 1998).

55. Quartin, "Emigração de Negros," 2.

56. A. Alves de Fonseca, "Informão" 11 June 1921 (Maço 9691/92, AHI).

57. NAACP to Helio Lobo, in Lobo to Ministro de Estado das Relações Exteriores, 19 April 1922 (Maço 9691/92, AHI).

58. Quoted in Representative Henry R. Rathbone (Ill.) to Frank B. Kellogg (Secretary of State), 11 May 1928, M519 roll 15: 832.111, NA; see also Quartin, "Emigração . . ."

59. "Effeitos da visita do sr. Abott ao Brasil. Os negros americanos pretendem provocar uma intervenção diplomatica para forçar o governo brasileiro a permitir a sua entrada e fixação em territorios nacionaes. As surpezas que offerecem as attitudes de nossos autoridades consulares" (translated in text), *A Patria,* 21 July 1923, n.p., in Maço 9691/92 (629), AHI.

60. "A immigração dos negros," *O Paiz,* 11 May 1923, n.p.; in Maço 9691/92 (629), AHI. See also "Effeitos da visita do sr. Abott ao Brasil . . ."; "Dr. Robert S. Abott," *Jornal do Commercio,* 11 May 1923, n.p., both in Maço 9691/92 (629), AHI.

61. Fonseca, "Informão," 3.

62. *Getulino,* 19 August 1923; "*leader*" in English in the original.

63. On the concept of "the cordial man," associated with Sérgio Buarque de Hollanda, see the *Revista do Brasil* Ano 3 no 6/87, org. Francisco de Assis Barbosa (Número Especial Dedicado a Sérgio Buarque de Hollanda).

64. "A mais santa e significativa fraternidade" and "importações sociaes da America Irmã" in Gervasio Moraes [N.B.: 'de' is absent here; I follow the paper's naming practice despite its apparent inconsistency], "A inquisição moderna," *Clarim,* 14 November 1926, 2. Moraes wrote this article three years after Abbott's departure, interestingly, after *Clarim* had begun the exchange with the *Defender* in which Leite found such reason for pride. It prompts me to wonder what specific reminder of Abbott might have sparked this rant. Perhaps another missive fired off to the ambassador?

65. *Getulino,* 19 August 1923.

66. Ottley, *Lonely Warrior,* 234.

67. Horacio da Cunha, "Os homens pretos e a instrucção," Clarim da Alvorada, 27 December 1925, 3. Agreeing, José Correia Leite claimed the achievements of "our racial brothers" (*nossos irmãos de raça*) "fills us with enthusiasm" in "E, apoz A Liberdade . . .," *Clarim,* 30 August 1925. Further Afro-Brazilian admiration for African American achievement (especially schools) is expressed in: "Os Pretos em São Paulo," *O Kosmos,* 16 November 1924, 2 (reprinted in Benedicto Florencio's piece in Getulino, 28 September 1924); "Os homens pretos e a Instrucção," *Progresso,* 23 June 1928; "Associação Nacional Para o Adiantamento da Raça Negra," *Progresso,* 31 August

1929, 4; *Progresso,* 24 March 1929. Booker Washington Theophilo, whose name itself bespeaks his parents' (and perhaps his own) identification with and admiration for the notable North American educator, described the African American milieu in 1925 as "the most advanced sphere of our race [*nossa raça*]" in a series of articles (which, interestingly, suggest that he studied at Williams College): "Negro!" *Clarim,* 27 September 1925, 3, continued in 15 November 1925 and 21 March 1926. In 1923, Abbott recounted his meeting with an Afro-Brazilian minister's son, Booker T. Washington de Castro. Was this the same person, and was he Olympio de Castro's son? If so, it is another point of entry for Abbott into the world of the São Paulo black press, and another point of contact between Afro-Brazilian groups in Rio de Janeiro and São Paulo. Abbott, "My Trip Through South America. Article 3—São Paulo."

68. "Josephina Backer, a condessa bailarinha, depois de reclamar no Velho Mundo a attenção para os *Pretos,* veio á America . . .," *Progresso,* 28 April 1929; "Occaso de um astro . . .," *Progresso,* 23 June 1929, 4; "Astro Negro," *Progresso,* 31 October 1929; "Uma trinca de . . . *Negros,*" *Progresso,* 24 November 1929, 6; "Separando o Joio do Trigo," *Progresso,* 24 November 1929, 5.

69. "A Formula Igualitaria Para Resolver a Questão Racial Americana."

70. Anon., "Associação Nacional Para o Adiantamento da Raça Negra," *Progresso,* 31 August 1929, 4.

71. They were following the leads provided by Diaspora Studies scholars such as Franz Fanon, Elsa Barkeley Brown, Evelyn Brooks Higgenbotham, and others who have forced a retheorization of identity and subjectivity throughout the academy.

6

An African American "Mother of the Nation"

Madie Hall Xuma in South Africa, 1940–1963

IRIS BERGER

In May 1940, a smartly dressed African American woman disembarked at Cape Town Harbour. The war in Europe had postponed her trip to South Africa and her upcoming marriage to A. B. Xuma, a highly respected physician who was soon to become president of the African National Congress. Then in her mid-forties, Madie Beatrice Hall knew little about South Africa and had scarcely met her prospective husband. She was also unaware that she was arriving in a country on the cusp of dramatic political transformation. Just as Afrikaner nationalists were laying the groundwork for a more systematized form of racism under the banner of apartheid, a new generation of Africans was beginning to formulate a militant challenge to the cautious moderation of its elders. As these opposing forces moved to the center of politics in the 1940s and 50s, they would, in different ways, create complex challenges for Hall as she sought to carve out a useful life in South Africa over the next twenty-three years.

Both Hall and her prospective husband came from unusually privileged circumstances. She had lived much of her life in Winston-Salem, North Carolina, where her father and brother were both physicians.[1] With normal school training from Shaw University, a BS degree from Teachers College in Winston-Salem, and an MA from Columbia University Teachers College, her education and family background placed her among the upper echelons of southern black women.[2] A. B. Xuma had spent thirteen years studying in the United States, primarily at Tuskegee Institute and the University of Minnesota.

Northwestern University awarded him a medical degree in 1926. Describing the sense of distinctiveness Xuma shared with many Africans who had studied abroad, historian James Campbell depicts him as "thoroughly African Americanized" in his institutional affiliations, speech, dress, and demeanor.[3]

Extremely lonely after his first wife, an Americo-Liberian, died in childbirth, Xuma resolved to find an African American bride. After enlisting the advice of friends who provided information on the personal and professional qualities and accomplishments of potential spouses, he organized an American "study holiday" in May 1937 to further his quest for a modern arranged marriage. His itinerary included International House at Columbia University where Hall resided. Discussing their courtship and marriage, Xuma's autobiography relates, "I must have played on her heartstrings because she is here in South Africa now even if the decision took place over a year after."[4] After noting that they married, he reveals little more about her or about their life together, adding simply, "She has been a devoted mother to our two children, an indispensable companion and devoted wife."[5]

By reducing Hall's life in South Africa to her roles as mother and wife, Xuma dramatically distorts a legacy that stretched far beyond her family responsibilities. By the time she left the country following her husband's death, Madie Hall Xuma had become a major community figure and a revered symbol of black achievement and pride. She had helped to revitalize the moribund Women's League of the African National Congress[6] and launched the Zenzele clubs, an influential network of women's organizations, eventually linked to the international YWCA, which provided African women with new opportunities for leadership and service. Her public presence made her an iconic figure to whom some admirers granted the honorary title (later bestowed on Winnie Mandela) of "mother of the nation." Like the black missionary women from the United States who preceded her in the 1920s and 30s, Hall embodied and promoted a powerful combination of Victorian womanhood, Christian devotion, and "American Negro" modernity.[7]

Evaluating Hall's accomplishments during her twenty-three years in South Africa is complex, however. Some contemporaries and historians have dismissed the Zenzele clubs for their domestic, apolitical orientation. While this judgment is not inaccurate, it fails to take into account that these clubs were linked to a profoundly political philosophy of African American advancement and racial uplift, which Hall emphasized repeatedly in public addresses and presentations during the 1940s. Hall also believed adamantly in women's rights, perceiving herself and her American compatriots as having "more advanced" attitudes toward women than South Africans. By the 1950s, however, women's politics were defined and validated primarily by their association with broader political struggles against apartheid; ideas of racial uplift had become an anachronistic survival of an earlier age. Furthermore, unlike some of the other African Americans discussed in this volume, Hall did not go to South Africa with the intention of seeking or affirming her African identity, but with the missionary ethos of helping the less fortunate. Nonetheless, through the organizations Hall founded and led and that have endured and adapted to changing conditions, her legacy to South Africa remains alive.[8]

Among the black women of her generation, Madie Hall shared many attributes with the South African social worker and activist Sibusiswe Makhanya. Born in the same year, 1894, Makhanya and Hall both attended Columbia University Teachers College and came from confident, close-knit families that raised them to feel pride in their heritage and self-confident in dealing with whites. Both women were committed to community uplift, emphasizing domesticity and welfare over political activism, and the two shared a strong belief in liberating women through education. The activities of the Bantu Youth League, which Makhanya founded, were remarkably similar to those of the YWCA groups that Hall initiated in Winston-Salem and South Africa. There was a difference in their personalities, however. Makhanya, in many ways a rebel since childhood, deliberately chose not to marry in order to carry on her work. While Hall might have remained single without Xuma's persistence, she was also more conventional; eventually he persuaded her to become his wife and launch a new life in South Africa.[9]

Anticipating South Africa

The most personal and detailed picture of Madie Hall's career emerges from the letters she wrote to A. B. Xuma from 1938 to 1940.[10] Despite this, Hall already had a life of accomplishments before meeting Xuma. She was educated at Slater State Normal School and Shaw University, where, disappointing her parents, she left with her classmates after a two-year teachers' training course and taught second grade at the Woodland Avenue School in Winston-Salem for five years.[11] Sent to Miami to heal after the flu epidemic of 1918, Hall met the prominent, pioneering black educator Mary McLeod Bethune, who invited her to teach piano at the school she had founded in Daytona, the Literary and Industrial School for Training Negro Girls. Bethune, an outspoken figure in the YWCA and founder of the National Council of Negro Women, became an important influence in Hall's life.[12]

Upon her return from Florida, Hall resumed the association with the YWCA that was to shape the rest of her life. She went first to Lynchburg, Virginia, as a social worker; when the white secretary at the YWCA in Winston-Salem (which Hall had helped to establish during her college years at Shaw) asked her to return as the secretary there, Hall did so. After they hired a trained secretary the following year, Hall went back to teaching, but continued to organize programs for school girls every afternoon. She also supervised adult night school classes in three counties of North Carolina under the Roosevelt administration[13] and organized a state federation of garden clubs. Before her father died in an automobile accident in 1935, he arranged for Hall to attend Columbia University to get her master's degree in education. It was here that she met A. B. Xuma, an encounter that would change her life.

Hall's letters to Xuma outline a world of professional accomplishment, warm relationships with her family, and a dense network of personal and organizational connections with other well-educated African Americans. She shared with other members of this group an intense concern with personal and racial progress and self-improvement, especially through education. Hall comes across in this correspondence as a dignified, strong-minded, independent woman, but someone relatively restrained in expressing her emotions. In making her eventual decision to go to South Africa, she seems drawn less by passion for a prospective husband whom she scarcely knew than by curiosity, a sense of adventure, and the idea that she could somehow be of service in her new home.

Hall's notions of service to Africans came from the long history of African American contacts with the continent, particularly through her membership in the African Methodist Episcopal Church, which had sent a steady stream of funding and personnel to South Africa since 1894.[14] On a more personal level, her old friends Susie and Max Yergan, the sources of her introduction to Xuma, had recently returned from fifteen years in South Africa.[15] Based at the Native College at Fort Hare as a representative of the international YMCA, Max Yergan, became good friends with A. B. Xuma. Foreshadowing Madie Hall's activities, Susie Yergan helped to organize the Unity Home-Makers Club, one of many groups across the country affiliated with the Women's Home Improvement Association.[16]

Her interest in Africa notwithstanding, Hall's first response to Xuma's letter proposing marriage was decisive and negative, underscoring her commitment to her work and her determination to preserve an independent life. Learning of his intention to travel to the United States, she replied firmly on August 26, 1938,

> I would not [underlined three times] have you incur that expense to see me unless you came of your own accord. It would not be fair to you nor to my American friends (male) of whom I am particularly fond—especially one—and I am sure I could not give you all of my time. I thought in the beginning we were only to be casual friends. I would be interested in your work and you in mine. I am sure we could get along nicely in a platonic manner but as far as romance goes I am not particularly interested. . . . as I told you in my last letter, marriage doesn't enter into my mind yet. It may be a long time before I can consider such a thing. . . . *romantically* I am not interested in you but *platonically* I am. Now, since we understand we can enjoy a beautiful friendship that can and will bring to both of us true happiness.[17]

Despite these strong reservations, by March of the following year Hall had made up her mind to go to South Africa and was actively planning an autumn trip. Available letters fail to explain this change of heart, but a later interview explains that the decision as divinely inspired, a result of hearing God's voice as she prayed for guidance about whether to go.[18]

Preparations for the trip, however, caused Hall to reflect explicitly and forcefully about her concern to maintain her independence. "I was glad to know that there would be no desire of yours to prevent me from living my own life—I couldn't live any other way—for to be free mentally and otherwise is the greatest part of my personality. I have enjoyed comfort and independence—I have been happy and free all of my life—to cramp me now means death to me—but I do trust you and do feel that somehow I shall be happy there in So. Africa with you. I am willing to sacrifice, if the sacrifice is not too hard."[19]

The letter also underscores her commitment to education and personal growth and her desire to contribute to society. "I have had excellent chances to marry but somehow I never accepted, waiting I suppose for something that would make me very happy. I believe that time has come—my education is what I have wanted it to be—time has also brought many experiences along lines of accomplishments etc. I really think the time is ripe for me to marry—If you think sincerely and definitely that I can serve there and that I, too can grow personally, I am willing to accept."[20] By May 5, Hall had resigned her position teaching first grade, relating, "I have definitely decided to cast my lot with you. Maybe I can be of some [underlined five times] service there."[21]

Although most of the letters are relatively restrained for someone on the verge of marriage, Hall's intense emotional involvement with Xuma leaps from the page on July 15, 1939 when she has not heard from him for some time. She writes with alarm, "I am wondering what on earth can be the matter. It was in June when I heard from you last. I have thought all kinds of things. Are you ill—the children—has something gone wrong? Tell, me, the suspense is too great!"

Her only other possible explanation is that Susie Yergan may have led Xuma to doubt the wisdom of marrying her. This suspicion reflected Hall's ambivalent feelings about Yergan, whom she mentions frequently in her letters. Describing an earlier opportunity to travel to South Africa on an exchange program, she relates, "I volunteered to go—she raised objections. I wonder now why! In my letter from her she has prefaced her 'go forward' with a negation. Is it possible that she does not want any other star to shine as brightly as the '*Yergans*'? She seems to think I will not like it in Africa. She did. *Why can't I.*" Hall then begs Xuma's forgiveness for writing these things, "but I can't understand your silence—when I'm just eating my heart out to know *what's ailing thee!* Please! Please! Please! let me hear from you real soon."[22] While the postal service rather than Xuma was responsible for this temporary interruption in communication, the letter conveys an emotional urgency absent in most of their correspondence.

Despite her obvious eagerness to depart for South Africa, Hall's basic optimism comes across in her reaction to an unexpected delay. Although she was scheduled to sail on October 5, 1939, the outbreak of war in Europe forced her to postpone the trip indefinitely. She responded to the wait and to her disappointment and loneliness with stoicism: "Things could be worse. We must accept situations and march bravely on. Something will work out someday, somehow."[23] To pass the time and to develop new professional skills that might be useful in South Africa, Hall took Xuma's suggestion and applied to study social work at Atlanta University, which had the first such program at a historically black institution.

In the course of her studies in Atlanta, where she met W. E. B. Du Bois (who was teaching there), Hall began to glimpse the meaning of poverty and racial domination in South Africa. Having come across the journal *Africa* in the library, she expressed shock at the extreme deprivation of the black community there. "I was quite concerned about native affairs in and around Johannesburg. Is it true that you people are on reservations 15 and 20 miles away from the city proper with no *sanitation, lights, water* and etc.? I thought you were on the outskirts of the city but within city limits like most of the southern towns in this country. I knew there were problems there but not to that extent."[24]

This passage suggests that, knowing little about South Africa, Hall imagined circumstances comparable to those in the United States. Reflecting on and responding to the differences she found would occupy much of her energy in South Africa, particularly during her early years there when she confidently assumed that her model of black American achievement could easily be transposed to her adopted country.

If conditions in South Africa surprised Hall, a letter she received several months later from Louise Ballan Gow must have startled her even more. Gow had lived in South Africa for fifteen years and was married to the prominent AME (African Methodist Evangelical) Reverend Dr. Francis H. Gow. Gow begins by cautioning Hall not to marry until she had looked around carefully to be sure she would like South Africa. Toward the letter's end, though, Gow finally tackles her real agenda: an alarming warning about Dr. Xuma. "Now I hope that you're a strong-willed self reliant girl who is able to stand up to a man—that's all—if you can do that then I'd say go, because Dr. Xuma is a fine young man, but a tyrant, an autocrat! There, it's out. We all know it."[25] Although no evidence remains of Hall's response to this unsolicited admonition, several of her letters to Xuma suggest that he, too, was receiving cautions about her—especially whether she would be an appropriate mother to his young children. "I glean from [your letter]," she wrote in September 1939, that "some of your friends are a bit afraid that I might mistreat your children."[26] In response, she reassures him of her love for children and her intense involvement in raising her sister's son. Given the anomaly in African society of a woman over forty who had never married, it is not surprising that his family and friends were questioning her suitability as a wife and mother. Some also objected to his marrying an American woman.[27]

In the end, neither of them heeded these warnings. Finally allowed to sail, Madie Hall reached Cape Town on May 17, 1940. She and Alfred B. (A. B.) Xuma married the following day and returned to Sophiatown, where he combined his medical practice with active community and political leadership. With her arrival in South Africa, Hall joined an exclusive group that included her husband, Sibusisiwe Makhanya, and early African National Congress (ANC) leader John Dube, all of whose experiences sustained and continually reshaped the close transatlantic ties between blacks in the United States and South Africa.

South Africa in the 1940s

Hall entered a country on the eve of momentous change. During World War II, African families flooded into the major cities as new jobs opened up for men and controls on population movement were loosened. With increasing numbers of black women in Johannesburg, family life became more settled. As the female population diversified, it was no longer possible to demonize all African women as prostitutes and beer brewers and to blame them for urban disorder as white officials had done in the 1920s and 30s. From among this "respectable" middle class of nurses, teachers, and housewives, Hall found women receptive to a new organization that encouraged them to develop a sense of pride, accomplishment, and self-assurance.

Demographic changes also contributed to shifts in political organization and attitudes. The ANC, founded in 1912 by a proud and respectable group of lawyers, ministers, chiefs and other recognized leaders, had survived nearly three decades as a cautious, moderate group of elite men. Their pleas for justice and their willingness to work as a coalition with liberal whites were met only with an increasing erosion of African rights. When Xuma was elected ANC president in 1940, he injected a new spirit of activism into the group. In seeking to strengthen its regional organization and to make it more responsive to a broader constituency, he prepared the ground for the upcoming "Youth League" generation of Nelson Mandela. This new group, which advocated aggressive though nonviolent mass action and rejected cooperation with whites, would oust him from leadership in 1949, a year after the National party came to power under the banner of apartheid. In assuming control of black politics, the Youth League was explicitly rejecting the politics of racial uplift shared by elite South Africans and African Americans of an earlier generation.

Connecting Two Worlds

During her twenty-three years in South Africa, the effort to forge connections between African Americans and Africans became a primary focus of Madie Hall Xuma's life. While she maintained close personal and professional ties in the United States through correspondence and travel, her speeches, interviews, and organizing made her a well-known figure in South Africa. A common theme motivated all these activities: a deep commitment to communicate to black South Africans what she perceived as the lessons of African American advancement and progress. In reply to a question in 1963 about why she had devoted her life to helping African women, Hall expressed a strong personal bond with them. "I regard them as my sisters. We share more or less the same background. It was my duty to share with them what we Americans know."[28] Thus, throughout her residence in South Africa, she never lost the attitude shared by her husband that African Americans had skills and understanding that could help Africans to "advance."

As a foreigner, however, Madie Hall Xuma was in an ambiguous position, straddling two worlds in a rapidly changing political environment. While widely admired and respected, she was also faulted for her aloofness and air of superiority; in addition, her light complexion set her apart from most Africans, who often treated her as colored.[29] Furthermore, many black South Africans resented the fact that Dr. Hall had married an American woman.[30] Following the advice of her husband, who clearly wanted his wife to be perceived as the African American that she was and not as a South African, Hall decided not to learn Xhosa, the language of Dr. Hall's people. (After a year, however, Hall mastered the click sound with which her married name began.)[31] Nonetheless, she made a memorable impression on South African social life. In a short story published long after Hall left South Africa, Mbulelo Mzamane's fictional character Mrs. Mazo represented Hall; excerpts accurately describe Hall's esteem in local society. "Mrs. Mazo brought her American graces with her. She became a social hit wherever she went and her ideas found very widespread support. . . . It was an honour to be invited to her house."[32]

Hall's attitude toward her position and towards Africa came from deep roots in African America history. W. E. B. Du Bois's influential argument that the "talented tenth" of college-educated blacks should assume leadership of the struggle for equality implied that cultural fertilization filtered down from the top to the masses of the people. In this view, racial leadership would come from those who had achieved educational, intellectual, and professional distinction. Extending the potential international reach of these elites, Du Bois also drew on nineteenth-century ideas that portrayed African Americans as the vanguard of the race as "technical experts, leaders of thought, and missionaries of culture for their backward brethren in the new Africa."[33] Madie Hall Xuma, with a master's degree from one of the most prominent universities in the country, fell squarely into the category of the "talented tenth." In 1940, only 1 percent of African Americans, male and female, had attended college for four or more years.[34]

Although emanating from America, elitist conceptions of progress were deeply rooted in South African culture thanks to the small but highly influential group of Africans, primarily men, who had studied in the United States during the preceding half century, many under the auspices of the AME church. In addition to Sibusisiwe Makhanya, the women among the talented tenth included A. B. Hall's exceptionally accomplished friend Charlotte Manye Maxeke, AME teacher, political activist, and social worker, and Eva Mahuma Morake, principal of the AME-affiliated Wilberforce Institute, who also assisted Xuma in his search for an American wife.[35]

As touchstones of progress, these American-educated Africans embodied not only elites to be emulated, but also a new transnational black identity that promised modernity linked to racial pride. In this transatlantic dialogue, black Americans became models of cultural sophistication and respectability, a people who had struggled to attain their freedom in part through political organizations such as the National Association for the Advancement of Colored People (NAACP) and, equally or more important, through education.[36] This "electrifying" narrative of a rapid rise from slavery to international acclaim in sports, arts, and education implicitly challenged white domination, proving that blacks were capable of running their own schools, hospitals, churches and businesses.[37]

Early in her marriage Hall devoted considerable energy to bringing this view of African American progress to her counterparts in South Africa. With reference to politics in the early 1940s, she held up the NAACP as a model for the African National Congress. According to historian Peter Walshe, "Not unnaturally she saw the South African scene almost entirely in terms of her American background, exhorting unity amongst congressmen, educational advance and economic self-help. The goal was to reach the 'promised land' in the same way as the Negro who was intent on acquiring 'the rights that are his as an American citizen.'"[38]

Hall found herself in a difficult position in moving to South Africa, however. As a foreigner, she sought to avoid direct political involvement and controversy.[39] But her marriage to a man who presided over the ANC until 1949 and who remained an active spokesperson for African rights made her a natural target of government reprisals.[40] Furthermore, although the women's clubs that Hall founded were not intended as political groups, her intention to "uplift" black South Africans by exposing them to the ideas and politics of their North American brethren was inherently subversive. Indeed, Walshe credits her influence with shaping the continued identification of the ANC with the civil rights movement in the United States.[41]

The ambiguities of Hall's situation were similar to those of other African American women in South Africa, who came to the country primarily as missionaries or as the wives of men in leadership positions. Writing of the period between 1920 and 1943, Amanda Kemp perceptively sums up these contradictions. While these black American women embodied many of the characteristics of idealized Victorian Christian wives and mothers, by their extensive travel, public leadership positions, and professional accomplishments, they defied traditional African ideas of wifely submission and obedience.[42] Although such independence among foreign women escaped local censure, African women such as Sibusisiwe Makhanya who led equally autonomous lives attracted criticism and resentment. Explaining why Makhanya never married, Shula Marks cites an interview with a family member: "You know amongst our people a woman has got to be very nice and humble. She wasn't. She was so outspoken. . . . [Young men say] 'I can't live with such a woman—she's a boss to me.'"[43]

Shortly after her arrival, Hall registered for an master's in social studies at the University of the Witwatersrand to further her understanding of South Africa. She also sought varied ways to bring the message of black American advancement to her new country. In a major undertaking, she produced a popular musical on African American life and shortly afterward, proposed a follow-up performance of *The Green Pastures,* a powerful parable of black liberation. During the 1940s when her husband presided over the ANC, she was a popular political speaker who continually voiced her ideas about African American progress. In an address to the Wilberforce Library Society, she presented an argument similar to that of later Africanists in South Africa: that the main tragedy of slavery lay in brainwashing blacks to believe in their own inferiority and to accept their servile status as a matter of course. Addressing such groups as the Bantu Nurses Association and the Daughters of Africa during her early months in Johannesburg, Hall also underscored the importance of women's collective activity.[44]

While Hall's speeches impressed Johannesburg audiences, she overwhelmed them with the theatrical production that she wrote, directed, and produced as a benefit for the ANC in 1943. She also acted the part of a washerwoman forced to abandon her baby on a creek bank when white men captured her. Entitled *American Negro Review: The Progress of a Race,* the musical was based on a performance staged in Winston-Salem, North Carolina, with a cast that included Marion Anderson. Hall's production, staged at the Bantu Men's Social Centre, drew an overflow crowd at its first performances on June 10 and 11. With hundreds of actors, the play used music and dance to dramatize a history of black advancement from slavery to freedom, culminating in achievements in science, politics, sports, and the arts. In five acts, the production reproduced precisely the narrative of black "progress" that elite members of America and South Africa shared. The play was so popular and attracted such enthusiastic audiences that numerous repeat performances were scheduled between June and December, raising over £200 for the ANC.

Advance publicity for *American Negro Review* emphasized the themes of black progress from slavery to freedom, highlighting the success that prominent black Americans had achieved by the twentieth century. The notices read, "After President Lincoln frees the slaves you will see the negro develop and taking advantage of the newborn freedom under the 'Stars and Stripes' until you get in [their areas] Marion Anderson, world premier contralto[;] the versatile Paul Robeson, sometime scholar, sportsman, and great actor and singer; Hattie Macdaniels, Actress; Joe Louis—world heavyweight champion; Professor George Washington Carver, famous botanical and Industrial Chemist."[45]

Following up on the resounding success of *Review,* Hall decided to continue her efforts to bring American drama to South Africa. She chose a play by Marc Connelly entitled *The Green Pastures,* which had run successfully on Broadway from 1930 to 1935. A less popular film version followed in 1936. Though greeted with mixed reviews by African American critics, the story had many elements that would have appealed to Hall and to black South African audiences. Based on a white southern fable of black life titled *Ol' Man Adam an' His Chillun,* Connelly transformed the original story into an empowering African American drama. Noah, Moses, Adam and Eve, Cain, Joshua, and most subversive of all, God, were black; they spoke their lines in rural southern dialect and interspersed their dialogue with renditions of popular spirituals. When a strong black Moses succeeded through his greater power in persuading an angry Pharaoh to "Let de Hebrew chillun go!," the political message rang clear.

This choice displayed an acute understanding of the parallels between South Africa in the early 1940s and the United States. In choosing a drama that "romanticized and memorialized the history of the rural black South that had been decimated by the northern black diaspora and, in disarming style, brought it to a broad national white audience for whom black life had been exotic,"[46] Hall understood precisely the extent to which the black South African exodus from the countryside during World War II represented a fissure with a rural past—although in South Africa that past had been deeply fractured through over a century of white conquest. By promising "the eventual carving of a black place in American society based upon individual dignity and merit,"[47] the drama spoke eloquently to the aspirations of black South Africans.

While the play's intent was less about explicit political action than about portraying black characters with strength and dignity, South African authorities correctly perceived the political implications of blacks appropriating Biblical legend. In December, 1943 Hall received her first indication that the South African state would act decisively to silence potentially subversive ideas: a letter from the Secretary of the Interior informing her that the work was unsuitable for presentation "as the play is calculated to give offence to the religious convictions or feelings of a section of the public."[48] As her first run-in with white authorities, this incident may have begun shaping her cautious attitude towards overt political confrontation.

In another apparently unsuccessful effort at making connections between African Americans and South Africans, Hall wrote and collected a group of stories about African children. Submitting them to the noted children's author Alice Dalgliesh, she explained that they were based on her two years of anthropological study "for the purpose of learning something of the traditions and customs of the African peoples in this country."[49] Reflecting the state of publishing in the United States at the time, Dalgliesh rejected the volume since she already had two books on her list about Africa; instead she offered the name of a New York literary agent.[50] There is no record that the book was ever published.

A lengthy 1944 speech in Bloemfontein to an African National Congress meeting once again forcefully emphasized Hall's message of black achievement to a receptive audience. She began by outlining the parallels between the children of Israel in Biblical times and African Americans, both taken from their homelands to a foreign land and purified and united through suffering. For African Americans, she argued, this separation was part of God's plan to place them in a "superior environment" where they would gain through exposure to civilizing influences and, through adversity, become a great spiritual force and a united nation. Here Hall reflected a prophetic Christian tradition that rejected the idea of black people as "cursed."[51] As in her dramatic production, she emphasized that after achieving freedom, African Americans developed an obsession for education as the key to producing a long line of successful professionals in banking, insurance, business, journalism, churches, and self-improvement associations.

Hall's intent was not simply to relate the history of black American success, but to convey a powerful message to her elite audience. Castigating the tendency of some of the most educated to separate themselves from the less fortunate, she chastised her listeners: "My friends to my sorrow I find that in this country some of the more fortunate people among our group who have had the opportunity for an education . . . draw off from the masses and become a class within themselves."[52] With this attitude, which she depicted as contrary to the scriptures, black South Africans would go nowhere as a race. "We cannot serve if we withdraw ourselves from the masses. We must give to them and share with them some of the things we have learned ourselves. Suppose I had taken that attitude—would I have been in Africa today. No."[53] She concluded her recitation of black American achievement with these words: "I bring this message to you as an incentive so that you may not despair of your continued disabilities and fetters that hang so heavily about you—but that you will gird up your loins and unite your people for action and press on."[54]

Although few records exist of Hall's other cultural and writing projects during the 1940s and 50s, at the time of her departure, she was writing a play about Africans brought to America as slaves, another reworking of the ideas she dramatized in her first theatrical production in South Africa.

The United States and South Africa: Mid-1950s

In the 1950s, the emphasis of Madie Hall Xuma's life changed as she withdrew from political visibility and became deeply involved in the international activities of the YWCA. With her husband no longer heading the most prominent black political organization in the country, her attention shifted completely to the Zenzele clubs and to the international women's networks of the YWCA, with which the clubs had affiliated. Furthermore, as apartheid began to disrupt and destroy the lives of black South Africans, her impressions of the stark contrast between the United States and South Africa intensified. While letters from her trips overseas depict a crowded schedule of parties, meetings, interviews, and conferences, at home in South Africa the government repeatedly harassed her by refusing to grant her permission to travel. Moreover, at a time when the policy of forced removals struck even affluent and influential blacks such as her husband, Hall portrayed African Americans as continuing to climb the ladder of upward mobility. Letters from her 1955 trip abroad, while underscoring her social and professional prominence in the United States and Europe and reinforcing her contrasting impressions of American and South African life and politics, also convey a sense of relief from the somber tone and the anxieties of South African life.

Hall's friends and relatives in the United States were intensely interested in South African politics. Commenting on this concern, she observed, "Politics gets worse by the day in South Africa. Everyone I meet knows and talks about the problems there. All seem deeply interested in them."[55] On May 25, 1955, she wrote to YWCA co-worker Margaret Hathaway, "So the Government goes merrily on. When they finally wake up—the Government and more especially the Nationalists' clique—it will find that most of the citizens will be against what it is doing."[56] Later in the month she wonders whether she should return directly to South Africa without stopping in Europe, noting her depression when she reads about the "goings on" there politically.[57]

Particularly distressing at this time, the government's policy of destroying selected black communities began to threaten the Xumas personally. As plans proceeded to uproot their home and Dr. Xuma's medical office in Sophiatown, Dr. Xuma again became a vocal and militant political leader in the unsuccessful campaign to stop the removal. Hall's advice to her husband on the question of moving his office reflects her strong religious outlook and the same optimism and stoicism she had expressed nearly twenty years earlier when wartime conditions threatened to derail her trip to South Africa. She wrote from the United States, "Now about establishing an office at Dube. You do what you think best. I believe the time for persecution of the Xumas has arrived. We'll take it gracefully, however & not panic. Somehow, I feel *God* [underlined twice in text] will work out everything in a just manner."[58]

By contrast with the personally threatening, repressive situation in South Africa, Hall perceived progress, prosperity, and optimism in the United States. She spoke glowingly of a "glorious" visit to the twenty-five-acre estate of friends in New Jersey,[59] and described enthusiastically a new black community in North Carolina: "My! Negroes are building beautiful Ranch houses here. Went to see two yesterday. One especially cost $65,000, not including the furnishings—one [sic] two acres of land. It is a show place in Durham."[60] Remarking on the active travel schedules of Americans, Hall wrote, "Americans are leaving for Europe & other places abroad by every means of transportation everyday—especially Negroes. Many conferences are being held in Europe by them."[61] Although she referred to "die-hards" in Winston-Salem who were obstructing integration by trying to construct two additional segregated high schools, she also expressed confidence that the NAACP would respond effectively.[62] In general, she felt that race relations had improved since the landmark Supreme Court decision on desegregation the previous year.[63]

As the threat of forced removals closed in on her own family, however, Hall grew more guarded in expressing opinions about South African politics in public. Reporting on a YWCA meeting outside London in August 1955, she related: "Every single reporter wanted to see me. We had to be very careful what we said to them."[64] This caution about political expression seemed deeply ingrained. When asked in 1963 why she was returning to the United States, she replied simply that her late husband had urged her to do so. The conversation continued, "Is it because of the racial atmosphere in South Africa?" She replied, "I have been in many embarassing [sic] situations, but I'd rather not talk about them." Asked if she had any plans to return to South Africa, she replied emphatically: "Definitely not South Africa."[65]

Uplifting Women

Madie Hall Xuma's attitudes regarding African Americans as more "advanced" role models for black South Africans also were at the root of her most enduring contributions to her host country: reviving the ANC Women's League and initiating the Zenzele clubs for African women. The name Zenzele, meaning "do it yourself," probably came from an already established women's movement on the eastern cape.[66] Like the founders of the black women's clubs in the United States at the turn of the century, Hall believed in the idea of the "talented tenth" who would turn their skills and talents to the betterment of the entire race. In a revealing examination of class attitudes, Mary Church Terrell, leader of the National Association of Colored Women (NACW), expressed these ideas frankly in explaining the club's motto "Lifting as We Climb." "In no way could we live up to such a sentiment than by coming into closer touch with the masses of our women. . . . Even though we wish to shun them, and hold ourselves entirely aloof from them, we cannot escape the consequences of their acts. So, that, if the call of duty were disregarded altogether, policy and self-preservation would demand that we go down among the lowly, the illiterate, and even the vicious to whom we are bound by the ties of race and sex, and put forth every possible effort to uplift and claim them."[67] By adopting the same motto for the Zenzele clubs in South Africa, Madie Hall Xuma was once again returning to her roots. Though much less explicit about her elitism than Terrell, the adage exemplified Hall's belief that "progress" was a dual process in which the individual achievement of the privileged would uplift the entire race.

But, perhaps more important an influence than the NACW was the YWCA, which had occupied much of Hall's adult life in the United States. During the time of her involvement from the early teens until the late 1930s, the number of black YWCA chapters in the United States expanded greatly, especially after World War I. Although all branches were segregated, interracial cooperation received an increasing emphasis from the early 1920s on. Sharing the elitism of the NACW, YWCA women emphasized mutual understanding between the "better classes" of each race, practicing a "politics of respectability" that would challenge racism by demonstrating that some African American wives and mothers also embodied the "white" values of morality, education, and culture.[68] In their emphasis on self-help, the YWCA also offered practical social services at a time when southern public institutions such as parks, schools, and recreational facilities were closed to blacks.[69]

In keeping with these ideas and trends, the black branch of the YWCA in Winston-Salem, which Hall helped to found as a student, was set up in a converted garage to provide recreational, educational, and social services along the same lines as those for whites. By the 1920s and 30s the YWCA had become a focus of black community activities with an estimated thirty-eight organizations using the building, including the Horton Branch of the Carnegie Library, the only such facility for blacks in Winston-Salem. As elsewhere in the United States at the time, the city's YWCA emphasized partnership across racial lines without challenging segregation or white domination of the organization. During the 1920s, interracial board meetings were held in the homes of the white members, and white women served on boards of the black branch. A 1931 lecture, "A Study of the Interracial Problem," indicates that the Winston-Salem YWCA, like the national movement, was grappling with issues of race, though without serious thought of forming a single integrated organization.[70]

Sharing the ethos of the NACW and the YWCA, central to Hall's conception of progress were Western ideas of domestic refinement. She was not the first foreigner to espouse such notions. A century-long missionary effort to reformulate family and domestic life among African converts preceded her. Expressing alarm at what they saw as the moral failings of local family structure, foreign Christians early on extended their religious zeal to condemn polygyny, bridewealth, and rites of passage from childhood to adulthood. They also sought to clothe their converts in "proper" European clothing, to replace round lodgings with "orderly" square houses, and to reorder the "unnatural" division of work between women and men.[71] While creating an ambiguous legacy for African women, these efforts forged a powerful new vision of womanhood connected with "civilization" and "respectability." What Madie Hall Xuma added to these earlier versions of domesticity was a prestigious association with African American culture that subverted the connection between modernity and whiteness at a time when educated Africans were open to embracing new identities and to challenging the association of black urban women with immorality. Though forced to live in squalid townships, many African women were drawn to new ways of creating beauty and order within their homes.

In addition to launching Zenzele, Hall played a major role in revitalizing the Women's League of the African National Congress. Expressing surprise when she first arrived that the organization had no women's affiliate and that women could not be official members, she became the League's first President in 1943 and was elected to a second term in 1946. As President, she encouraged women to organize within the framework of the ANC, which was then engaged in efforts to build up local branches around the country.[72] When the militant Youth League ousted her husband from leadership in 1949, she, too, lost her position. In the 1950s, when African women clashed with the government over its intention to force them to carry passes, the League became the leading force in organizing mass protests among women. By this time, however, her husband's differences with the ANC and her own increasingly apolitical orientation distanced her from the group she had previously led.

Thus, the Zenzele clubs (with a strong domestic focus during the 1940s and a greater emphasis on social service after their affiliation with the international YWCA in the 1950s) formed the center of Hall's life in South Africa, creating the legacy most commonly attached to her name. A 1963 interview elaborates at greater length on how she perceived these domestic skills. "In the past twenty years there has been a wonderful change in African homes, despite the low income. The women can prepare meals and entertain with confidence and they often do so. High teas, morning teas, luncheons etc. are prepared by them and served beautifully. They have also learnt how to dress, with right colour combinations, and how to sit, stand and walk correctly. When buying furniture for their tiny homes, they choose carefully, giving attention to design and colour."[73] These clubs attempted both to further African women's independence and to give them new domestic skills and ideas. Perhaps most important in the long run is that through these accomplishments, women gained self-confidence, knowledge of how to run an organization and raise funds, and a new collective identity as sophisticated homemakers. Annual exhibits and competitions brought their achievements into a public, sometimes competitive forum.

Women's accounts of their activities best convey the meaning of this experience. In 1947, R. Msweli, a founding member, wrote from Sophiatown about the self-confidence these new skills engendered in her: "The development the Club has roused in me could be the following:—(i) It has improved me socially and mentally (ii) It has removed inferiority complex in my person (iii) It has taught me to work cooperatively (iv) It has enable [sic] me to depend on myself regarding home management."[74] One report of the Witbank Zenzele Club praised its founder, F. Ndimande, as a "gallant daughter of Africa" who "carried the toch [sic] of light so high up that other women saw in the Zenzele the way to ultimate independence"; the report went on to thank Mrs. Xuma for her faith "in the total independence of the womanhood of this continent."[75] The Germiston club adopted the motto "Only the best is good enough." Reflecting this emphasis, a speaker at one of the group's meetings praised club work for encouraging "self-help and self-reliance," and for giving members the opportunity to "find pleasure and take pride in being able to create something and turning out a success."[76]

At times, however, handiwork seemed to take precedence over all other concerns. Apologizing for their lack of craft projects during the year, the 1949 Annual Report from Roodeport promised to "give all the branches a very big surprise next year." In fact, the group was not entirely inactive. During this "quiet time," members worked with European women to raise funds for the Margaret Ballinger Home. They also sought to remedy such critical community problems as a water shortage in the area and ill-treatment in the local hospital.[77] The portrayal of these social and political interests as a lapse from good Zenzele citizenship speaks clearly about the narrow range of the group's concerns.

While Zenzele clubs emphasized domestic themes in the 1940s, Hall did not believe that this concentration restricted women to the home. Rather, she perceived these domestic accomplishments as the mark of modern womanhood and respectability. Hall's letter to A. B. Xuma before their marriage (quoted previously, in which she insisted on her lack of interest in marriage) displays a strong belief in her own need for independence. Furthermore, she considered herself to have more advanced views on women's place in society than most South Africans. In a 1952 *Drum* magazine interview on the topic "Is Women's Place in the Home?," Hall criticized such restriction. Seeing her home country as more "modern" than South Africa, she argued that in the United States women and men worked "on a 50–50 basis" and that couples commonly spent leisure time together. "People have remarked to me in this country, 'You're always with doctor!' Yes, I'm always with doctor. That's done in modern society all over the world."[78]

In a speech to the white National Council of Women in 1953, Hall again underscored her view of African American women as role models. *Bantu World* gave the following report of her position: "No race can rise if its womenfolk are left behind. Traditionally . . . African women had no equal rights with men, but were not oppressed. The change came about with the arrival of Europeans. The African woman came into urban areas for work, and she projected herself as an individual. She qualified as a teacher, social worker and a nurse. African women are awakening and following the steps of their Afro-American people who have advanced."[79] In Hall's eyes, domesticity did not restrict women to household chores, but rather allowed them to enhance their lives and those of their families and friends by adding new skills and expertise to the tasks they already performed. To her, these skills were markers of class and culture that she shared with South African women, thereby "lifting" them to her own level of refinement. While the tone of this approach reflects the elitist attitudes of an earlier age rather than the militant ideologies of nationalism and self-determination that dominated political discourse by the late 1940s, Hall's emphasis on women gaining self-confidence and independence also connects her to a later era of gender politics.[80]

From Domesticity to Social Service

During the 1940s, Zenzele remained a small, exclusive movement. By 1950, the entire organization comprised only ten clubs, all in the Johannesburg area.[81] Most women viewed Zenzele as "a select society," "only for the upper classes," and for "high-flown people" who aspired to be "swanky." Explaining the reasons for this reputation, some argued that Hall "simply could not come down to the level of the African women," although others contended that she was trying to fight against elitism. Mia Brandel, however, the researcher who collected these impressions, added another reaction to Hall: "simple folks are afraid to receive her in their homes," fearful that she would see "how poorly [they are] furnished."[82]

In October 1951, however, a transformation began. Zenzele became affiliated with the World YWCA, initiating an expansive new phase in the organization's development. The local South African YWCA remained a segregated organization that resisted any effort to expand its membership across racial lines.[83] But with organizational and financial backing from the international body, the possibilities for launching more democratic and socially oriented women's groups could be realized. The moment was opportune, since widespread efforts during the 1940s, initiated by white liberals, had generated a training school for African social workers in Johannesburg and a growing network of community centers in black townships.

With a full-time staff person assigned to South Africa, Zenzele YWCA groups spread quickly through Natal, Zululand, and the Orange Free State in the early 1950s. Acknowledging the growing popularity of the clubs by 1954, an African employee of the Department of Bantu Education lauded Hall as "the mother of Africa," responsible for a "renaissance" among African women.[84] By 1954, the clubs had added new programs, deepened their purpose, and widened their scope. As new leaders emerged, youth programs and leadership training programs were developed and membership expanded to include colored women. Perhaps most importantly, Zenzele was shedding its primarily domestic concentration. "For one woman it may mean advising Youth Clubs; for another, teaching adult education classes; for another, leading a 'young couples' club; for others it may mean serving the community in other ways."[85]

Even after professional leaders were hired, Hall remained the general adviser to local Zenzele groups. Mia Brandel's contemporary account describes her as "the women's chief guide, instructor and friend," advising on how to conduct meetings, administer funds and keep minute books. "In her," Brandel adds, "the YWCA have found that rare treasure—a voluntary worker doing a professional job. . . . She has infinite tact and tremendous patience. Minor squabbles are brushed over lightly, major ones are remedied. She is kind-hearted, untiring and inaffected [sic], and obviously enjoys it all hugely. . . . Her prestige is immense. She is 'the first lady of the land.'"[86]

In addition to spatial expansion and professionalization, affiliation with the YWCA brought a newly articulated Christian overlay to the organization. The 1956 Annual Report had a different tone than reports during the 1940s, declaring: "The Purpose of the Association is to build a fellowship of women and girls devoted to the task of practising the principles of Christian living in all aspects of individual and community life. It aims to provide opportunities for the development of new interests and skills, constructive recreation, and acceptance of responsibilities in the community."[87]

This affiliation opened new opportunities for women to rise in a structured multiracial environment that placed strong emphasis on training female leaders. According to Hall, "One important job that Zenzele has been doing all along has been to train women to speak and become leaders of the community." Her interviewer adds that the Zenzele YWCA "has helped some of South Africa's most famous women on their way to the top," in part by creating opportunities for studying and working in the United States, England, and other parts of Africa.[88] Phyllis Mzaidume's successor as Transvaal General Secretary, Ellen Kuzwayo, was educated as a social worker at the Jan Hofmeyr School and elected to parliament in 1994. She became one of the most outspoken and accomplished members of her generation.[89] A career in the YWCA helped prepare Joyce Seroke to chair the Gender Commission created by South Africa's first democratic government.

YWCA affiliation also furthered Hall's interest in forging new connections between South Africa and the United States and between black and white women. During her 1955 trip to the United States, Hall reported to Margaret Hathaway on a model convention at the local YWCAs in Winston-Salem and New York. "I spoke for South Africa at both meetings. Many of the white girls told me I spoke so convincingly they were wondering if they too could not go to South Africa and give service."[90] Her language is interesting here, indicating that she conceptualized her work in South Africa in much the same way she had in the late 1930s—as "giving service." The letter continues: "I am so glad you are seeing some light in P.E. [Port Elizabeth] both for the Europeans and

Non-Europeans. I cannot tell you how happy I am over the progress of the work in South Africa looking at it from this angle. We have made genuine and steady progress throughout the years and I also believe the YWCA is filling a need in the lives of the African people. It makes me very happy indeed."[91]

With full-time staff, growing infrastructure and international support by the time Hall left the country in 1963, the clubs had blossomed into a national organization. Branches existed throughout South Africa and extended into Botswana (then Bechuanaland), Swaziland and Central Africa. Many African women had been trained in leadership skills, both in South Africa and overseas, and new Zenzele buildings were being planned around the country as the clubs took a greater interest in broad issues of social welfare and community organization. Through the Zenzele YWCA movement, large numbers of African professionals and volunteers assumed the "social housekeeping" positions that white women had dominated a generation earlier. Ellen Kuzwayo confirms this interpretation of a change in focus.

Kuzwayo states, "It was during this period in the life of the black communities in South Africa, when YWCA clubs were in operation, that a foundation of community-minded commitment was laid. Hitherto the women's groups or organizations outside the churches or political settings were focused much more on individual gain than on community development where community people work towards improving their surroundings and neighbourhood."[92]

With a similar emphasis, organizers of the campaign to construct a community center in Bloemfontein for young African women explained their goals: "By establishing a community centre we hope to decrease illegitimacy by providing facilities, such as sewing, domestic science, vocational guidance and religion and to keep young Bantu women, who leave school much too early, off the streets."[93] As Hall was preparing to leave South Africa, the new Zenzele Community Centre was under construction in the Soweto community of Dube as a monument to her. Built at a cost of R30,000 it was the first center of its kind in the country. The *Drum* reporter who interviewed her as she was preparing to leave observed, "The women of Zenzele called her 'Mummy.' As I left her, standing grey-haired and matronly I realised that that was what she was—'Mummy' to the new type of woman we are seeing in our townships now; 'Mummy' to the smart social workers and new feminine intelligentsia, who will take over the leadership from her."[94]

Assessing the Zenzele Clubs

While both her own remarks and the slogan Hall chose for the Zenzele clubs speak to the inspiration of black women's organizations in the United States, the strength of this influence raises questions about the initial exclusiveness and heavy domestic concentration of the Zenzele clubs. African American women's organizations such as National Association of Colored Women (the most prominent of the organizations) shared Hall's concerns with self-help and racial uplift, but their activities were hardly limited to the domestic sphere. Rather, these clubs sponsored a wide range of social welfare and community organizing activities seeking to help the needy, build and maintain public health clinics and hospitals, libraries, and settlement houses, and run orphanages, kindergartens, and homes for the elderly, working women, and unwed mothers.[95] By 1914, the National Association of Colored Women's Clubs claimed 50,000 members in over one thousand clubs. In addition to promoting individual and collective achievement and interracial understanding, the NACW articulated a broad range of goals: "To secure and enforce civil and political rights for ourselves and our group."[96] The YWCAs for which Hall had worked had a similarly broad, community-oriented focus. In short, they provided an infrastructure of social services more comparable to the South African YWCA in later years than to the original Zenzele clubs.

Hall's perceived elitism and the intimidating exclusiveness of the early clubs help to explain the narrowly domestic emphasis of Zenzele during the 1940s. In addition, as a newcomer to South Africa who spoke no African languages, Hall may have felt unable to mount a more ambitious effort on her own. Enlisting YWCA sponsorship in the 1950s enabled the Zenzele clubs to become more like their counterparts in the United States. The population of Johannesburg during the 1940s may provide another reason for this orientation. Although the number of educated black women in the United States was extremely small during the early twentieth century, the situation in South Africa was far worse. Even a high school diploma placed an African woman among into a small, elite category. Under these conditions, the number of women with the time and personal resources to organize a broader-based movement would have been extremely limited.

Conclusion

Part of a small group of African Americans who have lived in South Africa during the twentieth century, Madie Hall Xuma embodied the complexities and contradictions of this relationship and of the cultural and political transformations of the 1940s and 50s. She identified closely with South African blacks and their growing oppression under apartheid, and was married to a man whose political influence continued even after younger men displaced him in the ANC leadership. Yet she retained the early twentieth-century "missionary" attitude toward Africans as being in need of uplifting from those more "cultured" and more "advanced" than they were. Deeply committed to the NAACP as an organization fighting to expand the rights of African Americans, she identified herself as a foreigner in South Africa and, at least during the 1950s, hesitated to become directly involved in politics or even to take the risk of publicly criticizing the government. Fiercely protective of her right to live her own life and to travel freely for long periods, she founded a movement centered on domesticity at a time when household skills were often tied to women's subordination to their husbands. Finally, though personally privileged, Hall ended up leading two organizations that have had a long-lasting, popular influence.

By training a new generation of women leaders and creating the space for black women to assume control of community organizations long dominated by white volunteers and social workers, the Zenzele clubs became part of the more democratized and assertive spirit of the late 1950s and early 1960s. By that time, the creation of a distinct class identity was less important to younger urban women than it had been during the early 1940s. Following a long tradition of social welfare in South Africa, the younger Zenzele women devoted their energy as much to "lifting" others out of desperate circumstances as to individual "climbing." By acquiring leadership training under the auspices of the YWCA, many of them became role models of social and political engagement that went far beyond the cooking, embroidering, and flower arranging of the 1940s clubs. While standing apart from the protests against the pass laws that engaged women's political energies during the late 1950s and early 1960s, the YWCA movement in South Africa encouraged a new generation of women to become involved in their communities in ways that helped to nurture the locally based politics of the Black Consciousness era during the 1970s. By the late 1980s and early 1990s, as a new women's movement began to define its objectives, Madie Hall's words to her prospective husband expressing her desire to live her own life and "to be free mentally and otherwise" would have resonated as a sympathetic voice from the past.

Notes

I would like to thank Steven Gish for copies of his unpublished papers on A. B. Xuma, Lillian Williams for valuable conversations about African American women's history, and Ron Berger, Cheryl Johnson-Odim, and Modupe G. Labode for thoughtful critiques of earlier drafts of this article. In addition, Bob Edgar offered valuable suggestions and he and Robert Vinson have generously shared materials from the project on African-American Historical Linkages with South Africa. Funding from the Social Science Research Council and the Faculty Research Awards Program of the University at Albany is gratefully acknowledged. Thanks are also due to the *Journal of Southern African Studies*, which published an earlier version of this article. The journal is available at http://www.tandf.co.uk/journals/carfax/03057070.html (accessed December 10, 2008).

1. Her father was the city's first black doctor. Hall was accepted at the Howard University medical school at the same time as her brother was, but her father, whose female classmates faced difficult circumstances as doctors, refused to allow her to study medicine. See E.H. Wilson, *Hope and Dignity: Older Black Women of the South* (Philadelphia: Temple University Press, 1983), 144. I am indebted to Bob Edgar for bringing this source to my attention and for providing me with a transcript of Wilson's original interviews with Hall.

2. Because southern universities refused to integrate, talented students were sent north to pursue graduate degrees. Personal communication, Lillian Williams.

3. James T. Campbell, *Songs of Zion: The African Methodist Church in the United States and South Africa* (New York: Oxford University Press, 1995), 275–76. For a recent biography of A. B. Xuma, see Steven B. Gish, *Alfred B. Xuma: African American, South African* (New York: New York University Press, 2000). See also Richard D. Ralston, "American Episodes in the Making of an African Leader: A Case Study of Alfred B. Xuma (1893–1962)," *The International Journal of African Historical Studies* 6, no. 1 (1973): 72–93. The article includes interview material from M. H. Xuma on her husband's life.

4. A. B. Xuma, Untitled typescript autobiography. University of the Witwatersrand (UW), Box P, Folder 14, p. 37. See also Campbell, *Songs of Zion*, 276.

5. Typescript autobiography, 39.

6. For a discussion of women's earlier participation in the ANC, see F. Ginwala, "Women and the African National Congress, 1912–1943," *Agenda* 8 (1990): 77–93; and J. Kimble and E. Unterhalter, "'We Opened the Road for You, You Must Go Forward': ANC Women's Struggles, 1912–1982," *Feminist Review* 12 (1982): 11–35.

7. Amanda Kemp includes an excellent discussion of these women in her dissertation "'Up From Slavery' and Other Narratives: Black South African Performances of the American Negro (1920–1943)" (Ph.D. diss., Northwestern University, 1977), 140–63.

8. Interestingly, more recently, Hall's role as founder of the ANC Women's League has put her in the pantheon of "legendary women leaders," in the words of Pallo Jordan, South African Arts and Culture Minister, in a statement celebrating the historic women's anti-pass march of August 8, 1956. See www.southafrica.info/women/womensmarch50.htm. Leaving a contrary impression, a recent biography of Hall's friend Max Yergan, who provided the introduction to A. B. Xuma, depicts Hall as "an African-American socialite." See David Henry Anthony III, *Max Yergan: Race Man, Internationalist, Cold Warrior* (New York: NYU Press, 2006), 147.

9. Shula Marks, ed., *Not Either an Experimental Doll: The Separate Worlds of Three South African Women* (London: The Women's Press, 1987), 30–39, outlines Makhanya's life and accomplishments. Despite a letter to A. B. Xuma giving her birth date as 1900, all other evidence confirms Hall's birth in 1894.

10. These letters are part of the A. B. Xuma Collection in the William Cullen Library at the University of the Witwatersrand.

11. These details of her life come from an interview with Emily Wilson, Winston-Salem, May 28, 1980.

12. Bethune had been turned down when she applied to become a missionary in Africa; but whether she influenced Hall's decision to go to South Africa is unknown. She was among the strongest black voices against segregation and white domination in the southern chapters of the YWCA.

13. Bethune and many other black and white YWCA activists were active in implementing New Deal legislation. They were especially represented in the Works Progress Administration, the National Youth Administration, and the Women's Bureau, according to Nancy Marie Robertson, *Christian Sisterhood, Race Relations, and the YWCA, 1906–46* (Urbana and Chicago: University of Illinois Press, 2007), 144.

14. Campbell, *Songs of Zion,* discusses these contacts in great detail. See also Alan Gregor Cobley, *Class and Consciousness: The Black Petty Bourgeoisie in South Africa: 1924–1950* (New York: Greenwood Press, 1990), 117–29. Several times in her letters, Hall indicates that she had often wished to travel to Africa.

15. Yergan also had introduced Xuma to his first wife.

16. These clubs are discussed in "African Women's Self-Help: The Work of the Home Improvement Associations," *The South African Outlook* (May 1, 1940), 95–98, and Mrs. Max Yergan, "The Unity Home-Makers' Club," *The South African Outlook* (April 1, 1933), 78–79. Whether Madie Hall knew of Susie Yergan's activities and used them as a model, or whether Hall drew independently on her knowledge of black women's clubs in the United States is uncertain. After returning from South Africa, Susie Yergan returned to Shaw University as the Dean of Women. On Max Yergan, see Anthony, *Max Yergan;* David H. Anthony, "Max Yergan and South Africa: A Transatlantic Connection," in Sidney J. Lemelle and Robin D.G. Kelley, ed., *Imagining Home: Class, Culture and Nationalism in the African Diaspora* (London: Verso, 1994). Also see R. R. Edgar, *An American in South Africa: The Travel Notes of Ralph J. Bunche* (Athens: Ohio University Press, 1992), 338–39, for brief biographical sketches of Max and Susie Yergan. P. Ntantala presents a critical view of the Yergans in *A Life's Mosaic: The Autobiography of Phyllis Ntantala* (Berkeley and Los Angeles: University of California Press, 1992), 69–70.

17. UW, Letter from M.H. to Dear Alfred, August 26, 1938. ABX microfilm, Reel 6.

18. See Wilson, *Hope and Dignity,* 146–47.

19. UW, 21 April 1939, ABX.3904210.

20. Ibid.

21. UW, 5 May 1939, ABX.390505a.

22. UW, 15 July 1939, ABX.390715.

23. UW, 11 October 1939, ABX.391011.

24. UW, 11 November 1939, ABX.391117a.

25. UW, Letter from Louise Ballan Gow, 26 March 1940, ABX.400326.

26. UW, 22 September 1939, ABX.39022. See also UW, 19 June 1939, ABX.390619c.

27. Hall discussed the objections to her as an American in Wilson, *Hope and Dignity,* 147. Such concerns probably prompted her to misrepresent her age. Xuma had two children from his earlier marriage.

28. Jose, "Madie Hall Xuma," newspaper clipping (source unidentified).

29. Hall's light skin was the product of a white grandfather and great-grandfather and a half-white grandmother. She discusses this issue in Wilson, *Hope and Dignity,* 144, where she also notes on 148 that when she first arrived in South Africa, many colored people thought she would be working mainly with them. Her lack of knowledge of an African language probably contributed to this interpretation of her racial identity.

30. When Watson asked whether there was resentment of her, she replied pointedly, "Oh, Lord, yes." See Watson interview, 12. A June 4, 1980 article in the *Post* reinforces this point, noting that this chapter of her life "earned her the opprobrium of a few who believed the studious African doctor had no right to marry outside of his own people."

31. She explained in an interview, "Doctor said it was a waste of time for me to learn the [sic] speak it because they all spoke English," Watson interview, 10.

32. This story, "The Pioneer's Daughter," appears in Mbulelo Mzamane, *Mzala,* 2nd ed. (Randburg, South Africa: Raven Press, 1995). Additional details depicting Mrs. Mazo as the founder and first President of the YWCA make the association with Hall unmistakable. My thanks to Rob Nixon for bringing this source to my attention.

33. G. M. Frederickson, *Black Liberation: A Comparative History of Black Ideologies in the United States and South Africa* (New York: Oxford University Press, 1995), 109–10, 125, 151.

34. L. Gordon, "Black and White Visions of Welfare: Women's Welfare Activism, 1890–1945," in D. C. Hine, W. King, and L. Reed, ed., "*We Specialize in the Wholly Impossible*": *A Reader in Black Women's History* (Brooklyn: Carlson Publishing Co., 1995), 457.

35. Campbell's *Songs of Zion,* 282–94, presents an eloquent and insightful portrait of Maxeke. A. B. Xuma's pamphlet on her life, "Charlotte Manye (Mrs. Maxeke) or What an Educated African Girl Can Do," The Women's Parent Mite Missionary Society of the AME Church, 1930, celebrates her as the first black woman in South Africa to hold a college degree; Hall uses her story in part to argue for higher education for African women. The pamphlet includes a brief Foreword by W. E. B. Du Bois, Maxeke's teacher and friend at Wilberforce University.

36. This is a major theme of Campbell, *Songs of Zion.*

37. Recent works that explore in detail the "up from slavery" narrative and the power of "American Negro" ideologies in the construction of South African modernity include Kemp, "Up From Slavery"; Ntongela Masilela, "New Negroism and New Africanism: The Influence of United States Modernity on the Construction of South African Modernity," *Black Renaissance/Renaissance Noire* 2, no. 2 (Summer 1999): 47–59; and Cobley, *Class and Consciousness,* 117–29. Cobley argues that a fascination with black American achievements and freedom gripped African popular imagination in South Africa during the interwar decades.

38. P. Walshe, *The Rise of African Nationalism in South Africa: The African National Congress, 1912–1952* (Berkeley and Los Angeles: University of California Press, 1971), 340.

39. *Drum,* March 1963, 39.

40. These actions focused mainly on harassing her when she sought permission to travel outside South Africa.

41. Walshe, *African Nationalism,* 340.

42. In "Up From Slavery," 140–59, Kemp outlines these issues through the lives of Lucy Hughes, president of the AME-affiliated Women's Home and Foreign Missionary Society; and Charlotte Crogman Wright and Luella White, both married to prominent AME missionaries.

43. Marks, *Experimental Doll,* 39, citing a 1979 interview with H. M. S. Makhanya. Marks also alludes to resentment at Makhanya's sexual independence (54n117).

44. *Umteteli wa Bantu,* 2–3 November 1940.

45. Quoted from *Bantu World* and *Umteteli wa Bantu* in C. Ballantine, *Marabi Nights: Early South African Jazz and Vaudeville* (Johannesburg: Ravan Press, 1993), 52–53.

46. T. Cripps, "Introduction: A Monument to Lost Innocence," in M. Connelly, *The Green Pastures,* edited with an introduction by T. Cripps (Madison: University of Wisconsin Press, 1979), 12.

47. Ibid., 21.

48. UW, ABX.431221b.

49. UW, Letter of 11 July 1945, ABX.450711.

50. UW, Letter of 12 September 1945, ABX.450912.

51. My thanks to Modupe Ladobe for this insight.

52. UW, Notes, pp. 7–8. ABX microfilm, Reel 4.

53. UW, Notes, pp. 8–9.

54. UW, Notes, pp. 18–19.

55. UW, 28 May 1955, ABX.550528.

56. UW, 25 May 1955, ABX.550525.

57. UW, 25 June 1955, ABX.550625.

58. Ibid.

59. UW, 8 July 1955, ABX.550708.

60. UW, 28 May 1955, ABX.550528.

61. UW, 16 July 1955, ABX.550716.

62. UW, 25 May 1955, ABX.550525.

63. *Bantu World,* 1 October 1955.

64. UW, 26 August 1955, ABX.550826a.

65. Jose, "Madie Hall Xuma."

66. Florence Makiwane Jabavu founded a group called Zenzele in 1927 to teach domestic skills to rural women. Catherine Higgs refers to this organization in *The Ghost of Equality: The Public Lives of D.D.T. Jabavu of South Africa, 1885–1959* (Athens: Ohio University Press, 1997), 70. She adds that Susie Yergan's club was launched as a rival organization (214n182). Given the close political associations of Hall's and Jabavu's husbands, it is likely that Madie Hall Xuma knew of the earlier movement, although there is no direct evidence for this assertion; indeed she claimed in interviews that South African women did not know about clubs. Although Hall belonged to the Goler Memorial African Methodist Church in Winston-Salem, there is no evidence that she took part in AME women's associations in South Africa. A letter certifying her church membership in the United States is dated 1948, eight years after she had left home. See UW, ABX 480429.

67. A.F. Scott, *Natural Allies: Women's Associations in American History* (Urbana: University of Illinois Press, 1991), 147, quoting from B. Jones, "Mary Church Terrell and the National Association of Colored Women, 1896–1901," *Journal of Negro History* 67, no. 1 (Spring 1982): 28.

68. Robertson, *Christian Sisterhood,* 29. The notion of the "politics of respectability" comes from Evelyn Brooks Higginbotham, *Righteous Discontent: The Women's Movement in the Black Baptist Church, 1880–1920* (Cambridge, Mass.: Harvard University Press, 1993), chap. 7. Robertson quotes Lily Hammond, a white woman who wrote prolifically on race relations, as arguing that the "status of the Negro woman and Negro home in the minds of the privileged white women will determine the status of the race" (45–46).

69. Robertson, *Christian Sisterhood,* 7, 28.

70. Rick Mashburn, *Winston-Salem Sentinel,* n.d.

71. J. and J. L. Comaroff, "Home-Made Hegemony: Modernity, Domesticity, and Colonialism in South Africa," in K. T. Hansen (ed.), *African Encounters with Domesticity* (New Brunswick, N.J.: Rutgers University Press, 1992), 52–59.

72. She may have seen the Zenzele clubs as also having political potential. In a speech to the Daughters of Africa in 1942, Hall highlighted the achievements of the National Federation of Colored Women's Clubs in the United States as a collective organization recognized as black women's "political mouthpiece." Reported in *Umteteli wa Bantu,* 18 July 1942.

73. Jose, "Madie Hall Xuma."

74. UW, Letter dated 21 August 1947, ABX470821a.

75. UW, "Witbank Zenzele Club." ABX Box O, File 23.

76. UW, "Germiston Club Report," 1949, ABX.490000a.

77. UW, "Annual Report," 1949, ABX.490000b. The Margaret Ballinger Home in Roodeport, run by the European and African Association of Women, was a holiday convalescent home for children sent from clinics and hospitals.

78. *Drum,* September 1952.

79. *Bantu World,* 7 February 1953.

80. She would not, however, have shared later feminists' critique of the family or their emphasis on male domination; her concern was to stress a stronger sense of partnership between husbands and wives than she saw among her contemporaries in South Africa.

81. South African Institute of Race Relations (SAIRR), "Zenzele Women's Clubs." AD 1715.

82. SAIRR, Mia Brandel, "The Needs of African Women," Unpublished manuscript, 416. AD 1725.

83. Hall makes this point in *Hope and Dignity,* 147.

84. UW, Letter from D. P. Marolen to Dr. A. B. Xuma, 9 August 1954, ABX.540809. On July 30, 1955 *Bantu World* observed that new Zenzele YWCA clubs were starting all over the country.

85. Brandel, "African Women," 418.

86. Ibid., 415.

87. UW, "Zenzele Young Women's Christian Association of the Transvaal," Annual Report and Financial Statements, 1956, ABX.561231. There is no evidence from Zenzele documents that the clubs were affiliated with the YWCA from the beginning, contrary to claims in the recent history of the World YWCA.

88. Both quotes are from *Drum,* March 1963, 39.

89. Kuzwayo's autobiography, *Call Me Woman* (San Francisco: Spinsters Ink, 1985) includes an informative section on her work as Transvaal General Secretary.

90. UW, 25 May 1955, ABX.550525.

91. Ibid.

92. Kuzwayo, *Call Me Woman,* 167.

93. Unidentified clipping, 17 June 1964.

94. *Drum,* March 1963, 39–40.

95. S. J. Shaw, "Black Club Women and the Creation of the National Association of Colored Women," in Hine, King, and Reed, *Reader in Black Women's History,* 433–47.

96. Scott, *Natural Allies,* 147.

SECTION THREE

The Black Presence in the Pacific

7

The African Diaspora at the End of the World

CASSANDRA PYBUS

In 1912, police shot dead a young man in a remote mining hamlet in the Snowy Mountains of southeastern Australia. There was nothing really unusual about that, considering that at the inquest Thomas Conquit was described as part Aboriginal. He was shot while being arrested for lunacy, having declared he was on a mission to kill police who were part of a worldwide conspiracy to murder all black people.[1] That fact is what made this case unusual. The indigenous people of Australia trace their occupation of that continent back sixty thousand years or more. They do not see themselves as belonging to a worldwide black community.

The very distinctive name of Conquit makes it easy to trace the young man's connections through colonial records. His convict grandfather, Thomas Conquit, was transported from England to Australia in 1819 with a common-law wife named Frances Martin, who was described on his death certificate as Aboriginal. She was the daughter of John Martin, transported from England on the First Fleet in 1788, and Mary Randall, whose father and mother were also transported from England on the First Fleet. With these parents, Frances Martin could not possibly have been Aboriginal; but she *was* black. Her father, John Martin, and her grandfather, John Randall, were both African American. Her grandson correctly understood himself to belong to the African Diaspora, even if the authorities did not.

Randall and Martin were part of the cohort of eleven black convicts among the first party of convicts and marines that arrived in 1788 on the eastern coast of the barely charted southern land called New South Wales. These black convicts had all been sentenced in England to seven years "transportation beyond the seas": John Randall at the Manchester Quarter Sessions for stealing a watch chain; John Martin at the Old Bailey for stealing a bundle of clothing; Janel Gordon at Winchester for stealing clothing; James Williams at the Old Bailey for stealing clothing and shoes; John Coffin at Guildhall for stealing plates and some other things; John Williams at Kent Assizes for stealing a wooden cask of liquor, silver, clothes, etc.; Thomas Orford at the Old Bailey for stealing some items of clothing; Samuel Chinery at Exeter in Devon for stealing a linen shirt; George Francisco at the Old Bailey for stealing clothes from a man who allowed him to sleep in his shop; Caesar at the Kent Assizes for stealing twelve shillings; and John Moseley at the Old Bailey for impersonating a seaman to receive his wages.[2]

These men were illiterate. They provided no account of how they came to be in England and the detail of their defense was not recorded. The sparse, one-line entries in transportation indents provide few clues to their history. They had all been arrested in the period between 1782 and 1787, a time when the black population in England increased dramatically, especially in Greater London, where most were sentenced.[3] By 1785, the black population in that city was around ten thousand people and parish records indicate that the majority of that population was made of young men concentrated in parts of the East End, such as Stepney, Minories, Wapping, Shadwell, Limehouse, and Deptford.[4] It was the view of contemporary observers that this sudden influx of indigent black men, living by their wits and whatever they could steal, was a direct result of the American Revolution. Four or five thousand African Americans were fetched up in London in the aftermath of that war, nearly all of them runaway slaves who deserted their masters when promised their freedom by the British.

From the moment that hostilities commenced in the American colonies in 1775, enslaved men and women took to their heels with rhetoric about the inalienable rights of free people ringing about their ears, entrusting their aspirations for liberty not to their Patriot masters, but to the King's Men.[5] The British were happy to receive them and used these black recruits in many different ways. The army directly recruited runaways into regiments as soldiers or more commonly, as drummers and fifers and incorporated black recruits into a noncombat corps known as the Black Pioneers. Likewise, the Hessian regiments recruited African Americans as soldiers and musicians; some recruits were servants for officers in both Hessian and provincial regiments.[6] Even greater numbers served in the Royal Navy and aboard British privateers; as much as 10 percent of the massive British maritime force in America was black.[7] More important than any fighting role that African Americans performed and involving infinitely greater numbers were their jobs in the Barrack Master-General's, Quarter Master-General's, Wagon Master-General's, Commissioner-General's and Engineer's departments of the army. The British relied heavily on their workforce of runaways in British-occupied New York: black artisans worked on rebuilding projects and in the naval yards; black teamsters hauled provisions and collected firewood; black nurses and orderlies staffed the hospitals; black laundresses and needlewomen did the washing and sewing; black pilots guided the ships safely in and out of the port; black fiddlers and banjo players provided entertainment for balls and taverns; black jockeys rode the horses at the races; and black cooks, servants, and valets ensured the comfort of the elite. These workers were provisioned and usually paid for their services; they could be well paid if they had skills in demand, such as carpentry and piloting.[8]

The runaways who sought protection from the British were granted freedom by British proclamation, but to remain free once the conflict of the war had ended, they had to leave America and forge a problematic new life in far-flung corners of the British Empire. Between eight thousand and ten thousand black refugees were evacuated from America with the British in 1783, constituting a diaspora within a diaspora, with widespread distribution throughout the Atlantic world and beyond. The majority went to Nova Scotia and to England. Some were sent to the Bahamas, Jamaica, and St. Lucia, while a few hundred were fetched up in the unregulated territory of Mosquito Shore and the Bay of Honduras (present-day Guyana and Belize). Several dozen went as far as Germany. That some even made it to the end of the world, to the impossibly remote colony of New South Wales, indicates the complexity and scope of the diaspora created by the exigencies of war, imperial connections, and transnational processes of empire building.[9]

Few records document the hasty British evacuation of America, but one document, known as the Book of Negroes, lists three thousand African Americans removed by the British from New York in 1783. Among them was John Moseley, aged twenty-five, listed as being on the *Elijah* bound for Nova Scotia; but he never arrived there. I believe this was the same John Moseley tried at the Old Bailey in 1784 and transported to New South Wales. Locating him in this crucial document as well as having his unusually detailed court record allows the possibility of reconstructing his story as a window into the vicissitudes of the black struggle to find freedom in the Revolutionary Era.

In his account of himself in the Book of Negroes, Moseley said he "lived with John Cunningham, Portsmouth, Virginia as freeman; left him in 1776." His somewhat ambiguous claim not to have been a slave in Virginia must be read with caution, as Moseley provided no evidence of his emancipation. The only evidence of his free status, which allowed him to leave America, was a certificate from a British general at New York. Moseley may have been working in Portsmouth for John Cunningham, captain of an Irish ship and a regular visitor to the ports on the James River; but there is every reason to believe that Moseley was originally a runaway slave from a plantation. His name points to one of the grandest planters in the area, Edward Hack Moseley of Princess Anne County, the plantation located adjacent to Portsmouth.[10]

In July 1775, Edward Hack Moseley placed a notice several times over a period of a month for three runaway slaves between the ages of fifteen and eighteen that he named respectively Jack, Daniel, and Peter. Moseley was apparently unsuccessful in regaining his property. These were turbulent times in Virginia. The embattled royal governor, Lord Dunmore, had been forced to take refuge on a British warship on the James River, having enraged the rebellious colonists by announcing that any act against him would cause him to arm the slaves and give them freedom. Given that the planters of Virginia held some 180,000 people enslaved, to even hint at such a thing was truly shocking. Since Moseley was a friend of Lord Dunmore and had just been appointed royal lieutenant of Princess Anne County, his runaways probably did not make for the nearby British fleet. Rather, as Moseley suspected, they took refuge in either Portsmouth, Hampton, or Norfolk. The willingness of white artisans and tradespeople in these towns to shelter runaways rather than return them consistently angered planters. Fifteen-year-old Jack could well have gotten work with Captain John Cunningham, who had brought his ship, *Fanny,* into Portsmouth to mend a mast that had been damaged en route from Ireland.[11]

In November 1775, Dunmore carried out his threat and published a proclamation that he would free any slaves ready to bear arms for the king. He made no distinction between rebel and loyalist slaves. Dunmore's fleet of British schooners cruised up and down the river openly inciting slaves to come on board, spreading indignation and alarm throughout the tidewater. "Letters mention that slaves flock to him in abundance," the president of the Virginia Convention, Edmund Pendleton, wrote glumly to a friend.[12] Yet any stampede to the British was against huge odds. The danger was terribly real, and militating against irrevocable flight were the bonds of family from which the enslaved community drew its fortitude. By 1775, most enslaved people in the tidewater lived in families, certainly children with their mother and young siblings, and sometimes with their father, grandparents, aunts, uncles, and cousins. While the close-knit-kin networks of the tidewater did facilitate short-term runaways, by providing hospitality and shelter over a considerable distance, the bonds engendered were a powerful pull against making a decisive break from which there could be no return. Unless whole families ran away together—almost unheard of—a lifetime of separation from close kin was the consequence.[13]

Added to the psychological pressures of abandoning family was the fundamental difficulty of reaching Dunmore's fleet in the mouth of the James River. Enslaved people could only move about the country with signed passes, and plantation owners kept a close watch on their watercraft. Slave patrols were doubled throughout the region and armed militia were stationed along the Chesapeake shores. Savage penalties were imposed on anyone caught attempting to reach Dunmore. Notwithstanding the surveillance and intimidation, hundreds made the attempt. At the end of November, Dunmore could report "two and three hundred [runaways] already come in and these I form into a Corps as fast as they come. . . ." Those who got safely to Dunmore came mostly from Hampton, Norfolk, and Portsmouth, and were often maritime workers, especially pilots; others ran off with British forces when they cruised along the James River; still more absconded from plantations close to navigable waterways. They came on small crafts, and some came on foot, propelled by sheer willpower, swimming out to Dunmore's ships. Male recruits were sworn into a military unit called the Ethiopian Regiment, provided with weapons, and taught how to use them.[14]

Virginians were beside themselves with fury that slaves could be armed against them; their backlash against loyalist sympathizers was swift and savage. In late December, Edward Hack Moseley and his son were arrested and sent to Williamsburg to be examined by the Virginia Committee of Safety. John Cunningham also came under suspicion. His ship *Fanny*, loaded with British army provisions, was seized as a prize. Cunningham managed to persuade the Committee of Safety that he had been coerced into carrying supplies for the British and he was compensated for his loss of wages, even though his cargo was auctioned off. Soon after, he applied for permission to leave Virginia. This could have been the time that Moseley's young runaway, Jack, decided to throw in his lot with the King's Men. Eight years later John Moseley was twenty-five years old and working for the Wagon Master General's Department in New York.[15]

Although Edward Hack Moseley and his son were eventually granted parole, they were required to move at least thirty miles away from the shore, and to enforce submission, the Committee of Safety ordered the militia take their slaves. Here was both motivation and opportunity for the rest of Moseley's slaves to run off, including several young women with infant children and a grandmother in her mid-fifties, who took with her a husband and son from another plantation. They would have been terrified of being seized by the patriots and sent to work in the lead mines or sold away. The new government of Virginia was much in need of money and the sale of seized slaves was one way to raise it. They had already auctioned off eleven enslaved people whom Lord Dunmore had left behind at the governor's mansion in Williamsburg. Another eight seized slaves of defecting loyalists had been sent to work in the lead mines. An even more distressing prospect was that seized slaves could be sold to the West Indies, as was the intended fate of one of the Moseley runaways who was caught before he got to Dunmore. In May he was put aboard a ship to be transported to Antigua for sale.[16]

Dunmore believed he had created a formidable force in his Ethiopian Regiment, but he had not counted on the invasion of smallpox. While smallpox had been present in the colony at times before, there had never been any major outbreak and as a result, native-born whites and blacks had next to no immunity. When the disease first appeared in Dunmore's overcrowded flotilla, the British were largely immune, but disease hit the black recruits especially hard. They died by the hundreds. With advice from the naval surgeons, Dunmore moved his forces to a small island in Chesapeake Bay to inoculate the black recruits, but an influx of new recruits kept the contagion alive, wreaking havoc with Dunmore's military ambitions and killing off "a great many fine fellows." Dunmore reported that "there was not a ship in the fleet that did not throw one, two, three or more dead overboard every night." Virginians found diseased bodies drifting ashore on the tide the next day, as many as a dozen at a time. On the island, the dead were buried in shallow mass graves. Tragically, Dunmore continued to draw fresh black recruits at the rate of six to eight each day, most of whom succumbed to the disease as soon as they arrived. Moreover, those who recovered from the inoculation fell victim to an outbreak of typhoid fever that "carried off an incredible number of our people, especially the blacks," Dunmore lamented to the Secretary of State. In this dreadfully weakened condition, Dunmore's force was easily driven from the island in early July 1776, having lost about 70 percent of its number.[17]

The Virginia militia encountered a horrible sight when they entered the hastily evacuated camp. They were "struck with horror at the number of dead bodies, in a state of putrefaction, strewn . . . about two miles in length, without a shovelful of earth upon them." Many had burned to death, too sick to move when the militia set fire to their flimsy huts. Almost certainly some of the Moseley runaways were among the eight hundred or so who died. When Dunmore sailed north to New York in the first week of August 1776, he took with him about three hundred African Americans, being all that remained of his Ethiopian regiment, with their families. Among the survivors were at least nine of Edward Hack Moseley's runaways, a grandmother, six children, and two youths. Young Jack was also taken to New York, having made a dual escape from perpetual enslavement and from a horrible death from smallpox. Moreover, as he had been exposed to the disease and survived, he would be free of its ravages for the rest of his life.[18]

Behind the British lines in New York were between three thousand and four thousand black refugees who had flocked to the British in response to proclamations promising freedom. They came from as far as Massachusetts, South Carolina, and Pennsylvania, but most were from New York, New Jersey, Delaware, and Rhode Island, since the permeable borders of the occupied zone permitted runaways from adjoining colonies to merge into the throng of foreign soldiers and loyalist refugees without attracting scrutiny. One of the most significant acts for these self-emancipated people in New York was a change of name. Enslaved people were universally known by first names only, and even free black people were routinely denied the dignity of a surname. Choosing one's own name was a potent gesture of self-emancipation, with much more than symbolic value, as names marked one as enslaved as clearly as a brand. First names were commonly formalized from their infantilizing diminutive form: Toney to Anthony; Jem to James; Jack to John. More often than not, the new surname would reflect an inheritance from the past life, so the runaway Jack was transformed into John Moseley.

John was employed by the Wagon Master-General's Department and lived in "Negro barracks" across the East River at the wagon yard in Brooklyn, where laborers slept twelve to a room, supplied weekly with a lamp and a pint of oil for each room. Close by the wagon yards were the shipyards, where the massive British fleet was maintained. Over seven years, the opportunities for John Moseley to have become acquainted with British crew were boundless. A ship that was regularly in New York was HMS *Loyalist* and one of the several African American seamen on board that vessel was Amos Anderson, who became a friend of Moseley.[19]

The war came to an expectedly sudden close early in 1782 following the capitulation of British forces at Yorktown. In England, the government of Lord North collapsed. His replacement, Lord Shelburne, lost little time in granting independence to the rebellious colonies and opening talks for peace. For the black refugees in New York, this news was utterly demoralizing.

Promises of freedom made to them by successive British commanders had been contingent on the British winning the war and retaining control of the colonies. A runaway like Moseley knew that the nominal liberty runaways like himself employed within the British enclave counted for nothing to the Patriots. Unless the black allies of the British had papers of emancipation by their former owners, as very few did, they could expect to be returned to enslavement in perpetuity, for themselves, their children, and their children's children.

The man charged with negotiating the changed circumstances, Sir Guy Carleton, was appalled that the peace treaty stipulated the British could not evacuate "Negroes and other American-owned property." Being required to renege on the British debt of honor with regard to the offer of freedom to their black allies was not a duty he was prepared to perform. On his own initiative, he undertook to make good the promises made to the runaways. On May 5, he coolly informed the astonished George Washington that in his understanding of the treaty, the British government had never agreed "to reduce themselves to the necessity of violating their faith to the Negroes into the British lines under the proclamation of his predecessors." Warming to his subject, he further insisted that "delivering up Negroes to their former masters . . . would be a dishonorable violation of the public faith." Protesting furiously as he was bound to do, Washington understood the depth of feeling behind the words "dishonourable violation of the public faith." That night, he wrote to the governor of Virginia, "the slaves who have absconded from their masters will never be restored to them." So John Moseley escaped reenslavement to his former owner, who was now reconciled with the government of Virginia and demanding his property be returned.[20]

When the United States finally gained control of New York on 1 December 1783, they found that as many as five thousand Africans Americans had been systematically evacuated over the preceding thirteen months. Most of Edward Hack Moseley's surviving runaways went to Nova Scotia in July 1783. Whatever John Moseley's relationship to these people—son, grandson, brother, cousin—he seems to have chosen not to join them. In November 1783, John Moseley and Amos Anderson applied together to claim seaman's wages in London, having just been discharged from *HMS Loyalist.* Soon after that, Anderson was shanghaied and taken to the West Indies to be sold. Moseley must have known what had happened to Anderson, and he returned to the *Loyalist* with a certificate for Anderson's wages for an earlier voyage, where it had been erroneously noted that Anderson had deserted. Saying that Amos was sick in Wapping and could not come himself, Moseley induced the captain to sign the certificate to the effect that Anderson had not deserted. He was then able to claim Anderson's wages on December 30, 1783. One might have some sympathy for Moseley, who no doubt believed the money would never be claimed. Not able to find work in London, which was swarming with unemployed men demobilized after the war, he did not have recourse for poor relief, so he would have had desperate need of Anderson's unclaimed wages. Unhappily for Moseley, Anderson escaped from his re-enslavement, got a berth on the *Enterprise* from Rhode Island and was back in England in March, where he quickly established that his friend had defrauded him of his wages.[21]

At his trial at the Old Bailey on April 21, 1784, Moseley was sentenced to death and sent to London's Newgate prison, an overcrowded, stinking cesspit, where there were no beds, no proper sanitary arrangements, no medical attention, and next to no food, except for the prison issue of a three-halfpenny loaf supplemented by charitable donations and a weekly ration of dubious meat. For clothing, food, and bedding, a prisoner had to depend on bribes offered to the turnkeys by families, curious strangers, hawkers, prostitutes, and accomplices who streamed into the jail each day. Although Newgate had an infirmary, doctors could not be induced to enter it. The only time the keeper of Newgate paid any attention to the sick was when a burial was required. As John Moseley was a stranger in England and without an extended family to provide the necessities of life, he was condemned to a squalid existence that must have been utterly soul destroying. In this he probably made common cause with another man battling to survive in Newgate, the black sailor John Martin, who had been found guilty of theft in 1782 and was awaiting transportation to Africa.[22]

After nearly a year in stinking Newgate, Moseley was called to reappear before the Old Bailey on March 3, 1785, to be reprieved from hanging in favor of transportation to Africa. He was said to be twenty-seven years old. He had escaped the gallows, but on the other hand, to be sentenced to transportation to Africa meant a separation as profound as death. While languishing in Newgate, Moseley seems to have managed to father a child. In November 1785, a "mulatto" baby of three months named Jane Moseley was baptized in Marylebone. The baby was probably baptized in Thomas Coram's foundling home in Marylebone, which regularly took in children from Newgate.[23]

Moseley and Martin were among a hundred convicts from Newgate transferred to the hulk of the *Ceres* to await transportation to Africa. Convicts were selected for the *Ceres,* the House of Commons was told, because they were judged to be "of the most desperate and dangerous disposition, deserving for the sake of the public example of the greatest severity."[24] The hulk was more efficient and more humane than Newgate, but it was also much better regimented so that the opportunity for families and friends to come aboard the hulk to bring money and clothing, as well as food to supplement the provisions, was limited. Even though the food allowance was more substantial than Newgate, the hulk diet was conducive to scurvy and other illnesses that were compounded by damp, crowded, and confined living arrangements. Between July and December 1785, sixty men died on the *Ceres.* John Moseley was reported among the deceased, but this appears to be a case of misidentification as he was recorded as still on the *Ceres* a year later.

By 1786, all the convicted black men in London (with the exception of the youngest—John Williams, aged sixteen, and James Williams, aged seventeen) had been put aboard the *Ceres,* regardless of the severity of their sentence. Those eight black convicts waiting transportation to almost certain death in Africa represented 6 percent of the men on the *Ceres,* in contrast to the prison population, where black felons constituted less than 1 percent of the total population. As Africans, the prisoners may have been considered the most likely to survive abandonment in Africa, even though few observers had any doubts that the place would make short work of everyone assembled on the *Ceres.* As Edmund Burke sardonically observed at the same time Moseley received his pardon, a death sentence that had been commuted to transportation to Africa was nothing less than a "singularly horrid" death sentence "after a mock display of mercy." Africa was "the capital seat of plague, pestilence and famine," Burke told the House of Commons, where "the gates of Hell were open day and night to receive the victims of the law."[25]

Burke was one of the members of the House of Commons who had raised the alarm about the proposal for a penal settlement on the Gambia River and persuaded the parliament to establish a committee to investigate the proposal in April 1785. One after another, experts confirmed that Africa was a place of disease and death. Finally, and most damningly, the committee heard evidence from a long-time resident that even if the convicts landed "in the most healthy part of the country . . . only two at the most would be alive after six months." Evidence of that kind killed the Gambia proposal, giving Moseley an escape from certain death in pestilential West Africa.[26]

That left about thirteen hundred convicted felons awaiting transportation on five separate hulks and a government more than anxious to be rid of them. As Lord Sydney acknowledged, it was imperative to solve the problem, and with that matter in the forefront of his mind, he announced, "His Majesty thought to fix on Botany Bay" as the destination for his unwanted felons. Having hitherto shown complete disinterest in Botany Bay, Sydney now lauded the place for the "fertility and salubrity of the climate." Much was made of the glowing reports of Botany Bay that Captain James Cook provided on his return from his momentous voyage of exploration in 1770, but the particular appeal of Botany Bay lay in "the remoteness of its situation (from whence it is hardly possible for people to return without permission)."[27]

The first of the fleet carrying 740 convicts (fewer than 200 of them women) as well as another 200 marines, arrived at Botany Bay on the coast of New South Wales on January 18, 1788, after a voyage of nearly nine months. Those officers who went ashore found a place that deceived the eye. At first sight the country resembled a gentleman's park, with stately trees and grassy meadows, but in reality it could not have been more alien from the tranquility of pastoral England. Tormented by flies by day and being ready prey for swarms of mosquitoes after dusk, these eager young men looked in vain for the fine meadows they had been led to expect. Instead, the grass was long and coarse and the soil sandy. Massive tree trunks rose straight up for fifty feet or more, their narrow leaves providing little shade from the remorseless sun. The more closely the officers looked, the more bewildered they became. Botany Bay in no way resembled the salubrious descriptions offered by Captain Cook.[28]

Still, a start had to be made to create this latest outpost of empire, so a small work party of convicts from the transport ship *Scarborough* was landed each day to cut grass for the livestock and to attempt to clear a site. Happily, the Aboriginal inhabitants proved to be inquisitive rather than hostile and were especially curious to find a black man among the interlopers. None of the fleet's many diarists recorded exactly which black convict landed with the initial work party—there were three black convicts aboard the *Scarborough*—but it could well have been Moseley. A watching naval officer thought that the Aborigines were delighted to see "a man of their own complexion" attacking the landscape with strange weapons. He thought the Aborigines were puzzled when the black convict failed to understand their language, but this was his fanciful rendering of the unintelligible behavior of the indigenous people. For the Aborigines of Eastern Australia, isolated from other people for thousands of years, someone from Africa dressed in a convict uniform would appear just as alien as those with pale faces in the same funny clothes.[29]

On January 24, the entire fleet moved further north to settle at a more pleasing site named Sydney Cove. John Moseley was among the very first to step ashore, with a work party from the *Scarborough* ordered to clear the trees for settlement. Even though he must have been relieved to find himself on land, it would have been cruelly painful after 258 days at sea, lurching about on sea legs with scurvy-softened bones. As if it were not difficult enough to hew enormous trees when the earth appeared to be heaving beneath, the timber was so hard that it blunted the axes and twisted the inadequate crosscut saws. After two days of work in searing heat, Moseley and his fellow convicts had cleared enough ground for the rest of the fleet to disembark and start pitching tents among the tree stumps.

Within a few months, enterprising convicts had managed to construct huts from the soft cabbage palms that grew in abundance around the cove, rendered with mud and thatched with grass. Moseley shared just such a hut with John Randall, a runaway slave from Connecticut who was sentenced to transportation in Manchester in 1786.[30] Randall was known to play the fife and drum, so he was probably once a musician in a British regiment in America that had been demobilized around Manchester in 1785.[31] In a hut nearby lived Moseley's compatriot from Newgate, John Martin, who formed a lifelong friendship with Randall.

Of all the black convicts in New South Wales, it was Randall who fared best, possibly because of his army connections, given that many of the officers and marines at Sydney Cove were veterans of the American Revolution. Randall must have been deemed trustworthy as well as being an experienced shot with a musket, because he was given the job of shooting game for food. The position allowed him to maintain an independent existence within the ironbound penal system at Sydney Cove, ranging widely through the bush, often out for days at a time, tracking and shooting kangaroo.[32]

It is impossible to know much about how these black men lived during the first years at Sydney Cove, as only fleeting glimpses of convict life have survived and archeological evidence relates to a later period. Certainly all the heavy work of clearing and building had to be done by convicts who were still suffering the effects of scurvy. There were no beasts of burden; the task of carting the huge trees and stones fell on their puny shoulders. The black convicts may have had an advantage, as they were bigger and stronger than most, a head taller than almost every other convict at Sydney Cove. Unfortunately, ration allocation took no account of size or the amount of labor undertaken. With remarkable fairness, the governor had decreed that, regardless of status, every man would have the same weekly ration, which was nowhere near sufficient to sustain a child, let a alone a large adult at ten hours of back-breaking labor a day.

By the second year the settlement faced starvation. How Moseley managed his hunger is not known, but his association with John Randall may well have helped him through the famine years. As a game shooter, Randall worked unsupervised, so he had opportunity to get additional game for himself and his friends, which may explain why neither Moseley nor Martin ever came to the attention of the authorities through this terrible time. By contrast, the flamboyant Black Caesar was perpetually in trouble, having earned the lasting enmity of the judge advocate. Caesar distinguished himself very early as the strongest and best worker in the Sydney Cove, but as famine began to stalk the settlement the judge advocate believed Caesar was stealing food to feed a mighty appetite. In May 1789, Caesar headed into the bush armed with a musket and cooking pot, having decided that the terror of the unknown hinterland was less fearsome than starving to death in a brutal penal system. No matter how many times he was caught and savagely punished, this "incorrigibly stubborn black" would always abscond to the bush again. He became the most notorious convict in the colony, leading a gang of armed convict absconders who survived by plundering farms on the outskirts of the settlement. Although his dangerously glamorous career was soon terminated by bounty hunters, Caesar was the role model for a succession of flamboyant convict outlaws who continued to be celebrated in popular memory as men who'd "scorn to live in slavery bound down by iron chains."[33]

Unlike Caesar and several other refractory black convicts, Moseley stayed out of trouble and escaped official scrutiny, despite his conspicuous color. Marriage and baptismal records show that he did not marry nor father children in New South Wales, unlike Randall and Martin, who both married white convict women.[34] Perhaps Moseley still considered himself bound to the mother of his daughter in England. The records are silent about him until April 1800, when he received a conditional pardon. Like his two friends Randall and Martin, he was given fifty acres of land north of Sydney, where grants were given to emancipated convicts on the condition that after eighteen months they had cleared the virgin bush and raised enough crops for their subsistence. Those taking up the grants were given two pigs as initial livestock. To assist in clearing this utter wilderness, they were supplied with a hatchet, a tomahawk, two spades, and shovel.[35]

In the long run it was only Martin who proved to be the adequate farmer, with twelve of his fifty acres in grain within the first few years, though never anything more than "poor but industrious." Randall continued to hunt game for the governor and eventually sold his land in order to join the New South Wales Corps and resume his earlier career as a soldier. Moseley also escaped the vicissitudes of life as a small farmer, choosing instead to work for others as a free laborer. The census of 1825 lists him as was employed by a firm of merchants based in Sydney. That same year, Moseley was reissued a conditional pardon, this time giving his date of birth as 1764, suggesting that he was progressively lowering his age. He also gave his previous occupation as having been "a tobacco planter in America." By the census of 1828, which was the last record of his existence in New South Wales, he had further refashioned himself, claiming to be aged sixty, thereby shaving off a decade or more of his life. His occupation, he said, was as a self-employed dealer in Essex Lane, where he employed three young women as servants. So by way of a series of escapes, John Moseley finally found freedom and modest prosperity in Sydney where, with consummate irony, he could describe himself as a tobacco planter from America; his ultimate escape from a dehumanizing economy that categorized him as property.[36]

It was a cruel paradox that a bid for freedom during the Revolution brought Moseley and his fellow black convicts in chains to New South Wales, yet this is less a testament to their shabby treatment by their British allies than the tortuous process of negotiating freedom among Britain's poor. One only has to read British criminal indictments to see how hard life was for the laboring classes, for whom freedom often meant the capacity to chose between one form of servitude and another. A whole range of coerced labor, such as impressment and indenture, was used to harness the energy of freeborn Englishmen for minimal cost to the state, while a savage criminal code created a new category of unfree labor for Britain's imperial projects.[37]

There can be no doubt that penal servitude in New South Wales was coercive and brutal. Convicts were torn away from their families to be dumped at the end of the world and forced to labor on state projects, without a wage, for a period of four to twelve years. Arbitrary punishment was meted out that could scar them for life. Yet for all that, penal servitude was nothing like chattel slavery. Little distinguished the convict from those who guarded them. Many of the marines at Sydney Cove, like the seaman on the transport ships, had been impressed into service and were lucky if they were ever paid; they too faced excessively brutal punishment for minor misdemeanors. Everyone at Sydney Cove had to labor on state projects in the first decade of settlement in order to create a place to live; just as everyone had to scrabble for subsistence in the face of famine. When the government rations were cut to a quarter, everyone received the same allowance of food, from the lowliest convict to the governor. Most significant for the African American cohorts was that their children were born with the same status and privilege of any colonist. More than a dozen in the first generation of Australian-born children had African fathers, including the outlaw Caesar's daughter who received a land grant in the new colony of Van Diemen's Land in 1813.

For Moseley's compatriots Randall and Martin, to see their children with the privilege of the freeborn English, guaranteed by custom and law, was a significant achievement, probably worth all the bitter tribulations that had brought them to this strange place at the very end of the world.

During the next fifty years, close to a thousand black convicts were sent to the Australian penal colonies. A steady trickle of transported felons from England continued, but after 1820, the penal colonies began to receive a new kind of African convict: slaves transported directly from Mauritius and the British Caribbean. Their status as chattel was rarely stated on the official documentation, reflecting official squeamishness about complicity in the slaving business. An exception was a slave sentenced to life in St. Vincent known simply as Bruce, who was transported at some considerable cost, as his owner had to be compensated. Bruce's offence was probably an act of retaliation or rebellion because his owner had not managed to get his property returned.[38] Certainly that was the case for Sophie, a Malagasy woman transported from Mauritius who set fire to her owner's barn. Compensation paid for Sophie included the worth of the baby that Sophie had given birth to while in prison. Likewise Theresa, another native of Madagascar transported from Mauritius in the same year, was found guilty of assault after she tried to hit her master's daughter with a hoe as retaliation for the brutal treatment she had received. When the father tried to intervene, Theresa had seized his testicles and squeezed so hard that he fainted. He was well compensated for the loss of his troublesome property.[39] Also in Mauritius were two children found guilty of crimes; Constance, aged eight, and Elizabeth, aged twelve, had tried to poison their mistress and were transported for life.[40]

The traffic in convicted slaves dramatically increased as the anti-slavery movement in Britain grew louder and more persistent. After 1830, the slave colonies sought transportation as a means to control a dangerously restive slave population excited by rumors of impending emancipation. In December 1831, sixty thousand Jamaican slaves staged the largest slave rebellion in the British Empire at Montego Bay, which was put down with savage violence in January 1832. Subsequently, hundreds of slaves were vindictively condemned to death under martial law. After the orgy of execution during the first few months of 1832, prudence, combined with pressure from England, encouraged white Jamaicans to rid themselves of slave troublemakers in other ways. Transportation was an attractive option because it permanently removed the source of trouble, rather than inciting more trouble with continuous executions.[41] Alexander Simpson was convicted at a Jamaican Court Martial on 20 January 1832 of "making use of Seditious language, Joining and Engaging in Conspiracy, Traitorous, Rebellious or Hostile Acts against His Majesty's Government and against the peace and safety of the Island" and sentenced death, but unlike 344 slaves executed after the rebellion, he was transported to Australia on the convict ship *Jupiter*, arriving in May 1833.[42] Seven more rebels were also transported. The majority of convicts from the slave colonies, however, came to Australia during the period of apprenticeship. In these cases, the felonies for which they were convicted often masked the real crime, which was resistance to the continuation of unfree labor, widely perceived as slavery in a new guise.

During the period of the abolition of slavery there were also a number of slaves transported from the Cape of Good Hope with telltale names such as Adonis and Jacob. Most convicts from the Cape were not slaves, however, but indigenous Khoi-khoi men. The largest numbers of transported Khoi were soldiers from the Cape Rifles, tried by courts martial in the Cape, mostly for desertion.[43] The Khoi were thought to make excellent soldiers and the Dutch East India Company raised military units of Khoi, a tradition continued by the British. The high numbers of desertions suggest that this was a coercive rather than voluntary recruitment. Other Khoi-khoi were among a group of offenders emptied out of Robben Island in the early 1830, convicted of banditry and cattle stealing, which was colonial code for Khoi resistance. Ruthlessly pushed off their lands in the eighteenth century, the Khoi were forced into a debt peonage and near slavery in which they were obliged to indenture their children up to age 25 years. David Stuurman led a quixotic attempt to re-establish an independent self-sustaining Khoi community, for which he was dubbed "the last chief of the Hottentots." He and his followers were hunted down and imprisoned on Robben Island from where he was transported to New South Wales in 1823.[44] Several of his compatriots who had escaped from Robben Island were recaptured and transported a decade later. Peter Haley was a transported Khoi man who became one of Australia's notorious outlaws (known as bushrangers), until his flamboyant career was cut short by the hangman in 1836.

At least as many of the African diaspora who came to Australia were free settlers, often seamen. Since the Seven Years War, black seamen were a feature of British maritime life, and they made up about a quarter of the crew on American sea-going ships, with a higher ratio on the whaling ships that were so common in Australian ports.[45] Whaling concentrated the worst elements of the maritime industry, and desertion was a weapon in the limited arsenal of the seafaring man. For black sailors, desertion in any Atlantic port, or anywhere in the Caribbean, carried the very real fear that they would be caught and immediately reenslaved or traded into slavery elsewhere. A black man needed not fear being caught in the illicit slave trade in the distant ports of the penal colonies. These were also places where a man might get a new start, regardless of his background. This made the penal colonies very likely places to jump ship and many sailors did. Sometimes American whaling ships found themselves entirely bereft of crew.

This rash of desertion among American seamen reached epidemic proportions during the Victorian gold rush that began in 1851. Police records from the subsequent decade reveal dozens of African American men, often known as Black Jack or Black Harry or Black Pete, arrested in the goldfield regions for vagrancy or being a "rogue and vagabond."[46] These men invariably held mercantile occupations, such as sailors, cooks, or carpenters and probably jumped ship in the hope of finding gold, then found themselves stranded with no visible means of support. Thomas Johnson was one African American charged with vagrancy in 1865. This man, who gave his place of birth as North Carolina, was described as a woodcutter when he married the Irish woman Mary Gallagher in Melbourne on April 16, 1868.[47]

Soon after their marriage, Thomas Johnson and his wife moved to Sydney where their son Thomas Creiton Johnson was born in 1874.[48] In his adult years, the younger Thomas moved to the Western Australian colony, where in 1924 he married Elizabeth Barron, the daughter of a well-to-do pioneer pastoral family. Already quite an old man when he married, Thomas had poor luck with farming. When he died in 1937, he left Elizabeth pregnant with their fifth child and totally destitute. Four children were placed in the care at St. Joseph's orphanage. Nine years later, the fifth child, Colin, was also placed in care. Colin Johnson went on to transcend his miserable background in many ways. Calling himself Mudrooroo Nyoongah, he has become internationally renowned as Australia's premier Aboriginal writer.

It is one of the many tragedies of race relations in Australia that history has not recorded stories of settlers from the African diaspora. A willful ignorance about the multiracial beginnings of Australia has led to widespread misreading of racial identity. Should a claim for indigenous identity be revealed as incorrect as in the case of Colin Johnston, trauma and unhappiness result. But it is utterly unacceptable that African Australians can be rolled into a racial category with Aborigines. People of the African Diaspora who came to Australia, whether voluntarily or in chains, must be understood as part of—not apart from—the settler society that expropriated Aboriginal land. It is an insult to Aboriginal rights and indigenous culture that descendants of Africans can claim the same status and the same rights and privileges as the descendants of the indigenous people who were forcibly dispossessed and subjected to genocidal regimes.

Notes

1. I am indebted to Dr. Michael Powell, University of Tasmania, for this story.

2. Cassandra Pybus, *Black Founders* (Sydney: New South Wales University Press, 2006). Provides a detailed account of these black convicts.

3. Norma Myers, *Reconstructing the Black Past: Blacks in Britain 1780–1830* (London: Frank Cass, 1996).

4. My analysis of records of black baptisms for 1770–1800 for the parishes of Greater London, using data supplied by the Greater London Records Office, indicate that about 1 percent of baptized Londoners were black; however, the Records Office underestimates the black population, many of whom were not Christian. Analysis of trial records from the Old Bailey, the Middlesex and Kent Assizes in the period immediately after the American War reveal that about 0.9 percent of indictments were identified as black, but racial identity was not always specified in the court documents. In the more detailed records for the prison hulks and transportation ships, the percentage of black felons was 2 percent. An average of all three indicators suggests a population of about 1.3 percent of a population of 750,000; this is just under 10,000.

5. The defection of slaves to the British is discussed in Benjamin Quarles, *The Negro in the American Revolution* (Chapel Hill: University of North Carolina Press, 1961); Sylvia Frey, *Water from the Rock: Race and Resistance in the Revolutionary Age* (Princeton, N.J.: Princeton University Press, 1991) and most recently the revisionist interpretation of Cassandra Pybus, "Thomas Jefferson's Faulty Math: The Question of Slave Defections in the American Revolution," *William and Mary Quarterly,* 3rd series, 62 (2005): 244–64.

6. Gordon Fenwick Jones, "The Black Hessians: Negroes Recruited by Germans in South Carolina and Other Colonies," *South Carolina Historical Magazine,* 83 (1982): 287–302 and Todd W. Braisted, "The Black Pioneers and Others" in John W. Pulis, ed., *Moving On: Black Loyalists in the Afro-Atlantic World* (New York: Garland Press, 1999), 3–37.

7. A wealth of anecdotal evidence exists for black crews on Royal Navy ships, much of which is documented by Jeffrey Bolster *Black Jacks: African American Seamen in the Age of Sail* (Cambridge, Mass.: Harvard University Press, 1997). The majority of the black claimants to the Loyalist Claims Commission were seamen from the Royal Navy. Nearly every ship in the Royal Navy's American fleet carried a handful of African American crew members; some had as many as 20 percent, while the percentage on privateers might be even higher. British ships captured by the Patriots were found to have had a black crew of between 13% and 30 percent; see Quarles, *The Negro in the American Revolution,* 154–55.

8. For a more full discussion see Cassandra Pybus, *Epic Journeys of Freedom: Runaway Slaves of the American Revolution and their Global Quest for Liberty* (Boston: Beacon Press, 2006).

9. For a discussion of free black refugees in Jamaica see John Pulis, "Bridging Troubled Waters: Moses Baker George Liele and the African American Diaspora to Jamaica," in Pulis, ed., *Moving On,* 182–222. For the Bahamas: Michael Craton, "Loyalist Mainly to Themselves: the 'Black Loyalist' Diaspora to the Bahamas," in Shepherd, ed. *Working Slavery, Pricing Freedom: Perspectives from the Caribbean, Africa and the African Diaspora,* (New York: Palgrave, 2001), 44–64. For St Lucia: George Tyson, "The Carolina Black Corps: Legacy of Revolution, 1783–1798," in *Revista/Review Interamericana,* 5, (1975–76): 648–64. For the Mosquito Shore and British Honduras: Peter Linebaugh and Marcus Rediker, *The Many Headed Hydra: Sailors Slaves Commoners and the Hidden History of the Revolutionary Atlantic,* (Boston: Beacon Press, 2000), 269. For black refugees in Germany, see George Fenwick Jones, "Black Hessians," 287–302.

10. Book of Negroes PRO 30/55/100, National Archives of the United Kingdom (hereafter NAUK).

11. Runaway slave notices, Dixon & Hunter *Virginia Gazette,* August 26, 1775. For John Cunningham, see R.L. Scribner (ed.), *Revolutionary Virginia: The Road to Independence,* vol. V, (Charlottesville: University of Virginia Press, 1983), 360.

12. Pendleton to Lee, November 27, 1775, John D. Mays, ed., *The Letters and Papers of Edmund Pendleton,* vol. 1 (Charlottesville: University of Virginia Press, 1967), 133.

13. For Creole slave life: Alan Kulikoff, *Tobacco and Slaves: The Development of Southern Cultures in the Chesapeake, 1680–1800* (Chapel Hill: University of North Carolina Press, 1986); Lucia Stanton, *Slavery at Monticello* (Monticello, Vir.: Thomas Jefferson Foundation, 1996); Phillip J. Swartz, *Slavery at the Home of George Washington* (Mount Vernon, Vir.: Mt. Vernon Ladies Association, 2001).

14. Capture and punishment of runaways: Scribner, *Revolutionary Virginia,* vol. 4, 305, 485 and vol. 7, part one, 284.

15. Edward Hack Moseley: Scribner, *Revolutionary Virginia,* vol. 5, 141, 142, 207. For Cunningham: Scribner, *Revolutionary Virginia* vol. 5, 361, 408; and Purdie's *Virginia Gazette,* 19 January 1776. John Moseley, Book of Negroes PRO33/55/100, NAUK.

16. Forced removal: Scribner, *Revolutionary Virginia,* vol. 5, 369–71. For sale to the West Indies: Scribner, *Revolutionary Virginia,* vol. 6, 425.

17. For background on the smallpox epidemic see Elizabeth Fenn, *Pox Americana: The Great Smallpox Epidemic of 1775–82* (New York: Hill and Wang 2001) and Phillip Ranlet, "The British, Slaves, and Smallpox in Revolutionary Virginia," *Journal of Negro History* 84, no. 3 (1999): 218. Dunmore to Germain, 30 March 1776, C05/1373, NAUK; Dunmore quoted in W.B. Clarke, ed., *Naval Documents of the American Revolution,* vol. 5 (Washington, D.C.: United States Printing Office, 1970), 669; Dunmore to Germain, 26 June 1776, C05/1373, NAUK.

18. Fenn, *Pox Americana,* 60–61.

19. For housing and employment in New York: Ellen G. Wilson, *The Loyal Blacks,* (New York: Capricorn Books, 1976), 64; PRO30/55/84, NAUK; Wray Papers, vol. 7, Clements Library, University of Michigan. For HMS *Loyalist,* ADM36/8202. NAUK.

20. Substance of a Conference between General Washington and Sir Guy Carleton, May 6, 1783, in J. C. Fitzpatrick, ed., *The Writings of George Washington,* vol. 26 (Washington, D.C.: Government Printing Office, 1937) 402–6; Carleton to Washington, May 12, 1783, CO 5/109, f. 313, NAUK; Washington to Harrison, May 6, 1783; Washington to Carleton, May 6, 1783, in *Writings,* 406–14.

21. Moseley Trial: *Old Bailey Session Papers,* (OBSP) 1784–5, 532.

22. John Howard, *An account of the present state of the prisons, houses of correction, and hospitals in London and Westminster* (London, 1789). John Martin, OBSP, 1781–2, 454. Martin had probably just come off a ship from America or the West Indies.

23. Parish records for Marylebone, London Metropolitan Records Office.

24. "Minutes of the House of Commons respecting a plan for transporting felons to the island of Lemaine in the River Gambia," H07/1, NAUK. Duncan Campbell Letterbooks, Mitchell Library, State Library of New South Wales. *Ceres* lists, T1/637, NAUK

25. Burke, from *Cobbett's Parliamentary History of England from the earliest period to the year 1803,* vol. 25 (London, 1806–20), 430.

26. "Minutes of the House of Commons," H07/1. NAUK.

27. Sydney to Lords of Treasury, August 18, 1786, T1/369, NAUK.

28. The best account of the arrival and the first few years in New South Wales is Watkin Tench, *1788: Comprising a Narrative of the Expedition to Botany Bay and A Complete Account of the Settlement at Port Jackson,* ed. Tim Flannery (Melbourne: Text Publishing, 1996).

29. W. Bradley, *A Voyage to New South Wales: the Journal of Lieutenant, William Bradley RN of HMS Sirius, 1786–1792* (Sydney: Ure Smith, 1969), 62.

30. Randall's trial with another black man who probably died on the *Ceres* was reported in *Manchester Mercury* 19 April 1786.

31. The Irish radical Joseph Holt wrote of Randall, "the black played the flute and tambour" in *A Rum Story: The Adventures of Joseph Holt Thirteen Years in New South Wales, 1800–1812,* ed. Peter O'Shaughnessy (Sydney: Kangaroo Press, 1988), 66–67. The 63rd Regiment, originally raised in Manchester and later reconstituted as the West Suffolk Regiment, still had black drummers on its establishment a decade after 1785. For black drummers in British regiments, Peter Fryer, *Staying Power: The History of Black People in Britain* (London: Pluto Press, 1984), 81–86.

32. Randall joined the New South Wales Corps, which would only accept exconvicts if they were veterans from another regiment, which strongly implies he had been a soldier in the revolution.

33. The convict outlaw known as the "bushranger" is probably the most iconic figure in the popular imagination of contemporary Australia. The quote is from the

chorus of the celebration of the bushranger that is second only to "Waltzing Matilda" as Australia's national song.

34. Both Randall and Martin married twice. Randall's daughter Mary became Martin's second wife.

35. R. J. Ryan, *Land Grants 1788–1809: A Record of the Registered Grants and Leases in New South Wales and Norfolk Island,* Book 1a (Sydney: Australian Document Library, 1972), 12.

36. NSW Muster, 1822, A15241; NSW Muster, 1832, 33618; NSW Muster, 1828, M3314.

37. See Peter Linebaugh, *The London Hanged: Crime and Civil Society in the Eighteenth Century,* (Cambridge, Mass.: Cambridge University Press, 1992) and Douglas Hay et al., eds., *Albion's Fatal Tree: Crime and Society in Eighteenth Century England* (New York: Pantheon Books, 1975).

38. *Indents to Convict Ships,* 1820, Index to convict indents, 1788–42, microfiche 5969–5979, Archive Office of NSW.

39. Both these convicts are discussed in Clare Anderson, "Unfree Labour and Its Discontents: Transportation From Mauritius to Australia, 1825–1845," *Australian Studies* 13, no. 1 (1998): 116–33.

40. See Cassandra Pybus and James Bradley, "From Slavery to Servitude: The Australian Exile of Constance and Elizabeth," *Journal of Australian Colonial Studies* 9, no. 1 (2007): 29–50.

41. Ian Duffield "From Slave Colonies to Penal Colonies: The West Indian Convict Transportees to Australia," *Slavery & Abolition* 7, no. 1 (1986): 25–45.

42. Ian Duffield, "'Stated This Offense': high density convict micro narratives" in Lucy Frost and Hamish Maxwell-Stewart, ed., *Chain Letters: Narrating Convict Lives* (Melbourne: University of Melbourne Press, 2001), 117135.

43. C V Malherbe, "Khoikhoi and the Question of Convict Transportation from the Cape, 1820–1845, *South African Historical Journal* 1, no. 17 (1985): 19–50.

44. C V Malherbe, "David Stuurman: "Last Chief of the Hottentots," *African Studies* 1, no. 39 (1980): 60–64.

45. See Jeffery Bolster, *Black Jacks: Afro-American Seamen in the Age of Sail* (Cambridge, Mass.: Cambridge University Press 1997).

46. *Victorian Police Gazette* 1853– 61 and *Victorian Central Register of Prisoners,* micofiche McN 1383, National Library of Australia.

47. Births Death & Marriages Registry Victoria, 369/1868.

48. Births Death & Marriages, NSW, 1720/1874.

8

The Presence of (Black) Liberation in Okinawan Freedom

Transnational Moments, 1968–1972

YUICHIRO ONISHI

Throughout the period when Americans occupied Okinawa (1945–72), Okinawans expressed their deepest desire to return to Japanese prefectural status and rallied behind this cause. However, after U.S. President Richard Nixon and Japanese Prime Minister Sato Eisaku agreed on the terms of Okinawa's reversion to Japan in November 1969, the gravity of this political activism in occupied Okinawa rapidly moved to a different dimension. The leaders, officials, and policy makers on both sides of the Pacific expected that Okinawans would be celebrating the prospect of again becoming full members of the Japanese nation. Many did just the opposite. They took to the streets and headed straight to the military bases. They mobilized an islandwide opposition to the U.S. Civil Administration of the Ryukyu Islands (the occupation authority) and the Japanese government, and demanded the abrogation of this bilateral agreement and the immediate, unconditional removal of all military personnel, bases, and weapons. Far from realizing rehabilitation as full members of the Japanese nation, Okinawans contended that they faced two alien powers that were committed to maintaining colonial rule, racial domination, and a large military buildup on the islands.

The struggle for freedom meant many things to Okinawans, but it largely reflected ordinary people's aspirations to end the American occupation in general and the system of colonial and racial domination in particular. In the late 1960s and early 1970s, Okinawans framed the politics of reversion in a new way and demanded the rights of masses to struggle for self-determination.[1] Within this context of the politics of reversion, diverse groups of protest movements participated in the Okinawan freedom struggle both collectively and independently.

Peace activists from the United States and Japan, for instance, entered this politics of reversion by way of opposing the American war in Southeast Asia. Similarly, GIs stationed in bases in Okinawa entered the politics of reversion by way of challenging aggressive militarism and its manifestations in their daily lives. Black GIs, in particular, entered the politics of reversion by way of making connections between the Vietnam War, the violence of militarism, and the persistence of white racism at home and in military. Okinawans, above all, pushed this politics of reversion forward by opposing the indefinite military occupation by the United States and the reannexation of Okinawa by the Japanese government.

These diverse constituents, at critical moments, moved toward temporary alliances, even though each started from its own vantage point with different histories, goals, and interests. Human struggles against the militarized and racialized international security system appeared at the front and center of protest groups' activities. What was at work on the eve of reversion was the formation of a distinct system of critique that shaped diverse constituents' identities, worldviews, and political action. I argue that the alternative conception of political agency emerged out of cross-racial, cross-border, antiracist, anti-imperialist, and transnational struggles against "global whiteness."[2]

In a dynamic way, the participants of social movements around the world converged locally and took the giant steps to transform existing society dominated by bases, machines, guns, profit motives, and private property rights, all of which animated the "pursuit of whiteness."[3] Recognizing the perpetuation of this global system of domination based on race and class as the core problem of aggressive militarism in occupied Okinawa and abroad, the movement participants—Japanese and American peace activists, antiwar black and white GIs, and local people—entered the Okinawa freedom struggle. Many of them put the visions of black and Third World liberation to work and explored the interconnectedness of different histories, aspirations, and experiences through localized projects. A large part of this study of protest movement in postwar Okinawa is devoted to the analysis of grassroots organizing, particularly the local dynamics of the globalized movements toward black and Third World liberation. It shows the strategic, contingent, and flexible formation of the black radical tradition that helped to articulate the diverse groups' visions of struggles against global whiteness in occupied Okinawa.

Pan-Nonwhite Mobilizations Against Global Whiteness

In *The Politics of Culture in the Shadow of Capital* (1997), Lisa Lowe and David Lloyd call for the critical need to identify the politics of culture that have repeatedly survived the relentless, uneven expansion of inequality and exploitation, despite the logic of domination to conceal these realities. According to Lowe and Lloyd, the politics of culture is a kind of space where the aspirations of liberation would come into direct conflicts with material conditions. Although it echoes a classic Marxist formulation of contradiction, this space is far more complex, heterogeneous, and highly differentiated than the one characterized by the conflict between capital and labor. The dynamics of identity formations and political activism in Okinawa on the eve of reversion offers a case study to analyze the politics of culture in the shadow of global whiteness in Asia-Pacific.[4]

More specifically, it identifies a form of political activism that was not simply built around identity politics alone—be it identification with race, class, gender, and ethnicity—but was informed and transformed by the radical possibility of, as Angela Davis puts, "the creation of unpredictable or unlikely coalitions" across multiple identities and experiences working on a particular agenda. On the cusp of Okinawa's return to Japanese sovereignty, myriad human struggles moved across, below, above, and behind the United States, Japan, and Okinawa in dynamic ways and coalesced with the black freedom struggle and anti-Vietnam war protest in localized projects. The constituents of these struggles all imagined the nation as something other than existing colonial powers—the United States and Japan—and pursued the possibility of "nonwhiteness" in concrete ways.[5]

In this essay, I borrow historian David R. Roediger's formulation of nonwhiteness and make a critical inroad into the analysis of movements against global whiteness in occupied Okinawa in the late 1960s and early 1970s. In *Colored White: Transcending the Racial Past* (2002), Roediger offered commentaries on alternative routes to abolish the system and logic of racial domination called "whiteness" and identified the presence of nonwhiteness in the past and present as the key to radicalization. Nonwhiteness is conceptualized as a political construct and alliance, as well as a political choice and commitment. It is also conceived as a strategic political and cultural space occupied by the diverse constituents of social movements that could enable this space to become productive for a new politics and struggle.

Throughout this essay, I conceptualize the creation of unpredictable trans-Pacific and cross-racial solidarities against aggressive militarism as a study in pan-nonwhite mobilizations. During the course of participation in human struggles, the participants of protest movements in occupied Okinawa made up their minds to fight for social justice, a base-free society, and peace, rather than taking the path toward global whiteness to strengthen the militarized international security system. The dynamics of freedom struggles was such that these constituents insistently drew inspirations from black and Third-World liberation movements. They made conscious decisions to cross over into nonwhiteness to challenge military, racial, and colonial oppressions in solidarity with each other.[6]

While the protest movements splintered in myriad directions in the late 1960s in the United States, the activists of the Okinawan freedom struggle developed a network of alliances and identifications between and across the Pacific and that crossed over into black and Third-World liberation solidarity movements. They chose to support the initiatives of colonized and racially oppressed peoples and expressed utmost confidence in their self-activity. They called for a revolution in the dominant conceptions of thoughts, property, and rights; carved out a new space through transnational, cross-racial, anti-imperialist, and antiracist struggles; and created a new politics and a new form of life.[7] There existed what Herbert Marcuse once called "eros," which informed the dynamics of freedom struggles in occupied Okinawa in powerful ways, demonstrating "the deep affirmation of the Life Instincts in their fight against instinctual and social oppression" and "the prevailing reality principle of domination."[8]

Young and old activists and ordinary people who joined freedom struggles in occupied Okinawa cracked open the liberal consensus within the civil rights movement and in so doing articulated the connection between U.S. neocolonial and imperial adventures in the Third World and racial oppression and military violence in local communities. Especially in the aftermath of the assassination of Martin Luther King Jr. in April 1968, many of the movement's participants in the United States, Japan, and Okinawa took giant steps into the domain similar to that of eros: "nonwhite radicalism."[9] They synthesized multiple realities of violence—the violence of economic exploitation, the violence of the Federal Bureau of Investigation against blacks and other radicals, the violence of police and the National Guard, the violence of the imperialist war in Vietnam, the violence of militarism—and grasped the dialectical relations between the terror of state power and the emergence of a revolutionary subjectivity. By the late 1960s, revolts against the U.S. empire appeared everywhere around the world—campuses, streets, factories, towns, military bases, and battlefields. It generated global upheavals and captured the political imagination of human subjects struggling to create a new society.

Although these human desires for liberation were often disseminated through the media in the form of cultural commodities, a world-historical movement against racism, colonialism, and militarism always started at the grass roots, through which strategies, aspirations, and perspectives of social movements became "generalized, emerging here, then there, building up gradually in confined spaces, then erupting on a global level." The alternative form of a subjectivity and political agency critical of Cold War liberalism and U.S. imperialism emerged because ordinary people made a conscious decision, as King said on April 4, 1967 (exactly a year before he was killed), to "get on the right side of the world revolution . . . [and] undergo a radical revolution of values." These human actors made a political choice to step into nonwhiteness—and joined strikes and picketers; participated in sit-ins, teach-ins, rallies, and demonstrations; disseminated critical knowledge widely through the alternative media; and built coalitions and alliances locally and transnationally against global whiteness.[10]

The story of the dynamics of freedom struggles in occupied Okinawa does not have an exact starting point. The "winged seeds" of pan-nonwhite mobilizations moved through and below the United States and Japan; circulated across the Pacific; returned to all three places in a whirlwind; became buried under the soils they craved—Okinawan freedom, black liberation, anticolonial, and Third-World struggles; and sprouted instinctual strivings toward human liberation. This essay will first introduce a white American peace activist, Barbara Bye, whose political commitment intersected with the visions of nonwhite radicalism, especially the demands of Okinawan, black, and Third-World liberation movements locally and globally.[11]

Stepping into Nonwhiteness

Shortly after completing work as a Peace Corps volunteer in Côte d'Ivoire, Barbara Bye returned to the United States and became a committed activist, fighting on behalf of the Okinawan freedom struggle in the late 1960s and early 1970s. Like other Americans who entered the protest movements of the sixties, she devoted her time and energy in the struggle for social justice, peace, and the liberation of the oppressed. However, unlike others who became disillusioned or dropped out of radical politics by the late 1960s, especially with the disintegration of Students for a Democratic Society (SDS), she showed utmost confidence in creating a new society and pursued the possibility of nonwhiteness. She espoused a different conception of radical politics from earlier activists of the sixties, all the while remaining close to the spirit of resistance characterizing that period.

Bye took part in various experiments around the causes of global justice and peace, always doing small things, to transform the dominant society. She carried with her "seeds of catalysts" and planted them as she seized "points of gravity" in various experiments, operating with the belief that, as an active participant of the antiwar and black freedom movements, in Staughton Lynd's words, "if none of our experiments has yet been successful, one day soon it will be otherwise."[12] She did not measure successes of movements according to substantial gains made in electoral politics, legislatures, and courtrooms. She had markedly different attitudes toward activism and moved through many forms of nonwhite radical politics, especially in the context of the Third-World liberation movement, the anti-imperialist struggle, and the international peace movement.

Bye learned about Okinawa, U.S. imperialism in Asia-Pacific, the GI movement, and the peace movement in Japan when she participated in one of the largest antiwar demonstrations in American history in Washington D.C. in November 1969. Among half a million concerned citizens and activists who gathered on the Mall was Oda Makoto, a writer, a critic, and an antiwar activist from Japan. Just before the Sato-Nixon talks, the Committee of Concerned Asian Scholars invited him to be part of the cross-country lecture tour to educate ordinary Americans about colonialism in Okinawa and security imperialism in Asia-Pacific. Bye's encounter with Oda in Washington was the beginning of her involvement in the freedom struggles in Okinawa. She learned a great deal about the American imperialist thrust in Asia-Pacific and people's movements to challenge this global system of domination. She later told the reporter, "I came to realize how essential Japan was to America's Pacific-rim policy. . . . I decided to go to Japan for about two or three months and to see what makes the country tick. I . . . wanted to familiarize myself with the Japanese antiwar groups and with the American pressure."[13] Oda showed her the road to nonwhite radicalism.

Oda was not a stranger to the international peace movement, nor was he a mere sojourner in the United States. In 1958–59, he was a Fulbright fellow at Harvard University and backpacked across Europe and Asia on his way back to Japan. Upon his return, he published the chronicle of his world tour, titled *Nandemo Mite Yaro* (*I Want to See It All*) in 1961, which became a national bestseller and made him the voice of a new generation critical of Japanese conservatism. He spoke and wrote candidly about wars, revolutions, fascism, racial discrimination, and social problems in Japan and the United States. When the United States declared war against North Vietnam and started the bombing campaign, Oda, along with Japan's leading critics, such as Tsurumi Shunsuke, Tsurumi Yoshiyuki, Muto Ichiyo, Iida Momo, and Oe Kenzaburo, organized the peace movement in April 1965. Oda emerged as the icon of the movement calling itself "Betonamu ni Heiwa o! Shimin Rengō" (Japan's "Peace for Vietnam! Committee"), commonly known as Beheiren.[14]

Beheiren was conceived as a network of protest groups, where members came from diverse occupational, social, and political backgrounds. Some were intellectuals and critics, while majority of them were citizens concerned with the escalation of the Vietnam War and the Japanese involvement in it. Writers, composers, artists, professors, housewives, students, salarymen, foreigners in Japan, shopkeepers, and the elderly founded local chapters in their neighborhoods and operated without dues at the grassroots level. The members led petition campaigns and teach-ins, wrote and distributed pamphlets and flyers near U.S. military bases and installations, organized fund-raising to place an advertisement in major U.S. newspapers (the *New York Times* and the *Washington Post*), wrote letters to local and national newspapers and elected officials, joined demonstrations and rallies, and offered American deserters safety and shelter. Iida Momo, an active member and organizer, regarded Beheiren as "a catalyst to introduce fluidity into the too rigidly organized, and severely divided traditional movement." She explained that it emphasized the "voluntary action of every individual" and mobilized around the following principles: "Peace for Vietnam," "Vietnam for the Vietnamese," and "Against Japan's Collaboration."[15]

Many of the movement's participants, including Barbara Bye, were attracted to Beheiren precisely because it did not represent itself as a political organization, affiliate with a progressive political party, or participate in sectarian struggles. It operated independently of the politics of the Left. Leaders of Beheiren stressed that the movement offered a space where individuals concerned with war, militarism, and violence could learn about self, community, and freedom through practical activity. Historian Thomas R. H. Havens explained the philosophy of Beheiren's activism in this way: "The aim was self-awareness as a step toward helping one another build a society of democratic individualism. The purpose of joining a demonstration was not to merge with the mass of protesters but to achieve self-consciousness as an individual participant."[16]

Beheiren offered such a space for individuals to experience radicalization, instilling commitments "to work against all inhumanity and barbarism, including [those] that [reside] within" every individual. Its slogan, "Korosu na!" ("Stop the Killing!"), asked people to come to grips with their own role as killers and break away from this existence, especially their social contract with this coercive state. It encouraged them to transform their identities and help establish the necessary foundations to create a new polity, something other than the existing polity that buttressed the expansion of global systems of aggressive militarism and racial and colonial domination. Oda regarded the principle of civil disobedience as a political right, which needed to be exercised and practiced to "resist compulsion by the state."[17]

The members of Beheiren applied this right to veto—a refusal to be the accomplice to the coercive power of the state—as the basis of building the international solidarity struggle. From its inception, the movement showed solidarity with the Vietnamese liberation struggle. It also sought to strengthen solidarity with participants of the Black Freedom struggle and peace movement. The leaders of Beheiren, for instance, worked closely with activists of Students for a Democratic Society (SDS), Student Nonviolent Coordinating Committee (SNCC), the Black Panther Party for Self-Defense, and numerous peace groups, such as the Committee for a SANE Nuclear Policy (commonly known as SANE). Leaders of Beheiren were in close contact with David Dellinger, A. J. Muste, Noam Chomsky, Jean-Paul Sartre, Howard Zinn, Ralph Featherstone, Stokely Carmichael, Eldridge Cleaver, and Katherine Cleaver. Beheiren was committed to promoting internationalism and solidarity with people mobilizing resistance against the rampant pursuit of wealth, whiteness, and imperialist interests. It supported the emancipation of self from the militarized totalitarian state and the transformation of society "through concrete individual acts" in global scale.[18]

Oda's call for action to create a new form of reality caught Bye's attention in the fall 1969, capturing her radical imagination and stirring instinctual strivings toward human liberation. She heard Oda's speeches against the colonial domination of Okinawa and the U.S.–Japan Security Treaty in Washington at either the U.S. Imperialism and the Pacific Rim conference (November 13–14) or the anti-Nixon-Sato talk demonstrations (November 17 and 19). The conference attracted progressive groups working around antiwar, Black Power, youth activism, and Third-World issues, and it coincided with the Nixon-Sato talk on November 20, which was aimed at reaching a bilateral agreement on the "re-annexation of Okinawa." A day before the protest against the Nixon-Sato talk and demonstration outside the White House, Oda, along with conference participants, stayed up all night to make a large puppet representing a monster—the head depicted "Uncle Sam" and the tail,

"Sato." The monster and street performers showcased the skits, chanting in Japanese: "Ampo funsai!" (Scrap the treaty!); "Okinawa kaiho!" (Okinawa liberation!); and "Betonamu ni heiwa!" (Peace in Vietnam!). Some twenty people (including nine women) performed acts of civil disobedience in front of the White House and were consequently arrested by the police.[19]

In summer 1970, several months after first encountering the world of anti-imperialist coalition-building among people of color and antiracist whites, Bye came in contact with Beheiren in Japan. By then, Beheiren had already garnered strong citizen support. In particular, it had responded to repeated patterns of GI desertions from U.S. military bases on the Japanese mainland and organized around deserters and antiwar GIs. By the late 1960s, dissenting GIs in Vietnam, the United States, South Korea, the Philippines, Hong Kong, West Germany, mainland Japan, and Okinawa began to voice their opposition to American foreign policy and rebelled against the legitimacy of military authority. Many of them risked discharge under less than honorable conditions, outright imprisonment, removal from jobs, and transfer to isolated posts or battlefields—and built the GI movement against the military machine.[20]

In mainland Japan and Okinawa, GI organizing required efforts to cross barriers separating diverse constituents of protest movements—differences in language, politics, culture, ethnicity, and race. Early in 1969, a coalition of civilian groups in mainland Japan and Okinawa, transnational peace activists, and dissenting GIs began challenging aggressive militarism. They organized rallies and sit-ins, met and interacted through counseling activities, published underground newspapers, and disseminated information about repressive military life and the growth of solidarity struggles outside of bases. Barbara Bye arrived in Japan in the midst of the successful coalition-building campaign. Throughout the summer of 1970, she immersed herself in this organizing activity by taking part in the work of Pacific Counseling Service (PCS) and Beheiren.[21]

Bye's participation in this emerging GI movement helped her to mature intellectually. At the Iwakuni Marine Air Station in Yamaguchi prefecture in mainland Japan, she passed out antiwar handbills and copies of the underground GI newspaper *Semper Fi*. She spoke at rallies, showed unity with GIs across the barbed wire fences, and "rapped" with servicemen in coffeehouses, noodle shops, and bars. She not only consulted those seeking to oppose the Vietnam War but also exchanged perspectives on war and militarism with both GIs and the Japanese. She came into contact with some one hundred GIs and shared information about the procedures applying for conscientious objector status. (Some GIs seriously considered taking the administrative discharge option.)

Through the work of PCS and Beheiren, Bye sharpened her perspectives on institutional violence and the structural inequality called "global whiteness," connecting her work in Iwakuni to her own experience as a health extension worker for Peace Corps in Côte d'Ivoire from 1967 to 1969. She told a reporter, "I guess my Quaker religion was what originally propelled me into the antiwar, civil rights, and third world liberation movements . . . but I became secularized by my experience in the Peace Corps." "In the end . . . I realized that the wells, the latrines, the purified water—all that I had been doing—was insignificant. These countries need a much more profound change in the nature and structure of their government and system. I began to see the Peace Corps as an extension of American foreign policy, as something hindering social progress and supporting the status quo."[22] She acknowledged that she identified herself with "the left wing of Quakerism," but what she ultimately advocated was the self-activity of people struggling against the global systems of domination. Her commitment to work toward revolutionary change, especially socialism, was not defined in terms of Maoism or Marxist-Leninism, but rather was informed by the political philosophy of Beheiren and PCS, operating with the vision that the "ultimate trust of human beings must be based on the lives and hopes of people—not on the often self-serving interests of 'great men.'"[23] Bye's direct encounter with the essence of the colonial system in postcolonial Africa was crucial in making her realize the problem of global whiteness.

Many of the activists who participated in transnational coalition-building in occupied Okinawa on the eve of the Okinawan reversion raised the banner of an alternative agenda, which was far more radical than the domestic antiwar movement. By 1969, Bye had become highly critical of imperial and white supremacist dynamics underpinning Cold War liberalism. Like black radicals and anticolonial activists among American Indians, Asian Americans, Puerto Ricans, and Chicanos in the United States, she rejected the promise of the American dream, opposed militarism and racism, and struggled to liberate the oppressed from realities of underdevelopment, military violence, and colonial subordination.

While some of the participants of this transnational social movement invoked the language of rights embodied in the Universal Declaration of Human Rights, others went straight to black and Third-World liberation movements for inspirations, ideological strategies, and directions, and found a new form of life, agency, and subjectivity—the future—in nonwhite radicalism. In particular, as I will show in the next section, the black conception of soul, especially the politics of black emancipatory desire, functioned as a mode of imagining nonwhiteness and stimulated the radical imagination. It allowed diverse constituents of the freedom struggle in occupied Okinawa to challenge forms of an authoritarian and coercive power of the state that protected the legitimacy of bases, aggressive militarism, and especially of global whiteness.

The Radical Possibility of Nonwhite Coalition-building in Koza

Barbara Bye entered occupied Okinawa in the aftermath of a rebellion against U.S. domination in Koza (known today as Okinawa City) on December 20, 1970, and quickly started to work with Okinawans, antiwar white and black GIs, and transnational peace activists.[24] The incident that triggered the revolt was a car accident involving a local Okinawan worker and a vehicle driven by an American serviceman. The military police (MPs) hastily tried to clean up the scene of the accident, while local people surrounded the scene and protested. The MPs fired into the air to quiet the crowd. In response, residents overturned and set fire to the MPs' car. The urgency of the Koza rebellion spread quickly throughout the base town, and thousands of people joined this anti-imperialist struggle. They set fire to American personnel vehicles one after another and battled against MPs, U.S. armed forces, and Ryukyu police for nearly six hours. In the aftermath of the rebellion, the mayor of Koza, Oyama Asatsune, captured the crowd's sentiments in this way: "Fire was not set by local people in Koza; it was set as a result of the explosion of people's opposition to twenty-five years of U.S. domination. Since fire was burning inside of ordinary people, it could not be put off by water."[25]

Two days later, a group of black GIs from Kadena Air Force Base issued a dramatic appeal in support of the local people's struggle against the American military occupation. Their statement was printed both in Japanese and English at the local printing shop and distributed widely by the local chapter of Beheiren and other anti-base and antiwar civilian groups. Black GIs stressed the process through which they were radicalized during the course of the escalating American war in Vietnam and argued that they were "trying to become a part of the solution, not the problem."

> Black people have been fighting for Liberation for a long time. So have the Okinawa. Who can stop you from having what is rightfully yours? No One!!! . . . Black people have been discriminated against for over 400 years, and it hasn't stopped yet. The same with Okinawans; they've been discriminated against also. So you see we both are in the same situation . . . The Black GIs are willing to help and talk to Okinawans in order to form much better rela-

> tions between the oppressed groups, because we have so much in common. So why not get our heads together and come up with a solution to destroy the problem. The Black GIs are aware of the situation that brought about the riot, and this was truly a RIGHT-ON-MOVE. That's the only way [the U.S. will] bend.[26]

The appeal of dissenting black GIs to Okinawans was an effort to base their own liberation struggle within the localized project of the internationalist, anti-imperialist, antiracist, and anticolonial struggle in occupied Okinawa. They linked the liberation of Okinawa to the liberation of blacks and the Third World, as well as to the liberation of working-class GIs (both white and black) from the military's repressive system of control, discipline, and domination.

Antiwar black GIs of the Kadena Air Force Base recognized that they would not be liberated as long as the militarized international security system safeguarded property interests in whiteness. In the essay "Oppression: Causes and Effects," the GIs explained the logic of domination they described as whiteness and its destructive consequences not just for people of color but also for those who sought security and happiness in whiteness. They expressed, for instance, that neither blacks nor whites in the military had developed an effective method for explaining how the system of oppression affected the "people of all races," including whites. They acknowledged that some white GIs were "being oppressed by not being given a fair chance. They are also being oppressed by people hating them for associating with blacks or any person or color." Despite this reality, black GIs concluded that "so many white people feel that every black person hates them. So blacks think the same." They called upon black and white GIs to unite against racial oppression: "You can plainly see what the effects of oppression are, just look around, and listen to news and radio, last but not least STOP BEING SO NARROW MINDED!!!"[27]

Shortly before some three thousand copies of the dissenting black GIs' appeal for pan-nonwhite mobilizations against racial oppression appeared in print and on the streets of Koza in the aftermath of the Koza rebellion, Jan Eakes and Dianne Durst Eakes, young white radicals from California, had come in contact with black GIs and began to translate the vision of nonwhite radicalism in solidarity with them. Like many white college students, Jan Eakes became radicalized when he encountered the antiwar and Black Power movements in 1967and 1968. Dianne Durst Eakes, on the other hand, crossed over into radical politics while studying abroad in Taiwan, where she encountered the problems of underdevelopment.[28] In summer 1970, they entered Okinawa and started to develop working relationships with leaders of antiwar black GI groups and local antiwar/anti-base activists. They emphasized blacks' interests were not the same as those of antiwar white GIs, Okinawans, and transnational peace activists, even though all of them participated in the politics of liberation. Jan and Annie believed that people struggling against oppressions along race, class, and gender needed to establish their own terms of negotiation, self-identification, and democratization, all the while converging around a particular political project.[29]

Before the outbreak of the Koza rebellion on December 20, 1970, Jan and Annie screened the Black Panther Party's recruiting film, *Off the Pig*, and attracted a large audience, including the black GIs of the Kadena Air Force. Shortly after, these GIs started to brainstorm concrete actions. Some of them published their own underground newspaper at the Kadena Air Force base, while others led reading groups to discuss radical literature at the Eakeses's residence or held rallies on the street corners of Koza.[30] Both Jan and Annie identified the radical possibility of a nonwhite coalition among blacks, Okinawans, and antiwar activists. Uniting with them, they laid the groundwork for pan-nonwhite mobilizations against the American empire.

The Eakeses's regular contacts with dissenting black GIs culminated in the publication of the antiwar GI underground newspaper *Demand for Freedom* in fall 1970. The paper covered stories of repeated race-based patterns of harassment, discrimination, and mistreatment in the military and reminded readers not to be intimidated. In particular, articles expressed the right of black GIs to enjoy freedom of choice in military life, such as their choice of hairstyles or clothing. The first issue of *Demand for Freedom* also featured the transcript of a meeting between Okinawan base workers and black GIs. The purpose of this meeting was, as the editor stated, "to gain a better understanding of the oppression of the Okinawan people caused by the presence of the Amerikan military on their island, especially the workers on the bases, and to build a common struggle." In particular, black GIs talked about various forms of discrimination against Okinawan base workers. The restrooms for women on the base, for instance, were divided between "women" and "cleaning women." "Women" was written in English only, while "Cleaning Women" was written in both English and Japanese. This symbol of white supremacy certainly reminded them of the Jim Crow South. They also commented that base workers were overworked and were not properly compensated for the work they performed on the base. One black GI said, "Some of the jobs . . . that these people get, if they was back in the 'world' they would be makin' 8 dollars—9 dollars an hour" as welders, carpenters, plumbers, landscapers, and maids.[31]

Although *Demand for Freedom* showed evidence of cross-racial solidarity, anti-black racism was quite strong among ordinary Okinawans. They often singled out black GIs for provoking racial conflicts and committing violent crimes. Taxi drivers, bar owners, managers, and hostesses openly displayed hostilities toward black GIs and did businesses only with white GIs. They followed the ethics of Jim Crow. Certainly, racial segregation was not the official policy of the U.S. occupation authority. It was a de facto segregation, understood by every member of military personnel and local people. Since black GIs were excluded from certain businesses, such as restaurants, bars, strip joints, and brothels, they eventually staked out their own territory within authorized entertainment districts in base towns.

Teruya—the black district in Koza (also known as the Four Corners or the "Bush")—was one such district and the most prominent of them. Like other districts, the livelihood of local residents in Teruya depended on the prosperity of bars and brothels where a number of Okinawan women worked. These sex businesses thrived during the Vietnam era since they offered the quickest way to make money; Okinawans' labor played an important role in fulfilling the material, sexual, and psychological desires of American military personnel.[32]

Yet Okinawans' attitudes toward black GIs oscillated from rage and repulsion to empathy and affinity in the racialized landscape of base towns. Both blacks and whites policed the borders of racially segregated districts and clashed openly and violently if they stepped into each other's territory. Repeated incidents of racial conflicts threatened peace and security in the community but also affected local residents directly. In *Gayukten* (*The Reversal*), writer Isa Chihiro captured the complexities of race relations in Koza through the eyes of an Okinawan who understood the depth of white racism that affected both black GIs and Okinawans, but unequally. Teruya was, Isa wrote, a "soul town" for black GIs:

> Although I get mad whenever I encounter violence on the streets [between Black and White GIs], they [Blacks] do what they do, I think, because of whites. . . . They did not organize a district such as "The Bush" voluntarily. Rather, they did not have a place to go other than Four Corners; they were forced out of other GI districts in Koza by whites. They know that the Four Corners is a place where they will be treated equally. They can drink without being harassed and humiliated by whites, and they can talk with their brothers. For them, the Four Corners is the only place in Okinawa where they feel safe and at home. . . . Therefore, if whites were to enter Blacks' "sacred place," they would do everything to stop that encroachment. . . . I have heard

> that even though Black GIs wear the military uniform, they are not really a member of U.S. military personnel. Some refuse to pledge allegiance to the American flag since they are unwilling to express their loyalty to the country that they do not call home. It is quite shocking to know that Blacks are treated so poorly. I feel for them.
>
> . . . Like Blacks, there is no government that can represent us [Okinawans]; there are no laws that protect the lives of Okinawan people. All that we have are inequalities, as well as regulations and laws that protect the legitimacy of bases. They deny the rights of local people. In this regard, Okinawans are worse off than Blacks. Blacks, at least, articulate their rights and are eager to fight, but Okinanwas don't.[33]

Okinawans projected negative images of blacks and distanced themselves from them, but race relations in the base town reminded them of definite material limits in their own lives. In specific colonial settings, these two groups exchanged understandings for each other and created a space, where Okinawans' resentment toward the occupiers coalesced with black Americans' resistance to white supremacy. Both groups recognized that what lay beneath the machinery of U.S. militarism abroad and in Okinawa was American democracy's refusal and inability to view blacks and Okinawans as equals.

The protagonist in Isa's story exhibited the deeper understanding of a "soul town" as a place of enjoyment and its significance for black GIs struggling for freedom and autonomy. His worldview, however, showed that the black conception of soul functioned as a mode of belonging and identification for local people as well. At the height of the Black Power period in the late 1960s and early 1970s, the transnational circulation of black popular culture entered into the everyday life of Okinawans and helped to cultivate a space for cross-racial solidarities and nonwhite mobilizations against white supremacy. The consumption of blackness did not always activate the cultural logic of essentialism to perpetuate the racist stereotypes and caricatures.

Most recently, African American anthropologist John G. Russell has pointed out that some of the leading Japanese New Left intellectuals, especially those closely associated with Beheiren, read works of James Baldwin, Paul Robeson, Malcolm X, and Frantz Fanon; this led them to support African independence movements, the civil rights movement, and revolutionary black nationalism. The heroic representations of black freedom fighters in the diaspora helped some Japanese radicals to work out their ambivalence toward America, their own identity as Japanese, and their relationships to Japan's minorities.[34]

The bonds of affection between Okinawans and blacks, however, followed a different trajectory. The radical formations of a nonwhite alliance between these two groups were not made possible at the level of representation alone or through the consumption of soul culture. Both clearly exhibited "a transnational sense of black radicalism" and grasped something concrete.[35] Okinawan writer Takamine Tomokazu, then, a young reporter for *Ryukyu Shimpo,* recognized something emancipatory in the soul town Teruya and made a conscious decision to cross over into nonwhite radicalism. In 1968 and 1969, he followed the activity of dissenting black GIs in Okinawa and reported the manner in which the vision of revolutionary black nationalism intersected with the antiwar movement. He observed that blacks began demonstrating their opposition to the escalation of the Vietnam War and the persistence of racial discrimination in the military openly. Groups such as Black Hawk, Sons of Malcolm X, Mau Mau, Afro-American Society, People's Foundation, and Zulu represented diverse political opinions of black GIs on bases. Many, however, brought the ideals of black solidarity symbolically and in action. In Teruya, creative expressions of Black Power were visible in their everyday lives. However, behind the visible images, styles, and cultural practices of Black Power aesthetics—be they Afro haircuts, embroideries, hand slappings, finger snappings, clothing, dancing, or music, there existed conditions for cross-racial, anti-imperialist, antiracist, and antiwar coalition-building that informed the formation of nonwhite radicalism.[36]

According to Takamine, the group called Bush Masters, which emerged in the late 1960s, was particularly popular in Koza. Its membership fluctuated in years between 1969 and 1972, but the group claimed as many as one hundred members in 1969–70. Members often rented bar spaces and organized workshops to read, study, and discuss the Black Panther Party's literature, as well as other works on revolutionary politics, movements, and philosophy. They also participated in various aspects of community organizing in and around Teruya. Countless times, Bush Masters aided white GIs out of the black district when they mistakenly roamed into the area, so as to avoid racial confrontation. Moreover, when local residents of Teruya could not acquire adequate medical attention in local hospitals, Bush Masters took them to military base hospitals. They organized a blood drive when a local resident underwent major surgery. Some members of Bush Masters were concerned that black GIs repeatedly committed both petty and violent crimes in Teruya and threatened residents' welfare and security, so members often policed and patrolled the area. For example, when black GIs left restaurants, bars, or retail stores, they made sure they paid. If they did not have enough money, members helped to pay these bills. In his memoir, *Shirarezaru Okinawa no Bei-hei (The Unknown American GIs of Okinawa),* Takamine presented a deep understanding of the nexus of race and the American occupation and how Okinawans and black GIs, at particular moments in time and space, crossed over into nonwhiteness.[37]

Takamine fraternized with the members of Bush Master and other black GIs and took part in numerous local meetings and rallies, both as a reporter and an ethnographer. What drew him closer to them was a sense that out of their shared experiences with the violence of racism, militarism, and war, both groups projected a deep desire to transcend the burden of the racial past. He had come to interpret these groups as witnesses of racial terror locally and globally. One day in early 1970, while in a Teruya bar that he often frequented, he saw an engraving of a Bush Master's signature on a bathroom wall. It was scratched with a jackknife onto the mortar-made wall, which was covered with drawings of female nudity, depictions of sexual intercourse, and other graffiti.

> GOOD BY[*sic*] BROTHER
> I GO TO VIETNAM.
> J.B
> A MEMBER OF BUSH MASTER[38]

Takamine later said this signature embodied a conflation of a young black GI's anger, pain, and sorrow. Takamine expressed an affinity toward black GIs and stepped into the realm of black freedom to pursue the radical possibility of nonwhiteness. He knew that black soldiers were more often sent to dangerous missions and died in the combat zone than did their white counterparts; that the majority of them came from working-class backgrounds; that they entered military services because they could not find decent jobs after graduating from high school; that they enlisted, and often reenlisted, to support their families, to provide for aging mothers, or to assist their siblings through college; and that they did not have access to resources to secure exemptions, as did many white middle-class college students. He was also aware that they had to be reminded of a racial hypocrisy in the U.S. military at every turn, where, for instance, the overt display of symbols of white power on bases, not to mention their visible activities, were not subjected to disciplinary measures in the same manner as were black GIs' cultural practices.[39]

In *Shirarezaru Okinawa no Bei-hei,* Takamine presented the framework by which to understand the development of complex human relationships in the localized and heterogeneous space within base towns in occupied Okinawa. He mapped two historical developments, the Vietnam War and Okinawans' struggle for reversion, perpendicular to each other. He argued that the lives of ordinary Okinawans, dissenting American GIs (particularly blacks) and peace activists from the United States overlapped, despite differences in race, culture, class, and politics. He emphasized that they all struggled to make sense of themselves and cultural realities in the face of the violence, terror, and destruction of the American war in Vietnam and occupied Okinawa. He noted in passing in the book's epilogue that he had intended to title it *Machikado No Betonamu Sensou* (*The Vietnam War on the Street Corner*). What he had in mind was the conceptualization of occupied Okinawa as the microcosm of the world systems, where the forces of global whiteness uprooted and transformed the lives of diverse people, all the while providing opportunities to mobilize pan-nonwhite solidarities at local levels in powerful ways.[40]

On the eve of Okinawa's reversion to Japan, some Okinawans, especially students, intellectuals, and those affiliated with Beheiren and the GI movement, recognized the imperative of exercising the rights of masses to struggle for self-determination to pursue a different path toward peoplehood and nationhood, even though majority of Okinawans identified themselves as the Japanese. They seized their unsettling identity and projected their deep desire for human freedom onto oppressed people's "dreams of freedom."[41] Such a crucial moment of identification was evident in an Okinawan journalist's reporting of the emerging GI movement in Koza.

Like Takamine, the writer accurately reported that antiwar GI activity was grounded in the black radical tradition. The *Okinawa Times* journalist wrote, "Antiwar GI activity in Okinawa's bases grew out of Black GIs' struggle for freedom and became a model of activism for other dissenting American GIs. This was made possible as a result of people's belief that there existed something sensuous beyond differences in 'color' or 'class.'" The writer emphasized that the black freedom struggle against slavery and racial oppression was not simply a fight for formal equality confined within national boundaries to claim property and citizenship rights. It was a struggle for a new conception of peoplehood, statehood, and citizenship, aiming to abolish the structures of white supremacy. The Okinawan journalist continued, "By learning the important lesson from the strivings of dissenting GIs in Koza, Okinawans, too, need to materialize the ideals of '*Hansen*' [antiwar] and '*Jichi*' [sovereignty] and transform Okinawan identity concretely."[42] At the point of cross-racial, cross-border, antiracist, and transnational identifications between these two groups, an alternative conception of political right and human agency crystallized and emerged as a powerful force against global whiteness at the local level.

However much the presence of black liberation incited new political possibilities in U.S.-occupied Okinawa, enabling local people to think dialectically about their own conditions of racial oppression and imperatives for emancipatory projects, the manner in which Black Power GIs conveyed the revolutionary potential of black nationalism, was compromised by their gendered and sexual politics. When these GIs who wrote for *Demand for Freedom* expressed their dissent, their discourses of antiracism and anti-imperialism were couched in terms of combating emasculation and restoring black manhood. Such a rhetorical strategy unavoidably translated into, as black feminist critic bell hooks explains, "a discursive practice . . . that link[ed] Black male liberation with gaining the right to participate fully within patriarchy."[43] Such was the limitation of these black GIs' political project, for implied in the way they approached black male liberation was their desire to regain control of female sexuality.

For instance, in an appeal written to Okinawans and the Japanese to forge cross-racial solidarity, a black GI writing in *Demand for Freedom* emphasized that all of them faced the common enemy, "Amerik-ka." He continued, "You are not alone. You have 200 million people of color to depend on if everyone unites. POWER TO THE THIRD WORLD! POWER TO THE PEOPLE!"[44] Yet throughout this anti-imperialist and black nationalist narrative, the writer repeatedly cast Okinawans as students in need of tutelage by black men. A strain of colonial paternalism ran throughout. Although the writer recognized that U.S. imperialism in Asia-Pacific was responsible for the underdevelopment of Okinawa, he criticized Okinawans' uncritical acceptance of existing unequal power relations, seeing them as too accommodating in their relations with the American occupation authority. He wrote: "True, it gives many jobs, but now you're dependent on Amerik-ka. Amerik-ka is the one gaining because you're working your ass off for low wages, but yet to you it's fair or good."[45] Okinawan subordination, however, did not mean that ordinary people lacked initiatives to change their own unequal status. This writer's rhetorical strategy reinforced the privileged political position he occupied; he could not see himself as the agent of U.S. imperialism and sexual aggression.

Most significantly, the black GI writer's critique of Okinawa's dependency on "Amerik-ka" had little to say about one of the cornerstones of the base political economy, military prostitution. It failed to discuss the crucial role it played in maintaining the basic structures of white supremacy. He wrote: "Now Okinawa depends on its American visitors for income. Amerik-ka legalized prostitution in Okinawa for its soldiers. . . . Why legal here? To keep the Americans happy, or what? Now Okinawa depends on prostitution for a big income. Ameri-ka has made Okinawans, your friends, into viscious [*sic*] businessmen. They value the dollars more so than their fellow brothers and sisters."[46] Rather than pointing out the interconnectedness of patriarchy, racism, and capitalism and the problem of a heteronormative political outlook, however, the writer turned to the criticism of Okinawan men, saying that they privileged business interests over human and social concerns of their people struggling for freedom. What his narrative revealed was not only his blindness to the nexus between his gendered and sexual desires to recuperate manhood and control women's bodies but more important the implication of his limited conception of human liberation in making coalition work productive. An Okinawan male observer acutely pointed out such an epistemic failure: "Black GIs say that Okinawan male managers and female hostesses discriminate them. But have they ever considered what it would be like for Okinawan women to sell their bodies to live?"[47]

Perhaps Takamine Tomokazu recognized the deep irony of this failure in thought. He commented in the closing section of his memoir *Shirarezaru Okinawa no Bei-hei* that the limitation of these black GIs' political engagements became glaring when violence against Okinawans and women in particular ensued, impeding the very progress of anti-imperialist and antiracist coalition-building and simultaneously producing the racialized representations of black GIs as aggressors and criminals. Black GIs' masculine dissent was rendered moot in the discursive terrain. Indeed, as black feminist scholar Rose Brewer explains, "These are complex social relations involving multiple sites of oppression, occurring in conjunctive, disjunctive, and contradictory ways to generate a system of race, color, gender, sexual, and class oppression."[48]

Despite this, the eve of Okinawa's reversion to Japan in the late 1960s and early 1970s represented not the end of the Okinawan freedom struggle, but the beginning. Although Okinawa's return to Japanese prefectural status was finally realized in May 1972, the massive buildup of U.S. armed forces did not come to an end. To this day, Okinawa continues to bear the heavy burden of bases in the name of defending the "free world." Okinawa is a host to more than 30 bases and installations, which constitute 75 percent of all U.S. military bases stationed in mainland Japan and Okinawa combined, even though Okinawa only has 0.6 percent of Japan's total land area. Approximately 28,000 of the 45,000 U.S. troops in Japan and 22,000 dependents are based in Okinawa. The key bases are mostly concentrated in the southern part of the island, although this area is the most populated. For instance, the U.S. Air Force occupies 83 percent of the total area of Kadena Town so more than 14,000 Okinawans are forced to live on the remaining 17 percent of the land. Since the U.S.–Japan Mutual Security Treaty continues to guarantee the huge military buildup in Asia-Pacific, the triangular colonial relations of power between the United States, Japan, and Okinawa are still firmly in place, keeping the bases concentrated in Okinawa.[49] Thus, contemporary Okinawan people's movement is ongoing, and these stories of efforts to build solidarities in the past have potential to establish grounds for a new kind of resistance, just as the entry of black GIs in the Okinawan freedom struggle on the eve of reversion broke new ground. It offered radical possibilities of unlikely cross-racial, transnational, cross-border, and anti-imperialist alliances that were crucial to the struggle against global whiteness, even when these groups were unable to critique the heteronormative political orientation and transcend the racial past, which had deep historical roots in the system of U.S. colonial rule in Okinawa and globally.

Notes

Funding from the MacArthur Interdisciplinary Program on Global Change, Sustainability, and Justice and from the Department of History at the University of Minnesota supported fieldwork and archival research for this article. I would like to thank the staff and archivists at the Swarthmore College Peace Collection, Urban Archives (Temple University), Center for the Study of Cooperative Human Relations (Saitama University), and Okinawa City Hall for their assistance. My thinking on transnational activism was sharpened by feedback from Takamine Tomokazu, Furukawa Hiroshi, David Roediger, Erika Lee, Peter Rachleff, George Lipsitz, Earl Lewis, Ernest Allen, Jay Wendelberger, Joel Helfrich, Toru Shinoda, and Sophia Kim. Finally, I express my thanks to editors of this volume for their support and patience throughout the revising process.

1. Mikio Higa, "The Reversion Theme in Current Okinawan Politics," *Asian Survey* 7 (March 1967): 152–64. Also, see Mikio Higa, *Politics and Parties in Postwar Okinawa* (Vancouver: University of British Columbia, 1963).

2. Vron Ware, "Global Whiteness: A Multilateral Approach," *Souls* 4 (Fall 2002): 70–73.

3. The phrase is borrowed from David Roediger's essay entitled "The Pursuit of Whiteness: Property, Terror, and National Expansion, 1790–1860." See David R. Roediger, *Colored White: Transcending the Racial Past* (Berkeley: University of California Press, 2002), 121–37.

4. Lisa Lowe and David Lloyd, ed. *The Politics of Culture in the Shadow of Capital* (Durham: Duke University Press, 1997); Robin D. G. Kelley, *Freedom Dreams: The Black Radical Imagination* (Boston: Beacon Press, 2002).

5. Angela Davis, "Reflections on Race, Class, and Gender in the USA," interview by Lisa Lowe, in *The Politics of Culture,* 322.

6. See especially David R. Roediger, "Nonwhite Radicalism: Du Bois, John Brown, and Black Resistance," in *Colored White,* 97–102.

7. Alice and Staughton Lynd, "Liberation Theology for Quakers," in *Living Inside Our Hope: A Steadfast Radical's Thoughts on Rebuilding the Movement* (Ithaca, NY: ILR Press, 1997), 44–45.

8. Herbert Marcuse, *The Aesthetic Dimension: Toward a Critique of Marxist Aesthetics* (Boston: Beacon Press, 1978), 10–11, 62–63.

9. The phrase is borrowed from Roediger's essay, "Nonwhite Radicalism."

10. George Katsiaficas, *The Imagination of the New Left: A Global Analysis of 1968* (Boston: South End Press, 1987), 8; Martin Luther King Jr., "Beyond Vietnam," address given at Riverside Church Meeting, New York City, Tuesday 4 April 1967, in *Dr. Martin Luther King, Jr., Dr. John C. Bennett, Dr. Henry Steele Commager, and Rabbi Abraham Herschel Speak on the War in Vietnam,* ed. Clergy and Laymen Concerned about Vietnam and forward by Dr. Reinhold Niebuhr (New York, 1967), 15. The pamphlet is in Box 44, SANE—Greater Philadelphia Council Records, Urban Archives, Manuscript Collections, Temple University (hereinafter abbreviated as SANE).

11. I have borrowed the phrase "winged seeds" from a Li-Young Lee's prose poem, *The Winged Seed: A Remembrance* (New York: Simon & Schuster, 1995).

12. Staughton Lynd, "The First New Left. . . . and the Third," in Lynd, *Living Inside Our Hope,* 88.

13. Thomas R. H. Havens, *Fire Across the Sea: The Vietnam War and Japan, 1965–1975* (Princeton, N.J.: Princeton University Press, 1987), 57–67; Ivan Hall, "Hotel Room is Jail for Bucks Pacifist in Japan," *Philadelphia Bulletin,* 19 November 1970, Box 17, SANE.

14. Havens, *Fire Across the Sea,* 57–67.

15. Momo Iida, "Report on Anti-War, Peace Movement in Japan (Gist)," in *Report on Japan–U.S. Two Nation Conference for Peace in Vietnam* (October 1966), 23, Box 1, A Quaker Action Group Records, Swarthmore College Peace Collection (hereinafter abbreviated as QAGR); Lynne Shivers on Beheiren, Box 1, QAGR; Kuninaga Hiroko, "'*Beheiren' undo: Ninshiki to kankei no tenkai*" (Senior Paper, Tsukuba University, 1996), Yoshikawa Yuichi Papers, Center for the Study of Cooperative Human Relations, Saitama University; Sekiya Shigeru and Sakamoto Yoshie, ed. *Tonarini dasohei ga ita jidai: JATEC, Aru shimin undo no kiroku* (Tokyo: Shiso no kagakusha, 1998); Yoshiyuki Tsurumi, "Beheiren: A New Force on the Left," *AMPO: A Report from the Japanese New Left* 1 (1969): 5, 9.

16. Havens, *Fire Across the Sea,* 62.

17. Oda Makoto, "Making of Peace: Principle, Action, and Declaration," in *Two Nation Conference for Peace in Vietnam,* 15; "Actions for the Peace in Vietnam," in *Two Nation Conference for Peace in Vietnam,* 10; Oda Makoto, "*Beheiren*" *kairoku de nai kaiko* (Tokyo: Daisan Shokan, 1995), 44–48, 55–72, 73–87, 239–56.

18. Oda, "Making of Peace," 15.

19. Ibid., 17; Hall, "Hotel Room is Jail"; Havens, *Fire Across the Sea*, 57–63, 199–204; Oda Makoto, "Washington kara no houkoku," in *Shiryo: Beheiren Undo*, vol. 2, ed. Beheiren (Tokyo: Kawade shobo shinsha, 1974), 218–22; "Conference: U.S. Imperialism and the Pacific Rim," Box 23, QAGR.

20. David Cortright, *Soldiers in Revolt: The American Military Today* (New York: Anchor Press, 1975), 70; David Cortright and Max Watts, *Left Face: Soldier Unions and Resistance Movements in Modern Armies* (New York: Greenwood Press, 1991); Robert D. Heinl Jr., "The Collapse of the Armed Forces," *Armed Forces Journal* 108 (7 June 1971): 30–38; Richard R. Moser, *The New Winter Soldiers: GI and Veteran Dissent During the Vietnam Era* (New Brunswick, N.J.: Rutgers University Press, 1996).

21. Richard DeCamp, "The GI Movement in Asia," *Bulletin of Concerned Asian Scholars* 4 (Winter 1972): 109–18; Sekiya and Sakamoto, *Tonarini dasohei ga ita jidai*, 107–200.

22. Hall, "Hotel Room is Jail"; Kakega Kyoko, "Iwakuni no ninen," in Sekiya and Sakamoto, *Tonarini dasohei ga ita jidai*, 168–77.

23. Hall, "Hotel Room is Jail"; "And This is Being Done," CDG-A, Pacific Counseling Service, Swarthmore College Peace Collection.

24. After working with PCS in Iwakuni, Barbara Bye left for Okinawa. Upon returning to mainland Japan on October 30, 1970, she was denied entry at Haneda International Airport in Tokyo. Japanese immigration authorities determined that Bye violated tourist visa provisions by working under false pretenses (meaning that she participated in "political" activities). Both the Justice Ministry and the Tokyo District Court upheld the ruling. Bye appealed to a higher court, but the court upheld the earlier rulings on December 26, 1970. While awaiting the trials, she remained under arrest at the airport hotel. Beheiren groups organized the "Free Barbara" campaign, which also reached across the Pacific where her mother Mary Bye actively solicited support from elected officials and antiwar groups at local and national levels. In the end, Bye lost the case and returned to Okinawa in February 1971. A small collection of "Free Barbara" campaign documents, including letters, fact sheets, and clippings, are in Box 17, SANE.

25. Takamine Tomokazu, *Shirarezaru Okinawa no Beihei* (Tokyo: Kobunken, 1984), 67–68. On the Koza Rebellion, see Takamine, *Shirarezaru Okinawa no Beihei*, 45–84; Fukugi Akira, "Koza: Gekihatsu suru Okinawa no kokoro," *Sekai* (February 1970): 42–51; *Asahi Shinbun*, 19 July 2000; Isa Chihiro, *Enjou* (Shio shuupan, 1981); "Koza Uprising," *AMPO: A Report from the Japanese New Left* 7/8 (1971): 1–5; Okinawa-shi Heiwa Bunka Shikou Ka, ed. *Beikoku ga mita Koza bodo* (Okinawa: Okinawa City Hall, 1999).

26. *Demand for Freedom* 3 (25 December 1975), 3, GI News Periodical, Swarthmore College Peace Collection (hereinafter abbreviated as GI News Periodical).

27. Ibid., 2, 4.

28. Eakes, *Senso no kikai wo tomero!*, 35–40. "Jan Eakes to tomo ni," published by Beheiren, 15 February 1971, Yoshikawa Yuichi Papers, Center for the Study of Cooperative Human Relations, Saitama University. On Dianne Durst Eakes's biography, see *Fujin Minshu Shinbun*, 12 February 1971, Yoshikawa Yuichi Papers, Center for the Study of Cooperative Human Relations, Saitama University.

29. Stokely Carmichael and Charles V. Hamilton, *Black Power: The Politics of Liberation in America* (New York: Random House, 1967); Eakes, *Senso no kikai wo tomero!*, 40–42, 70–74; "Jan Eakes to tomoni," vol. 2, 4 March 1971, Yoshikawa Yuichi Papers, Center for the Study of Cooperative Human Relations, Saitama University.

30. Eakes, *Senso no kikai wo tomero!*, 120–21, 166–67; Takamine, *Shirarezaru Okinawa no Beihei*, 211–14.

31. *Demand for Freedom* 1 (7 October 1970), GI News Periodical.

32. Takamine, *Shirarezaru Okinawa no Beihei*, 201–4; Michael S. Molasky, *The American Occupation of Japan and Okinawa: Literature and Memory* (New York: Routledge, 1999), 53–69; Cortright, *Soldiers in Revolt*, 205; Charles C. Moskos Jr., "The American Dilemma in Uniform: Race in the Armed Forces," *The Annals of the American Academy of Political and Social Science* 406 (March 1973): 103–5.

33. Isa, *Enjou*, 31–32 (my translation). Unlike Isa's piece, the *New York Times* journalist did not report the complexities of cross-racial encounters and interactions between black GIs and Okinawans. See Takashi Oka, "Okinawa Town Has a Black Enclave That White G.I. Enters at His Peril," *New York Times*, 24 November 1970.

34. John G. Russell, "Consuming Passions: Spectacle, Self-Transformation, and the Commodification of Blackness in Japan," *positions* 6 (Spring 1998): 113–77.

35. May Joseph, "Soul, Transnationalism, and Imaginings of Revolution: Tanzanian Ujamaa and the Politics of Enjoyment," in *Soul: Black Power, Politics, and Pleasure*, ed. Monique Guillory and Richard C. Green (New York: New York University Press, 1998), 131.

36. Takamine, *Shirarezaru Okinawa no Beihei*, 204–14; Touma Kensuke, "Okinawa no kuroi chikara," *Datso hei tsushin* 4 (15 October 1969), in *Beheiren News shuksatsu ban, 1964–1974* (Tokyo: Beheiren Betonamu ni Heiwa wo! Shimin Rengo, 1974), 696. Also, see *Beheiren News*, 1 February 1971, in *Beheiren News shuksatsu ban, 1964–1974*, 396, 400; Milton White, "Malcolm X in the Military," *The Black Scholar* 1 (May 1970): 31–35.

37. Takamine, *Shirarezaru Okinawa no Beihei*, 204–7; Cortright, *Soldiers in Revolt*, 205–6.

38. Takamine, *Shirarezaru Okinawa no Beihei*, 199.

39. Ibid., 161–64, 210; Christian G. Appy, *Working-Class War: American Combat Soldiers and Vietnam* (Chapel Hill: University of North Carolina Press, 1993), 17–37; Wallace Terry II, "Bringing the War Home," *The Black Scholar* 2 (November 1970): 2–18; Julian Bond, "The Roots of Racism and War," *The Black Scholar* 2 (November 1970): 20–23.

40. Takamine, *Shirarezaru Okinawa no Beihei*, 259–60.

41. The phrase is borrowed from Robin D. G. Kelley, *Freedom Dreams: The Black Radical Imagination* (Boston: Beacon Press, 2002).

42. *Okinawa Times*, 7 February 1971 (my translation).

43. Quoted in Devon W. Carbado, "The Construction of O. J. Simpson as a Racial Victim," in *Black Men on Race, Gender, and Sexuality: A Critical Reader*, ed. Devon W. Carbado and foreword by Kimberlé Williams Crenshaw (New York: New York University Press, 1999), 190.

44. *Demand for Freedom* 2 (16 November 1970).

45. Ibid.

46. Ibid.

47. Takamine, *Shirarezaru Okinawa no Beihei*, 215.

48. Rose M. Brewer, "Black Radical Theory and Practice: Gender, Race, and Class," *Socialism and Democracy* 17:1 (2003), available at http://www.sdonline.org/33/rose_m_brewer.htm (accessed May 8, 2008).

49. Jens Wilkinson and Koshida Kiyokazu, "Overview: Time to Scrap the Security Pact," *Ampo Japan Asia Quarterly Review* 27 1 (1996): 14–17; Gwyn Kirk, Rachel Cornwell, and Margo Okazawa-Ray, "Women and U.S. Military in East Asia," *Foreign Policy In Focus* 4 (July 2000): 1–3, available at www.fpif.net/briefs/vol4/v4n09wom.html (accessed December 3, 2008); Koji Taira, "The Okinawan Charade—The United States, Japan, and Okinawa: Conflict and Compromise, 1995–96," JPRI Working Paper #28 (January 1997), available at http://www.jpri.org/publications/workingpapers/wp28.html#Taira (accessed October 23, 2008); Masahide Ota, "Governor Ota at the Supreme Court of Japan," in *Okinawa: Cold War Island*, ed. Chalmers A. Johnson (Cardiff: Japan Policy Research Institute, 1999), 205–14; Masamichi Sebastian Inoue, John Purves, and Mark Selden, "Okinawa Citizens, U.S. Bases, and the Dugong," *Bulletin of Concerned Asian Scholars* 29 (October-December 1997): 82–86.

SECTION FOUR

Race and Nation

9

Becoming British by Beating "Black" America

National Identity and Race in the Molineaux-Cribb Prize Fights of 1810 and 1811

JOEL T. HELFRICH

Tom Crib is a British man, he's cast in British mould,
With a heart like a lion, of courage, stout and bold,
A brave black man is Molineaux, from America he came,
And boldly tried to enter with Crib the lists of fame.

The Black stripp'd, and appeared of a giant-like strength,
Large in bone, large in muscle, and with arms a cruel length,
With his skin as black as ebony—Crib's as white as snow,
They shook hands like good fellows, then to it they did go.

—Pierce Egan, *Boxiana*

Introduction

On a cold, wet December day in 1810, a black American named Tom Molineaux and a white Englishman named Tom Cribb engaged in a bare-knuckle bout. Under questionable circumstances, Molineaux lost.[1] Nine months later they battled each other in another bloody contest and Molineaux lost again. These classic boxing matches tell us much about nineteenth-century British history. During the early 1800s, British nationalism was taking a distinctly new form after two decades of wars with continental Europe, particularly Napoleonic France.[2] Molineaux affected and reflected British nationalism at this critical stage. Scholars have dealt at length with France's influence on

British nationalism. However, the role of other countries in this process is also of importance, even if largely forgotten by research. Most scholars ignore America's role in this reshaping and they miss the larger conclusions that can be drawn about the new forms of British nationalism.[3] The early nineteenth-century British prize ring provides an intriguing starting place to look at British national and racial identity. Molineaux provides an excellent case in point. In fact, American blackness had a bigger role in the British prize ring during the Regency period (1811–20) than any historian has ever noted.[4]

Both fights between Molineaux and Cribb occurred during the buildup to the War of 1812, a period characterized by rising tensions between the United States and Britain. Since the Revolutionary War, both nations had struggled to define their national boundaries. Along with hundreds of other free blacks traveling to and living in Britain at the time, Molineaux helped to consolidate and solidify a British national identity; his movements throughout Britain and Ireland and his fights, especially with Cribb, illustrate just how porous the Atlantic world was. He was able to move freely throughout the British Isles even as Britain engaged in war, racism flourished, and blacks saw themselves socially and economically shunned by white society.[5] Molineaux's life was one of significant mysteries and stunning silences. Nonetheless, what we know about Molineaux from outside sources situates him squarely as a subject for a study of British nationalism in the early nineteenth-century North Atlantic world.[6] According to an observer of his boxing skill, Molineaux's arrival and battles "have not only added greatness, but given stability to the English character."[7]

This essay is less about the fights between Molineaux and Cribb than the meanings they took on, as well as the representations of the fighters as embodying the collective feelings, beliefs, and qualities of Britain. By looking at a particular moment in the history of the African Diaspora in order to understand the making of British nationalism, this essay presents a different interpretation than historian Linda Colley's seminal work, *Britons: Forging the Nation, 1707–1837*, that naively puts forth an argument that British patriotism was antiracist and humanitarian. A cursory look inside the British prize ring shows that Britons were not charitable nor were they antiracist. By studying race, white racial attitudes in Britain, black figures in the Atlantic world, and the ways in which popular culture such as boxing helped racialize Britain's national identity, we can gain a deeper understanding of the making of British nationalism during the early nineteenth century, as well as the role that the Molineaux-Cribb prizefight played in that making.

* * *

That Tom Molineaux was the first American to fight in England for a heavyweight title is only the beginning of his story. The popular tale regarding Molineaux's earlier life in America is interesting. He was born into slavery in Georgetown, in what is now the District of Columbia, on March 23, 1784.[8] He grew up on a plantation outside of Richmond, Virginia. There, Molineaux began his boxing career by defeating an unknown opponent from a neighboring plantation, and in the process impressing his slave master, an aristocrat named Algernon Molineaux, with his performance. According to the commonly circulated story, Tom was promised his freedom and $500 if he could defeat a slave named Abe from a nearby plantation.[9] Tom defeated the contender and headed north as a freedman. For unknown reasons, he left the United States and arrived in London, possibly in early 1810, three years after England adopted policies prohibiting its engagement in the international slave trade. Upon arrival, Londoners directed Molineaux to the Horse and Dolphin on St. Martin's Street near Leicester Square, the house and pub owned by William Richmond, an ex-slave and his fellow countryman. A great pugilist himself, although not a heavyweight, Richmond won boxing matches against larger white competitors, but never fought for a title. He soon acted as Molineaux's guide, friend, philosopher, instructor, and corner man in the ring.[10]

Molineaux landed in the world's largest city and made a name for himself as he moved among several different types of people and classes. Sports helped him move between classes: the boxing community, the press, and some members of the general public took note of him—all of which demonstrate the significance of his presence. Molineaux and Richmond were not the only black faces in London. As scholars have illustrated, thousands of blacks lived in London at the time, but it was because of their celebrity status that Molineaux and Richmond attracted the most attention. Molineaux first appears on the record in Britain in 1810.[11] At twenty-six years of age and not long after his arrival in England, Molineaux became famous by defeating Bill Burrows ("The Bristol Unknown") and "Tough" Tom Blake.[12] One observer, Francis Place, who knew most of the well-known boxers of the time, took note of Molineaux.[13] Place, "the radical tailor of Charing Cross," had much to say about boxing. In fact, he began collecting newspaper articles about sports shortly after the first fight between Molineaux and Cribb.[14]

The skill, and particularly the physical power, that brought Molineaux fame also brought resentment because he threatened British conceptions of race.

The press increasingly contrasted Tom Cribb's intelligence with the "beastly" qualities of Molineaux. This emphasis comforted and placated the British, who felt that Molineaux was a threat in the ring and possibly a threat to a sport that they imagined was their own. In the United States, no one cared, possibly because Americans viewed boxing as a "savage" sport; perhaps that is why Molineaux left America.[15] In Britain, however, boxing was seen in a much different light. Although it has been around since ancient Greece, boxing has a particular history in the early modern period, especially during the Regency period, because there is something uniquely British about boxing. It was a way of settling challenges; indeed, it was a way of demonstrating British superiority. In fact, while the French were renowned for foils and the Italians for daggers, the British fought a much harder, dirtier game with their fists, according to Pierce Egan. Many boxing enthusiasts considered Egan, the most famous boxing journalist at the time, the first boxing historian. He seemed to be writing for the nation, and, in 1812, he created his tour de force, the monthly serial work titled *Boxiana, or Sketches of Modern Pugilism,* which provided biographical sketches of fighters, round-by-round descriptions of fights, and other information about the sport and its participants. Egan printed *Boxiana* in monthly paperbound sections and sold copies by subscription.[16] Egan noted that "in Holland the long knife decides too frequently; scarcely any person in Italy is without the stiletto; and France and Germany are not particular in using sticks, stones, etc. to gratify revenge; but in England, the FIST only is used. . . . The fight done, the hand is given in token of peace; resentment vanishes, and the cause generally bound in oblivion. This generous mode of conduct is not owing to any particular rule laid down by education—it is an inherent principle—the impulse of movement—acted upon by the most ignorant and inferior ranks of people. . . ."

Egan had no reservation about stating that "pugilism" was "a national trait." In point of fact, he had "no hesitation in declaring that it is wholly—*British!*"[17] Stated Egan, "By Boxing we will raise our fame, 'Bove any other nation."[18]

Because of the importance placed on boxing in Britain, Molineaux received more attention there than in America. His opponent, a white coal porter named Tom Cribb, received slightly more attention in Britain than did Molineaux. As historian Norman McCord points out, "Men like Tom Cribb [and Molineaux] were better known than many political activists" such as Francis Place, William Cobbett, Robert Wedderburn, Thomas Spence, George Cannon, and Thomas Evans, "who have figured more prominently in the received historical record."[19] Such insight establishes the significant role that Molineaux and Cribb played in British society. When linked to the importance of boxing in Britain, it is easy to see how, in December 1810, they took part in what could be called the fight of the early nineteenth century.

When the first challenge came from Molineaux in 1810, many Englishmen were worried that this black American, who had already made a name for himself as a result of two bouts against English fighters, would take the English title.[20] Many Britons deemed England's honor to be at stake, and the fight attracted huge interest. The buildup to the fight was exceptional; not since the fight between Richard Humphries and the Jewish boxing champion Daniel Mendoza twenty years earlier had a fight been so anticipated.[21] Both the "Fancy" (the elite social class of men who followed sports, especially prizefighting, in early nineteenth-century England) and the "flash" (the underworld of showy thieves and other disreputables in London) worried that Molineaux would win. While Molineaux's Americanness earned him little favor, his blackness raised a whole different set of issues and concerns regarding connections between national (hometown) and racial pride that were hard to separate. At the time, it was said that "some persons feel alarmed at the bare idea that a black man and a foreigner should seize the championship of England, and decorate his sable brow with the hard earned laurels of Cribb."[22] To many Britons, the fight between Molineaux and Cribb "appeared somewhat as a national concern, and ALL felt for the honor of their country, and deeply interested in the fate of their Champion, TOM CRIB."[23]

Molineaux's fight with a boxer named Rimmer that occurred in May 1811, between the two Molineaux-Cribb fights, deserves mention because of the bigotry that the spectators exuded. This fight also helps to explain why fighting against a *black* American was so important. The *Bell's Weekly Messenger* acknowledged, "The antipathy against a man of colour being considered a pugilist of first rate, has caused a good many uncharitable declarations, and the ardour of those people so illiberally disposed, aided by the assistance of those who had taken the odds, broke the ring in a moment, and suspended the men in action. . . ."[24] Because of the tensions, the battle between Rimmer and Molineaux moved outside of the ring. At that point, fifteen thousand spectators began brawling. This behavior was not unusual for early nineteenth-century sporting events.[25] Only the effort of Cribb, who was present, helped to stop the mayhem, restore the ring, and allow Molineaux to continue his hammering another six rounds until Rimmer could no longer stand. Although the British ended their participation in the slave trade, their racism, like that Molineaux experienced in America, ran rampant.

The epic battles between Molineaux and Cribb, the British champion, saw two contestants from opposite worlds, as well as opposite sides of the Atlantic, face off. The first battle set the scene for the greatest bare-knuckle event of the nineteenth century, possibly of all time. Budd Schulberg aptly notes that the British sporting world was more worried about Tom Molineaux than Napoleon.[26] (In fact, this is probable because by 1810 Napoleon was no longer a threat, with Wellington scoring victories in Spain and Portugal.) Indeed, boxing was a welcome diversion to the British populace. Additionally, the fight was also significant in that it challenged the myth of British fair play. The match was hard fought, but by the twenty-eighth round it was clear that neither fighter could have continued; they had expended their adrenaline and their legs and arms were tired, the logical result of nearly an hour of fighting and "fibbing." Egan ended his round-by-round description of the fight by recalling that "Molineaux . . . proved himself as courageous a man as ever an adversary contended with. . . . In the 28th round, after the men were carried to their corners, Cribb was so much exhausted that he could hardly rise from his second's knee at the call of 'Time.' His second, by a little maneuvering, occupied the attention of the Black's second, and so managed to prolong the period sufficiently to enable the champion to recover a little, and thus assist him to pull through."[27] However, Fred Henning, in his late nineteenth-century work, *Fights for the Championship,* described the scene thus:

> In the twenty-eighth round Thomas Molyneaux fairly won the fight. Tom Cribb could not come to time, and Sir Thomas Apreece [an umpire] allowed the half-minute to elapse, and summoned the men three times. Still, Cribb could not come, and the Black awaited the award of victory, his just due, in the centre of the ring. But during the excitement Joe Ward, [Cribb's second,] rushed across the ring to Bill Richmond [Molineaux's coach and second], and accused him of having placed two bullets [weights] in the Black's fist. This was, of course, indignantly denied, and Molyneaux was requested to open his hands, proving that nothing was there.
>
> The ruse, however, succeeded, and gave Cribb the opportunity to come round. . . .[28]

Apparently, there was more to the ruse than just the suggestion that Molineaux had bullets in his hands. The crowd was unruly and broke the ring, and Cribb's seconds tried to break Molineaux's fingers.[29] The common skullduggery in the fight world allowed Cribb to gain the upper hand and a few rounds later Molineaux gave up.

That Cribb probably secured victory through unfair means was shocking to Britons. "In the Regency period," as historian J. C. Reid mentions, "Englishmen were very conscious of being Englishmen, and the national pride which still, to a degree, attaches to the performances of a touring football team or cricket eleven was focused passionately on the feats of boxers."[30] In this atmosphere, and with the outcome of the fight, "the honour of England, and Cribb's victory . . . [were] hailed as not only a personal, but also a national, triumph."[31] Such nationalistic references to the Molineaux-Cribb fights, of course, were not uncommon. According to Egan, Cribb answered the call "to protect the honor of his country, and the reputation of *English Boxing*."[32] Cheating in and of itself was against the British notion of a "fair fight." Many Britons felt Cribb, who they perceived as a gentleman boxer, should have won without help. Contemporary London newspapers were filled with stories about the incident during the subsequent months.[33]

Although Molineaux lost the fight, both he and his managers were undeterred in their quest to win the championship. Several days later, Molineaux called for a rematch. The London newspapers printed his "Pugilistic Challenge to Mr. Thomas Cribb," and it was later copied in the New York *Evening Post:*

> Sir,—My friends think that had the weather on last Tuesday on which I contended with you, not been so unfavourable, I should have won the battle; I therefore challenge you to a second meeting, at any time within two months, for such sum as those gentlemen who place confidence in me may be pleased to arrange.
>
> As it is possible this letter may meet the public eye, I cannot omit the opportunity of expressing a confident hope, that the circumstance of my being of a different colour to that of a people amongst whom I have sought protection, will not in any way operate to my prejudice.
>
> I am, sir,
> Your most obedient humble servant,
> T. Molineaux[34]

For those who read newspapers in an attempt to keep up with the events of sporting culture, in its heyday at this time, the challenge would have been immediately evident. "As it is possible that this letter may meet the public eye" was less a conjecture than a fact; his promoters certainly would have sent it to all the newspapers they knew. Also, as Schulberg suggests, "Molineaux had alluded to the 'unfavorable weather' but the champion and his friends, their consciences not entirely clear, knew the dangerous foreigner was not referring to the elements alone."[35] What matters here is the flair and brash Americanness used in issuing the challenge and that by delivering it, Molineaux became an active agent—more so than any scholar has noted—in the project of inventing his own persona.[36] By using the London press, he and his promoters were able to get his challenge to Cribb and, more important, to the "Fancy" and general public. Most important, the phrasing in the second paragraph of Molineaux's squib demonstrates that he challenged racial conceptions. The fight pitted America versus England, and England was again worried. After all, it was widely believed that if Cribb's attendants had not cheated, Molineaux would have won.[37] His honor questioned and the fate of the nation on his shoulders, Cribb accepted the challenge, and the rematch was arranged.[38]

As the September 1811 fight date approached, the tensions between the United States and Britain were escalating. This was the eve of the War of 1812.[39] Many Britons questioned "whether OLD ENGLAND should still retain her proud characteristic of conquering" and feared that Molineaux, "an AMERICAN, and a *man of colour*, should win the honor, wear it, and carry it away from the shores of Britain."[40] Although Molineaux stood in especially well for America during the buildup to the War of 1812, he did not win his rematch. He returned to London with a broken jaw, in fact.

Egan offers the best insight regarding both the excitement that the "Fancy" felt—which was clearly linked to ideas about national identity—and the bigotry that they articulated. "The joy experienced . . . by the *flash* side," after Cribb beat Molineaux, "cannot be described—and considering all the disadvantages under which MOLINEAUX fought this battle, he performed wonders. It is not meant to be urged, that MOLINEAUX had not fair play throughout the fight *in the ring*—it is well known that he had." Egan noted,

> the *Black* had to contend against a prejudiced multitude, the pugilistic honour of the country was at stake, and the attempts of MOLINEAUX were viewed with jealousy, envy and distrust—the national laurels to be borne away by a foreigner—the *mere* idea to an English Breast was afflicting, and the *reality* could not be endured:—that it should seem, the spectators were ready to exclaim—"Forbid it heaven, forbid it man!" . . .
>
> It was from this sort of impression which operated upon the feelings of the auditors that MOLINEAUX had more to fear from, than even the mighty prowess of his brave opponent—the applause and cheering was decidedly upon the part of the CHAMPION [Cribb]; in fact, the *man of colour* received, generally, a very different sort of reception, occasioned, we apprehend, from the extreme anxiety manifested by the friends of *Crib* for one to stand long against him.[41]

At one level, Egan's statements suggest that he was aware of the national pride that Britain had displayed and the prejudice that Molineaux received. On another level, although Egan himself certainly felt that national pride, he was still instrumental in his efforts to relay to the general public the idea that in the rematch Molineaux was afforded the "fair play" that the British were noted for—indeed, the fair play that was absent in the first fight. Egan concluded his comments regarding Molineaux by discussing his skill and demeanor. Molineaux was, according to Egan, "inferior to none in point of courage and *bottom;* and considered a most excellent two-handed fighter. Full of fight, he exchanges *hits* with great alertness, and stops with considerable dexterity. Remarkably civil and unassuming in his demeanour, considering his wants for education, MOLINEAUX has rendered himself to the Fancy, if not a decided favourite, at least an object of considerable attention. To Richmond, he is most undoubtedly indebted for a considerable portion of that superior pugilistic science which he possesses. . . ."[42] Egan recognized that Molineaux was a skilled fighter who had carried himself in a peaceful way outside the ring and was worthy only of goodwill from the people of Britain.

Media and Race

After the second fight, huge crowds assembled for the separate returns of Cribb and Molineaux to London.[43] Cribb was likened to a general returning from a victorious battle; his "reception on the road was as flattering as a gallant officer could have met with, bearing a narrative of any glorious exploit against a foreign enemy."[44] Upon his return to London a few days later, Molineaux attracted large crowds. His reception, however, included more gawkers than fans with a hospitable interest in his well-being.[45] The condescension against Molineaux was unbearable. When reporting of the rematch with Cribb, which took place at Crown-Point, a short distance from Thistleton Gap and twelve miles from Stamford, the *Stamford Mercury* revealed that "the prejudice against the black colour seems to exist as much in the country as in London."[46]

The racism that Molineaux experienced while abroad is comparable with the anti-Semitism Daniel Mendoza felt during his reign in the late eighteenth century.[47] As was the case with the Molineaux—Cribb fights, there was huge publicity for Mendoza's fights. In fact, many authors have compared Molineaux's fights against Cribb to Mendoza's three contests against his ex-pupil, Richard Humphries, from 1788 to 1790. The fights were similar in terms of promotion, crowd size, the ferocity of the battles, and the extent to which racial and ethnic slurs were exchanged between members of society and Molineaux or Mendoza.[48]

What follows may be the best glimpse of the real Molineaux. Several nights before the second fight with Cribb, an ugly crowd confronted Molineaux. He and "his friend Caleb went out to promenade . . . but when the public curiosity to see the hero manifested in so violent a manner, the black Memnon was quite confounded, and shrunk back with the delicacy of a sensitive plant."[49] This suggests the violence of the era, even in the countryside (although many ruffians had, indeed, traveled from London), but also the personality of Molineaux. In this example, as in the earlier reference by Egan, we get a feeling that Molineaux had a reserved "demeanor" on the streets.[50] But every author who has looked, if only briefly, at Molineaux's life, suggests that he was also a nuisance or a tyrant.[51] For example, historian Dennis Brailsford suggests that Molineaux was "out of control" and accustomed to "fine clothes, endless food, heavy drinking and constant womanizing." According to Brailsford, Molineaux "appeared always as the powerful, angry and uncontrolled black, a regular drinker and a man whose first inclination in any new town he arrived at was to seek out the local stews and the fanciest of their providers of comfort."[52] However, the examples above from the English press suggest that he was neither a hulk nor a bruiser outside the ring. Common sense tells us that Britain would never have allowed him to act as a tyrant. Although the anti-slave trade laws ended the trade within the British realm, technically nothing could prohibit sailors from selling Molineaux into slavery in the Caribbean. Nonetheless, such unwarranted analyses regarding Molineaux's persona persist. Examples that run counter to the commonly held beliefs regarding Molineaux offer us the best glimpse of the man—a powerful and fierce competitor inside the ring, yet shy, reserved, and rational when going about his daily business in Britain.

Although the British feelings against Molineaux were severe, the British press was sympathetic because of the lengths he had come to fight in England. He had to rely on his friends. As the press pointed out, "Molineaux, it is said, had provoked a good deal of vengeance, and vapouring professions of what he would do to Cribb. These are certainly sufficiently disgusting and repugnant to the spirit of the Englishmen. . . . But it ought not to have been forgotten that Molineaux is a stranger—that he gave a proof of his courage by offering a general challenge—and that he came to the fight unsupported by friends of note, while the champion had all the *flash men* in his train."[53]

For his efforts in saving the nation from the mauler the British deemed a threat to *their* sport, the tributes kept pouring in for Cribb. Because he beat Molineaux, the boxing community of London, made up of both landed gentry and the "flash," presented Cribb with numerous gifts, medals, honors, and other accolades. Troubadours and authors wrote dozens of songs and poems about him, most of which mentioned Molineaux, and compared Cribb to pugilistic champions such as Mendoza and John Jackson. Shortly after his second match with Molineaux, the boxing community held a reception dinner. The *Bell's Weekly Messenger* recounted the scene in an article whose headline read "A Milling Grubbing Match." Those promoters and boxing enthusiasts present offered a toast to "Tom Crib[b], the Champion of England, who has nobly and successfully combated for the laurels of native championship, against a Moor."[54] Another toastmaster stated that the "innovating hand of a foreigner, when lifted against a son of Britannia, must not only be aided by the *strength* of a lion, but the heart also."[55] Later that year, "About 100 of the *gentlemen* patrons and practisers of the science of boxing assembled. . . . After a sumptuous banquet, a superb silver vase of the value of 80 guineas was produced, as the reward of the celebrated pugilist *Cribb.*"[56] According to *The Times,* Cribb awkwardly accepted the loving cup, which was "ornamented with Cribb's heraldic bearings; and is supported by a figure, representing the sable Molineaux, kneeling under its weight."[57] Molineaux, on this trophy, was like other blacks in the British Empire, most of whom remained enslaved. The burden of supporting the economy of the nation and the task of enriching white citizens, in this scenario, symbolically rested on his shoulders.

In 1810 and 1811, the Molineaux-Cribb fights were a main topic of conversation among the "Fancy"—indeed, among all Britons. Tales regarding the fights and dozens of artists' depictions of Molineaux and Cribb circulated throughout Britain and Ireland. Furthermore, because sailors wrote about the fame of Molineaux and Cribb in their journals, the stories circulated among those living in other parts of the Atlantic, as late as 1831. Other popular representations, such as poems and songs, clearly traveled to the peripheries of Britain, as well as its former colonies. Indeed, the reverberations were felt in 1818, long after Molineaux left London, by artists and authors such as Théodore Géricault and Thomas Moore.[58] American newspapers reprinted stories regarding some of Molineaux's fights; moreover, they mentioned Molineaux and Cribb in articles that appeared as late as the 1820s.[59] As many of the poems and songs that survive suggest, Molineaux's name became a household word in Britain.[60] At least two American sailors imprisoned in Dartmoor during the War of 1812 mentioned Molineaux in their diaries. Josiah Cobb, in writing about boxing within Dartmoor's walls, noted that sailors in prison wanted to be like Cribb and Molineaux, "of boxing celebrity, the most renowned heroes in all Christendom."[61] Benjamin Waterhouse, another sailor, stated: "We take two or three London newspapers, and through them know a little what is going forward in the world. We find by them that . . . Molenaux, the black bruiser, engross[es] the attention of the most respectable portion of *John Bull's family.*"[62] Waterhouse's reference to John Bull, the personification of England or an Englishmen, suggests how Molineaux garnered mass appeal.[63] Given the Prince Regent's (later, George IV) fascination with boxing and familiarity with many British fighters, many of whom attended his coronation ceremony in 1820, it is likely that he knew a great deal about Molineaux.

Nonetheless, Molineaux's popularity seemed annoying to some Britons. Years after the fights, Scottish-born painter Sir Henry Raeburn (1756–1823) lamented, "The thing is damned, sir—gone—sunk: nothing could be more unfortunate: when I put up my Scott for sale, another man put up his Molyneux. You know the taste of our London beer-suckers: one black bruiser is worth one thousand bright poets; the African sells in thousands, and the Caledonian won't move;—a dead loss, sir—gone, damned; won't do."[64] Raeburn directly attacks the class of people within the sporting community by referring them as "beer suckers." Admittedly, he was upset about losing money, but he was also concerned with threats to British national identity. As Raeburn's quandary—his failure to sell a portrait of the most famous Scottish writer—suggests, the cultural "working out" of large issues in the ring affected the larger British population.

Conclusion

In 1810, Molineaux became the first American to fight for a heavyweight title in England. The next title fight that matched an American with an Englishman and attracted similar attention occurred in 1860, a half-century later, when a white American boxer named John Camel Heenan fought Tom Sayers, notably known as "The Napoleon of the Prize Ring," to a draw in two hours and twenty minutes.[65] Although a persona non grata among early nineteenth-century elitists in America who snubbed athletics in general and boxing in particular, Molineaux was a kinesthetic genius in Britain during the Regency period who left spectators (many of whom were of elite stock), as well as competitors, open-mouthed. Additionally, it is possible to relate his success in life, and at various times in the ring, to the fact that athletic competition is one area of endeavor in which African Americans have been quite successful.[66]

Authors focused on binaries—Cribb's intelligence and the "science" of the "civilized" white versus the brute strength and laziness of Molineaux—for a reason: Molineaux threatened racial attitudes in Britain. The contested nature of the first fight supports this. Pierce Egan had downplayed the fact that the British tried to harm Molineaux. Egan, like at least some Britons, feared losing to an American, especially a black man, and could not accept Molineaux's apparent victory in the first fight. As we have seen, there was more to the disruption during the fight than Egan admitted in his *Boxiana.* Molineaux threatened basic elements of British national identity. This is supported by the fact that, regardless of how he obtained his freedom, Molineaux was "free" to travel, and that he was a skilled, strong boxer. That the British classified him as a "savage" illustrated that they were dismissive. To the British public it was essential that Cribb be portrayed as an intelligent, gentlemanly fighter in order to portray Britons' collective mind-set, expertise, and benevolence, or "their boasted fairness, prowess, and modesty," as one American put it in a letter to a newspaper.[67]

Historian Elliott Gorn wrote, "For decades proponents of boxing had argued that the ring upheld the values of fair play and equal opportunity."[68] Molineaux was afforded the equal opportunity to fight—indeed equality—and yet the English prize ring failed to offer him a level playing field. During the first fight, British spectators rushed into the ring and attempted to break his fingers in order to give Cribb more time to recover. Cribb's seconds then accused Molineaux of cheating, a testament to the fact that he was not offered fair play. Although Molineaux's second fight with Cribb was fair, in the sense that it was not interrupted by unruly spectators, Cribb had by that time completed several months of intense training in Scotland and easily won the contest.

The title fights between Molineaux and Cribb are more than defining moments in sports history. In fact, their story transcends the history of sports and can offer much to scholars who marginalize sports in general and boxing in particular.[69] Britain was defining and forming its identity in an international way, not only in opposition to other European nations but also in opposition to America. British national identity and the roles of race and of Americans—more precisely, a black American—in that moment have not been given enough attention. In fact, few historians look at America's effect on Britain during the Regency period, which overlapped with part of America's Early National era. Yet, many international men, from various countries, challenged British national identity.[70] Moreover, when historians who look at the Regency period discuss the role of outside influences on identity, they usually restrict their vision to the east—France in particular, but also Europe in general.[71] British nationalism, while clearly defined by the Napoleonic wars, was also defined by its racist ideology. The two were profoundly connected. Britain's former American colonies contributed significantly to the racialized component of British nationalism. Part of this contribution came from the high-profile presence of black boxers from the United States, such as Tom Molineaux, whose experiences in Britain show that the boxing ring racialized nationality. Sporting events, particularly those in the ring, were places where issues of national identity and race negotiated themselves.

Notes

I wish to thank those scholars who responded with questions and comments when I presented preliminary findings for this paper at the British Association for American Studies Conference (1999); the Race, Ethnicity, and Migration Conference (2000); and the Diaspora Paradigms Conference (2001). I also wish to thank the members of the Early American History Workshop at the University of Minnesota, especially Rus Menard, Lisa Norling, and John Howe who helped narrow the focus of an unwieldy essay. Thanks go to Simon Newman, Patrick Myler, and Don Ross who read this paper in various stages and offered helpful suggestions that clarified its argument. Special thanks go to David Roediger, Kirsten Fischer, Yuichiro Onishi, Jason Eden, Will Cooley, Anna Clark, Lou Andolino, and several anonymous reviewers for their suggestions and helpful hints. Thanks especially to Yashasvini Helfrich and Valerie D'Arienzo for their support, encouragement, and patience. Vegan kudos!

Epigraph. Pierce Egan, *Boxiana,* vol. 1 (London: 1812), 480–81. Quoted in Paul Geoffrey Edwards and James Walvin, *Black Personalities in the Era of the Slave Trade* (Baton Rouge: Louisiana State Press, 1983), 201.

1. The family name is spelled differently in different documents, sometimes as "Molineaux" but also as "Molineux," "Molyneaux," and "Molyneux." I have used Molineaux throughout, except in quotations from newspapers and books, because that spelling appears most often.

2. Especially important on my thinking about issues of race, nationalism, and identity in Britain are Linda Colley, *Britons: Forging the Nation, 1707–1837* (New Haven, Conn.: Yale University Press, 1992); Roxann Wheeler, *The Complexion of Race: Categories of Difference in Eighteenth-Century British Culture* (Philadelphia: University of Pennsylvania Press, 2000); Iain McCalman, *Radical Underworld: Prophets, Revolutionaries and Pornographers in London, 1795–1840* (Cambridge, Mass.: Cambridge University Press, 1988).

3. Linda Colley states, "Everyone knows that the War for American Independence created a new nation. . . . But it did more than this. It helped forge a very different Great Britain in which both men and women would have to work out their ideas of patriotism as never before." Yet in Colley's ultraconservative look at Britain at this time, she talks little about the affect of America or the role of sports and sporting society in Britain. See Colley, *Britons,* 145.

4. For example, see Hugh Cunningham, "The Language of Patriotism," in Raphael Samuel, *Patriotism: The Making and Unmaking of British National Identity* (New York: Routledge, 1989), 1:57–89; Colley, *Britons,* 145, 170–73. Simply, all U.S. boxers in England—a handful about whom we know something—were black. See Paul Magriel, "Tom Molineaux: Career of an American Negro Boxer in England

and Ireland, 1809–1818," *Phylon* (December 1951): 336. Numerous black American fighters—among others, Sam Robinson, Harry Sutton, Massa Kendrick—followed in Molineaux's footsteps, but none fought for a heavyweight title. Their stories are, so far, best documented in Peter Fryer's excellent work *Staying Power: The History of Black People in Britain* (London: Pluto Press, 1984), but more study is needed. On March 18, 1811, *The Times* (London) reported that there was, in fact, a "fraternity of black millers" in London.

5. It has been suggested that black Americans in the Atlantic world were afforded a relative ease of movement during the War of 1812 that was not granted to whites in similar instances. For example, black American sailors captured off the tip of South Africa by the British navy were somewhat free to move about and find jobs while their white shipmates were imprisoned at the Cape. See Keletso E. Atkins, "The 'Black Atlantic Communication Network': African American Sailors and the Cape of Good Hope Connection," *Issue: A Journal of Opinion* 24, no. 2 (1996): 23–25.

6. The bibliography of works that briefly mention Molineaux is voluminous and indicates that although historians, scholars, and popular boxing enthusiasts have realized that there is a magnificent story in the life of Molineaux, they have failed to seriously investigate his importance in history and, as a result, have written little about him in their works. Indeed, more than thirty-four popular secondary works mention Molineaux's name, but none has attempted to piece together his life and uncover the significance of it, particularly his role in issues regarding the formation of identities, race, and nationalism. For a bare-bones biography of Molineaux, see Magriel, "Tom Molineaux," 336; Michael Harris Goodman, "The Moor vs. Black Diamond: Thomas Molineaux, Tom Cribb, and the British Prize Ring," *Virginia Cavalcade* 29, no. 4 (1980): 164–73; Patrick Myler, "The First Great Black Heavyweight: How Tom Molineaux was Robbed of the World Title," *The Ring* (December 1994); Howard B. Furer, "Tom Molineaux: America's First Black Sports Hero," *The New England Journal of History* 51, no. 2 (1994): 4–13.

We should applaud popular historians and boxing enthusiasts. They are, after all, the ones who have been the first to look at Molineaux's life. Historians could learn much from the efforts of many of the popular sporting enthusiasts. Molineaux's life receives little more than mention in twenty-one other "historical" studies, including Peter Linebaugh and Marcus Rediker's recent work, *The Many-Headed Hydra: Sailors, Slaves, Commoners, and the Hidden History of the Revolutionary Atlantic* (Boston: Beacon Press, 2000), 321. William H. Rhoden devotes an entire chapter titled "The Plantation: The Dilemma of Physical Bondage" of his recent work, *$40 Million Slaves: The Rise, Fall, and Redemption of the Black Athlete* (New York: Crown Publishers, 2006), to Molineaux.

7. Egan, *Boxiana*, 361.

8. International Genealogical Index Record (Salt Lake City, Utah).

9. Nat Fleischer, *Black Dynamite: The Story of the Negro in the Prize Ring from 1782–1938*, vol. 1 (New York: C. J. O'Brien, 1938), 34–35. In other accounts, the sum of money also ranges in different sources from anywhere between $100 and $500.

10. For a more complete biography on Bill Richmond, see Fleischer, *Black Dynamite,* 1:21–23; Trevor C. Wignall, "Coloured Fighters," in *The Story of Boxing* (New York: Bretano's, 1924), 251–64; Alexander Johnston, *Ten—And Out!: The Complete Story of The Prize Ring in America* ([1927] rev. ed., New York: Ives Washburn, 1936), 19–21; Nat Fleischer, *The Heavyweight Championship: An Informal History of Heavyweight Boxing from 1719 to the Present Day* ([1949] rev. ed., New York: G. P. Putnam's Sons, 1961), 28–32, 34; Edwards and Walvin, *Black Personalities in the Era of the Slave Trade,* 186–92.

11. A significant amount has been written in the past two decades regarding black migration to England and black populations in England. See works by James Walvin, Folarian Shyllon, Peter Fryer, Peter Linebaugh, Marcus Rediker, and Gretchen Gerzina, amongst others, for examples of other blacks in London. Also see John Thomas Smith, *Vagabondia* (London: published for the proprietor and sold by J. and A. Arch, 1817), esp. Plate XIII, depicting "Joseph Johonson, a black sailor, with a model of a ship *Nelson* on his cap" and Plate XIV, showing "Charles M'Gee, a notorious black man, whose father died at the age of 108. He usually stood at the Obelisk at the foot of Ludgate Hill." Molineaux's first fight in England was mentioned in *Bell's Weekly Messenger* (London), 26 August 1810.

12. Molineaux must have known when he was born because several of the newspapers reported his age correctly. *Bell's Weekly Messenger* (London), 26 August 1810. See Dennis Brailsford, *Bareknuckles: A Social History of Prize-Fighting* (Cambridge, Mass.: Lutterworth Press, 1988), 60.

13. Francis Place, *The Autobiography of Francis Place (1771–1854),* edited with an introduction by Mary Thale (Cambridge, Mass.: Cambridge University Press, 1972), ix, but also 20, 50, 74. See also, Dudley Miles, *Francis Place, 1771–1854: The Life of a Remarkable Radical* (New York: St. Martin's Press, 1988); McCalman, *Radical Underworld.*

14. See The Francis Place Collection, Microfilm Reel 25, "Manners. Morals.—Sports.—Poor.—Emigration. 1810–1840," British Library.

15. For contemporary examples of American disgust with prizefighting, consult *Niles' Weekly Register* (Baltimore), 31 January, 18 July, 18 October 1818; *Niles' National Register* (Baltimore), 3 December 1842. See also Elliott J. Gorn, *The Manly Art: Bare-Knuckle Prize Fighting in America* (Ithaca, N.Y.: Cornell University Press, 1986); Brailsford, *Bareknuckles,* 139–50, esp. 145.

16. By 1813, Egan had produced enough material to enable him to turn his serial into a single book-length volume, and by 1829, he published *Boxiana* as a five-volume set. Egan also wrote plays, songs, novels, epigrams, and a dictionary of slang. James B. Roberts and Alexander G. Skutt, *The Boxing Register: International Boxing Hall of Fame Official Record Book,* 2d ed. (Ithaca, N.Y.: McBooks Press, 1998), 482. See also J. C. Reid, *Bucks and Bruisers: Pierce Egan and Regency England* (London: Routledge & Kegan Paul, 1971); James Huntington-Whiteley, *The Book of British Sporting Heroes,* with an introduction by Richard Holt (London: National Portrait Gallery Publications, 1998), 16. A. J. Liebling suggests that the first Molineaux-Cribb fight was the catalyst for the Egan's publication of *Boxiana* and for his subsequent success.

Liebling, *The Sweet Science* ([1951]; New York: Penguin Books, 1956), 9. Saul David underscores Liebling's comment in *Prince of Pleasure: The Prince of Wales and the Making of the Regency* (New York: Atlantic Monthly Press, 1998), 288.

17. Quoted in Reid, *Bucks and Bruisers,* 21. Emphasis in original. Also cited in *The Book of British Sporting Heroes,* 16.

18. Egan, *Boxiana,* 481.

19. Norman McCord, *British History 1815–1916* (New York: Oxford University Press, 1991), 126.

20. *Bell's Weekly Messenger* (London), 26 August 1810.

21. See *The Times* (London), 13 December 1810.

22. Henry Downes Miles, *Pugilistica, the history of British boxing, containing lives of the most celebrated pugilists; full reports of their battles from contemporary newspapers, with authentic portraits, personal anecdotes, and sketches of the principle patrons of the prize ring, forming a complete history of the ring from Fig to Broughton, 1719–40, to the last championship battle between King and Heenan, in December 1863,* 3 vols. (1863; Edinburgh: J. Grant, 1906), 1:253; Magriel, "Tom Molineaux," 331. See Edwards and Walvin, *Black Personalities in the Era of the Slave Trade,* 202–3.

23. Egan, *Boxiana,* 401. Emphasis in original.

24. *Bell's Weekly Messenger* (London), 26 May 1811. Also see *The Times* (London), 28 September 1811.

25. On the rowdiness of the crowds at sites of popular entertainments, see Elliott J. Gorn, "'Good-Bye Boys, I Die a True American': Homicide, Nativism, and Working-Class Culture in Antebellum New York City," *Journal of American History* 74, no. 2. (September 1987): 388–410; Elliot J. Gorn, "'Gouge and Bite, Pull Hair and Scratch': The Social Significance of Fighting in the Southern Backcountry," *American Historical Review* 90, no. 1, Supplement to Volume 90 (February 1985): 18–43. See also Norman Clark, *The Boxing Referee* (London: Methuen & Co. Ltd., 1926), 2–3; Joe Robinson, *Claret and Cross-Buttock or Rafferty's Prize Fighters* (London: Allen and Unwin, 1976), 13; John Durant and Edward Rice, *Come Out Fighting* (New York: Essential Books, Duell, Sloan and Pearce, 1946), 13; Brailsford, *Bareknuckles,* 61–62.

26. Budd Schulberg, "The Battle of the Bare-Knuckled Champions," *True Magazine* (Fawcett Publications, Inc., 1953; reprt. in *1965 Boxing Yearbook* [London: True Magazine by Atlas Publishing and Distributing Co. Ltd., 1965]), 28, 30. See Reid, *Bucks and Bruisers,* 13.

27. Quoted in Magriel, "Tom Molineaux," 332.

28. Quoted in ibid. See also Fred Henning's account of the Cribb versus Molineaux fights in Denzil Batchelor, *Best Boxing Stories* (London: Gaber and Faber, 1953).

29. *Bell's Weekly Messenger* (London), 29 September 1811; David Remnick, *King of the World: Muhammad Ali and the Rise of an American Hero* (New York: Random House, 1998), 222.

30. Reid, *Bucks and Bruisers,* 13.

31. Ibid.

32. Egan, *Boxiana,* 408 (emphasis in original).

33. See especially *The Times* (London), 19, 25, and 29 December 1810; *Bell's Weekly Messenger* (London), 23 December 1810 and 29 September 1811.

34. *The Times* (London), 25 and 29 December 1810; *Bell's Weekly Messenger* (London), 30 December 1810, p. 7. Reprinted in *Evening Post* (New York), 13 February 1811.

35. Schulberg, "The Battle," 32.

36. I borrow this phrasing from Cheryl Harris's wonderful article on Sojourner Truth, "Finding Sojourner's Truth: Race, Gender, and the Institution of Whiteness," *Cardozo Law Review* 18, no. 309 (1996): 361.

37. See *The Times* (London), 30 December 1810–25 May 1811; *Bell's Weekly Messenger* (London), 30 December 1810–26 May 1811.

38. See *Bell's Weekly Messenger* (London), 30 December 1810, pp. 1 and 7. See *The Times* (London), 25 May 1811.

39. See Schulberg, "The Battle," 30; Gorn, *The Manly Art,* 34.

40. Egan, *Boxiana,* 409. Emphasis in original.

41. Ibid., 367–68. Emphasis in original.

42. Ibid., 369–71. Emphasis in original. Quoted in Edwards and Walvin, *Black Personalities in the Era of the Slave Trade,* 202–3.

43. *The Times* (London), 1 October 1811.

44. *Bell's Weekly Messenger* (London), 6 October 1811.

45. Ibid.

46. *The Stamford Mercury* (Stamford, England), 26 September 1811; *Bell's Weekly Messenger* (London), 29 September 1811. In a fascinating essay on boxing fans' responses to black heavyweights, Frederic Cople Jaher shows that race and national (hometown) cheering are hard to separate: "White America Views Jack Johnson, Joe Lewis, and Muhammed Ali," in *Sport in America: New Historical Perspectives,* edited by Donald Spivey (Westport, Conn.: Greenwood Press, 1985): 145–92.

47. An interesting parallel can be drawn between Molineaux and boxers who came before him in Britain. The former heavyweight champion Daniel Mendoza (1788–1836), fittingly called "The Light of Israel," was Jewish and a hero to Jews in Britain in the late eighteenth century. We can speculate that the black community in London had similar regard for black prizefighters. For more on Daniel Mendoza, see his treatise *The art of boxing with a statement of the transactions that have passed between Mr. Humphreys and myself since our battle at Odiham. By Daniel Mendoza, P.P.* (London: Printed and sold for Daniel Mendoza, No.4, Gapel Court, and No.2, Paradise Row, Bethnal Green, 1789) and *The memoirs of the life of Daniel Mendoza* (1826), edited and with an introduction by Paul Magriel (New York: Batsford, 1951); Roberts and Skutt, *The Boxing Register,* 28; W. C. Heinz, ed., *The Fireside Book of Boxing: A Collection of Pugilism's Greatest Literature & Art* (New York: Simon and Schuster, 1961), 288–90; Whiteley, *The Book of British Sporting Heroes,* 16, 166–67.

48. See Schulberg, "The Battle," 32; Roberts and Skutt, *The Boxing Register,* 28; Whiteley, *The Book of British Sporting Heroes,* 16, 166–67.

49. *Bell's Weekly Messenger* (London), 29 September 1811.

50. See Egan, *Boxiana,* 369–71, quoted in Edwards and Walvin, *Black Personalities in the Era of the Slave Trade,* 202–3.

51. See, for example, Magriel, "Tom Molineux"; Myler, "The First Great Black Heavyweight"; and Goodman, "The Moor vs. Black Diamond," but also recent popular representations of Molineaux in George MacDonald Fraser's novel *Black Ajax* (London: Harper Collins, 1997), a play on BBC Radio titled "Cribb and The Black" (1999), and the countless authors that have mentioned him. See Egan, *Boxiana,* 361, when Egan calls Molineaux "a rude, unsophisticated being." On page 370, Egan states that Molineaux is "civil and unassuming in his demeanor."

52. Brailsford, *Bareknuckles,* 62. Thanks to Will Cooley for this source.

53. *Bell's Weekly Messenger* (London), 6 October 1811, p. 7. Italics in original. See also Magriel, "Tom Molineux," 334–35.

54. *Bell's Weekly Messenger* (London), 13 October 1811.

55. Egan, *Boxiana,* 419 (emphasis in original).

56. *The Times* (London), 3 December 1811. Italics in original. See Egan, *Boxiana,* 418–19; Gorn, *The Manly Art,* 21–22.

57. *The Times* (London), 3 December 1811.

58. Heinz, *The Fireside Book of Boxing,* 300. Rupert Christiansen, *The Victorian Visitors: Culture Shock in Nineteenth-Century Britain* (New York: Grove/Atlantic, Inc., 2002), 33.

59. *Evening Post* (New York), 13, 18 February 1811; *The Republican, And Savannah Evening Ledger* (Savannah, Ga.), 23 July 1811; *Niles' Weekly Messenger* (Baltimore), 20 May 1815, 30 October 1824; *The Analectic Magazine* (Philadelphia), November 1817.

60. Heinz, *The Fireside Book of Boxing,* 300. See Thomas Moore, *The Journal of Thomas Moore,* 6 vols., edited by Wilfred S. Dowden, Barbara Bartholomew, and Joy L. Linsley (Newark [and] London: University of Delaware Press [and] Associated University Presses, 1983–91), 1: 73, 78; 3: 1296–97, as well as several sections that deal with "Gentleman" John Jackson. Gorn, *The Manly Art,* 34.

61. Josiah Cobb, *A Green Hand's First Cruise, Roughed Out From the Log-book of Memory, of Twenty-Five Years Standing: Together With a Residence of Five Months in Dartmoor,* 2 vols. (Baltimore: Cushing & Brother, 1841), 1:34.

62. Benjamin Waterhouse, *A Journal of a Young Man of Massachusetts, Late a Surgeon on Board an American Privateer, who was captured at sea by the British, in May, Eighteen Hundred and Thirteen, and was confined first, at Melville Island, Halifax, then at Chatham, in England. . . . and last, At Dartmoor Prison. Interspersed with Observations, Anecdotes and Remarks, Tending to Illustrate the moral and political characters of the Nations. To which is added, a correct engraving of Dartmoor Prison, Representing the massacre of American prisoners. Written by Himself. The second edition, with considerable Additive and Improvements* (Boston: Rowe & Hooper, 1816), 75.

63. For more on the image of John Bull, see esp. Jeannine Surel, "John Bull," translated by Kathy Hodgkin in Samuel, *Patriotism,* 3:3–25.

64. Allan Cunningham, *The Lives of the Most Eminent British Painters and Sculptors,* vol. 2 (New York: J. & J. Harper, 1831–34), 237. Also quoted in Hugh Honour,

"Black Models and White Myths," *The Image of the Black in Western Art,* 4:2, forward by Amadou-Mahtar (Cambridge, Mass.: Harvard University Press, 1989), 30. Thanks to Paul Gilroy for these citations.

65. See Durant and Rice, *Come Out Fighting,* 15–17; Alexander Saxton, *The Rise and Fall of the White Republic: Class Politics and Mass Culture in Nineteenth-Century America* (New York: Verso, 1990), 212; Elliott Gorn and Warren Goldstein, *A Brief History of American Sports* 3rd ed. (New York: Hill and Wang, 1995), 65–66; Brailsford, *Bareknuckles,* 128–37, esp. 134.

66. See Jaher, "White America Views Jack Johnson, Joe Lewis, and Muhammed Ali." See also Gorn, *The Manly Art;* Jeffrey T. Sammons, *Beyond the Ring: The Role of Boxing in American Society* (Urbana and Chicago: University of Illinois Press, 1990); Gorn and Goldstein, *A Brief History of American Sports;* Gerald Early, *The Culture of Bruising: Essays on Prizefighting, Literature, and Modern American Culture* (Hopewell, N.J.: Ecco Press, 1994); Gerald Early, ed., *Body Language: Writers on Sport* (St. Paul, Minn.: Graywolf Press, 1998); Nelson George, *Elevating the Game: Black Men and Basketball* (New York: Harper Collins, 1992); and Rhoden, *$40 Million Slaves.*

67. *Niles' Weekly Register* (Baltimore), 30 October 1824.

68. Gorn, "'Good-Bye Boys, I Die a True American,'" 396.

69. Some significant studies, however, stand out. See books by Benjamin Rader and Richard O. Davies. Dave Zirin's work is also important, notably *What's My Name, Fool?: Sports and Resistance in the United States* (Chicago: Haymarket Books, 2005) and *Welcome to the Terrordome: The Pain, Promise, and Politics of Sports* (Chicago: Haymarket Books, 2007). On sport culture, particularly boxing, see Gorn, "'Gouge and Bite, Pull Hair and Scratch,'" 18–43; Gorn, *The Manly Art;* Gorn, "'Good-Bye Boys, I Die a True American,'" 388–410; Sammons, *Beyond the Ring;* Gorn and Goldstein, *A Brief History of American Sports;* Early, *The Culture of Bruising;* Early, *Body Language.*

70. See Fryer, *Staying Power,* particularly his appendix of nineteenth-century black pugilists from the United States, Canada, the Caribbean, and Africa. Also see Peter Fryer, *Aspects of Black British History* (London: Index Books, 1993).

71. For example, see most of the essays in Samuel, *Patriotism,* 3 vols., esp. Cunningham, "The Language of Patriotism," 1:57–89, esp. 63; Colley, *Britons,* 145, 170–73; Roger Wells, "English Society and Revolutionary Politics in the 1790s: The Case for Insurrection," *The French Revolution and British Popular Politics,* edited by Mark Philp (New York: Cambridge University Press, 1991): 188–226; Sara E. Melzer and Kathryn Norberg, *From the Royal to the Republican Body: Incorporating the Political in Seventeenth- and Eighteenth-Century France* (Berkeley: University of California Press, 1998); Marilyn Morris, *The British Monarchy and the French Revolution* (New Haven, Conn.: Yale University Press, 1998).

10

"Colored Germans There Will Never Be"

Colonialism and Citizenship in Modern Germany

FATIMA EL-TAYEB

Germany engaged in formal colonialism only for a short period, lasting for little more than thirty years, from 1884 to the First World War.[1] It still is a widespread popular belief, therefore, in Germany and beyond, that the possession of African and Pacific territories had no lasting impact on either the colonizing or the colonized societies; an assumption that was long supported by colonialism's scholars' negligence of the German Empire. While this exclusion of Germany from colonial history has been effectively questioned by a number of scholars in recent years, another, related assumption lives on largely unchallenged: the supposed unaffectedness of Germany by racist thinking or the existence of "race issues" within its own population.[2] The extreme racism of the National Socialist state is paradoxically ignored here by claiming that anti-Semitism and racism are fundamentally different ideologies. Anti-Semitism thus appears as Germany's "substitute" for the racism prevailing in other Western countries, rather than as being related to it. This claim has a number of problematic consequences: Nazi policies against nonwhites remain largely unexplored; the influence of scientific racism, less concerned with Jews prior to 1914, on Nazi anti-Semitism is often underestimated; and the binarism of Jews and Germans inherent in many analyses not only repeats exclusionary models but also erases the history of various German ethnic minorities.

In this essay, I will put forward a different argument, proposing that colonialism had a lasting influence on German society, namely in offering a model for gradually excluding "non-Germanic" citizens from the definition of *German.* By looking at the role colonialism played for definitions of what "Germanness" meant (as expressed in legal policies around citizenship as well as the cultural debates and social interactions accompanying them) I am hoping to show how German colonialism was both fed by and produced racialized notions of national identity, notions whose traces have been visible in German citizenship policies throughout the twentieth century.[3] I will concentrate on one particular episode: the 1905 ban on interracial marriages in "German South West Africa" and its historical context. This measure and the debates surrounding it were important beyond its immediate effect on the colony. While the number of persons directly affected was small (only about fifty "mixed marriages" were registered when the law was implemented in South West Africa),[4] its implications were much more far-reaching: the law was based on beliefs about the relation between *Germanness* and *whiteness,* which were shared by a substantial number of Germans, independent of their political beliefs. It is impossible to associate biological and racist definitions of citizenship with reactionary political groups alone. Scientific explanations of human relations, based on Darwin's evolutionary model of the "survival of the fittest" were popular across the political spectrum, as were eugenic population theories (which in turn had inspired Darwin). Policies such as the sterilization of the "genetically inferior" or the exclusion of the "racially foreign" from the body of citizens were discussed among nationalists and race scientists as well as feminists and socialists.[5] *Race* was the central concept within all these debates, be it in relation to the "optimization of the German race" or in consolidating a world order based on a race hierarchy first developed by Enlightenment thinkers such as Blumenbach and Kant. The "internal" racial thinking of eugenicists or sexologists, supposedly concerned only with the "white" or "Germanic race," is not usually associated with racism, but the race hierarchy and its dogma of clearly separable, biologically defined races with immutable and disparate characteristics was a necessary point of reference within those internal discourses as well.[6]

This becomes obvious in the debates around the apartheid laws in German South West Africa introduced by the local governor in 1905. The laws aimed at excluding "racially mixed" children of white German settlers married to African women from the German citizenship to which they were entitled by law. This was the first time, thus, that German identity was explicitly linked to *race* not only culturally and socially but also legally. The context of colonial domination, and more specifically the suppression of a colonial revolt, provided an immediate justification, but as will become obvious, arguments of both defenders and enemies of the measure centered on questions of German national and racial identity rather than colonial policies.

From the late nineteenth century onwards, *colonial enthusiasm,* declaring Germany's right and duty to take a place among the world's leading nations, had swept the country. Such a leading position, so the argument went, necessarily demanded a colonial empire.[7] Part of the imperialist movement's success can be explained by the opportunity of public activity it offered to the fast-growing urban middle class, whose economic importance was not yet accompanied by political influence.[8] Simultaneously, the conservative government instrumentalized the movement to direct social tension out of society, construct a common national goal, and isolate its opponents, particularly the Social Democrats, as "unpatriotic traitors." Colonial enthusiasm thus put progressive forces on the defensive and strengthened the position of the nationalist organizations. The latter skillfully used the new mass media—popular magazines and newspapers, exhibitions, and even film—to popularize their vision of an imperialist, modern Germany. Thereby, they were able to incorporate the general population into the political process in a hitherto unknown way.[9] While the overseas empire was not necessarily of central interest to the average German, the constant propaganda worked to convince him of his nation's superiority and of the advantages of the government's imperialist politics. The German colonies thus from the beginning had complex, at times contradictory, functions. Economically, they were marginal at best, never even getting close to fulfilling hopes of making Germany independent of the resources imported from French and British territories. Neither did they offer a home to the substantial number of Germans leaving their motherland each year. Of all the colonies, only German South West Africa was deemed fit to house a large settler population and even there, the number of German colonialists was as low as 12,000.[10] Ideologically though, the colonies were of central importance. Germany became a colonial power only thirteen years after the nation was founded; the establishment of a national identity and of an imperialist empire thus largely coincided.[11] The connection between these two vast material and ideological transformations was further strengthened by a third chronological coincidence: the late nineteenth century was also the high point of social Darwinism. Accordingly, this ideology played an important role in defining Germanness both within (i.e., which inhabitants of Germany were to be considered "Germans") and without (i.e., in clarifying what set Germans apart from other peoples and more specifically, what made them destined to rule over "inferior" populations in Africa and the Pacific). The different levels of identity politics mentioned above continuously intermingled so that to fully comprehend one, it is necessary to take into account the others. This might seem self-evident, but the question of whether German colonialism affected concepts of national identity is rarely asked. While this essay cannot offer an exhaustive answer, it will raise a number of issues demonstrating the importance of exploring this relation. The specific questions concerning us here are, how much was the perception of colonized peoples, especially in German South West Africa, shaped by notions of "Germanness" derived from the struggle to create a national identity (prior to and after 1871); and how, in turn, did racialized notions of "German," used to justify colonial domination, work to divide and rank the German population according to a racial hierarchy?

The nationalist organizations popularizing the colonial idea had close allies in the social Darwinist scientists, whose influence was rapidly growing around the beginning of the twentieth century in Germany and internationally. In the wake of Darwin's theory of evolution and the fast development of natural, "exact" sciences that had followed it in the late nineteenth century, social Darwinist disciplines had developed in all Western nations. Eugenics, sexology, and race science aimed at uncovering the "natural laws" governing human interactions. This promise of a set of unambiguous, scientific explanations replacing contested philosophical models of human nature proved attractive to conservatives and progressives alike. While most social Darwinists politically associated themselves with ultraconservative nationalist groups, their ideas quickly spread throughout society, into conservative as well as socialist or feminist circles, even clearly affecting their most outspoken opponent, the Catholic Church.[12] While a number of social Darwinist positions remained contested, such as the propagation of eugenic sterilizations, the widespread agreement on questions of race became obvious in the public debate around "miscegenation" in the colonies.

Social Darwinism provided a supposedly neutral, that is, a scientific argument for colonialism. And while academic disciplines concerned with human societies, such as history, sociology or psychology, considered the race scientists' ideas on the "white" and "yellow" race oversimplified and extreme, they did not doubt that "race" itself was a useful category in analyzing historical and social processes. Furthermore, concerning their attitude toward the black race, the social Darwinists were rather mainstream. That Africans constituted the most primitive kind of humanity, separated from the civilized Europeans by a wide biological gap, was a notion that had been well established by the early twentieth century.[13] In Germany neither the academic community nor society in general questioned the truth of these social Darwinist beliefs. Accordingly, the country's self-image of racial superiority was severely shaken when the Herero and Nama in Germany's most important colony, South West Africa, began a revolt in 1904 that, despite the use of an unheard number of soldiers and amount of money, could not be suppressed until 1907.[14] The German military responded with a genocide, justified by the troops' commander Lothar von Trotha, who claimed the revolt as "the beginning of a race war."[15] Within this logic, extermination or slave labor were the only options for rebellious "natives," and after the war, the Germans established a system of control and oppression that in its completeness was unique in the world (and later became the model for the South African apartheid system).[16] It included the destruction of the traditional community and family structures, complete expropriation, mass deportations, and forced labor for natives above the age of eight.[17]

The war in South West Africa, lasting much longer than expected, generated much publicity in Germany. In 1906 the parliamentary opposition, Social Democrats and the Catholic Center Party, voted against further war credits and parliament was dissolved. The ensuing elections, dubbed "Hottentotten-Wahlen" ("Hottentot elections," *Hottentotts* being the derogatory name for the Nama), ended in a disaster for the Socialists as the conservative government had managed to present the colonial war as a cause that united patriotic Germans and isolated those groups that questioned the colonialist practice. The immense publicity that went with the election campaign not only further established the racist ideology within the German society, but it also brought violations of the code of strict racial separation into focus, most importantly miscegenation.[18] By then, the race scientists' obsession with the dangers of racial mixing had become common wisdom.[19] The conviction with which the *Leipziger Neueste Nachrichten* excluded persons of "colored" ancestry from the community of potential German citizens shows the extent to which social Darwinist theories had become popularized: "The German Empire will have many colored subjects in the future, but colored Germans there will never be, since color and other signifiers mark the human bastard with the inextinguishable sign of its descent and according to these signs, it will be named and ethnologically classified."[20]

The above statement was a reaction to the South West African situation, into which we will look in detail. But the scientific argumentation employed here claimed universal significance. In the eyes of social Darwinism's proponents, the declining purity of the superior races was the single most important explanation for the downfall of civilized nations, and the perseverance or reconstruction of this purity therefore the foremost duty of science and society.[21] This extremely negative attitude logically sprang from the assumption of a strict racial hierarchy, an idea that was popular far beyond social Darwinist circles in early twentieth-century Germany—and far beyond Germany. The international social Darwinist community transcended national and political borders, it was equally popular in capitalist Britain and the socialist USSR; forced "eugenic" sterilizations of "the genetically inferior" were as frequent in the United States as in Sweden. Eugenicists worldwide were in constant exchange and shared certain basic beliefs, central among them the existence of a "white race" that, especially in its Germanic variety, formed the crown of human evolution; of its counterpart, "the black race" that, by its gene pool, was doomed to internal inferiority; and of "racial mixing," especially between those two races, as the greatest threat to civilization and root of all evil. German race scientists were among the leading in the world and these three topics dominated their studies and publications as well as those of scientists from other nations. And nothing threatened the "natural order" more than a blurring of the supposedly clear boundaries between the races: the existence of persons with a mixed heritage undermined the dogma of the different races being clearly separable and actually mutually exclusive. Accordingly, "mixing" between the black and white race was condemned as unnatural and disastrous not only for the offspring itself but for all mankind. And "mixed blood" as the ultimate threat to the West meant miscegenation as the ultimate sin. German social Darwinist literature abundantly explored this topic, often in reference to Egypt or Persia whenever the downfall of great ancient cultures was explained, and the Americas when current threats to civilization were debated.[22] In the first decade of the twentieth century, the focus moved from "racial mixing" as a general threat to the white race to that of a concrete threat to the German nation. The war in South West Africa had caused a heightened public interest in the colonies and a disturbance of the "natural racial hierarchy" caused by interracial relationships was routinely used to explain the inexplicable: the continued, successful resistance of "primitive peoples" against the superior German war machine. While white women with black spouses had long been subjected to public scorn on all levels, certain white men now became "race traitors" as well; not by having sexual relationships with black women, but by legitimizing those relationships through marriage and thereby allowing "black blood" to pollute the white nation.[23] In 1905, the war was still raging, the South West African governor Friedrich von Lindequist declared: "Among the long term effects of the revolt will be a large number of mulattos . . . This cannot be prevented. The government has to make sure, however, that these bastards won't be accepted as equal German citizens. A compromise of considering them legitimate children and natives at the same time is not practicable. Therefore, the marriages themselves have to be outlawed."[24]

Accordingly, on October 1, 1905, Lindequist enacted the first German colonial anti-miscegenation law, aimed at excluding "mulattos" from the privileged group of "Germans."[25] Persons having a combined German and African heritage were unacceptable within the dominant ideology of both race and nation: "white, Germanic" and "black, African blood" were considered polar opposites, one encapsulating humanity's best, the other its worst qualities. A humanist imagery of colonialism as was often employed toward Samoa with its "almost white" population and in which the Germans appeared as benevolent patriarchs, wisely ruling over their lesser developed "cousins" was absent for the African colonies.[26] The Protestant church offered the only alternative model to the strict separation between whites and natives in South West Africa: the Rheinische Mission, present since 1842, opened two homes in Keetmanshoop and Okahandja exclusively housing children of African German descent. This "mixed-race offspring" was to be brought up separated from both parents, but infused with loyalty to German culture and the white race and a firm sense of superiority over "full-blooded natives."[27] Thus, the church hoped, one would create a loyal caste of mediators between rulers and ruled. The plan was contested among missionaries and firmly rejected by the governors who, beginning with Lindequist in 1905, preferred an unambiguous binarism of "whites" and "natives." Hopes of expanding the existing homes finally died, when the Department of Colonial Affairs refused to grant them financial support.[28]

While segregationist laws were certainly not unique in the colonial period, the German regulations were especially severe: not only civil, but also religious marriage ceremonies were outlawed, even though the latter held no legal power whatsoever.[29] Furthermore, the "natives" to whom the discriminating laws applied were defined by the High Court in Windhoek as "all persons with a native ancestor, however far removed," meaning an unconditional "one-drop rule" going far beyond everything practiced even in the U.S. South.[30] And finally, the Anti-miscegenation law was applied retrospectively, that is, not only future relations were prohibited but existing, formerly legal marriages were nullified; German men who failed to separate from their African wives lost their civil rights (including the right to vote, buy property, and receive government funding), and their children, formerly legally treated as Germans/"whites" were relegated to the status of "native," meaning among other things that they were expelled from schools and could not be legal heirs to their fathers.[31]

While these colonial practices confirmed to the dominant German ideas of who and what a German was, they created a conflict with existing German laws: *race* was the central category in legally defining identity within the colony, but it did not officially exist in the German legal system, where *nationality* was inherited patrilinear, that is, every legitimate child of a German father was considered German, independent of the mother's race or nationality. The 1905 anti-miscegenation law, the "native laws" (*Eingeborenenverordnungen*) of 1906, and a number of provisions specifying both, regulated and restricted relations between "whites" and "natives," severely limiting the latter's civil rights. The laws did not clearly define, however, who was to be considered a *native*. The Windhoek High Court in its definition followed "common practice" in employing a strict one-drop rule. A number of formerly "legally white" German settlers thus lost not only their status as "whites" when their native ancestry was discovered, but also the status of "German." Local courts in interfering with German citizenship regulations clearly went beyond their competence, but Governor Theodor Seitz backed them toward colonial authorities in Berlin (additionally refusing to register the children of legally married interracial couples entering the colony to avoid having to officially classify them as "German").[32] It was common practice to have two legal systems in the colonies: natives were subjected to special regulations (or, in minor matters, allowed to practice their precolonial laws), while German laws extended to the settler population. Local South West African authorities had upset this system by claiming the right to legally define who a German was, basing their definition on racial categories explicitly and univocally tying *Germanness* to *whiteness*. Theoretically German laws had clear precedence over colonial regulations, but in practice both legal systems existed in parallel, depending on where one was. That meant for example, that biracial couples could legally marry in Germany, but were treated as breaking the law as soon as they entered the colony.

This legal uncertainty had multilayered effects on Germany itself. Many African German couples in the colonies sent their children to Germany, where they were legally considered "citizens" not "natives." There, they added to the small black German community, which had existed since the fifteenth century.[33] Social Darwinist and colonial publications, which had followed the developments in South West Africa closely, in the wake of the colonial war now increasingly focused on the threat the colonial "mongrel population" posed to Germany's racial purity. Both the professional journalists of the conservative press and the missionaries and lawyers giving their "expert opinion" in colonial magazines took pains to rest their arguments not on ideology alone but to invoke "scientific facts" in support of their position.

Thus, they reasoned less with the political danger that a population of color with full civil rights might pose to German rule in the colonies than with an eternal and worldwide "war of the races," based on biological antagonisms, in which each battle was a step toward the destruction or survival of the white race. Accordingly, relationships between white settlers and African women lost all individuality or privacy and became hostile acts of war, while African Germans quite contrary to being incorporated into the German *Volk* became "the enemy"—more dangerous even than "pure blacks" as they were infiltrating the "Germanic race."[34] "Children of such marriages overwhelmingly inherit the characteristics of the parent belonging to an inferior race, i.e. the colored woman. Secondly, it has been scientifically proven that each European living with a Colored or Half-Colored for an extended period, will irrevocably sink to the level of his wife."[35]

Some authors advocated extending the colonial practice of treating non-white and German as exclusive categories onto the motherland itself. They generated an extensive public debate, mostly taking place in the colonial and conservative mainstream press.[36] Positions taken in the debate thus stayed within a limited range. There was no rejection of German colonialism or the social Darwinist race hierarchy and controversies centered on how (not whether) to limit the civil rights of Germans of African ancestry. Among those debating were principled social Darwinists who did not mind how large—or rather small—the mixed-race population was, because for them one drop of black blood was enough to poison the whole German nation. Accordingly, they favored a radical change of laws: Miscegenation was a crime against nature and all sexual contacts between the races had to be outlawed—in the colonies and Germany itself. The proponents of this most extreme position could use the authority of Germany's (and one of the world's) leading expert on "racial mixing," the anthropologist Eugen Fischer. In closing his study on the "Rehobot Bastards" in South West Africa, conducted in 1908 and published in excerpts since 1909, Fischer gave German politicians scientific advice on the question of miscegenation: "If there is the probability, or even the mere possibility that bastard blood damages our race . . . any absorption must be prevented. I take this to be so absolutely obvious, that I can consider any other point of view only as that of complete biological ignorance . . . this is about the survival—I choose my words consciously—of our race, this has to be the main criterion, ethical and legal norms just have to be secondary to that."[37]

Those authors unconcerned with miscegenation as a matter of principle took a more pragmatic stand. Their interest lay in preventing any person of African ancestry from becoming a German national. Accordingly, they focused on the legitimate children of white settlers and black women, favoring an addition to German laws that would explicitly exclude them. In 1908, the influential Colonial Society topped its list of recommendations to the government with the demands that "no colored can acquire the German nationality, marriages between coloreds and whites in the colonies cannot be registered. [And] Children of those marriages are considered coloreds."[38]

Catholic and Protestant churches introduced a third position into the debate by opposing any restriction of marriage rights. Nevertheless, they too condemned interracial marriage and racial mixing—there were fundamental disagreements in ideology between social Darwinism and Christian churches, but the race question was not among them. The biological inferiority of the black race was as self-evident to the churches as it was to politics. And to proselytize Africans meant to present Christian Europe as the only universal civilization, vastly superior to the primitive and barbaric African traditions. The attempt to refashion Africans according to the image Europeans had of them was as much in the interest of the missions (who thereby held the only key to salvation for the "natives") as it was central to colonial politics. Yet the discussion around mulattos and miscegenation also showed the conflict arising from the churches' support of colonial politics and the racist ideology behind it while they simultaneously insisted on certain basic "Christian demands"—thought the churches' opposition mainly sprang from the fact that governors in the colonies had not only outlawed civil but also religious marriage ceremonies. That was trespassing into a territory the churches considered exclusively their own and accordingly they insisted on their authority in this particular matter. This position led to renewed social Darwinist attacks on the churches, attacks that the latter perceived as unfair. After all, official church statements never forgot to condemn racial mixing, for reasons that directly derived from social Darwinist race theories, but they also argued that anti-miscegenation laws would not solve the problem, since the majority of biracial children were illegitimate. Their existence was considered a natural consequence of the scarcity of white women in the colonies and the solution therefore lay in an increased immigration of female Germans.[39] Until this was achieved, legal wives, even African ones, were morally preferable to concubines. These marriages' legality, however, need not generate any civil rights.[40] Ultimately, the opposition to the anti-miscegenation legislation was largely a fight for influence; as long as the government was ready to lift the ban on religious marriages ceremonies, the churches were ready to accept limited civil rights for African Germans: "Christian morality demands—our opponents might say—that the colored wives and mulatto-children acquire the German nationality with all legal consequences. Christian morality wants to force the bastardization of the German nation! No, that is not the conclusion. Christianity simply demands that a possible relation between the white [man] and the colored woman should be legitimate, it does not judge on its legal position. Should the German government think it wise to refuse the colored elements entry into the community of citizens, Christianity will not protest."[41]

The government institution having jurisdiction over the colonies, the Ministry of Colonial Affairs, was thus caught between the demands of an increasingly aggressive racist nationalism and the limits provided by German laws. The conflict escalated around the question of nationality during the tenure of Wilhelm Solf, former governor of Samoa, as colonial secretary (1911–18). The South West African regulations interfered with German laws by denying citizenship to a group of people solely because of their race, but the decisions of the South West African courts, always unconditionally backed by the governors, got increasingly radical, finally even expatriating those biracial residents who already held the German citizenship. The secretaries of colonial affairs, interior, foreign affairs, and justice all agreed that anti-miscegenation laws were a prerogative of the German government, not the Colonial authorities and that legitimate children of German men inherited their father's nationality, no matter what their race might be.[42] This neither impressed the courts in South West Africa nor the governor; both continued their policy of equating nationality with race. That the secretary of colonial affairs could not stop this insubordination possibly was connected to the fact that he himself was a committed supporter of anti-miscegenation laws; contrary to the local governors, though, his prime concern was their compatibility with German laws—if he considered it given, he had no qualms in applying them. In one case, for example, Solf tried to have an army officer expatriated when it became known that the man's great-grandfather had been a Herero: according to German law, nationality was inherited through the father, making the man, who had never left Germany, legally a "native."[43] The colonial department's policy of generally refusing to naturalize Africans also aimed at preventing them from settling in Germany and marrying German women.[44]

To achieve legal compatibility, Colonial Secretary Solf introduced an anti-miscegenation bill into parliament in May 1912. It was considerably mellower than the already existing regulations, but being the first proposal introduced on government level it could have functioned as a precedent and opened the way for a general measure.[45] This tactic likely would have succeeded had it not been for the Catholic Center Party, which, being well informed about the colonial situation through its missionary connection, with the support of the socialists initiated a competing measure aimed at outlawing marriage restrictions based on race. The debate in parliament was largely similar to the one that was already happening outside of it. All factions agreed on the undesirability of interracial relations; supporters of the government measure concentrated on the dangers of racial mixing and miscegenation, contrasting black bestiality with German culture, while its enemies insisted on the ineffectiveness of anti-miscegenation laws. And while the debate's topic was relationships in the colonies, almost exclusively between white men and black women, speakers drew more attention to the threat of black men having sexual relations with white German women; they used the most effective racist stereotype of the black rapist and reminded the assembly of instances of white German women seeking relations with black men, cases causing immensely negative publicity and which had been condemned by all political parties, including the opponents of the anti-miscegenation law.[46] Forced onto the defensive, the opponents of the anti-miscegenation law made it clear that they too principally rejected racial mixing and that their insistence on the legality of interracial marriage did not extend to full civil rights for black spouses and children. Instead they distinguished between private and public law: while German men should have the right to marry whomever they wanted, the interests of the nation weighted heavier than those of the individual— these national interests prohibited the inheritance of citizenship by mixed-race children. Despite such concessions, parliament rejected the anti-miscegenation legislation in May 1912. In practice, however, all parties agreed that "German" and "white" belonged together. Furthermore, the secretary of colonial affairs and the governors of the colonies refused to acknowledge the parliamentary decision, so the marriage bans were effective until Germany lost its colonies in the First World War.

The exclusion of and discrimination against African Germans in the colonies, and the public debate around it, set an example for the treatment of the "racially inferior" within the German nation. The term *Volk* (people) lost its cultural connotation and was more and more seen as an equivalent of "race," supporting the attitude that whoever was not part of the "Germanic race," was not part of the "German *Volk*" and therefore not of the German nation. This attitude was also reflected in the citizenship law of 1913. In 1912, shortly after the debates on the colonial anti-miscegenation laws had ended, negotiations for a new citizenship law began and with them, the conflict around the policies of exclusion continued. On the one side, the conservative National-liberal Party declared, "The . . . aim of the law is to prevent unwelcome foreigners from becoming Germans; one wants to exclude non-German blood from inclusion in the German fatherland."[47] On the other, the Social Democrats demanded the introduction of jus soli ("law of the soil") elements, namely a conditional *right* to naturalization for "foreigners" born in Germany, "because these persons *are* German" as MP Eduard Bernstein declared.[48] In the sessions of the parliamentary commission preparing the law, the confusion over the terms "race," "nation," and *Volk* became obvious. On the motion of defining in the law not who was a citizen, but who was a German as "whoever holds the citizenship of a German state," the minutes note: "This suggestion was rejected by the commission since it neglects the notion of nation, of race, and ignores the ethnic aspect. If 'citizen' is replaced by 'German,' the consequence would be that a German without citizenship, a German-Austrian, a Baltic could not consider and feel himself German anymore, while the Slav who gained the citizenship would be German."[49]

The artificially constructed contrast between "citizens" and "Germans" was not resolved; instead, it became obvious that for the majority of those involved in the legislative process, the latter category was the important one. The final motion favored the expression "German is whoever is of German blood" and suggested unqualified citizenship rights for "ethnic Germans" abroad and their descendants.[50] The latter group was granted dual citizenship, while in all other cases, this possibility was completely rejected as implying jus soli and thereby threatening the central principle of German national identity. The association with jus soli usually was enough to discredit any political measure. Social Democrats' attempts to introduce a right of naturalization for "foreigners" born and brought up in Germany were thus rejected as was the Liberal Party's motion to grant citizenship to the children of German women married to men not holding any citizenship—aimed at the families of stateless Danes in northern Germany, the motion was denied with explicit reference to children of racially mixed parentage who thus might become Germans.[51] Only in the case of foundlings, whose ancestry was impossible to know, did the commission allow a jus soli element: they should be considered members of the state they were found in. But even this was rejected by the government, which argued that this might include those who "could by no means be German: Mongolian or Negro-children." The final compromise stated that foundlings were assumed to *descend* from a member of the state they were found in—supposedly automatically excluding "Mongolians and Negroes."[52]

The government and a majority in parliament rejected anything that vaguely implied jus soli elements, trying to make naturalization as difficult and the status of immigrants as insecure as possible. Accordingly, the Social

Democrats' demand to facilitate naturalization for foreigners with longtime residency in Germany was without the least chance. "Foreign elements" were to be kept out lest they "taint" the German nation and immigration to be limited to "ethnic Germans" who would immediately be granted citizenship. Since the assumed "foreignness" was a biological one, it could not be overcome by assimilation. Not only "German blood" but "foreignness" as well was bequeathed from generation to generation, ad infinitum. The revision of the citizenship law was aimed exclusively at the "preservation of Germanness abroad," not at the indigenous "foreign" population.[53] Accordingly, in 1913 parliament, without the support of Social Democrats, passed a law cementing the principle of blood for the rest of the millennium: national identity was not built around a community of citizens, but around a community of "blood" (something that was only reversed with the revised citizenship law of 1999). That this necessarily meant exclusion and division of the population according to scientifically sanctified but highly questionable racial categories became increasingly obvious, and it is no coincidence that blacks, viewed as "the lowest race" and therefore as most "ungerman," were its first victims. Using the small, but highly visible, group of black Germans as a vehicle, a public discourse constructed a necessary, "logical" connection between "German" and "white" that left blacks as the absolute "other" and black Germans as a contradiction in terms; the fact that both in the 1920s and the 1950s, black Germans again became symbols for a threat to the country's "identity," that is, "racial purity," shows that these mechanisms continued independently of changing political systems.[54] Despite its far-reaching consequences, the early twentieth-century German discourse on race has been virtually forgotten. Its reexamination is important not only for the sake of a complete and accurate history of European colonialism, but also in light of recent developments such as the formation of a united Europe. Current struggles around the definition of a common European identity again focus on questions of culture and ethnicity—too often in an exclusionary manner uncomfortably reminiscent of the debates outlined here.

Notes

1. While German princedoms and merchants had been involved in colonialism and the slave trade for centuries, between 1884 and 1898 Imperial Germany formally acquired "East Africa" (parts of today's Kenya, Rwanda, Burundi, Tanzania, and Mozambique), Cameroon, Togo, and "South West Africa" (today's Namibia), as well as a number of Pacific islands (Samoa and part of Papua New Guinea). By the end of the First World War, Germany had lost all its colonies. For more information on the

involvement of Germans in colonialism and the slave trade, see, for example, Susanne Zantop, *Colonial Fantasies: Conquest, Family, and Nation in Precolonial Germany, 1770–1870* (Durham, N.C.: Duke University Press, 1997); and Sara Friedrichsmeyer, Sara Lennox, and Susanne Zantop, eds., *The Imperialist Imagination: German Colonialism and Its Legacy* (Ann Arbor: University of Michigan Press, 1998).

2. Zantop, *Colonial Fantasies;* Friedrichsmeyer, Lennox, and Zantop, *Imperialist Imagination;* and Lora Wildenthal, *German Women for Empire, 1884–1945* (Durham, N.C.: Duke University Press, 2001).

3. Citizenship is a complex and contested issue in Germany on many levels. For all of the twentieth century, national belonging was legally based on the jus sanguinis, the "law of blood," meaning that only persons descending from Germans had an unconditional right to citizenship (including those "ethnic" Germans whose families had lived abroad since centuries), while persons born in Germany of non-German parents were legal foreigners even if they never left the country. (They could acquire the German nationality by application, but this was considered a favor granted by the state to deserving individuals, not a group right.) The close association between citizenship and blood created a number of problems, such as an ethnicized definition of "Germanness," meaning in practice that whoever does not *look* "German" in the public eye is consistently treated as a foreigner regardless of the actual citizenship. An even more problematic effect of the jus sanguinis are the millions of people born and brought up in Germany but treated—legally and socially—as strangers in their own country because their parents (or grandparents or great-grandparents) migrated to Germany from somewhere else (most often Turkey). Since 2000, children born in Germany of legal non-German residents do automatically possess German citizenship, but because a bitter, polemical and often racist campaign accompanied this law, it is the result of a number of awkward compromises, among them a ban on dual citizenship, which will certainly cause problems in the future. See Rogers Brubaker, *Citizenship and Nationhood in France and Germany* (Cambridge, Mass.: Harvard University Press, 1992); Georg Hansen, "Deutschsein als Schicksal: Ein aktueller Rückblick: Das Reichs- und Staatsangehörigkeits-gesetz von 1912/13," *Frankfurter Rundschau* 10, no. 2 (1999): 7; and Fatima El-Tayeb, "Germans, Foreigners, and German Foreigners: Constructions of National Identity in Early 20th Century Germany," in: *Unpacking Europe: Towards a Critical Reading,* ed. Salah Hassan and Iftikhar Dadi (Rotterdam: Museum Boijmans Van Beuningen, 2001).

4. The number of children born out of wedlock of German-Namibian parentage was significantly higher, though: in 1909, 4,284 "mulattos" were registered in South West Africa. See Theodor Grentrup, *Die Rassenmischehen in den deutschen Kolonien* (Paderborn 1914), 32.

5. See, for example, Atina Grossman, *Reforming Sex: The German Movement for Birth Control and Abortion Reform, 1920–1950* (Oxford: Oxford University Press, 1995) and Peter Weingart, Jürgen Kroll, and Kurt Bayertz, *Rasse, Blut und Gene: Geschichte der Eugenik und Rassenhygiene in Deutschland* (Frankfurt am Main: Fischer, 1996).

6. Weingart, Kroll, and Bayertz, *Rasse, Blut und Gene.*

7. As Zantop and others have shown, German colonial fantasies since the seventeenth century had largely concentrated on the American continent where the vast majority of the millions of German emigrants ended up. (In 1890, e.g., 3.5 million Germans left the country while only 430,000 entered it.) See Brubaker, *Citizenship and Nationhood,* 118. When the German Empire finally entered the realm of colonizing nations in 1884, it had to be satisfied with scattered African territories, though.

8. In Imperial Germany, parliament, or the *Reichstag,* which was elected by the body of male citizens, had only limited influence on political decisions. The emperor named the government and needed its approval only on budget issues (which thus became the *Reichstag*'s most important weapon). While parliamentarian majorities reflected shifts in society, such as the growth of the urban working and middle classes, this did not necessarily mean more political influence for the groups representing the popular vote. See Wolfgang Mommsen, *Imperial Germany 1867–1918: Politics, Culture, and Society in an Authoritarian State* (London, New York: Arnold/St. Martin's Press, 1995).

9. This populist agitation notwithstanding, members of these organizations, especially of the German Colonial Society (DKG), belonged to the old political and new financial elites, a fact that added to their influence. See Arthur J. Knoll and Lewis H. Gann, *Germans in the Tropics: Essays in German Colonial History* (New York: Greenwood Press, 1987), 19.

10. Theodor Grentrup, *Die Rassenmischehn in den deustchen Kolonien* (Paderborn: Schoningh, 1914), 34.

11. Max Weber, for example, declared in 1895, "We have to understand that the German unification was a juvenile foolishness committed at an old age, which had better been avoided because of its costliness if it is the end and not the beginning of German imperialism (*Weltmachtpolitik).*" Max Weber Gesamtausgabe, Landarbeiterfrage, Nationalstaat und Volkswirtschaftspolitik, Schriften und Reden, Bd. I/4,2, Wolfgang J. Mommsen/Rita Aldenhoff (ed.), Tübingen 1993, 571.

12. Mannfred Gothsch, *Die deustche Völkerkunde und ihr Verhältnis zum Kolonialismus* (Baden-Baden: Nomos Verlag, 1983); Grossman, *Reforming Sex;* and Weingart, Kroll, and Bayertz, *Rasse, Blut und Gene.*

13. Nothing was more damaging here, probably, than Georg Wilhelm Friedrich Hegel's judgment of Africa as "the continent without history." In effect it placed Africans outside the realm of humanity but, nevertheless, for almost two centuries was not really taken into question. Georg Wilhelm Friedrich Hegel, *Vorlesungen über die Philosophie der Geschichte* (Stuttgart 1945), 144.

14. For details see Helmut Bley, Kolonialherrschaft und Sozialstruktur in Deutsch-Südwestafrika 1894–1914 (Hamburg: Leibniz Verlag,1968).

15. Commander Trotha to Chief of Staff Schliefen, 4 October 1904, quoted in ibid., 203.

16. The League of Nations made the former "German South West Africa" a South African mandatory in 1920.

17. Horst Drechsler, *Südwestafrika unter deutscher Kolonialherrschaft* (Berlin: Akademie-Verlag, 1966; Bley, *Kolonialherrschaft und Sozialstruktur.*

18. The German Colonial Society printed fifteen million leaflets and had one million copies of their pamphlet "Germany, Hold on to Your Colonies!" distributed as insets in newspapers and magazines (Pierard, in Knoll and Gann, eds., *Germans in the Tropics,* 31). Bernhard Dernburg, who became colonial secretary in 1906, was instrumental in forming the "Colonial Action Committee." Consisting of influential intellectuals such as the social historian Gustav Schmoller or Eduard Bernstein, member of parliament and leading Social Democratic theorist, the committee devoted itself to making the colonial war the central topic of the 1907 elections, a strategy that was largely successful. See Gustav Schmoller, Bernhard Dernburg, Walter Delbrück, et al., *Reichstagsauflösung und Kolonialpolitik* (Berlin: Wedekind, 1907).

19. Both "heterogeneous" and "homogenous racial mixing," (i.e., between "races" and European "subraces") were central themes of the social anthropologists around the *Politisch-anthropologische Revue.* The other important German social Darwinist faction, associated with Alfred Ploetz's Eugenic Society, devoted far less space to the topic but nevertheless shared the social anthropologists' sentiments. The society's cofounder, Rudolf Thurnwald declared in 1911, "Today more than ever the problem of degeneration on the one hand and the tide of the colored races on the other uncoil the race question from different angles . . . We will stand more and more confused and helpless before the problems of our times, if we will not decide to base our interpretations and great balances of life and work on the theory of inequality of men." In Ludwig Schemann, *Die Rasse im Schrifttum der Neuzeit* (München: Fromm, 1931), 43, 44.

20. Leipziger Neueste Nachrichten, 8 March 1906.

21. The tone was set by Arthur de Gobineau's *Essai sur l'inégalité de races humaines,* published 1853–55 and of fundamental importance for German race scientists. See E. J. Young, *Gobineau und der Rassismus. Eine Kritik der anthropologischen Geschichtstheorie* (Meisenheim: Anton Hain, 1968).

22. For an overview see Schemann, *Die Rasse.*

23. The German press, both left and right, repeatedly branded white women in (alleged) relationships with black men as "treacherous." Often such condemnations occurred in connection with public exhibits of "natives," the so-called *Voelkerschauen.* These were extremely popular in Imperial Germany, as in the rest of Europe, and hardly ever went without media-incited scandals around the "shameless behavior" of female German visitors. See Fatima El-Tayeb, *Schwarze Deutsche: Ders Diskurs um "Rasse" und nationale Identität* (Frankfurt/New York 2001), 151–61.

24. Governor Lindequist to Colonial Department, 23rd October 1905, BAB (Bundesarchiv Berlin [Berlin National Archive]), R 1001, 5423/1, p. 72.

25. Its status as the main German settler colony set South West Africa apart from the nation's other African territories, in which a small group of German officials organized the economic exploitation of resources and people. These differences aside,

settlers and colonial authorities were united in their hostility toward intermarriage as is shown by a 1912 inquiry from the colonial secretary to governors and settler councils of all colonies ("Rundschau," *Koloniale Zeitschrift* (1912): 867).

26.For example, Paul Rohrbach, *Die Kolonie* (Frankfurt am Main: Kutten & Loening, 1907); Wilhelm Solf, *Kolonialpolitik: Mein politisches Vermächtis* (Berlin: Reimar, 1919).

27. Bericht der Kommission für Innere Mission in den deutschen Schutzgebieten, 1909, EZA, 5/2916, 197–206. About 80 percent of German settlers in South West Africa were Protestant, though both Catholic and Protestant missions were active in Germany's largest colony (ibid.).

28. Central-Ausschuß für die Innere Mission der deutschen evangelischen Kirchen to Reichskolonialamt (RKA), 31 March 1911, Bundesarchiv Berlin, R 1001, 5423/1, 158; and Governor South West Africa to RKA, 23 June 1911; BAB, R 1001, 5423/1, 179.

29. Clearly, this ban on religious ceremonies had symbolic meaning: "racial mixing" supposedly violated human, natural, *and* religious laws. The local colonial authorities also used the ban to assert their power toward the Christian missions, a message that was well understood in the mission's headquarters—while the majority of local missionaries supported the law unconditionally, their superiors in Germany and the Catholic Center party fought the provision extending to religious ceremonies (Grentrup, *Die Rassenmischehen,* 65–91).

30. Decision of the High Court Windhoek in the case Karl Ludwig Baumann, 12 March 1913, BAB, R 1001, 5424, p. 51.

31. El-Tayeb, "Germans, Foreigners, and German Foreigners."

32. See for example the cases of Willy Krabbenhöfft (Willy Krabbenhöft to the president of the Progressive Party, 18 September 1913, BAB, R 1001, 5418/2, 331–35); Ludwig Baumann ("Der Fall Baumann," Deutsch-Südwestafrika-Zeitung, 18 March 1913); and the correspondence between Colonial Secretary Wilhelm Solf and Governor Theodor Seitz on the Windelberg family (Governor Seitz to Solf, 11 September 1913, BAB, R 1001, 5418/2, 276; Solf to lawyer Windelberg, 3 December 1913, BAB, R 1001, 5423/1, 272).

33. The vast majority of the children fathered by German settlers were illegitimate, though, and did not have any claim to German citizenship.

34. The "mulatto" who was able to physically pass for white but was "black" inside, torn between admiration and hatred for the superior white race, was a stock character of both German colonial fiction and scientific treatises. See Reinhold Grimm and Jost Hermand (Hg.), *Blacks and German Culture* (Madison: University Press of Wisconsin, 1986). The trope reappears in descriptions of the Westernized, culturally and racially "mongrelized," Jew.

35. Frankfurter Zeitung, 18 April 1906, in BAB, R 1001, 5417/1, 25.

36. See, for example, the Colonial Society's *Deutsche Kolonialzeitung,* the liberal *Koloniale Rundschau,* and conservative newspapers such as the *Leipziger Neueste Nachrichten,* but also the Social Democratic *Sozialistische Monatshefte,* representing the Sozialdemokratische Partei Deutschland's revisionist, pro-colonial faction.

37. Eugen Fischer, *Die Rehobother Bastards und das Bastardisierungsproblem beim Menschen* (Jena: 1913), 303 (italics in original). In the Weimar Republic Fischer became head of the Kaiser-Wilhelm Institute of Anthropology, the world's largest center for eugenic and anthropological research, and successfully continued his career under the National Socialists (being directly involved in the mass sterilizations of black Germans) and in the Federal Republic. He built his reputation on publishing "the first scientific study of racial mixing." Using new methods, namely Mendel's laws, he came to the same old conclusions: "mongrels" were inherently inferior, dangerous and unnatural. Interestingly enough, to this day his work is considered groundbreaking. See Benno Müller-Hill, *Murderous Science: Elimination by Scientific Selection of Jews, Gypsies, and Others in Germany, 1933–1945* (Oxford: Oxford University Press, 1988).

38. "Bericht über die Jahreshauptversammlung in Bremen, 12. Juni," Deutsche Kolonialzeitung (DKZ) 1908, 441.

39. The "import" of white women to the colonies was the stock solution that all enemies of anti-miscegenation laws put forward, assuming that this shortage was the only reason for interracial relationships. Governor Lindequist, though, had already denied the argument's validity in 1905: "One cannot say . . . that the increase in the white female population reduced the number of marriages between whites and native women." The Governor of South West Africa to the Colonial Division of the Department of Foreign Affairs, 23 October 1905. In BAB, R 1001, 5423/1, p. 71.

40. See Alfred Acker, "Zur Frage der Rassenmischehe," *Koloniale Rundschau* 1912, 462–68; Denkschrift der Versammlung des Missionsausschusses des Zentralkomitees der Katholikenversammlungen Deutschlands, 16 August 1912; and Denkschrift des Ausschusses der deutschen evangelischen Missionen, in Grentrup, *Die Rassenmischehen,* 56–61.

41. Grentrup, *Die Rassenmischehen,* 90, 91. See also Denkschrift des Ausschusses der deutschen evangelischen Missionen, 3 September 1912, 61.

42. Referat 1 A 5 to Solf, no date, BAB, R 1001, 5418/2, p. 252.

43. Only a formality let the measure fail. See RKA an Generalkommando des Gardekorps, 18 December 1913, BAB, R 1001, 5424, p. 79.

44. BAB, R 1001, 4457/6, p. 122.

45. The proposal basically stated that interracial marriages were to be prohibited and the prohibition would take effect immediately. All legitimate biracial children born before that date should be considered "white"; all those born after the deadline would be "natives." See *Deutsche Kolonialzeitung* 1912, 194.

46. The trope of the bestial black rapist, used to justify racist oppression, was a common trait of Western discourses on race, and various members of the conservative parties favorably mentioned the U.S. solution to this supposed problem, that is, lynching. Protocol of the Parliamentary Session 7 May 1912, BAB, R 1001, 5417/1, pp. 143, 162, and 164.

47. Beck, quoted in Hansen, "Deutschsein als Schicksal," 7.

48. Hansen, "Deutschsein als Schicksal," 7.

49. Bericht der 6. Kommission zur Vorberatung der Entwürfe a) eines Reichs- und Staatsangehörigkeitsgesetzes und b) eines Gesetzes zur Abänderung des Reichsmilitärgesetzes, Reichstag, 13. Legistlaturperiode, I. Session 1912/13, EZA, 5/340, 3.

50. See Hansen, "Deutschsein als Schicksal."

51. BAB, R 1001, 61 Kol DKG 1077/1, 230.

52. Bericht der 6. Kommission zur Vorberatung, 8.

53. Brubaker, Citizenship and Nationhood, 117.

54. Fatima El-Tayeb, "'Blood Is a Very Special Juice': Racialized Bodies and Citizenship in 20th Century Germany," *International Review of Social History* 44 (1999), Supplement 7.

11

Race, Color, and the Marxist Left in Pre-Duvalier Haiti

MATTHEW J. SMITH

It is obvious that color prejudice exists in the social relations of Haitians . . . But the color question is an effect not a cause. . . . It is in these terms that we, as Marxists, understand the problem. It is precisely because our adversaries are not Marxists that they look only at the superficial aspect of the color question. . . . But now recent events are compelling the masses to appreciate [the thesis of the Parti Socialiste Populaire], that color is nothing, class is everything.

—Étienne Charlier, "Rapport annuel," January 1948

They [the socialists] ask us, why we address the color question. Is this not contrary to Marxist doctrine? Our approach is that color prejudice is an historic reality in Haiti to which the Haitian black falls victim. The Parti Communiste d'Haïti is the party of reconciliation between blacks and *mulâtres.*

—"Declaration du bureau politique du P.C.H," 1947

In today's Haiti we consider false any communist movement that is not directed by the black majority.

—Haiti's radical labor daily, *Chantiers,* February 2, 1946

Introduction

In 1934, at the end of almost twenty years of military occupation by the United States (1915–1934), the black republic of Haiti began a transformation that was to determine the course of its political history between the occupation and the Duvalier era (1957–1986). The experience of foreign occupation and its intensification of historical color divisions between a light-skinned elite and a black majority created the conditions for a revival of Haitian nationalism marked by an emphasis on black consciousness. At the same time, members of the Haitian intelligentsia were attracted to radical political ideologies as a solution to Haiti's social and economic problems. During the two decades following the occupation, this effervescence led to the creation of several political movements, all of which advanced contrasting proposals for social change in the island. In the mid-thirties, Marxism emerged as one of the more prominent radical political discourses. From the beginning, it did not exhibit a significant influence over the country's largely poverty-stricken populace. Haitian Marxism remained urban-based and elite-driven throughout its early career. Nonetheless, Marxism, in tandem with the more popular *noirisme,* a variant of black power, and the burgeoning labor and student movements defined the way in which post-occupation Haitian politics evolved. This influence was clearly demonstrated in the revolutionary movement of 1946, started by young Marxists and resulting in the inauguration of the first democratically elected black president of the postwar period, Dumarsais Estimé. With the election of François Duvalier in September 1957, the Marxist Left, which came to form two decades before, was brutally silenced.

This essay explores the formative years in the development of Haitian Marxism, a history that has been largely overlooked in scholarship on modern Haiti.[1] It examines in particular the development and expansion of the Haitian Marxist movement with particular focus on its ideas and debates. Similar to Marxist movements elsewhere in the Caribbean during this period, Haitian Marxists supported socialism as a solution to the country's economic and political woes. Yet their left-wing ideas were distinguished from those of their counterparts in the diaspora in their treatment of race and color. That Marxists in Haiti had to address these issues was inevitable, given the racial circumstances of the occupation in which the U.S. policy of appointing members of the light-skinned elite to leadership positions exacerbated internal tensions in the island republic. As this paper argues, in challenging the political legacies of the occupation, the Marxist parties in Haiti presented a political alternative that went beyond both traditional Marxism and the more popular *noirisme* in its heterodoxy. For both the socialists and communists, issues of color and race became important parts of their radical agendas. Whatever their positions on the "color question," the collective force of the Marxist Left influenced the way political actors addressed issues of political legitimacy and state power. Although both parties failed to build a large constituency among the urban proletariat and their leadership seldom extended beyond the capital, the ways they approached these questions presented a persistent challenge to the reigning power elite. This threat had two results: on the one hand, it provided impetus for other radicals and influenced the course of events, as evinced by the role Marxists played in the revolutionary movement of 1946. On the other hand, the presence of an organized Marxist Left forced the state into a more defensive mode and contributed to the rise of an intensely repressive state. State repression only partially explains the failure of the Marxist Left by the fifties. The contentious battle between the socialists and the communists kept the movement disunited at the time when its potential to attain state power was at its greatest. Ultimately it was the combination of these two factors that accounted for the movement's dissipation in the late fifties.

The essay is divided into three parts. The first part provides a brief overview of Haitian radicalism during the occupation and examines the sociopolitical circumstances that gave rise to Marxist party formation in the thirties. This theme is elaborated in the second section, which details the history and ideas of the Communist Party in the thirties. The paper then addresses the crucial period between the revolution of 1946 and the fall of Estimé in 1950, the peak years of the Marxist Left. Special attention is given to the debate between the two leading Marxist parties. Finally, some brief conclusions on the role of Haitian Marxism in Caribbean political history are drawn.

Resistance and the U.S. Occupation

The long presence of a foreign power created an opportunity for the development of a formidable nationalist movement in Haiti. Ostensibly launched for the collection of loans and to restore civil order, the occupation did not take long to reveal its imperialistic character. The reinstitution of the slavish corvée work system, which found Haitian peasants working in chain gangs to construct railroads, was but one example of marine abuse. The nature of the occupation gave rise to immediate popular resistance. Despite its early successes, in 1919 the guerilla peasant movement led by Charlemagne Péralte had been quashed by the marines.[2] In Port-au-Prince, however, less direct forms of resistance continued. Among a new generation of elite urbanites who were resentful of the U.S. presence, a strong sentiment of nationalism emerged. Several factors explain this. First, the reforms of President Lysius Salomon (1879–88) created greater access to secondary education for urban blacks. By 1919 the numbers of enrolled students in urban schools had more than doubled its turn-of-the-century figures.[3] To this must be added the centralization of power in the capital facilitated by the occupation. Although a small number of black professionals had lived in Port-au-Prince since independence, these changes guaranteed greater access for non-elites to the professional ranks. To manage these developments, the occupiers manipulated Haitian color politics, appointing members of the elite to high-ranking government and army posts. All of these changes made tense the social order in a city already swelling with the pressures of rapid urbanization and increased professionalization.

It was, however, the activities of a new generation of writers, scholars, and poets who had exploited the educational opportunities and achieved prominent places among the intellectual elite that were most important. Several members of the elite returned to Port-au-Prince in the mid-twenties following years of study in Europe, where they became intrigued with developments in black consciousness in Paris and the European interest in the Harlem Renaissance. These writers expressed their views in several journals and discussion groups. By 1925 they formed a discussion group, La Nouvelle Ronde, whose principal aim was to draw attention to the literary innovations of Harlem and French writers and to apply them to the Haitian situation.[4]

In July 1927 most of the members of La Nouvelle Ronde founded *La Revue Indigène.* Although the journal ran for only six months, it proved extraordinarily influential. Among its collaborators were Max Hudicourt, Jacques Roumain, Étienne Charlier, Carl Brouard, and Jean Price-Mars. The indegenists called for a new national program that explicitly privileged Haitian culture over French. They stressed the significance of Haiti's African heritage and promoted its inclusion in the development of a uniquely Haitian literature. Though small and short-lived, the publication of *La Revue Indigène* represented an important shift in Haitian nationalism. Intellectuals responded to the cultural shock of U.S. occupation by celebrating the virtues of Haiti's indigenous culture. More importantly, this cultural movement created an outlet through which young radicals could meet and debate on the political course post-occupation Haiti should take.

In spite of this attribute, the loose coalition of nationalist writers associated with *La Revue Indigène* fast unraveled. A growing militancy among the urban youth stirred the more radical of the indigenous writers to political organization. In 1928 Jacques Roumain, who at twenty-three had already been incarcerated twice earlier in the year for alleged seditious activity, felt that the literary thrust of *Revue* was far too indirect to affect meaningful political change. Energized by the broad appeal of anti-occupation sentiment in the city, Roumain and his colleagues sought to express their growing political consciousness in other ways. With Georges Petit, he formed the Ligue de la Jeunesse Patriote Haïtienne. More political than the literary movement, the Ligue was one of the first attempts to mobilize youth from diverse social backgrounds.[5]

At the same time, militant political activism against the occupation reemerged. At the end of 1929 a student strike at the Haitian-American agricultural school in Damien in the outskirts of the capital, escalated into a large urban strike. Anti-U.S. feelings were further heightened on December 6 when marines fired into a demonstration of discontent peasants in the southern town of Marchaterre, killing twenty-five and wounding another seventy-five. In the aftermath of these events, the United States sent a commission to Haiti to investigate the state of the occupation and suggest a new policy. The combination of popular resistance, the Wall Street crash of 1929, and international criticism of U.S. gunboat diplomacy forced the United States to reconsider its foreign policy toward Latin America. Following the commission report, President Hoover issued a gradual dismantling of U.S. military presence in Haiti.[6]

"La Peste Rouge": The Communist Party in the Thirties

If 1930 marked the beginning of the end of the occupation, it also meant a shift toward a stronger left-wing tendency among revolutionary nationalists in Haiti. The student movement in 1929 demonstrated the potential of urban popular resistance and served to energize the more radical members of the indigenous movement. On the national political scene, the repercussions of this fervor were readily apparent. The next president, Stènio Vincent, was a light-skinned politician who despite his social position grew up poor and was deprived much of the privileges of others in his class. He was also an intellectual whose call for a lessening of U.S. control was a sharp contrast to the accommodation of the previous two regimes.[7] Positioning himself as a nationalist, he won much support in the 1930 presidential campaign. Vincent was keenly aware of social tensions in Haiti and skillfully retained support throughout his administration by appointing officials from both sides of the class and color divide. Vincent's promise that 1934 would be a "second liberation" attracted several members of the indigenous movement of the twenties.[8] Jacques Roumain, who resigned as president of the Ligue, campaigned for Vincent in the 1930 election. The expectations of profound change under a nationalist president would die fast.

Both the U.S. State Department, still reeling from the red scare in the United States earlier in the decade, and the new government feared that the Damien strike would unleash a wave of communist-inspired movements across the island. Among U.S. officials in Haiti, this fear was especially strong. One somewhat paranoid report on the strike claimed that in certain southern cities, leftists actively worked for the "organization of schools to train youths for the duties of communist leaders."[9] Though unfounded, these accusations indicate persistence on the part of U.S. authorities to confuse nationalist and racial movements with communism. They were also sufficient to worry the new government. Vincent, conservative by nature, responded to this potential threat with force. His persecution of political dissidents from the Left and Right and his surprisingly flaccid response to the 1937 massacre of Haitians in the Dominican Republic frontier aroused popular opposition.[10] By 1934 his regime became increasingly dictatorial.

Marine withdrawal, therefore, had the dual effect of creating a political environment brimming with expectation and fragmenting with the collapse of the nationalist movement. Before the occupation ended, the nationalist union was already splintering. These divisions, to be sure, were not entirely attributed to the political structure left by the occupiers. Within the nationalist movement existed a bitter ideological cleavage. These tensions grew out of the political changes that followed the events of 1930, when many nationalists, like Vincent, found themselves part of the new government. It was also part of the response of younger members of the indigenous movement, exposed to the attraction of Marxism among black activists and intellectuals during the interwar years. For them the cultural realignment of the indigenous movement was far too limited.[11] Thus once the nationalist movement imploded, Haitian radicals actively pursued other political alternatives.

Marxism had been a popular ideology among some of the collaborators of *La Revue Indigène,* but never commanded any organized following in the twenties.[12] The leading exponent of Marxism during this period and the figure most responsible for its growth was Jacques Roumain. Arguably the most renowned intellectual of twentieth-century Haiti, Roumain was born in Port-au-Prince in 1907 to a well-respected, elite family. He attended at the best schools in Port-au-Prince before traveling to Switzerland and Spain, where he studied agronomy and became heavily influenced by European cultural movements. On his return to Haiti in 1927, the young Roumain developed a reputation not only for his talents as a writer and poet, but also for his commitment to social justice. His activism took a sharp turn by the mid-thirties as he fast became disillusioned with Vincent's conservative policies.

In 1934, after two years of underground activity, Roumain formed the Parti Communiste d'Haïti (PCH) with fellow poet Christian Beaulieu. From the early thirties, Roumain began to stress material and class-related problems as being the most central issues in politics.[13] He argued that U.S. imperialism, the source of the nationalist movement, remained vibrant in Haiti despite *désoccupation* and required a more unifying strategy of combat. Since the anti-occupation movement emerged from the urban proletariat and the peasantry, a political philosophy that sought to liberate them was best suited for Haiti. "I am a Communist," wrote Roumain in 1932, "I have renounced my bourgeois origins."[14]

Roumain, like his contemporaries, held a romantic view of the country's mostly peasant majority and glossed over much of the reality of peasant life. He also had a naïve expectation of the likelihood for communist change in a country riven with poverty and social divisions.[15] Nonetheless, his devotion to the communist cause was both compelling and inspiring. By calling for a cross-class alliance, communism also exposed the veiled hypocrisy of the nationalist movement. As Roumain concluded, "The Nationalist movement was incapable of fulfilling its promises because these promises collided with the nationalist bourgeoisie . . . the knaves of imperialism and cruel exploiters of the peasants and working class."[16]

But in formulating a critique of the nationalist movement, the communists had to contend with several issues, none more vexing than the "the color question." Following the split in the nationalist movement, a group of young black radicals began to extend the call for a non-elite form of indigenous culture to include a more authentic form of political rule. In other words, certain members of the indigenous movement argued for a form of government based on black—not *mulâtre*—leadership. For Roumain, this *noiriste* black supremacy was dangerous to the political future of the island.[17] The country's political problems were founded on its dependency and post-independence exploitation; not the divisions among social groups. The party's views on "the color question" were publicized in the summer of 1934 with the release in pamphlet form of its manifesto, *L'Analyse Schématique.* In this document largely written by Roumain, the PCH dismissed the growing emphasis on color among black radicals. In Haiti, they argued, color was important only because it was "used as a mask by black politicians and *mulâtre* politicians to hide the true problem of class struggle. . . . The duty of the PCH, which is 98 [percent] black because it is a worker's party, is to put the proletariat on guard against the black intellectuals who would like to exploit to their gain their justifiable anger."[18] This position, as will be further explained, would create bitter divisions and weaken the force of the Marxist Left in the postwar years.

The party's treatment of the "the color question" had much to do with the composition of its leadership. During the Vincent years, the leading members of the party, Étienne Charlier, Anthony Lespès, and Roumain's brother Michel, were all young, vibrant, and determined radicals. There were also black party members from the northern and central provinces. Yet the social status of the principal members, all sons of the elite, served to alienate them from other radicals hostile to the bourgeoisie. Non-elite radicals who supported a *noiriste* perspective did not take seriously the convictions of elite radicals. Furthermore, the social circumstances of the Vincent regime in which the more privileged government positions were awarded to *mulâtres* convinced the *noiristes* that the struggle was one of color, not class. For these reasons, communists found no solidarity with other radical groups.

In the thirties, however, the Communist Party was the only organized radical group and thus the subject of close scrutiny. The local press made much of the communist presence in Haiti, arguing that "the nation must be like a guard at the door, blocking the passage of *la peste rouge*."[19] Many conservatives believed Communism threatened the unity *Vincentisme* seemed to represent. One newspaper went as far as calling for a fascist type of dictatorship to combat communist influence.[20] The PCH did attempt to organize dock workers and the urban working class in this initial phase of activity.[21] There is also evidence that small cells formed in the provinces, particularly Gonaïves in the center and Les Cayes in the south.[22] Nonetheless, open communist activity was ephemeral. Although Roumain and the others in the party had supporters from their earlier nationalist activities, few of the unemployed majority in the capital were receptive to Marxist doctrine. Notwithstanding the social differences between the PCH leadership and the small urban laboring classes, the Great Depression left many Haitian workers grateful for employment and less willing to organize. More important, the government and the U.S. State Department were gravely concerned with the formation of a communist party in the country and took immediate measures to suppress it.[23]

In 1936, the Vincent regime, which had closely followed Roumain's political activities, outlawed the party because it was spreading "violent" and "anarchistic" ideas, dangerous to the "Haitian social order."[24] The previous year Roumain and several other leftists were arrested for subversive activities and sentenced to two years in prison in a much-publicized trial.[25] On his release in 1937, Roumain spent several years in exile in Europe, the United States, and Cuba where he worked closely with radical intellectuals.

The younger members of the Communist Party continued the work of indoctrination in the late thirties and unsuccessfully attempted to start a union of bus operators.[26] However, government repression and the exile of its leader weakened the movement. The PCH once again became clandestine.

Marxist radicals did reemerge in the wake of the popular protest against the massacre of 1937, but they remained largely unorganized. In 1943, Christian Beaulieu died. His colleague Roumain had returned to Haiti in 1941, where after a failed effort to reorganize the communists, he became the director of the Bureau d'Ethnologie, and later *chargé d'affaires* of Mexico; he later succumbed to cirrhosis of the liver in 1944.

The deaths of Jacques Roumain and Christian Beaulieu dealt a severe blow to the Communist Party. The international stature of Jacques Roumain, who by the early forties was one of the more popular figures in Latin American intellectual circles, had brought Haitian radicalism within the ambit of diasporic resistance movements. His loss seemed to jeopardize this. The Haitian government assumed that "the communist threat" died with Roumain. But Marxism and black consciousness found new avenues of expression. More importantly, a militant sector of the urban youth from both elite and non-elite backgrounds, inspired by the war, found in Roumain an idol. René Depestre, one of the more prominent of the young Marxists, summarized this sentiment in his poem, *Le baiser au leader:* "Camarade Roumain you are our ideal. You are our flame. You are our God. [You] cried a voice and the present choir will respond."[27] The vision these youth held of postwar Haiti was of a democratic nation free from dictatorship and with social and economic equality. For progressive Haitians, the events at the beginning of 1946 promised all that and more.

The 1946 Moment and the PCH-PSP Conflict

More than any other period, the revolutionary movement of 1946 was the most decisive moment in the history of the Haitian Left. The overthrow of Vincent's equally repressive successor, Élie Lescot, that year created a real opportunity for political renewal. Considered in a broader context, it was the first popular movement against U.S. impositions in postwar Latin America.

The increased tensions that led to the movement can in fact be traced to the last years of Vincent's presidency. In the wake of the 1937 massacre, students, urban workers, and members of the Garde demonstrated their disgust with the government through urban protests and an aborted coup. Though Vincent was able to maintain social order, his attempt to secure a third presidential term in 1939 found no support from the National Assembly or the United States. He thus backed Lescot, his former ambassador in the United States, as his successor in 1941. Lescot was less adept than his predecessor in disguising his *mulâtrisme.* He employed various means of co-optation and repression to suppress his opponents. In 1944 he extended the duration of his presidency retroactively to seven more years, thus further alienating any possible support.

Lescot's attitude of politics as usual was but one factor that prompted a rise in leftism. Migration from the countryside to Port-au-Prince increased significantly during the early forties, spurred on by deteriorating conditions in the interior and the promise of employment in the capital. Census reports indicate that by the end of the decade, nearly half of the population of Port-au-Prince was born outside of the city.[28]

The spread of revolutionary ideas was furthered by the continuing expansion of the black middle-class. Largely comprising professionals and semi-professionals, the growth of this new *class politique* clamoring for greater inclusion in state affairs threatened the political control of the elite. That Lescot's vision of a modern Haiti privileged the educated light-skinned elite over the black middle-class added fuel to a combustible social situation. Not surprisingly, members of this new middle class became sympathetic to radical ideas. By the last two years of the war, with the victory of the Allied forces secure, global expectations of democracy and social justice echoed loudly in Haiti. A spate of radical groups emerged. Roumain's former associates, Charlier, Hudicourt, and a young journalist who participated in the Damien strike, Max D. Sam, deepened their devotion to the Marxist cause and in 1944 launched the radical journal, *La Nation*. Less than a year after its inaugural issue appeared, *La Nation* was closed down by Lescot and Hudicourt was forced into exile. Nonetheless, the circulation of a Marxist paper in the mid-forties was evidence that despite repression, Marxism remained an attractive political alternative among the radical intelligentsia.

As prominent as the *La Nation* group was, it was not the most important of the Marxist groups to form during the Lescot years. Among the medical students at the national university, an interest in Marxism began to grow. These young radicals, from both black and *mulâtre* families, were greatly influenced by Roumain and his work. They also drew inspiration from intellectual developments in France, particularly the Surrealist movement of the thirties. In December 1945, the founding father of Surrealism, André Breton, visited Haiti. Although Surrealism was waning in France at the time and it never held much of an influence on Roumain and the generation of the thirties, Breton was held in high regard by the young intelligentsia who admired the anti-elitism in his work.[29]

The conjuncture of radical ideas on the local scene and the changing international context occasioned by the war created an explosive situation far greater than Lescot could anticipate. During the first week of January 1946 the powder keg was lit. The New Year's edition of the radical student newspaper, *La Ruche,* led by the Marxist university students, featured several veiled critiques of the regime. An infuriated Lescot ordered the immediate banning of the paper and the arrest of its student editors. In response, on the morning of January 7, students from the medical school of the national university, along with other radicals, organized a protest march that over the course of the next three days escalated to a general strike. Lescot was deposed, a temporary military regime installed, and a spate of political groups surfaced.

Given the dominant role played by the young Marxists in the organization and execution of the strike, it was inevitable that an organized Marxist movement would reemerge. During the first week of February a cadre of Roumain sympathizers resurrected the PCH.[30] Swept by the immediate fervor following the strike, the party likened the events of January 7 to the Russian Revolution of 1917, an opportunity for meaningful change.[31] The party's initial program, which sought to build a "Socialist Soviet Republic of Haiti," advocated *inter alia,* the socialization of all industries and land, Soviet-style organization of all political institutions, and the democratization of the Garde, which was to be renamed "the people's army."[32] Following harsh criticism by regional communists, the party later outlined a far more tempered twenty-point minimum program for Haitian development, with the most radical provisions being the revision of all contracts signed by Lescot and Vincent, the participation of women in public office,[33] a democratic and socialist constitution, labor union organization, reduction of working hours, and a repeal of the 1936 anticommunist legislation.[34] Though modified, the proposals of the PCH were, nonetheless, out of step with the direction that international communism was taking after World War II.

A more important characteristic of the party was the PCH's staunch anti-imperialism. Jacques Stephen Alexis, a young editor of *La Ruche,* was among the most vociferous communist opponents of American imperialism. Alexis pointed to the Inter-American economic climate as being far more decisive to the future of Haiti than the battles among presidential hopefuls. The Soviet opposition to the imperialistic design of Britain and the United States, he argued, was the only real hope for underdeveloped countries.[35] His colleague Theodore Baker was equally condemning: "We are anti-imperialist. For thirty years we have been controlled by America and have not seen the benefits . . . when we vote in a few months it should be against all those who since 1915 have worked toward our ruin."[36] Such sentiments had their antecedents in Roumain's 1934 critique of the nationalist movement.

Although claiming to subscribe to Roumain's ideas, the reinvigorated PCH was markedly different in its political views and membership. The leader of the party was Félix d'Orléans Juste Constant, a black Episcopalian pastor from the central Arcahaie region, who had been a communist since the thirties. Edris St. Armand was the party's general secretary. Most of the *La Ruche* radicals were drawn to the PCH and the party they formed in the wake of the strike, the Parti Démocratique Populaire de la Jeunesse Haïtienne (PDPJH), became the youth arm of the PCH. The main paper of the party, *Combat,* first appeared on February 6. The party's membership during these years is difficult to determine. By the party's own account, *Combat* had a subscription of approximately 1,000 readers throughout the country, and according to State Department intelligence reports, there were 1,307 registered members.[37] What is clear, however, is that in 1946, the PCH was the only political party that had any experience in party organization. It was also considerably more active than its earlier incarnation.

The party was based principally in the capital, although there were cells in the provinces, the biggest being in the Grande Anse region in the south.[38] Despite its efforts to gain international recognition, the PCH had no apparent links with Russia or regional communists. On the contrary, Caribbean Marxists took issue with the party. The Cuban PSP (Partido Socialista Popular), for example, dismissed them outright as "infantile leftists" with a "puerile character" and an unrealistic program. They also criticized the authenticity of a communist party headed by an Episcopalian preacher.[39]

In spite of regional criticism, the PCH attempted to strengthen its base in the early part of the year by joining the Front Révolutionaire Haïtien (FRH), a coalition of eleven radical groups that officially formed on February 8. The black politician and lawyer Emile St. Lôt led the FRH and Juste Constant was one of two vice presidents. On the afternoon of the eighth, shortly after the formal meeting of the FRH, a parade was held in downtown Port-au-Prince in which thousands of the urban workers of the city participated, many carrying red flags and wearing red bands with revolutionary slogans and singing the Communist International and the Haitian National anthem.[40] The parade was a true first in Haiti and evidence of the initial strength of the leftist elements of the FRH.

The most important issue raised by the communist support of the FRH, was its new position on "the color question." The Front was decidedly pro-black and heavily *noiriste* in its outlook. Both St. Lôt and the other vice president, the popular labor leader Daniel Fignolé, were firmly devoted to black nationalism and campaigned for a black non-elite president. The PCH's support of this view marked a conscious reversal of the position taken in *L'Analyse Schématique*. On the one hand, the party, which was now predominantly black, was adapting itself to popular currents of black nationalism; on the other hand, it was using Marxism to apply to the Haitian situation and not vice versa. What is most apparent, then, is an ambiguity in the party's interpretation of Marxism. For the communists of the forties, the class struggle formed an intimate part of color divisions, and the relationship could not be ignored. This position was stated clearly in a *communiqué* issued in late March. "The Parti Communiste d'Haïti is the true revolutionary party in Haiti, closest to the black masses, unlike the *mulâtre* petit-bourgeois who have been the main beneficiaries of the Vincent-Lescot regimes . . . The [party] opposes the accusation that this position makes it racist and sectarian. For us Marxism is not a dogma but a guide for action. We consider the color question to be one of the most essential aspects of the class struggle in Haiti, and it cannot be ignored without losing all connection with reality and surrendering the most important quality of a sincere Marxist, the cause of the proletariat."[41]

This approach was an important departure from its earlier views. It was also inherently problematic. By refusing to hew to an orthodox Marxist line in dealing with color issues, the Haitian Communist Party lessened its chances of acceptance. We have already noted the regional reaction to the party. In Haiti a similar skepticism emerged. Conservatives viewed the party's acceptance of *noiriste* politics as an electoral maneuver to secure political power. *Noiristes* from the beginning found no solidarity with the communists, despite their similar advocacy of black power. More important, the taint of communism in a world rapidly dividing between East and West compelled the *noiristes* to distance themselves from the communists in order to gain necessary U.S. support in the upcoming presidential elections. It is therefore unsurprising that the Communist Party withdrew from the FRH in March, claiming that the "historical role" of the Front had ended.[42] Still, the party maintained its position as a pro-black communist organization.

The privileging of class struggle over color politics became the clarion call of the other major Marxist party to form at the beginning of 1946, the Parti Socialiste Populaire (PSP), the nucleus of which was the contributors of *La Nation*. Max Hudicourt, following a brief exile in New York, returned to Haiti the week Lescot left the country, and became the party's leader. The party's other principal members were Lespès, Charlier, Jules Blanchet, Albert Mangonès, and Max D. Sam. The Marxist convictions of the party members differed somewhat as Hudicourt, though having strong socialist sympathies, retained a liberal outlook. The other members of the party were more fervently socialist. Generally, however, the structure and approach the party closely resembled that of the Dominican Republic and the Cuban PSP (Partido Socialista Popular) with which it was aligned. The party's socialist program was also far more in keeping with Marxist currents of the period.

A further contrast with the PCH was the party's relationship with the burgeoning labor movement. Trade unions figured prominently in 1946, with over twenty-five emerging during the course of the year.[43] The first labor group established after the revolution was the party-controlled Fédération des Travailleurs Haïtiens (FTH), led by Fernand Sterlin; however, anticommunist protests forced it to split the following year.[44] The PCH, to be sure, did have a notable presence in labor organization. The Ligues Ouvrières, which existed in many working class areas, bore communist influence. Nonetheless, the level of labor organization was comparatively stronger in the case of the PSP.

Perhaps the most important feature of the PSP was its philosophy, which represented the starkest radical contrast to *noirisme*. Like Roumain, the light-skinned intellectuals in the PSP privileged class struggle over color issues as the most important threat to Haitian society. They argued that a reorientation of the polity based on color would not bridge the country's fundamental economic cleavage.

As one would expect, this position created a vibrant polemic between both Marxist parties. The PSP, according to the Communist Party, avoided the "the color question" because the party membership was largely bourgeois and thus fearful of the threat that a black government might pose to its status.[45] Indeed, several members of the PCH, including St. Armand, were once associated with Hudicourt and Charlier in the thirties but parted ways with them on the color issue.[46] In defense of the party, General-Secretary Lespès argued that the PSP had no allegiance with the conservative or reactionary bourgeoisie that, in fact, remained staunchly opposed to it.[47] The PSP, furthermore, argued that the program of the *noiristes,* with which the PCH was in agreement, was dangerous for the country and would only supplant the elites with the small landowning class of capitalists and speculators who had begun to side with them. Recalling the vibrant debate between the two parties, Max Sam maintains that the PCH was "not the true Marxist party in Haiti. They were only racist . . . we [the socialists] were mainly *mulâtre* in our leadership. That is true. But the people were with us nonetheless."[48]

The official position of the PSP was that color was unimportant to the future of Haiti. Whether a black president won or not, if the dependency on the United States and the economic strength of the bourgeoisie were not reduced, the problems of the Vincent-Lescot era were destined to be repeated.

The emphasis on color by both the PCH and the *noiristes* was, according to Lespès, "a new tactic by the bourgeoisie to divide the democratic forces." By focusing on color, the PCH, he argued, "polarized the Revolution."[49] Yet despite this insistence on Marxist adherence, the socialists recognized that color was indeed crucial to Haitian politics. The party demonstrated as much by supporting Edgar Néré Numa, a black deputy from the southern town of Les Cayes, in the presidential campaign. The decision to back Numa, according to Sam, was not because Numa was black, but because he appeared to have been the candidate most sympathetic to the goals of the Socialist Party even though he himself was never a member.[50] Still, the fact that a light-skinned candidate would never win in the heated political climate of 1946 was not lost on the PSP. They were well aware, as Sam concedes, that Haiti was not prepared for socialism and that a strong nationalistic president with no ties to *noiriste* factions would be the most realistic option.[51]

As far as the PCH was concerned, the socialist support of non-Marxist Numa was a poorly disguised attempt to steal the thunder from the radical Left and return Haiti to the pre-1946 status quo. Only a Marxist candidate, they argued, could support a Marxist program. In keeping with this view, the Communist Party president Juste Constant ran in the presidential election. Earlier in the year, he unsuccessfully ran for office as both senator and mayor of Port-au-Prince in the controversial legislative elections. He had some support among the urban workers but was never a challenge to the charismatic and far more popular Fignolé, who galvanized considerable support for his candidate Démosthènes P. Calixte.

By June, the dominance of the *noiriste* forces on the political scene made clear that a black president was the only choice in the August election. The provisional military government that oversaw the election was not prepared for a far left candidate to win and thus blocked the success of both the PSP and PCH candidates. Dumarsais Estimé, a black school teacher and former minister of education under Vincent, was favored by the powerful *noiristes* not only because he opposed oligarchic control, but also because his personal career seemed to best reflect the advance of the black middle class. Faced with this defeat, the PCH began to support the new administration, as did the younger radicals. Following a disastrous attempt to form a coalition government that included several socialists, the PSP withdrew its support of the new government and became its leading opponent.

During the first two years of his presidency, Estimé allowed the socialists and communists to organize freely. The divisiveness between the two groups, however, raged. The disunity took its toll on both parties. In April

1947, the PCH, by then suffering from a lack of funds, internal conflicts, and rising state repression of leftists, officially dissolved. Taking its inspiration from the Browder-influenced CPUSA, the party decided to collaborate with rather than challenge the government.[52] Some of the more radical members of the party such as St. Armand attempted to rekindle communist activity by forming the Parti Ouvrier Progressiste d'Haïti (POP) later that year. But with very little support, the POP floundered and was eventually absorbed into the PSP.[53]

With the dissolution of the PCH and the ascension of the *noiristes* to state power, the PSP remained the only organized left party in Haiti. Following the suicide of its leader Hudicourt in 1947, the party moved more closely to a stronger Marxist line. As the only Marxist party in the island, the Socialist Party attracted much attention. A U.S. embassy report offered the following evaluation of the party in 1948: "The PSP is the only organized political group in Haiti and as such inspires certain respect as well as fear. The danger that this party will take over the reins of government in Haiti is not imminent, but it exists and will tend to increase unless checked by governmental repression or a marked improvement in the economic situation."[54]

Whatever fear state and foreign interests had of the PSP, they were soon quelled when Estimé, under increasing pressure from the United States, issued a presidential decree banning all communist parties in 1948. *La Nation* continued throughout his regime, but was shut down permanently during the military coup that led to Estimé's overthrow in 1950. General Paul Magloire, a staunch conservative with little tolerance for leftism, led the military regime that replaced Estimé. Magloire sanctioned a greater degree of state repression to reduce the threat of political opposition. In the following years, members of the PSP remained politically inactive largely out of fear of government reprisals.[55] The tumultuous electoral campaign of 1956–57 that led to Duvalier's victory found the Marxist Left unprepared, fragmented, and impotent.

Between the fall of Estimé in 1950 and the ascendancy of Duvalier in 1957, the communist movement remained clandestine. The *noiriste* victory over the communists that began in 1946 was solidified with Duvalier's triumph. International factors also served to weaken communism's appeal. Although the region was never a focal point of conflict, the rapidly changing cold war context of the 1950s facilitated greater repression of communists in Latin American countries. A far more militant form of communism briefly emerged in the wake of the Cuban revolution. It, however, abruptly ended with the 1961 assassination of Jacques Stephen Alexis, who was then leader of the Parti Entente Populaire (PEP), the only significant communist organization in the island. The murdering of several other leading communists by Duvalier in the sixties and the exile of the remaining members of the party brought to an end thirty years of active Marxist struggle in the country.

Conclusion: Haitian Marxism in Comparative Perspective

The political history of leftism in Haiti during the two decades following the U.S. occupation was one of great import to the direction of national politics. Several points support this conclusion. As this paper has argued, despite its size and sporadic existence, the Marxist movement from its inception engendered considerable attention from government and foreign interests. Other non-Marxist radicals exploited the fear of communism in order to gain political advantage. *Noiristes* contested the equally pro-black PCH not only because of their genuine anticommunist sentiments, but also because they feared association with a communist party would lessen their chances of electoral victory.

This overreaction toward Haitian Marxists, which dates from 1930, is, of course, not peculiar to Haiti. What is important to consider here is that Haitian radicals were fully aware of the confusion U.S. interests had between communism and other race-based nationalist movements; a confusion that led U.S. officials to mistake anticommunist *noiristes* with Marxists. For example, Estimé's opponents in the United States often called his progressive government "communist" despite the passage of anticommunist legislation under his regime. What this suggests, therefore, is a great deal of ambiguity in perceptions of Marxism in Haiti. The increasingly repressive nature of the Haitian government in the late forties was both an attempt for the *noiriste* state to distance itself from Marxism, as it was a fear of the spread of leftist ideas in the country.

Notwithstanding the ultimate failure of the Marxist Left in Haiti, the preceding overview suggests several possibilities for comparative assessment. The postwar context of Haiti mirrored developments elsewhere in Latin America—increased democratization following the Allied victory; greater strength among left-wing forces; heightened militancy, a collaboration between Communism and labor, and eventually, greater repression of communist parties.[56]

Scholars of modern Haiti have emphasized the contradictions in the programs of Haitian Marxists, particularly the PCH, and, as a result, and have typically been dismissive of the movement. David Nicholls in his exceptional work on the period has argued Marxism in Haiti was nothing more than a small "movement among intellectuals from elite families."[57] Yet to disregard the movement on these grounds is to obscure its most peculiar feature, namely the way in which the parties articulated issues of race and color in their program. If Roumain and Beaulieu had consistently avoided color issues and *noiriste* discourse in the thirties, the 1946 variant of the PCH explicitly recognized that the color struggle in the country was as important as the class struggle. Indeed their treatment of this was unsophisticated and often reactionary. Still, it was a basic tenet of the party's program and a marked departure from traditional Marxist analysis. Although they argued otherwise, the members of the PSP also recognized the importance of color to the Haitian political situation, a point clearly acknowledged in Étienne Charlier's writings in *La Nation* during the Estimé years.[58]

The greatest failing of the Haitian Marxists was their near-constant division. By treating color divisions as the source rather than the outcome of the vast social chasm, the post-1946 PCH remained isolated from the socialists and lessened the chances to build a strong Marxist movement. For their part, the socialists, the more articulate faction of the Marxist Left, suffered from a lack of popular support and remained on the periphery of the radical movements by the late forties. Division prevented any meaningful front against the military dictatorship of the fifties and contributed to the personalization of national politics by the following decade.

It is also significant to note that Haitian Marxism surfaced at a time of political crisis. The euphoria that accompanied the end of the occupation forced progressive Haitians to reconsider issues relating to national identity, political legitimacy, and independence. Although Haiti was the second-oldest independent nation in the Americas, the U.S. occupation demonstrated just how fragile that independence was. Leftism became a response to the abuses of a bourgeoisie desperately clinging to a status quo threatened by a new politicized class.

As much as the debate on the "the color question" served to divide Haitian Marxists, it also forms one of the movement's unique features, as it was a notable departure from the approach of Marxist parties elsewhere in the diaspora. In the British and Hispanic Caribbean, for example, issues of race and color remained unresolved tensions. To be sure, these differences in approach derive from different political and social contexts defined by a struggle for racial recognition as in the case of Cuba, and a gradual shift in political power from Britain to a local middle-class elite as in the case of Trinidad and Jamaica.[59] Nonetheless, even in the intensely race-conscious atmosphere of the Caribbean during the sixties and seventies, issues of race and culture remained peripheral to regional Marxist movements. Issues of race, as Cedric Robinson has argued in his provocative study, *Black Marxism,* were typically addressed by black Marxists when they went beyond the parameters of Marxist orthodoxy and became part of what Robinson has termed the "black radical tradition."[60]

It is true that the PCH under Roumain explicitly critiqued color-based arguments in favor of a strict Marxist philosophy. However, this seemingly traditional approach to Marxism cannot be divorced from its context. It is no coincidence that the leading leftists of the thirties—Roumain, Charlier, and Hudicourt—were all part of La Nouvelle Ronde and the indigenous movement. That Haitian Marxism was born out of the indigenous movement of the twenties and the ideological plurality that accompanied it emphasizes a symbiotic relationship between culture and political theory in Haitian radical discourse. This link with local cultural movements was, in fact, an important constant throughout Marxism's career in Haiti. This factor partially explains the ease with which the PCH could support a *noiriste* discourse in the forties, and younger Marxists could fervently champion surrealism. It also explains the marked lack of adherence to Marxism-Leninism in Haiti that was inherent in other left-wing parties in the Caribbean. What we therefore find in the Haitian case is a conscious attempt to incorporate issues of race and color into Marxism.

In Haiti it could scarcely have been otherwise. The Haitian state, after all, was founded on black nationalism, a factor that was not lost on leftists in the forties. To varying degrees, all Haitian radicals accepted notions of black pride and viewed race as a source of social unification. This unity fell apart once the political structure of the occupation evolved into sharply divided lines partially based on color. Thus racial solidarity underlined the anti-occupation resistance and color divisions kept the Left weak.

Nevertheless, the fusion of black radicalism with Marxian class-consciousness in Haiti challenges conventional views that black consciousness in the Caribbean remained antagonistic to Marxism. In this regard, the experience of the Haitian Left in the thirties and the forties can be viewed as foreshadowing developments elsewhere in the postcolonial Caribbean.

It is against this background, then, that Haitian Marxism must be appreciated. Not simply as a brief moment in the trajectory of the country's tortured political past, but rather as one significant manifestation of the complex of ideas rooted in a long tradition of resistance.

Notes

Unless otherwise stated, all translations are mine.

First epigraph. From "Rapport annuel de Secrétaire général Étienne D. Charlier À l'Assemblée générale du Parti (Janvier 1948)," reprinted in *Trente ans de pouvoir noir en Haïti: tome premier, L'Explosion de 1946: bilans et perspectives* (Montréal: Collectif Paroles, 1976), 255, 258.

Second epigraph. From reprint in *Combat,* March 15, 1947.

1. With few exceptions, scholars of modern Haiti have long overlooked the political history of the Haitian left. The best available study is Michel Hector's *Syndicalisme et socialisme en Haïti, 1932–1970* (Port-au-Prince: Henri Deschamps, 1989). J. Michael Dash addresses the elite origins of the Marxist movement in his highly regarded work *Literature and Ideology in Haiti, 1915–1961* (Totowa, N.J.: Barnes and Noble, 1981). Although these and other studies provide much insight on the social movements of the period, there remains much more work to be done on the role of the Left in the evolution of twentieth-century Haitian politics.

2. The scholarly literature on the occupation is large and of varied quality. The most notable studies include Roger Gaillard's excellent multivolume work, *Les blancs débarquent* (Port-au-Prince: Henri Deschamps, various years). Hans Schmidt, *The United States Occupation of Haiti, 1915–1934* (New Brunswick, N.J.: Rutgers University Press, [1971] 1995), Brenda Gayle Plummer, "Black and White in the Caribbean: Haitian-American Relations, 1902–1934" (PhD dissertation, Cornell University, 1981). Mary A. Renda's recent *Taking Haiti: Military Occupation and the Culture of U.S. Imperialism, 1915–1940* (Chapel Hill: University of North Carolina Press, 2000), offers a provocative new reading of the meaning of the occupation and its links with cultural developments in the United States On Péralte and the *caco* peasant resistance movement, see, for example, Georges Michel, *Charlemagne Péralte and the First American Occupation of Haiti* (Dubuque, Iowa: Kendall/Hunt Publishing, 1996).

3. Georges Corvington, *Port-au-Prince au cours des ans: la ville contemporaine, 1922–1934* (Port-au-Prince: Henri Deschamps, 1991), 235.

4. On the background and activities of these writers, see Michel Rolph-Trouillot, "Jeux de mots, jeux de class: les mouvances de l'indigénisme," in *Conjonction* 197 (1993): 29–48.

5. Carolyn Fowler, *A Knot in the Thread: The Life and Work of Jacques Roumain* (Washington, D.C.: Howard University Press, 1980), 59.

6. On the strike at Damien see Rulhiere Savaille, *La greve de 29 - la première grève des étudiants haïtiens 31 octobre, 1929* (Port-au-Prince: Éditions Fardin, 1979). The details on the Forbes Commission are discussed in Magdalene Shannon, "President's Commission for the Study and Review of Conditions in Haiti and its Relationship to Hoover's Foreign Policy," in *Caribbean Studies* 15, no. 4 (January 1976): 53–71.

7. On Vincent's political views, see his voluminous collection of speeches and articles, *En posant les jalons* (Port-au-Prince: Imprimerie de L'État, 1939–45).

8. For example, in 1936 the journal *La Réleve* devoted an entire issue to Vincent likening 1934 to 1804 and labeling him the "Second Liberator" of Haiti. See *La Réleve* (Mars-Mai 1936).

9. Commandant of the Garde d'Haïti to the American High Commissioner, February 18, 1930, Port-au-Prince, Record Group 59, 838.00/1830, United States National Archives "Decimal File Dispatches from U.S. Ministers to the Department of Sate," Internal Affairs-Haiti, 1930–1939," Microfilm Publication microcopy no. 1246, roll 1.

10. Over the past decade there has been a growing literature on the massacre and its effect on Haitian diplomacy. See, for example, Miguel Aquino, *Holocaust in the Caribbean: The Slaughter of 25,000 Haitians by Trujillo in One Week* (Waterbury, Conn.: Emancipation Press, 1997), Thomas Fiehrer, "Political Violence on the Periphery: The Haitian Massacre of 1937," *Race and Class* 32, no. 2 (1990): 1–20, and Richard Turits and Lauren Derby, "Historias de terror y los terrors de la historia: la matanza haitiana de 1937 en la República Dominicana," *Estudios Sociales,* 26:92 (April-June, 1993): 65–76.

11. On the relationship between Caribbean radicalism and political activism in the United States, see, for example, Winston James, *Holding Aloft the Banner of Ethiopia: Caribbean Radicalism in Early Twentieth-Century America* (London: Verso Press, 1999).

12. On the role communism played in the early nationalist movement, see Michel Hector, "Sobre los albores del movimiento comunista en Haití, 1927–1936," in Michel Hector Auguste, Sabine Manigat, and Jean L. Dominique, ed., *Haití: la lucha por la democracia (clase obrera, partidos y sindicatos)* (Puebla: Universidad Autonoma de Puebla, 1976), 13–100.

13. Fowler, *A Knot in the Thread,* 303.

14. Jacques Roumain to Trisan Rémy n.d. (ca.1932), reprinted in *Haïti Journal,* January 4, 1933. The circumstances surrounding this correspondence are discussed in Fowler, 307.

15. Some of Roumain's romanticism regarding the applicability of communism to Haitian peasant life is revealed in his most celebrated novel, *Gouverneurs de la rosée* (Port-au-Prince: Imprimerie de L'État, 1944).

16. *L'Analyse Schématique,* 33, Typescript, Bibliothèque Haïtienne des Frères de L'Instruction Chrétienne, Institut St. Louis de Gonzague, Port-au-Prince, Haiti.

17. During the 1930s, *noiristes* fused the cultural nationalism of the indigenous movement of the twenties with racial theories of biological determinism to argue for a political system founded on black supremacy. The central figures in this movement were Lorimer Denis and a young François Duvalier. Although *noirisme* endured several transformations prior to Duvalierism, its roots can be traced to these years. The best discussion of the ideological influences on the *noiristes* of the thirties is David Nicholls, "Ideology and Protest in Haiti, 1930–1946," *Journal of Contemporary History* 9, no. 4 (1974): 3–26.

18. L'Analyse Schématique, 23.

19. Taken from the article "L'Anticommunisme Haïtien" in *La Rèleve* no.6 (December 1936): 32.

20. *Le Matin,* November 27, 1936.

21. The early mobilization activities of the PCH are discussed in the 1936 trial of Jacques Roumain, the details of which appeared in *Le Nouvelliste,* October 23, 1934. See also Mats Lundahl, "The Rise and Fall of the Haitian Labor Movement," in Malcolm Cross and Gad Heuman ed., *Labor in the Caribbean: From Emancipation to Independence* (London: Macmillan Caribbean, 1988), 92–93. On Roumain's literary career, see Fowler, *A Knot in the Thread,* and Roger Gaillard, *L'Univers romanesque de Jacques Roumain* (Port-au-Prince: Henri Deschamps, 1966). For a more critical assessment of his political activities, see Hénock Trouillot, *Dimension et limites de Jacques Roumain* (Port-au-Prince: Éditions Fardin, 1981).

22. Combat, February 6, 1946; Trouillot, Dimension et limites de Jacques Roumain, 104.

23. J. C. White to Secretary of State, Enclosure no 1, "Communist Activities in the Republic of Haiti," Port-au-Prince, USNA RG 84, 838.00B/130644.

24. *Le Nouvelliste,* November 23, 1936.

25. Secrétaire de L'État de L'Interieur à Secrétaire de La Justice, January 11, 1935, Corréspondence Général, Archives National de la République d'Haïti, Port-au-Prince, vol. 1272.

26. On unionism among the bus drivers in the mid-thirties, see *Le Nouvelliste,* November 23, 1936.

27. René Depestre, *Étincelles* (Port-au-Prince: Imprimerie de L'État, 1945), 20.

28. Figures based on "Recensement de la ville de Port-au-Prince, 24 Janvier 1949" Section I Table 1, Edmond Mangonès Collection, Bibliothèque Haïtienne, Collège du Petit Séminaire St Martial, Port-au-Prince, box 312; and Lundahl, "The Rise and Fall of the Haitian Labor Movement," 93.

29. On Breton's influence on the Marxist youth in Haiti, see, for example, Paul Laraque, "André Breton en Haïti," *Nouvelle Optique* 26 (Mai 1971): 126–38, and the special edition "Surréalisme et révolte en Haïti," *Conjonction* 193 (April/May/June, 1992).

30. The PCH and the PSP, discussed in detail below, were not the only Marxist groups to form during this period. In their book, *Written in Blood: The Story of the Haitian People, 1492–1995* (Lanham, Md.: University Press of America, [1979] 1996), 496, Robert and Nancy Heinl mention a small Maoist party (of which little is known) that formed in the capital in early February. René Salomon, a radical black medical doctor and teacher, also formed a small yet ideologically fascinating party, the Parti Socialiste Haïtien (PSH) in February as well. PSH's program fused socialist theory with a fierce black nationalism. Their position was made clear in an early issue of their organ, *Classe Moyene et Masse,* May 1, 1946: "We are in a battle to replace the rights of the authentic blacks . . . We will fight for this in order to establish a new

nation." The party was, however, short-lived and records on its activities are scarce, hence its exclusion from the present discussion.

31. *Combat,* February 6, 1946.

32. Ibid.

33. The party's support of the women's movement deserves mention. Suffrage was not a reality for Haitian women until the election campaign of 1956–57. Nonetheless, a women's movement had been in existence from at least the twenties and was always closely aligned with progressive movements in the country. For example, the wives of several leading politicians in the thirties formed their own Ligue Feminin. The relationship of this with the Marxist movement is difficult to evaluate. Unfortunately the work on the Haitian women's movement is woefully inadequate. See, however, Myriam J. A. Chancy, *Framing Silence: Revolutionary Novels by Haitian Women* (New Brunswick, N.J.: Rutgers University Press, 1997), chap. 1.

34. *Combat,* March 12, 1946.

35. On Alexis's views, see his article in *Combat,* July 12, 1946. For his address to the party regarding the upcoming elections, see Wilson to Secretary of State, "Memorandum Describing meeting of Communist Party of Haiti on July 26," Port-au-Prince, USNA RG 59, 838.00B/7–2946.

36. *La Ruche,* March 2, 1946.

37. Jack West (civil attaché for the American Embassy), "Report on Information regarding the Communist Party of Haiti," attachment to Wilson to Secretary of State, "Memorandum on the size of the Communist Party of Haiti," July 21, 1946, USNA RG 59, 838.00B/7–2176. Although this figure was most likely exaggerated, it does indicate the impact that Marxism as a political alternative had at the beginning of 1946.

38. *Combat,* March 12, 1946.

39. The Cuban PSP's assessment of the Haitian Communist Party appeared in their organ *Hoy,* and was reprinted in the Haitian PSP's *La Nation,* March 14, 1946. The Cuban PSP's decision not to recognize the PCH appears to have been shared by other Latin American communist parties, many of whom followed the developments in Haiti with great interest. For further comparison between the Cuban Communists and the PCH, see Robert J. Alexander's *Communism in Latin America* (New Brunswick, N.J.: Rutgers University Press, 1957), 297. For the PCH's response to these critiques, see *Combat,* March 19, 1946.

40. Orme Wilson to Secretary of State, February 12, 1946, Port-au-Prince, USNA RG 84, 838.00B/2–1246; Roger Dorsinville, "Les 'Authentiques' et le cercle enchanté du pouvoir," in *Trente ans de pouvoir noir en Haïti,* 46.

41. The communiqué appeared in *Combat,* March 19, 1946.

42. Wilson to Secretary of State, March 26, 1946, Port-au-Prince, USNA RG 59, 838.00B/3.2646; *Combat,* February 14, 1946.

43. For details on the unions that emerged see Mats Lundahl, "The Rise and Fall of the Haitian Labor Movement," in Cross and Heuman, *Labor in the Caribbean,*

96–97; and Jean-Jacques Doubout and Ulrick Joly, *Notes sur le développement du mouvement syndical en Haïti* (Port-au-Prince: Henri Deschamps, 1974).

44. Hector, Syndicalisme et socialisme en Haïti, 65.

45. *Combat,* March 23, 1946.

46. Harold H. Tittman to Secretary of State, "Study of Contemporary Leftist Elements in Haiti," June 11, 1948, Port-au-Prince, USNA RG 59, 838.00B/6–1148.

47. *La Nation,* March 23, 1946.

48. Max. D. Sam interview with author, Pétionville, Haiti, May 7, 2001 (hereafter Sam interview).

49. *La Nation,* March 13, 1946.

50. Sam interview.

51. Ibid.

52. *Combat,* April 26, 1947.

53. Hector, Syndicalisme et socialisme, 92.

54. Harold H. Tittman to Secretary of State, "Study of Contemporary Leftist Elements in Haiti," June 11, 1948, Port-au-Prince, USNA RG 59, 838.00B/6–1148, 15.

55. Sam interview.

56. On the changing political climate in Latin America after the Second World War, see Leslie Bethell and Ian Roxborough, ed., *Latin America Between the Second World War and the Cold War, 1944–1948* (Cambridge: Cambridge University Press, 1994); Martha K. Huggins, *Political Policing: The United States and Latin America* (Durham, N.C.: Duke University Press, 1998); David Rock, ed., *Latin America in the 1940s: War and Postwar Transitions* (Berkeley: University of California Press, 1994).

57. Nicholls, "Ideology and Protest in Haiti," 16. See also his now-standard survey of Haitian political history, *From Dessalines to Duvalier: Race, Colour, and National Independence in Haiti* (London: MacMillan Press, [1979] 1996).

58. Charlier's provocative articles appeared in *La Nation* throughout 1950. See also his *Aperçu sur la formation historique de la nation haïtienne* (Port-au-Prince: Presses Libres, 1954).

59. On the Cuban case, Alejandro De La Fuente's *A Nation For All: Race, Inequality, and Politics in Twentieth-Century Cuba* (Chapel Hill: University of North Carolina Press, 2001) provides an excellent analysis of how race was treated in the radical agendas of labor and communist militants. Several works deal with the political developments in Jamaica during the struggle for self-government. See, for example, Trevor Munroe, *The Politics of Constitutional Decolonisation-Jamaica, 1944–1962* (UWI Mona: Institute of Social and Economic Research, 1972); Aggrey Brown and Carl Stone, ed., *Perspectives on Jamaica in the Seventies* (Kingston: Jamaica Publishing House, 1981); and Evelyn and John Stephens, *Democratic Socialism in Jamaica: The Political Movement and Social Transformation in Dependent Capitalism* (Princeton, N.J.: Princeton University Press, 1986). All offer fairly good treatments of the political dynamics that prevailed in Jamaica in the tumultuous period 1938 to 1980. The

autocritique of the Worker's Party of Jamaica (WPJ), *Contributions to Rethinking: Issues in the Communist Movement* (Kingston: Worker's Party of Jamaica, 1987) also has some provocative admissions of the party's exclusionary policy to racial and cultural issues, as does Trevor Munroe's *Jamaican Politics: A Marxist Perspective in Transition* (Kingston: Heinemann Publishers, 1990). For Trinidad, Selwyn Ryan's *Race and Nationalism in Trinidad and Tobago: A Study of Decolonization in a Multiracial Society* (University of the West Indies–St. Augustine: Institute of Social and Economic Research, 1972) is most insightful.

60. Cedric J. Robinson, *Black Marxism: The Making of the Black Radical Tradition* (London: Zed Publishers, 1983). In recent years, Robinson's thesis has been addressed in several works on radical black movements in the Anglophone Caribbean. See, for example, Anthony Bogues, *Caliban's Freedom: The Early Political Thought of C. L. R James* (London: Pluto Press, 1997); and Rupert C. Lewis, *Walter Rodney's Intellectual and Political Thought* (Detroit, Mich.: Wayne State University Press, 1998).

12

"Considered Coloured or Honorary White"

African Americans in South Africa

DAWNE Y. CURRY

In 1937, future Nobel Prize recipient Ralph Bunche began his three-month South African journey.[1] As a two-year Social Science Research Council fellow, his goal was "not [to conduct] research per se but instead to hone his fieldwork skills by examining the methodology anthropologists used to study culture and contact between Western and non-Western societies."[2] As an observer, Bunche visited Cape Town, the Eastern Cape, Durban, Bloemfontein, Pretoria, Basutoland (Botswana) and Thaba Nchu and Mafeking. He lived among so-called "coloureds" and whenever he traveled to northeastern Alexandra Township, southwestern Soweto or other "black spots," he did so under the escort of Friends of Africa founder and white liberal William Ballinger. Not only did Bunche observe his host culture, he also wrote down his impressions. One journal entry dated November 18, 1937, explains how South Africa's white minority used technology to separate races. Bunche wrote, "There are two elevators—one with an operator for Europeans, and a self-operating one for non-Europeans."[3]

Bunche observed that Africans exerted physical strength to attain conveyance in public buildings whereas whites received mechanized service. In using technology to differentiate, white South Africans connoted superiority and inferiority based on the level of mechanization offered. This not-so-subtle policy underscored the government's attempt to reinforce the prevailing ideology of segregation, which from 1910 to 1948 affected almost every facet of South African life, from restrooms and buses to separate residential areas. Its origins, as Alistair Sparks shows, hark back to 1652, when Dutch settler Jan van Riebeeck planted an almond hedge bush to separate Europeans from the indigenous Khoisan and to protect the colonists' cattle. This vegetation, as Sparks indicates, helped the Dutch in their plan to create an "island" separate from Africa.[4] David Welsh, by contrast, traces the roots of segregation to colonial Natal, where Native Agent Theophilus Shepstone demarcated ten reserves for exclusive African occupation.[5] George Fredrickson supports Welsh's contention by pointing out in *Black Liberation* that the ingredients for a segregationist policy developed before 1902; however its formalization, (which he further notes in this work and *White Supremacy)* occurred years later, when the Union of South Africa formed in 1910.[6] John Cell concurs. Cell emphasizes that the rise in industrialization sparked the need for a continual labor supply, which in turn prompted government officials to lobby for and legislate laws that began to separate races.[7]

Bunche contributes to the conversation not by discussing segregation's origins but by highlighting its application and institutionalization. He, along with Eslanda "Essie" Robeson (wife of famed actor, singer, and activist Paul Robeson; mother of Pauli, a Hartford Seminary graduate and civil rights pioneer) analyze segregation through lived experience.[8] In many ways, Bunche's excerpt and the stories of other African Americans that follow, which historicize the eras of segregation, apartheid, and post-liberation, show how African Americans faced racism abroad and interpreted it. Bunche faced racism firsthand as an elevator passenger, and then he went on to the movie theaters and observed how cinema space reinforced the policy of segregation with whites and coloureds attending certain shows, Africans on other days, or all race groups watching the same film but in separate sections. In observing the allocation of space, Bunche compares the American South to South Africa using language that reflects his American roots. He wrote, "Non-Europeans can go into the Palladium Cinema . . . providing they get an advance permit for them to attend from the manager. They, are of course, are put in a Jim Crow section."[9] Bunche's travel narrative provides a comparative framework for analyzing his observations similar to the methodology that Fredrickson employed in his two opuses. Fredrickson delves into the history of political organizations while also noting ideological beliefs of South Africa's black populace and the white minority government that oppressed them. He blends the top-down approach with subaltern voices; however, the construction of race resides with the elite rather than South Africa's everyday people and foreigners such as African Americans who visited.

Earlier writings on African American interaction with black South Africans highlight the period from 1890 to 1925 and focus on race consciousness and secular and church movements. These works examine the collective role of African Americans rather as David Anthony (1994), Robert Edgar (1992), and Iris Berger (2001) do; they center their study on specific individuals, their political ideologies, and observations of a foreign land.[10] My work continues this tradition by discussing the social construction of race using three key episodes during my tenure in South Africa. These racial encounters of a South African kind reveal how notions of identity are embedded in lived experience but also in social mores. A central theme, however, does weave together these different methodological approaches. Attitudes of African Americans towards their African counterparts feature as a point of analysis. African Americans either treated black South Africans as surrogate siblings or as brethren. Despite their categorization as "honorary white," African Americans such as railway laborer John Ross also endured discrimination based on skin color, as when a white employer verbally abused him in 1893. To the story of African Americans we now turn.

African American Presence in South Africa: A Selected Historical Overview

African American presence in South Africa dates back to the eighteenth century, when sailors who were aboard ships docked in Cape Town and settled there, as well as in Port Elizabeth and Durban on the country's eastern coast.[11] By contrast, others migrated into the interior. One such person was ship steward Yankee Ward, who earned substantial fortunes from mining the diamond fields. With his windfall, Ward opened up hotels in the Eastern Cape's Kokstad and the Transvaal's Johannesburg. Sailors were not the only people traveling to Africa's southern tip; vocalists and missionaries were also prominent.

For five years, the Virginia Jubilee Singers or the Virginia Concert Company, established and directed by Orpheus McCadoo, toured the nation, rendering songs, minstrel shows, and presentations. On their first concert date, the troupe opened at the Vaudeville Theatre in Cape Town on the evening of June 30, 1890.[12] There in "The Mother City," the variety group performed classic Jubilee hymns such as "Steal Away Jesus" and "The Gospel Train," in addition to performing minstrels such as "Massa's Dead," "The Old Folks at Home," and "Old Black Joe." English colonists had introduced minstrel shows to various South African audiences as early as 1850; therefore, depictions of performances that mimicked and ridiculed black Americans were not a new form of entertainment, nor were they seen as potentially threatening to the status quo of racial etiquette.[13] Instead, "'acting the nigger, acting out white fantasies about blacks, was ideally suited as a rationalisation (sic) of the anxieties of white settlers in South Africa attempting to come to terms with the strength of precapitalist social formations."[14]

By contrast, African American missionaries did not fare as well. Their campaigns to proselytize and to introduce "the gospel" to their indigenous black congregants raised immense concern among white people, who viewed their intrusion into domestic affairs as threatening. Many former adherents began leaving the "approved" Christian mission stations to establish their own religious and educational institutions. One of these people, John L. Dube, attended a missionary school at Edendale near Durban. This church minister founded *Ilanga lase Natal,* a newspaper with a circulation of over one thousand subscribers and containing editorials focusing on issues of land, voting, housing, and political rights for Black South Africans. Dube spent approximately seven years in the United States from 1887 to1892, and again in 1897 to 1899. According to R. Hunt Davis Jr., Dube was among the many itinerant scholars who "fus[ed] black American educational ideas with the movement of independence and protest among South Africans in South Africa."[15]

Besides using his newspaper to arouse the sensibilities of black people, Dube also formed the Ohlange Institute in Natal in 1901. Modeled on Booker T. Washington's Tuskegee Institute and with its focus on industrial education, it was by 1910 "the only fully successful school for Africans in South Africa that, after a decade and a half of direct black American presence, was . . . under the control and guidance not of Afro-Americans [or of whites] but of Africans."[16] South African government officials wanted to curtail this type of direct cooperation and potential encounters between diasporic and continental Africans; after the conclusion of the South African war in 1902, they severely restricted the number of African Americans entering the country.[17]

Regardless of why African Americans traveled to South Africa, British officials or members of the later-unified Republics of the Transvaal, the Cape, the Orange Free State, and Natal labeled these temporary visitors and permanent residents as "honorary whites." To attain this status, certain conditions had to be met.[18] Sojourners had to acquire a temporary permit and then seek affiliation with an organization, preferably directed by white people, and they had to occupy a post that could be easily filled by an indigenous black South African.

When visiting South Africa in 1934 while writing her extensive *African Journey,* Eslanda Robeson answered a question a reporter posed: "How much European blood have you?" She responded rather "mischievously" but truthfully, "Some Spanish, English, Scottish, Jewish, American Indian, with a large majority of Negro blood. I consider myself a Negro."[19] Even though Robeson stood among a throng of newspaper correspondents and cited all known components of her racial and ethnic heritage, she still proclaimed allegiance to blackness. Robeson also used the specific white people who granted her second-class citizenship to legitimize her "chosen" and "situational" race. Had Robeson been born in South Africa rather than in the United States, she would have faced the possibility of having the term "coloured" conferred on her.

During the early nineteenth century, white settlers at the Western Cape distinguished themselves from persons of color (Malays, Indonesians, Khoisans, and free blacks). Slaves resided under a separate racial category. During the decades following slavery's abolition in 1834, many Africans who ultimately served as part of the laboring class began migrating to the Western Cape to experience the fruits of the mineral revolution and the process of industrialization. This influx led to the formation of a distinct "coloured" identity, based partially on descent from European settlers, and as Chris Saunders maintains, generations of incorporation into colonial society.[20] The problem with this racial category was that its members were often depicted as occupying an intermediate position, as described in *Between the Wire and the Wall,* or as Victor Turner described, residency in a liminal space.[21] Even though coloureds spoke Afrikaans rather than English, they were not fully accepted into white society. Nor were restrictions such as association or ancestry emphasized until apartheid's advent in 1948. Until then, people such as Eslanda Robeson could have assumed a coloured identity because of a light-brown complexion.

Robeson's sojourn to South Africa highlights the period when Bunche visited—that of segregation. A whole series of legislative measures, ranging from the color bar in the mining industry to race-designated residential areas governed South African social, political, and economic life. With squatting prohibited and seven percent of the land set aside for African occupation courtesy of the 1913 Natives Land Act, the government further embarked upon its plan to entrench territorial segregation. African encroachment of the rural areas basically ended with the passing of this act, as many reluctantly left the farms where they survived by subsistence or were well off, and entered into a cash economy by working in the mines, in factories, or white suburban homes.

With this influx of Africans into the cities, government officials ultimately decreed another law, the 1923 Natives Urban Areas Act (NUAA), to regulate the population influx. First implemented in Johannesburg's Malay Location, the NUAA provided "the mechanism for excluding Africans from white urban areas."[22] African areas languished when compared to white areas, creating slumlike conditions. Before the First World War, government officials failed to upgrade the Malay Location and other slums, citing insufficient funds.[23] As these slums proliferated and became disease ridden, so did white concern. The Malay Location experienced the Spanish influenza epidemic in 1918. Other places, such as Alexandra, faced an increase in cases of smallpox, typhoid, dysentery, and other diseases, resulting in that township's near expropriation in the 1930s and 1940s. Seen as health menaces, these sites gave government officials fodder to continue separating blacks and whites physically. Little concern existed for Africans placed or located near environmental hazards.

Mine dumps and sewage sites served as geographical buffers from the black and white worlds.[24] Robeson noted these mine dumps without citing their location and describes them as "great, depressing mountains of slag-whitish looking ashy dirt and clinkers washed clean of all gold dust, and just piled up and left."[25] African homes stood amidst these heaps. Bunche writes, "As we drove along Portland Avenue-Brixton, we could see Orlando in the distance—off behind a huge mine dump, and looking like a huge assemblage of dog houses with shiny tin roofs."[26] Equating dog houses with African homes analogizes poverty with geography. Bunche further questions, "Is it assuming a pattern in South Africa that Colored (as at Bokmakierie) and Native (as at Pimville) locations and housing projects should be built alongside sewage disposal farms?"[27] Near environmental hazards, African locations served as reservoirs of cheap, pliable labor for whites rather than as places where people lived free of fear, disease, and poverty.

Such a laboring force required transport. In Alexandra, African workers commuted nine miles to their places of employment. Because government officials made no provision for the defrayment of transport expenses until 1944, when it enacted the Employer Travel Subsidy,[28] Alexandrans boycotted the buses on four occasions during the 1940s to protest a penny fare increase from 4d to 5d.[29] This inconvenience reinforced segregation. Although Bunche and Robeson note the different living areas, the issue of transport surfaces only to explain the unfamiliarity of Jim Crowism. Bunche makes this point while Robeson remains uncharacteristically silent.

Robeson chooses instead to highlight the relationship between employment and job proximity by using domestic servants as an example to highlight the government's ability to maneuver around prescribed laws for whites' benefit. She uses as her terrain one of the oldest Capetown townships, Langa, situated some seven miles from the city center. Its history dates back to 1855, when a health scare similar to Port Elizabeth's origin prompted officials to create a separate African residential area. In analyzing Langa, Robeson compares American and South African segregation while underscoring the latter government's concerted effort to create separate living spaces for its African inhabitants. She writes, "As a Negro citizen of 'democratic' America, segregated colored sections of cities is not unknown to me. But these still further segregated *locations* are something different altogether."[30]

Not only does Robeson offer this comparison, but she takes the time to articulate their differences. She discerns two types of physical spaces created expressly for Africans: "The Colored people in South Africa, as in America, are allowed to live in certain sections of the city proper, or in the immediate outskirts of the segregated Colored sections . . . They must live in the *locations* (urban areas) and in the *reserves* (rural areas), which are special areas for them, entirely removed from the cities." Initially thought of as rural frontier land, locations ultimately became known as residential sites occupied by Africans in urban South Africa.[31]

Jennifer Robinson,[32] who wrote extensively on space and power, discusses how the state manipulated grids of habitation by making them easily discernable, or as James C. Scott argues in *Seeing Like a State,* legible.[33] According to Robinson, these locations represented perfect systems of control.[34] This aspect seems to elude Robeson, save this insight: "Natives in domestic service . . . may live on or near their employer's premises, for the convenience of the employer."[35] Robeson examines the issue of control by citing the state's ability to determine living arrangements as opposed to the layouts of African locations and what that possibly presented. Through these silences and amplifications, Bunche and Robeson inform us about the construction of race through geography, poverty, and labor distinctions. Such categories connoted racial identity. Blackness and whiteness figured prominently with other distinctions such as coloured or Asian left murky. In underscoring everyday formations of segregation and domination, Bunche and Robeson document their perceptions of similar racial systems. They did not, as their counterpart Max Yergan, side with South Africa's segregationists or apartheid's architects.

Max Yergan, physician, YMCA secretary, and missionary, resided in South Africa from 1912 to 1930. Yergan also served in the capacity of a State Department-sponsored speaker in the early 1950s. In that position, Yergan discussed progress towards racial reconciliation in the United States rather than exposing the country's hypocrisy or basically telling the truth about various lynching incidents, as well as noncompliance with some major Supreme Court decisions among other concerns of injustice. Instead of condemning racism abroad, Yergan seemed to honor the unwritten code of ethics governing what Mary Dudziak refers to as cold war civil rights activism: paint a positive (white) international image of America, rather than reveal the (black) skeletons in the nation's racial closet.[36]

Eslanda Robeson failed to adhere to this "agreement," as did her husband Paul, CRC Chairman William Patterson, and famed dancer Josephine Baker, resulting in passport revocation, or in Baker's case, a concerted effort by governmental officials to cancel all of her Latin American, European, and Central American scheduled tours.[37] Baker had renounced her American citizenship for that of France; therefore the limitation of her physical mobility differed from Paul Robeson, who could not leave American shores and was compelled one time to perform near the Canadian border so that aficionados of his craft could attend.[38] Yergan enjoyed full citizenship status not only in the United States, but also in South Africa. As his chronicler David Anthony reveals, "The nationalist regime, advocating its far-reaching policy of 'separate development' or Apartheid, greeted Yergan with open arms in 1949. So pleased were they with the enigmatic African-American that the South Africa Foundation, the public relations arm of government, would repeatedly serve as Yergan's hosts in the 1950s and 1960s."[39] To show his allegiance, Yergan "mouthed a plethora of pointless platitudes in praise of apartheid, seeing 'separate development' as the only realistic solution to a complex South African drama."[40]

In discussing differing interpretations of politics and race, Yergan opted for the exclusionary, far-removed version that accepted and embraced a culturally manufactured construction of race and class, while Robeson proposed the fictive kin model, which denounced "honorary whiteness." All of those categories intersected, yet their architects defied race- and even gender-prescribed notions. Eslanda Robeson altered patriarchal structures when she transcended the Victorian spheres to not only enter the public arena but also to share the intellectual stage with her male contemporary. She also defiantly proclaimed her blackness. Yergan, on the other hand, dismissed that strategy and instead employed the pall of whiteness to socially elevate himself as a man and as an American, rather than a person possessing darker skin. In the case of Yergan, gender and nationality trumped race, whereas the converse was true for Robeson, who stated, "If an example is needed, I am African."[41] Madie Hall Xuma also showed solidarity with Africans, but not without taking a superior position.

Born in North Carolina in 1894, Madie Hall Xuma immigrated to South Africa in 1940 and resided there until her husband, Dr. Alfred B. Xuma, passed away in 1963. Madie Hall Xuma entered South Africa at a time when Africans flooded the cities and bus boycotts abounded. Government legislation also colored her South African experience. Enacted in 1950, the Population Registration Act and the Group Areas Act, which formed part of a larger governmental plan to transform South Africa's landscape into strict racialized enclaves, enforced separate development. As a resident of swanky Dube, Soweto, Xuma experienced racial separation. Class distinctions also informed her outlook. Dube housed a professional stratum, which served to alienate Xuma from the masses and further reinforce her aloofness, though she often poured on the charm when necessary.[42] Three years before her departure to the United States, a watershed in South African history grasped international imagination. On March 21, 1960, a peaceful protest turned into carnage as sixty-nine fleeing people struck from the back died. Following the Sharpeville Massacre, the government cracked down on opposition by banning the ANC and the Pan Africanist Congress (PAC), an ANC splinter group founded in 1959 by former university professor and at one time South Africa's most feared man, Robert Sobukwe. Xuma's ideology, which centered on female empowerment and education, developed within this political context.

Xuma promoted and built up the Zenzele self-help clubs she founded. In this volume, Iris Berger shows how Xuma constructed blackness through the notion of womanhood. She felt an innate bond with Africans as this quotation reveals: "I regard them as my sisters. We share more or less the same background. It was my duty to share with them what we Americans know."[43] While noting shared descent and heritage, Xuma also revealed her responsibility as a surrogate sibling. Sharing knowledge underscores her ethnic chauvinism as it conveys a hierarchical structure that privileges geographical location and American nationality. Berger further solidifies this notion: "As touchstones of progress . . . American educated Africans embodied not only an elite to be emulated but also a new transnational black identity that promised modernity linked to racial pride."[44] As an "honorary white," Xuma pushed for unity among South African women and used her clubs to further that aim.

Conferment of "honorary white" status was not limited to black foreigners; even those residing within South Africa could attain such notoriety. The vehicle of racial transference, in this case, was education. On his fifth day in the country, November 23, 1937, Bunche recalled a conversation he had with his acting secretary, Peter Dabula, concerning education and the elevation of status. Bunche describes how a police officer stopped a group of educated Africans, who, after hearing them speak, apologized to them because of their verbiage. Noting his mistake, the officer insisted that these educated Africans wear badges to avoid further molestation.[45] While education served as the whitening tool, it also had the potential of providing a cloak of security, since the police officer alluded to providing badges for these "honorary whites" to ensure that they would not be "blackened" by interrogation or have further restrictions placed upon their physical mobility. An identifying marker such as a badge potentially could erase the anonymity and invisibility of an educated black person, but also increased the risk of rendering them highly more visible (white) in the eyes of state authorities.

Edgar noted other examples that Bunche documented three strategies his subjects used to engage in passing: lighter-skinned children attended "border line" or "fading" schools; accepted coloureds posing as Europeans passed to obtain cheaper accommodations; or Capetonian Africans married coloured women so that they could live in the urban areas.[46] The first strategy, which entailed physical complexion, did not guarantee an identity makeover. Needed in the complete "transformation" were the assumption of a European name and the renunciation of birthright. However, transference of racial identity assured the possibility of a better education, whereas people who preferred to "downgrade" their status by assuming a coloured racial identity (the second strategy) found it economically expedient to do so. The last strategy concerned the matter of holy matrimony. Persons seeking to pass through marriage rites availed themselves of the courts and the formality of signed contracts to transfer racially, thus contesting their imposed racial inscriptions of identity by choosing to "whiten" or "blacken" themselves.

In 1948, the Nationalist Party lessened this fluidity between racial populations when it came to power and began entrenching major cornerstones of Grand Apartheid, which documented race by residential location and by ethnicity. Legislative measures also, as Deborah Posel explains, heightened discipline, regulation, and surveillance, while also asserting racial difference.[47] To institute this policy, government officials reclassified South Africans. One of the more celebrated reclassification cases was that of Sandra Laing. Born into a white family, Laing, who possessed kinky hair and a darker complexion, faced reclassification in 1967. Even though DNA tests proved that her father was white, government officials ignored the results and had Laing register as a "coloured." During an interview with a *Guardian* correspondent, Laing underscores the political ramifications of her reclassification: "It was a step into another world, from ruling caste privilege to the oppression and poverty of townships."[48] Further removal of privileges came with a personal decision at the age of fifteen to marry a Zulu-speaking vegetable seller named Petrus Zwane.[49] Laing, a former white/reclassified coloured, and Petrus, a black, ultimately resided in Swaziland, where their interracial relationship mattered less and they could live freely as husband and wife.

Laing's story coincides with major changes within South Africa and the continent. In 1970, for example, government officials created the Bantustans, ten homelands where Africans developed along their own lines culturally and politically but remained economically tied to South Africa. As states recognized only by South African officials as independent countries, Bantustans represented another way in which the government reinforced the idea of blackness using the geographical landscape. The seventies also witnessed the end of Portuguese colonial rule in Angola and Mozambique in 1975. In these territories, the ANC and PAC had established bases from which to launch counter-insurgent measures in South Africa, a country that had by June 16, 1976 reached its boiling point, when the Soweto uprising started.

Ignited by the imposition of Afrikaans as a medium of instruction, the Soweto uprising was a major watershed. It marked the first overt protest since 1960, when the government clamped down on resistance following the Sharpeville Massacre. Affecting hundreds of African communities, this uprising featured the youth as the primary catalysts, many of whom armed themselves with stones and petrol bombs in opposition to the state machinery of casspirs and hippos. When the uprising ended in 1977, hundreds had lost their lives or had fled the country to neighboring African states or elsewhere around the continent and the world. By that time, Laing and her husband had experienced marital problems and the family became divided as she placed her children in social welfare. Laing also tried to mend the relationship with her biological family in the 1980s, only to learn of her father's death and her mother's refusal to see her. While Laing dealt with her personal problems, violence enveloped the townships, forcing former President P. W. Botha to declare a partial state of emergency in 1985.

Protesting police brutality, substandard education, and housing shortages among other issues aroused the consciousness of everyday people and prompted the government to unleash its full muscle as it sent in armed troops and casspirs to quell rebellions emerging in the townships. None of this daunted Joyce F. Kirk, who journeyed to the country during the aftermath of this turbulent time to conduct research. Her work, *Making a Voice*, which discusses African resistance to segregation in Port Elizabeth, documents her experience when trying to rent a Capetonian flat. "Upon seeing [Kirk], English woman Mrs. Smith, said 'Oh, you sounded so American.' [She] responded; I am American!"[50] Following this exchange, the two women viewed the apartment, and Kirk agreed to take the flat with the understanding that during the following day, they would make financial arrangements.

Initially the meeting between prospective landlady and tenant revealed Mrs. Smith's own limited understanding of nationality. She had immediately assumed Kirk was a safe person to rent to because she was an American. However, in her mind, that meant white. Smith did not even conceal her surprise, and made a major faux pas when she denied Kirk her nationality. The discussion did not end there, for the next conversation involved Mrs. Smith informing Kirk of another potential tenant, a man who had expressed an interest in staying for a longer period than he had proposed. Smith then requested payment in advance. Kirk agreed. Forty-five minutes later the phone rang again. It was Mrs. Smith. This time she reneged on the arrangement completely. An enraged Kirk hung up the phone, disappointed and complaining bitterly about apartheid. She writes, "Every time someone asks me about 'honorary' white status for foreign blacks in South Africa, during . . . official apartheid, . . . I think of Mrs. Smith and others who continually treated me as a nonperson, as they did most black people in South Africa."[51] Apparently Mrs. Smith was not the only one to express this sentiment. Even foreigners shared this belief. Journalist Keith Richburg was one such proponent.

In his description of a nighttime car chase by two white South African males, Richburg sought refuge in Alexandra's crime-infested bosom. Richburg was a visitor to South Africa during its transition from minority to majority government in the early to mid 1990s when the country witnessed turmoil and uncertainty about its future. Several reasons account for this uncertainty. Violence ran rampant. In one of the more celebrated cases of death, a Polish immigrant assailant felled South African Communist Party (SACP) and Umkhonto we Sizwe (Spear of the Nation) leader Chris Hani. As a plot initiated by the far Right in South Africa, Hani's death was an attempt to derail negotiations to end apartheid, as was the creation of a third force and the fomentation of ethnic rivalries. Alexandra Township also witnessed these tensions. Hostel-dwelling Zulus took over the homes of Xhosa residents and displaced them, causing many to live in churches, centers, and in shacks. Besides these misfortunate occurrences, exiles from all around the world and the African continent returned home. Nelson Mandela, poised to become the first democratically elected president, led the country in the interim—all while Richburg sped to save his own life. After realizing that the journalist intended to enter Alexandra, the unidentified white men aborted their chase. Richburg breathed a sigh of relief as he made a U-turn and headed back to the white suburbs and the safety he craved.

His reflection reveals ideas about black solidarity or lack thereof, to which he writes, "I was sure that those same township blacks who might have jumped to my aid against the common white enemy would likely just as soon as put a brick aside my head and leave me lying in a ditch for the keys to the car and the wallet in my pocket."[52] Richburg assumes that commonalities based upon skin pigmentation assured him safety in Alexandra. When the journalist retracted this thought and admitted that he could face possible harassment, he transferred his racial identity by assuming whiteness because of his acquisitions, such as the fancy sports car he drove or the money he allegedly possessed. He altered the positive nature of blackness from the definition of sanctuary to a den of fear. The definition of whiteness remained the same, as the author confessed to his desire to leave Alexandra and return to the white suburbs he labeled safe. The night car chase and his Alexandran escape route reveals Richburg's awareness as a potential victim, but also how privilege could make him a target. Race served to unify but another category of identity, class, served to divide. This perception is no different from the other itinerants reviewed. The selected African Americans reviewed invariably inscribed their own conceptions of race based upon a shared history and a shared understanding of racial construction in America. In assuming a position of authority, these African Americans distanced themselves from their African heritage and aligned more with their American upbringing.

I, on the other hand, did the opposite, but even my natural willingness to align myself with blacks did not guarantee that South Africans conferred blackness on me. In my experience (an odyssey that began in 1997 and continues today), I learned how South Africans formulated conceptions of race when they labeled me as a coloured. Each time South Africans made that assumption, I wanted to sing that old James Brown song, "Say it Loud, I'm Black and I'm proud." But I refrained. I did, however, investigate why South Africans chose that nomenclature over other possible alternatives, and at the same time I learned how sightings of inscription often lead to misunderstandings and improper labeling. In documenting three racial encounters of a South African kind, I show how the conceptualization of race by everyday people often challenged and reinforced its institutional definitions.

My Racial Encounters of a South African Kind

The issue of race mixing and its relation to colouredness as a determining feature of identity makeup is highly problematic and extremely contentious.[53] Zimitri Erasmus, who edited and contributed to *Coloured by History Shaped by Place* and wrote at a time when coloured identity was undergoing reassessment, supports this contention. Erasmus writes, "Coloured identities are not about 'race mixture' but are the result of borrowing from other subaltern cultures."[54] Mohamed Adhikari also shows how coloureds had agency and participated in the making of their own identity.[55] Erasmus's notion eluded my Alexandran informant but reinforced Adhikari's argument when Margaret Mangoti defined coloured in the traditional manner by explaining that her Afrikaner father married her Xhosa mother.[56] She also applied this same notion of interracial mixing to me when she assumed that I had a white parent.[57] Even when I explained that I had black parents, this homemaker, whom I had thought was black and married to a black man, exclaimed, "Somebody in your family's past was white, that's why you can be considered Coloured here."[58] Mangoti, as did Algernon Austin in his study, *Achieving Blackness,* used ancestry to further her argument. In analyzing Henry Louis Gates's reaction to the Zanzibari people identifying themselves as Arab rather than as African, Austin writes, "If one's father was defined as an Arab, then one was an Arab even if one's mother was African."[59] Mangoti's husband, who traces the line of descent maternally, defies the one-drop rule that historically defined Zanzibaris and African Americans. His affiliation with his mother's identity not only complicates this notion, but also shows how the social construction of race works on the ground rather than its theoretical paradigm. A conversation between Lisa and me at a Kaiser Chiefs-Orlando Pirates football game at Johannesburg's First National Bank Stadium (FNB) will illustrate this point and further tease out the inherent complexities of coloured identities and blackness.

During halftime, Lisa initiated a frank discussion about South African race politics. Recounting this story at a time when South Africa embraced the idea of a rainbow nation while contending with one of the world's highest AIDS statistics (with one in five affected),[60] Lisa began by listing her perceived categorizations of coloured. Lisa stated, "There are first-class, second-class, and third-class Coloureds. First-class Coloureds are white, like . . ." and she abruptly stopped speaking. I asked, "Were you going to say white like me?" Lisa said that yes, I would be a first-class coloured because of my light skin, whereas Tonya, a mutual friend, could be regarded as second-class coloured because she could pass for a black South African since she has light-brown skin. "Third class," she further elaborated, "look like us, Black South Africans, but aren't one of us because their first language is Afrikaans and not isiZulu, Sesotho or other languages spoken by Black people."[61] Tonya had the ability to pass as black, and Lisa as a third-class coloured; however, language impeded their transference. Each woman spoke a different first language; Lisa's mother tongue was Sesotho, and Tonya's Afrikaans.[62]

Within this story lies an important comparison. Complexional variations distinguished both coloureds and African Americans. However, they were expressed differently. Instead of the hues depicted as light, brown, or dark, Lisa utilized what she termed as "class," a term often used to connote differences in transport and amenities offered or restricted. Not included in this discussion were the different categories of coloured identities. The 1959 Population Registration Act recognized coloureds as the following: Cape Malay, Cape Coloured, Indian, Chinese, "other Asiatic" and "other Coloured. From Lisa's perspective, the coloured population represented a monolithic entity with no distinctions, except of course skin degradations, whereas Michele, who represents a Cape Coloured, acknowledged the regional differences among coloured people to show the diversity.

Aside from connoting uniformity among coloureds, Lisa also raises the issue of "passing." Historically, the definition of "passing" occurred because people wanted to attain economic opportunities, better education, or live in the urban areas. That meant that coloureds often assumed European names and renounced their birthright or Africans married coloureds to live near the city center.[63] People seeking to pass via marriage rites availed themselves of the courts, and the formality of signed contracts to transfer racially. These "rites of marriage" agreements signified another way people living under the veil of South Africa's segregated living conditions could contest their imposed racial inscriptions of identity by choosing to "whiten" or "blacken" themselves. Elsewhere on the continent, identity change took another form, as Algerians renounced nationality for gains in the liberation struggle.

During the Battle of Algiers and in the film with the same name, Algerian women removed their veils and began emulating European culture.[64] Donning European dress and hairstyles, they eluded police officers at checkpoints and moved easily between the dimly-lit Casbah (black) and the highly illuminated European city (white) to plant bombs in cafes and other designated sites. In the film, for example, an Algerian woman orders a Coke and secretly pushes a purse containing a bomb under her barstool. A European man sitting next to her smiles and seems disappointed when she chooses to leave. Minutes later the bomb explodes. As more explosions take place, ambulances parade down the streets and crowds begin to gawk—French Algeria is under siege. Such women, who renounced their Algerian identity publicly by removing their veils, first surfaced as anonymous and innocuous, but in reality they were trained insurgents. However, as long as they dressed as Europeans, their "secret" identity remained intact and allowed them to cross national borders.

Writing extensively on race, Michael Banton argues that groups create boundaries that determine insider and outsider status. Boundaries, Banton further purports, are permeable. An exchange that took place in KwaZulu-

Natal's Ulundi further illustrates Banton's point and reinforces the Battle of Algiers story.[65] Recognized as Dingane's birthplace, the home of a successful nineteenth century military battle, entrance to Umfolozi/Hluhlwe Game Reserve, and the province's Royal Capitol, Ulundi became the site where I did a one-month immersion experience. It was there that I earned the very sparingly given title of black. The story unfolds as follows. While visiting the local airport named after Chief Mangosuthu Buthelezi, a receptionist complimented me on my hair and asked if it was like black people's hairstyles. In isiZulu, I responded affirmatively and stated that I was also black. The clerk, who was standing alongside the surprised receptionist, exclaimed that I was one of them because I spoke their language, and therefore included me in spite of my American nationality and "complexional brilliance."[66]

Erasmus cautions us, however, to not assign moral authenticity or political credibility to "blackness" or "Africaness," something which my anecdote fails to reinforce.[67] In the past, especially during the South African struggle and the age of Black Consciousness (1969–70s), Steve Biko defined "black" as being any oppressed person. Asians, coloureds, and Europeans as well as Africans fit his categorization.[68] Although the definition continues to have elasticity in contemporary times, there is some limitation, as Banton argues and the vignettes show, to inclusion and exclusion, such as language, complexion, nationality, and voice, among other criteria.

Conclusion

African American travel narratives provide a unique opportunity to obtain a glimpse into historical racial trends, particularly in the manner in which they are transmitted by visitors to a foreign country. African Americans who came before me used their nationality to privilege and to distinguish themselves from their African counterparts. This inherent feeling of superiority showed the mentality of those African Americans and the impact that similar systems of segregation had upon their psyche. As descendants of the motherland, they implemented a policy of "divide and rule" among African people, similar to the example of Americo-Liberians, who formed a settlement in the West African country and systematically excluded the indigenous Africans. African Americans who visited during the era of segregation looked upon South Africans as surrogate siblings. Ethnic chauvinism not only threaded their narratives but also weaved together observatory remarks to critical comparisons. Comparisons often centered on travel, accommodations, the landscape, and race relations.

My essay also tied together regions of experience. In a period when black majority rule defines the day and the reconsideration of coloured identities abounds, the three examples given show how South Africans socially construct race and choose a racial category based on historical notions of identity. In *Becoming Black,* Michele Wright discusses the significance of "othering" historically by alluding to Frantz Fanon and G. W. F. Hegel before offering her interpretation. Wright explains that in a hetropatriarchal society, males serve as the subjects with females relegated as "others." She also notes how racial sameness can lead to other cases of otherness.[69]

In the vignettes highlighted, African Americans became the "African" other when they adopted the title of "honorary white" or when South Africans ascribed coloured identity. This act of othering between two traditionally alleged subordinates shows a power differential based on Western conceptions as well as an African notion. First constructed by the apartheid regime where coloureds occupied the second rung and Africans the last, then reformulated based on personal experiences, this African notion of otherness recognizes sameness but fails to incorporate difference. This difference relates to history, culture, language, ethnicity, and other identity markers. Instead of recognizing the differences, black South Africans and African Americans subjugated each other and made themselves the subject.

Notes

Portions of this article originally appeared in *Safundi: Journal of South African and American Studies,* 22 April 2006.

1. Bunche received the Nobel Peace Prize for his role as mediator in the Middle East crisis in 1950.

2. Robert Edgar, ed., *An African-American in South Africa: The Travel Notes of Ralph J. Bunche* (Athens: Ohio University Press, 1992), 1.

3. Ibid., 159.

4. Allistair Haddon Sparks, *The Mind of South Africa* (New York: Alfred A. Knopf, 1990), 30.

5. David John Welsh, *The Roots of Segregation: Native Policy in Colonial Natal, 1845–1910* (Cape Town: Oxford University Press, 1971).

6. George Fredrickson, *Black Liberation: A Comparative History of Black Ideologies in the United States and South Africa* (New York: Oxford University Press, 1995), 95.

7. John Cell, *The Highest Stage of White Supremacy* (Cambridge: Cambridge University Press, 1982).

8. Eslanda Robeson graduated from Columbia University in 1923 as an analyti-

cal chemist. She later went on to earn a doctorate in anthropology from Hartford Seminary.

9. Edgar, *An African-American,* 168–69; R. Hunt Davis Jr., "The Black American Education Component in African Responses to Colonialism in South Africa: (ca. 1890–1914)," *Journal of Southern African Affairs* 111, no. 1 (January 1978): 60–75; Veit Erlmann, "'A Feeling of Prejudice': Orpheus M. McAdoo and the Virginia Jubilee Singers in South Africa 1890–1898," *Journal of Southern African Studies* 14, no. 3 (April 1988): 331–50; Clements Keto, "Black Americans and South Africa, 1890–1910, *Current Bibliography on African Affairs* 5 (July 1972): 383–406; Robert Vinson, "African Americans in South African-American Diplomacy: A Case Study in Race and Citizenship Debates, 1895–1925," *Negro History Bulletin* 61 (1998): 245–67; Joyce F. Kirk, *Making a Voice: African Resistance to Segregation in South Africa* (New York: Westview Press, 1998).

10. David Anthony, "Max Yergan and South Africa: A Transatlantic Interaction," in Sidney Lemuelle and Robin D. G. Kelley, ed., *Imagining Home: Class, Culture and Nationalism in the African Diaspora* (London: Verso, 1994); Edgar, *An African-American;* and Iris Berger, "An African American 'Mother of the Nation': Madie Hall Xuma in South Africa, 1940–1963," *Journal of Southern African Studies* 27, no. 3 (September 2001): 547–66.

11. Edgar, *An African-American,* 2.

12. Erlmann, "'A Feeling of Prejudice,'" 335.

13. Ibid.

14. Ibid.

15. Davis, "The Black American Education Component," 69.

16. Ibid, 76.

17. Edgar, *An African-American,* 18.

18. Ibid.

19. Eslanda Robeson, *African Journey* (New York: John Day Co., 1945), 33.

20. Christopher C. Saunders, *Historical Dictionary of South Africa* (Lanham, Md.: Scarecrow Press, 2000).

21. Gavin Lewis, *Between the Wire and the Wall: A History of South Africa "Coloured" Politics* (New York: St. Martin's Press, 1987); Victor W. Turner, *The Ritual Process: Structure and Anti-Structure* (Chicago: Aldine Publishers, 1970).

22. Lewis, *Between the Wire;* Turner, *The Ritual Process;*Susan Parnell, "Sanitation, Segregation and the Natives (Urban Areas) Act: African Exclusion from Johannesburg's Malay Location, 1897–1925," *Journal of Historical Geography* 17, no. 3 (1991): 272. Besides increasing the percentage of African-occupied land from 7 percent to 13 percent, the 1923 Natives Urban Areas Act also controlled the influx of Africans into the cities, thereby stiffening legislation concerning the carrying of identity passes for men; enforcement for women came later in 1955.

23. Ibid.

24. Edgar, *An African-American,* 167; Robeson, *African Journey,* 72.

25. Robeson, *African Journey*, 72.

26. Edgar, *An African-American*, 215.

27. Ibid.

28. Meshack Khosa, "Black Bus Subsidies," *GeoJournal* 22, no. 3 (November 1990), 252. Even when government officials promulgated the 1944 Employer Travel Subsidy, the onus of collecting the subsidy rested with Africans.

29. See Alf Stadler, "A Long Way to Walk: Bus Boycotts in Alexandra, 1940–1945," in Phil Bonner, ed., *Working Papers in Southern African Studies* (Johannesburg: Ravan Press, 1981), 228–57.

30. Robeson, *African Journey*, 37.

31. Kirk, *Making A Voice*, 6.

32. Jennifer Robinson, *The Power of the Apartheid State: Power and Space in South African Cities* (Oxford: Butterworth-Heinemann, 1996).

33. James C. Scott, *Seeing Like a State: How Certain Schemes to Improve the Human Condition Have Failed* (New Haven, Conn.: Yale University Press, 1998), 253–83.

34. Jennifer Robinson, "A Perfect System of Control? Territory and Administration in Early South African Locations" *Environment and Planning: Society and Space* 8 (1990): 135–62.

35. Robeson, *African Journey*, 37.

36. Mary L. Dudziak. *Cold War Civil Rights: Race and Image of American Democracy.* (Princeton, N.J.: Princeton University Press, 2000), 66.

37. CRC stands for Civil Rights Congress.

38. Dudziak, *Cold War Civil Rights*, 63–75.

39. David Anthony, "Max Yergan and South Africa: A Transatlantic Interaction," in Sidney Lemelle and Robin D. G. Kelley, ed., *Imagining Home: Class, Culture and Nationalism in the African Diaspora* (London: Verso, 1994), 197–98.

40. Ibid.

41. Edgar, *An African-American*, 25.

42. Berger, "An African American 'Mother of the Nation,'" 553.

43. Ibid.

44. Ibid, 554.

45. Edgar, *An African-American*, 174.

46. Ibid., 29.

47. Deborah Posel, "What's in a Name? Racial Categorisations under Apartheid and Their Afterlife," *Transformation* 47 (2001): 54.

48. Rory Caroll, "The Black Woman with White Parents," *Guardian* (March 17, 2003). See Judith Stone, *When She Was White: The True Story of a Family Divided by Race* (New York: Miramax/Hyperion, 2007).

49. Caroll, "The Black Woman with White Parents"; Stone, *When She Was White.*

50. Kirk, *Making a Voice*, xx–xxi.

51. Ibid, xxi.

52. Keith Richburg, *Out of America: A Black Man Confronts Africa* (New York: BasicBooks, 1997), 194.

53. Personal communication with Noor Nieftagodien, University of Witwatersrand, Johannesburg, South Africa, 2002.

54. Zimitri Erasmus, ed., *Coloured by History, Shaped by Place: New Perspectives on Coloured Identities in Cape Town* (Cape Town: Kwela Books and South African History online, 2001), 16–17.

55. Mohamed Adhikari, *Not White Enough, Not Black Enough: Racial Identity in the South African Coloured Community,* (Athens: Ohio University Press, 2005), 36.

56. Dawne Y. Curry, "An African American Constructs and Confronts the Social Construction of Race in Post-Apartheid South Africa," *Safundi* 22 (April 2006), 16–17. Regarding this sublime idea of miscegenation, I had assumed that my informant Margaret Mangoti, who is publicly and governmentally recognized as a coloured, had married a black man because when I met him the day before, that's what I had mentally concluded. I then posed a question concerning how the two of them coexisted interracially when apartheid's "immobile grid for . . . racial classification [had segmented the] entire population." See Deborah Posel, "What's in a Name?" 54. Margaret Mangoti is a pseudonym.

57. Curry, "An African American Constructs," 16–17. I explained to Mangoti that the one-drop rule did not apply to coloureds in South Africa in the same manner that it applied in the United States. "Correct me if I am wrong," I said in the midst my explanation, "the term 'coloured' has historically defined people of various extractions such as Indian, Chinese, Portuguese, White, Malay, or black, unlike [in] the United States where people considered the progeny of these sexual unions as black rather than another racial category." This interpretation differs from the one accepted in the United States because of its inclusion of interracial relationships other than those between blacks and whites. In South Africa, "white blood" conferred a higher governmental status than in the United States; the one-drop rule made a person black in the United States. In other regions or countries (such as those in Latin America, the Caribbean, and South Africa), this small percentage of blood made them white or a racial category other than black, such as *preto* or *pardo* in Brazil. The historical differences were important for understanding how South Africa and the United States interpreted race and socially constructed it to legislate policies that officially defined blackness, whiteness, and Creolization.

58. Erasmus, *Coloured by History,* 16.

59. Algernon Austin, *Achieving Blackness: Race, Black Nationalism, and Afrocentrism in the Twentieth Century* (New York: New York University Press, 2006), 8.

60. Graham Pembrey, "HIV and Aids in South Africa," available at http://www.avert.org/aidssouthafrica.htm (accessed May 12, 2008).

61. Personal communication with Lisa (pseudonym) at First National Bank Stadium, Johannesburg, South Africa, 2002.

62. Curry, "An African American Confronts," 21–22.

63. Edgar, *An African-American,* 174.

64. Frantz Fanon, *A Dying Colonialism* (New York: Grove Press, 1965).

65. Michael Banton, *Racial Theories* (Cambridge: Cambridge University Press, 1987), 125; Curry, "An African American Confronts," 11–12.

66. This is the statement I uttered in isiZulu, "Yebo, Ngingumuntu omyama wase-Melika." Curry, "An African American Confronts," 12. I will explain my arrival in Ulundi. When the lady of the house arrived, she greeted everyone, rapidly passing by until coming to me and exclaiming "*Umlungu!*" ("White!"). The only way I could prove my blackness was to share a personal photograph showing a former boyfriend. Everyone picked the Hispanic guy, not the dark-skinned man. After further explanation, one woman emphatically stated, "[She said] she's black, so let her be black."

67. Erasmus, *Coloured by History,* 17.

68. Steve Biko and Aelred Stubbs, *I Write What I Like: Selected Writings* (Chicago: University of Chicago Press, 2002).

69. Michele M. Wright, *Becoming Black: Creating Identity in the African Diaspora* (Durham, N.C.: Duke University Press, 2004), 3–24.

Contributors

DAWNE Y. CURRY is an assistant professor of history and ethnic studies at the University of Nebraska–Lincoln (UNL) where she teaches courses in African history. Her scholarly areas of interest include African protest struggles, intellectual history, comparative black history, and women's and gender studies. Curry's published work has appeared in *Safundi: the Journal of South African and American Studies* and the *International Journal of Interdisciplinary Social Sciences.* Curry has received numerous fellowships including the Fulbright Hays, the Social Science Research Council (SSRC) International Pre-dissertation Fellowship, and the SSRC Peace, Justice and Global Transformation Fellowship as well as UNL-sponsored fellowships. Curry is currently working on a manuscript tentatively titled *A Decade Past Quiescence: Alexandra and the 1970s.*

ERIC D. DUKE is an assistant professor of history in the Department of Africana Studies at the University of South Florida (USF) where he teaches courses in African American, Caribbean, and African Diaspora history. His scholarly interests include race and nation-building, decolonization, black diaspora politics, black radicalism, intraracial relations, and identity construction. He has received fellowships from the American Historical Association, National History Center, U.S. Department of Education, and multiple USF-sponsored fellowships. Duke's research focuses on decolonization and nation-building in the Anglophone Caribbean in the twentieth century, and the multiple perceptions of this struggle within imperial, regional, and diaspora politics. He is currently working on a manuscript tentatively titled

Out of One . . . Many Nations: Conceptualizing a "United West Indies" in the British Caribbean and Diaspora.

MARSHANDA A. SMITH is a PhD candidate in comparative black history at Michigan State University, where she has served as a research assistant and instructor. Her scholarly areas of interest include African American women's history, gender studies, comparative history, nineteenth-century U.S. history, and the civil rights movement. Smith's dissertation, "Centering Black Women Faculty Accomplishments: Breaking Barriers at Michigan State University, 1967–2007," examines the lives, ideologies, and contributions of important African American women from four different decades after the modern civil rights movement. She is currently a research associate in the Department of African American Studies at Northwestern University.

IRIS BERGER is professor of history, Africana studies, and women's studies at the University at Albany, State University of New York, and a past director of the Institute for Research on Women. Her books include the award-winning *Religion and Resistance: East African Kingdoms in the Precolonial Period; Women and Class in Africa,* coedited with Claire Robertson; *Threads of Solidarity: Women in South African Industry, 1900–1980; Women in Sub-Saharan Africa: Restoring Women to History,* with E. Frances White; and *South Africa in World History.* She is also an editor of the *Oxford Encyclopedia of Women in World History.* In 1995–96, she served as the elected president of the African Studies Association.

JOHN CAMPBELL is a senior lecturer at the University of the West Indies (UWI) in St. Augustine, Trinidad. His scholarly interests include slavery, manumission, and the meaning of freedom. He received two major awards for scholarly and teaching achievement at UWI: the Chancellor's Award for Excellence (2007) and the Guardian Life "Premium" Teaching Award (2006). Campbell has published and edited books in the Caribbean including *Readings in History: Resource Materials for Caribbean Advanced Proficiency Examinations (CAPE),* and *Caribbean Civilisation.* He has published several articles and book reviews in *The ARTS Journal, Caribbean Quarterly,* and the *Jamaican Historical Review,* and a chapter in *Beyond the Blood, the Beach and the Banana: New Perspectives in Caribbean Civilisation.*

AFUA COOPER is the Ruth Wynn Woodward Endowed Chair in the Department of Women's Studies at Simon Fraser University. She holds a Ph.D. from the University of Toronto in the history of the African diaspora with specialties in Black Canadian history. Dr. Cooper's most recent history publication, *The Hanging of Angélique: The Untold Story of Canadian Slavery and the Burning of Old Montréal,* was nominated for the 2006 Governor-General's Award, and has been translated into French as *La Pendaison d'Angélique* by Editions de L'Homme. She also co-authored *We're Rooted Here and They Can't Pull Us Up: Essays in African Canadian Women's History,* which won the Joseph Brant Award for history, and *The Underground Railroad, Next Stop: Toronto.* In addition, Dr. Cooper has published scholarly articles on the theme of gender, slavery, and abolition, several volumes of poetry, curated multiple exhibits in Canada on the history of Black North Americans in Canada, and authored two forthcoming historical volumes for young adults on the struggle for freedom and against slavery.

FATIMA EL-TAYEB is an assistant professor for African American culture and film in the Department of Literature at the University of California–San Diego. Originally from Germany, she was active in black, migrant, and feminist organizing there and in the Netherlands. She is a former member of the Amsterdam-based Queer People of Color collective *Strange Fruit,* co-author of the movie *Everything Will Be Fine,* and co-founder of the Black European Studies Project. Her first book, published in German, explored the relationship between race and national identity in early twentieth-century Germany. She has published a number of articles on the interactions of race, gender, and sexuality, most recently "Blackness and Its (Queer) Discontents," in: Nagl and Lennox, ed., *Remapping Black Germany* (Amherst: University of Massachusetts Press, forthcoming) and "'The Birth of a European Public': Migration, Postnationality, and Race in the Uniting Europe," *American Quarterly* (forthcoming). She is currently working on a book on the racialization of migrants and minorities in contemporary Europe and the queering of ethnicity as a minoritarian counterstrategy. In 2008–9, she is an Andrew W. Mellon postdoctoral fellow and visiting professor at the University of California–Los Angeles.

STEPHEN G. HALL is an assistant professor of history at Ohio State University. His scholarly areas of interest include African American historiography and intellectual history, the modern African Diaspora, and American history in the nineteenth and twentieth centuries. His scholarly work has appeared in *William and Mary Quarterly, Pennsylvania Magazine of History and Biography, Journal of the Gilded Age and Progressive Era,* and *Journal of American History.* He has received fellowships from Schomburg Center, W.E.B. DuBois Center for Afro-American Research at Harvard University, National Endowment for the Humanities, Ford Foundation, Gilder Lehrman Foundation, and most recently the Carter G. Woodson Fellowship at Emory University's Manuscript, Archives, and Rare Book Library (MARBL). He the author of *A Faithful Account of the Race: African American Historical Writing in Nineteenth Century America*. He is currently working on a monograph tentatively titled *Framing Global Visions: African American Historians Write about the World, 1885–1954*.

JOEL T. HELFRICH is a doctoral candidate at the University of Minnesota. His dissertation, "Sacred Sites, Scientific Rites: The Struggle over *dził nchaa si'an* (Mount Graham), 1871–2002," examines the struggle for a sacred place in Arizona. He holds the conviction that a myopic focus defeats the most important work any historian does: being an informed and informative member of society. He sees the environment as a site where much of his historical training can be brought to bear, so he continues to pursue those interests as well as others. He teaches at Monroe Community College in Rochester, New York.

BEATRIZ G. MAMIGONIAN earned a PhD from the University of Waterloo in Canada. She is a professor of history at the Universidade Federal de Santa Catarina in Brazil. Her research interests focus on the impact of abolitionism on the Brazilian slave system throughout the nineteenth century and its human consequences. She is the coeditor (with Karen Racine) of *The Human Tradition in the Black Atlantic, 1500–2000* (forthcoming) and she is completing a book manuscript on the fate of the Africans who were emancipated in the course of the suppression activities in Brazil.

YUICHIRO ONISHI is an assistant professor of African American and African studies and core faculty in the Asian American Studies Program at the University of Minnesota–Twin Cities. His published work has appeared in *XCP: Cross-Cultural Poetics* and *Journal of African American History*. Currently, he is working on a book manuscript titled *Transpacific Racial Strivings: How Black Americans, the Japanese, and Okinawans Found Solidarities*.

CASSANDRA PYBUS is Australian Research Council research chair in history at University of Sydney, Australia. She has published extensively on Australian, American, and Transatlantic history with research interests in social history, colonial history of the British Empire, slavery, and the history of labor. She has authored eleven books; her most recent are *Epic Journeys of*

Freedom: Runaway Slaves of the American Revolution and their Global Quest for Liberty; Black Founders; and *Many Middle Passages: Forced Migration and the Making of the Modern World,* co-edited with Emma Christopher and Marcus Rediker.

MICOL SEIGEL is an assistant professor of African American and African Diaspora studies and American studies at Indiana University–Bloomington. Her work on cultural politics, transnational method, prisons and policing, and race in the Americas (particularly the United States and Brazil), can be found in *Hispanic American Historical Review, Radical History Review, Journal of Latin American Cultural Studies, Revista Brasileira de História, Black Music Research Journal,* and in her book *Uneven Encounters: Making Race and Nation in the Americas.*

MATTHEW J. SMITH is a lecturer in the Department of History and Archaeology at the University of the West Indies–Mona. He works on Haitian political and social history in the nineteenth and twentieth centuries. He is the author of *Red and Black in Haiti: Radicalism, Conflict, and Political Change, 1934–1957.*

Index

THE NEW BLACK STUDIES SERIES

Beyond Bondage: Free Women of Color in the Americas *Edited by David Barry Gaspar and Darlene Clark Hine*

The Early Black History Movement, Carter G. Woodson, and Lorenzo Johnston Greene *Pero Gaglo Dagbovie*

"Baad Bitches" and Sassy Supermamas: Black Power Action Films *Stephane Dunn*

Black Maverick: T. R. M. Howard's Fight for Civil Rights and Economic Power *David T. Beito and Linda Royster Beito*

Beyond the Black Lady: Sexuality and the New African American Middle Class *Lisa B. Thompson*

Extending the Diaspora: New Histories of Black People *Dawne Y. Curry, Eric D. Duke, and Marshanda A. Smith*

The University of Illinois Press
is a founding member of the
Association of American University Presses.

Composed in 10.5/13 Adobe Minion Pro
with Frutiger display
by Jim Proefrock
at the University of Illinois Press
Manufactured by Sheridan Books, Inc.

University of Illinois Press
1325 South Oak Street
Champaign, IL 61820-6903
www.press.uillinois.edu